KT-494-231

There is a trollop in the air. A trollop who divests my husband of his marriage vows, then attempts to cleanse her damned soul in the fruity balm of lemon. A trollop hung up on lemon-yellow Wonderbras. What's wrong with plain ordinary white?

Who *is* this person?

I turn up the label. Size 36D. Now I'm the first to praise generously where praise is due, especially if I'm flattened by the competition. But when it's a proven fact that generous breasts are one of Ronan's most important life priorities it's not so easy.

In fact, I want to take a knife and slash everything in sight.

Lemon.

Calm down, Julie!

There may be no need to panic. Having a size 36D silken lemon-yellow brassiere disgrace our front doorknob should not necessarily worry me. In and of itself.

After all, it could be, for instance . . . what if it's Ronan's sister?

Except.

I know it's not his flaming sister.

Brian Gallagher has practised as a barrister, but now writes full time. He lives with his wife in Dublin. *The Feng-Shui Junkie* is his first novel.

The Feng-Shui Junkie

Brian Gallagher

ORION

An Orion paperback
First published in Great Britain by Orion in 2000
This paperback edition published in 2000 by
Orion Books Ltd,
Orion House, 5 Upper St Martin's Lane, London WC2H 9EA

Copyright © 2000 Brian Gallagher

The right of Brian Gallagher to be identified as the author
of this work has been asserted by him in accordance
with the Copyright, Designs and Patents Act 1988.

All rights reserved. No part of this publication may
be reproduced, stored in a retrieval system, or transmitted,
in any form or by any means, electronic, mechanical,
photocopying, recording or otherwise, without the
prior permission of the copyright owner.

A CIP catalogue record for this book
is available from the British Library.

ISBN: 0 75283 710 9

Typeset by Deltatype Ltd, Birkenhead, Merseyside
Printed and bound in Great Britain by Clays Ltd, St Ives plc

To Martina,
for her love and inspiration

Acknowledgements

A debt of gratitude to Jonathan Lloyd at Curtis Brown, whose magic touch zapped my dream to reality. Thanks for all your help, guidance and availability. A big hug goes to Tara, Hannah, Carol and Diana.

At Orion, I'm indebted to my editor Malcolm Edwards. Thanks also to Susan Lamb, Helen Richardson and Selina Walker for their untiring support, and to Lucie Stericker for her artwork. And to the whole team who have helped turn this into something better than I'd have imagined.

Thursday, 16 June, afternoon

1

. . . you see, he thinks I'm touchy by nature, a bit moody, mercurial, cantankerous (is that spelt right?), unbalanced even . . . but I don't know.

I mean, you don't get to where I've got in life by being congenitally irritable. You don't get to being a venerated legal professional in a power suit, with an MGF 1.8i convertible, by surrendering to biorhythms and breaking down at magic-mood roundabouts when everyone else is full speed ahead. In a world which treats a woman like a lollipop for the eyeballs, I think I am a model of self-restraint, forbearance and dignity. I am good-natured. No, in fact, I think I'm a saint. After all, have I not up to now been a positive, moderating and pacifying influence on the rotten piece of whale-shit that is my husband Ronan? And does all this not imply a certain balance of mind on my part? A certain equanimity, a degree of sanity? You don't think so?

But.

No one's perfect. There are exceptions. Like when I return home two days early from holiday to discover another woman's lemon-yellow Wonderbra hanging from the inside knob of our hall door and the place smelling like a Cantonese bidet – ignore me if I begin to lose it. Temper, principles, dignity, cool. Everything.

I slam the front door behind me and glare at the offending yellow undergarment as if it recently hatched from a snake egg and might at any time spring up and bite. There's something outrageous about it. Defiant. *Conscious.* As if it's been hung there to ward off evil spirits.

I take a breath.

'Ronan?'

It's more a command than a question.

1

There's no response. Just silence. A silence with a peculiar buzz, not to be confused with the faint purring of the fridge or the happy gurgling of the aquarium in our living-room. No, it's a guilty silence. It's as if Ronan and his hump piece have been sweating guilt into the fresh air of our apartment and it's clung to the walls like paint.

'Ronan!'

Again, nothing.

He must be out. Of course, he's not expecting me back from my holiday until Saturday.

I sniff into space.

It's a strangely sweet, bitter smell. If not perfume, then some kind of aromatherapeutic ointment or herbal infusion, around which Ronan would not be seen dead. It lingers in the sunless hallway. It is warm and moist. It seems to be coming from the bathroom.

Lemon, that's what it is.

There is a trollop in the air. A trollop who divests my husband of his marriage vows, then attempts to cleanse her damned soul in the fruity balm of lemon. A trollop hung up on lemon-yellow Wonderbras. What's wrong with plain ordinary white?

Who *is* this person?

I turn up the label. Size 36D. Now I'm the first to praise generously where praise is due, especially if I'm flattened by the competition. But when it's a proven fact that generous breasts are one of Ronan's most important life priorities it's not so easy.

In fact, I want to take a knife and slash everything in sight.

Lemon.

Calm down, Julie!

There may be no need to panic. Having a size 36D silken lemon-yellow brassiere disgrace our front doorknob should not necessarily worry me. In and of itself.

After all, it could be, for instance . . . what if it's Ronan's sister?

Except.

I know it's not his flaming sister. Ronan has been warned to keep her away from this apartment. She's thirty and brings her cat, Ginger, with her everywhere she goes. I love life. I hate cats. Ginger moults like a hair factory during a Hoover recession. This annoys me so intensely that I have offered to stir-fry her guts in our new wok if she ever again steps into our apartment. In soya oil.

Do I sound horrible yet?

So no, I don't think it's his sister.

I fling my black leather Giorgio Armani bag against the banana-coloured couch on the right: my only token of defiance against the minimalist luxury of our apartment.

I take a left into the kitchen, a sniffer dog baying for blood . . . And when I see what lies here on the floor I stop dead, gripping the counter top beside me.

You are strong. You can cope. There is an explanation. Ronan loves you. Stop being stupid. Be calm. You're a lawyer, goddamnit. Relax. Let's not make a meal out of this.

I mean, just because there's a shitload of women's garments lying scattered all over our kitchen floor is no reason to hit the roof.

In and of itself.

2

Okay, Julie, simmer down now.

Think dignity. Think respectability. You've got neighbours. You've got a reputation to maintain. You've got self-respect. You've got pride. You may well have blood pressure.

Ever so silently, therefore, I hyperventilate.

You see, it's not just the cream-coloured high heels perched on the kitchen table like a museum piece, one poised defiantly on its heel and the other lying defeated on its side next to a half-full bowl of nachos and a crudely mauled pair of croissants and three empty bottles of Châteauneuf-du-Pape and two of our sparkling wedding-ware Duiske glasses.

Nor is it just the elegant cream ladies' jacket hanging from the back of one of the chairs, its accompanying cream blouse and skirt lying in a light clump beneath the kitchen table.

Nor is it the light-tone tights in the fruit bowl, sitting in a puffy ball alongside two oranges, three apples and one overripe mango.

This alone demands immediate compensation. But it gets worse: a pair of Ronan's boxer shorts snuggling across the electric kettle like an art nouveau tea cosy; a pair of black trousers and a black polo-neck sweater bunched up near the door like a pile of dirty washing; Ronan's black leather belt, lying snake-shaped on the floor beside the fridge, the pin from the thick metal buckle sticking straight up into the air like something I'm too polite to mention; Ronan's wine-coloured jacket dropped right in the middle of the floor two feet away from where I'm standing, its silken magenta insides spilling out like something else I'm too polite to mention.

My body is shaking uncontrollably, as if a pneumatic drill has got to work on my backbone. My mind is racing like it's on the Matterhorn ski slope and there's a thousand-foot drop coming up any second now. Voices from deep inside me are spewing out quite the most dirty-mouthed abuse I have ever heard, including vocabulary I've never heard in my life.

I am speaking in tongues. Four-letter words, juicy and foul, are spouting from my gullet. And several vile six- and seven-letter words too. The walls around me seem to quiver and quake and shrink in fear. I am a fire-spitting bitch-ape who craps on etiquette, screaming strings of filth into our homely kitchen . . .

. . . don't go away.

Just see it as slight turbulence in a sea of sanity.

This is a nightmare. It's like something out of a horror film. Except that horror films – however hard they try – don't generally lift off the screen and punch you hard in the smacker.

Well clearly, they lunched together. Now I happen to believe that extramarital friendships are healthy: they prove that marriages can still work. Even in kitchens.

But instead of shaking hands nicely and parting as friends, Ronan faltered (as men do) and ripped off his acquaintance's garments before they'd even emptied the bowl of nachos. And relied on Newton's laws of gravitation to do the rest.

But the Wonderbra on the doorknob? What objective meaning, what absolute aesthetic significance can be assigned to that? And what about her knickers? Where are they?

His sister!

4

He's been seeing some slut behind my back.

Where are the kitchen scissors? Call me gruesome, but I want to sever Ronan's balls from their sockets and make them both watch at scissor-point while I stamp his testicles on the floor and she, gasping, helplessly ogles future generations of herself and my husband being scrunched mercilessly by my metal heel against the hard ground.

This doesn't mean, I want to stress, that I'm not essentially a placid person by nature.

I slink out to the hall and through the doorway to the right leading to the bedrooms. I enter ours: the thin blinds on the large window are drawn, casting a sharp rectangle of shuttered light on to the spacious pine floor.

The white duvet of our low bed is pulled untidily across. Underneath one pillow lie Ronan's neatly folded T-shirt and boxer shorts. Underneath the other is a skimpy yellow night-dress. Not mine, I wish to stress. Neatly, I replace the pillow.

Draped across the pine art-deco chair is a fluffy white angora polo-neck jumper. Also not mine. Sitting on the chair is a small light-brown night case. In it are a woman's clothes and articles. No identifying features such as names or addresses.

No lemon-yellow knickers anywhere in sight.

I check the wardrobes. Next to his suits there hangs a long fawn dress and a smart mustard-coloured velvet jacket neither of which I have ever seen before.

On top of the chest of drawers is a blue bottle of factor fifteen suntan lotion. The exterior is smeared and greasy. On the floor at the foot of the bed is a pair of Ronan's shoes. Something makes me go to the wardrobe again. His rubber flip-flops: they are missing. I check for his bathing togs. Missing. Also missing is the striped blue and green beach gown, which I almost brought on my holiday.

Now I'm peering out of the bedroom window down at the communal swimming pool. It is small and glistening blue like the earth seen through space, surrounded by a hedge and a wooden fence.

There they are.

Lying together in their shades by the pool, alone, like they

5

own the place. Ronan is in his Adidas shorts, leaning over a newspaper stretched open on the ground, his left foot scratching his right calf. A blonde woman is lying on her back beside him on top of my sky-blue beach towel, her knees joined like twin peaks. Underneath her head is my rolled-up striped beach gown. She's propping up a blockbuster novel: from here I can just about make out Jackie Collins splayed in spidery red lettering. She's in a skimpy two-piece, this time in sunset yellow. She has a fantastic figure.

Has he no mercy?

Does he not care who might recognize him? This is where we live. This is where we swim. This is where we sunbathe. We are known, by sight. I am known, by sight: regularly I am spotted, returning home with my briefcase. With shopping bags. With Mother. My life is here. My home. My refuge, my shelter from a harsh world. My reputation, my pride, my dignity – if it is *anywhere* it is here.

And what does he do? He pastes his tight-thonged whore with a spatula on my neighbours' faces.

Of course, even if he is recognized, the chances of me discovering the insult were never going to be great, in this dungeon of sociability and camaraderie that is our de luxe apartment block.

I tear out my cellphone and input his number. I wait. It bleeps in my ear. It rings simultaneously from the pool below. Ronan makes a sudden movement towards his canvas bag, takes out his phone, presses a button and shoves it back in his bag.

'*This is Ronan Fitzgerald. Please leave a message after the tone.*'

Scumbag, I crave to communicate, but I don't. These things are better done in person.

'Hi, Ronan,' I articulate in this beautiful, sweet voice. 'It's Julie. Could you call me?'

I storm the bathroom. The jacuzzi. She has contaminated our jacuzzi. That sweet lemony scent. In here it is overpowering. The culprit is standing on the jacuzzi ledge: Bergamot Essential Oil. I pick up the bottle and read the label, getting a good idea of the pleasant sensations this woman enjoyed in my bath: 'This oil is expressed from the peel of the citrus fruit. It has an uplifting, sweet, fruity odour and can be used to make a pleasant and refreshing massage or bath oil.'

What to do?

I need a drink.

I rush back out through the hall and into the lounge. It's so bright in here I have to blink. The room is rinsed in splashes of midsummer sunlight, flooding through four giant windows which combine into one large seascape canvas, framed by the dark-blue pelmet and curtains.

I fling open the french windows to let out their love stench and head straight to the drinks cabinet. Jameson's: an essential ingredient in coping. I pour, staring the whole time at our coffee table. Where is our wedding photo?

Response: Ronan has hidden it. The bastard didn't wish to stain the perfect romance.

My glass overflows and a whiskey puddle is now shimmering like jelly on the floor. I take a sip, then furiously kick at the puddle, flicking droplets around the room.

Our beautiful home.

The white drinks cabinet and bookcase, the white leather suite, the pale marble floor flecked with grey, the white walls, the widescreen digital TV on the wall, the art-deco coffee table, the dark glass dinner table at the far end of the room beside the aquarium, the hung Paul Klee modern art . . .

The crucible of our dreams.

I escape through the french windows out on to the balcony. I lean against the railings. My head is spinning, my mind still skiing the white slope in freefall. Make-up is streaming down my cheeks, I know, because blobs of it are falling on to my black polo-neck jumper and plopping on to the balcony floor like droplets of dirty rain.

The bottle I am holding is like an oil pipeline straight into my veins. It's starting to make me feel a whole lot better.

I strip open a fresh packet of cigarettes, light a double-barrel and suck away at it like a maniac.

What am I going to do?

A hazy sun spreads its lustful heat over my face, fanned by a thermal puff of air. The light-blue of water is set against the deeper blue of the sky across whose giant orb endlessly slant fluffy clouds. Across Dublin Bay is the incessant play of ships crossing back and forth. Closer, the sea's white fingertips lap gently against your ears and mingle with the tinkle of boat masts, music in the light June breeze.

Over to the right is the catamaran terminal. One departed for Holyhead only a short time ago. It travels fast; now it is a small dark square on the horizon. It will return in approximately four hours.

Further right again is the sun-yellowed arm of Dun Laoghaire pier, articulated like a crab limb across a mile of water. Its massive shoulder meets the coastline only two hundred metres from our apartment.

All this beauty.

It has made me so happy. Us.

And now?

They have met secretly in *my* apartment. They have stripped their clothes off in *my* kitchen. They have had sex in *my* bedroom. In *my* bed.

And it's *my* marriage. Even if, like everything else here, I strictly own just half. But this doesn't give him even half a right to jerk it off with another woman for a few minutes' joy. It's *my* life and he's threatening to destroy the whole of it, and he hasn't got that right.

Not without asking me first.

3

Of course, the holiday was Ronan's idea.

It all started last week on our comfortable leather couch. We were on the point of moving to a more intense, groping phase of our mutual-lust session when I suddenly spat it out. 'Ronan, I want a baby,' I said.

He froze. Ever so gently, he separated himself and beheld me at arm's length. Then he stood up. Rubbing his chin, he peered down at me suspiciously for signs of emotional dysfunction.

He rushed out to the balcony to make a series of phone calls.

When he returned I asked him what all that was about. Staring out at the blue day, he replied that I required a period of 'intensive care in an alternative environment' (his shorthand for a break) to get myself together again. And since I wasn't too busy in the Law Library at present, he had just booked a week for two in the Cliff Castle, to begin the following Sunday.

'What's that? A sanatorium for the unhinged?'

'It's a hotel cum health farm,' he replied. 'It'll do you good.'

I thanked him for being so thoughtful and told him I felt privileged indeed to be married to a man who could display such touching concern over my mental state. 'But', I added, 'it's not a holiday I need, Ronan. It's a baby.'

Standing by the french doors, with that slightly supercilious half-smile of his, he gently explained to me my problem. Job-stress, he said. It was giving me strange ideas.

It was understandable, he lectured, that with my every waking moment filled by 'turgid legal problematics' (to quote) such as trusts, probate, conveyancing and drafting defences for psycho-paths and murderers (he has this romantic idea about my job) I should hanker after something more . . .

He paused. '. . . primordial.'

'Primitive, you mean.'

'I can understand this innate urge,' he said.

'You can?'

'Of course I can.'

He sat down beside me to talk, a rare enough event – at least on a sofa. His voice became all sugary and soft, a give-away sign that he'd just switched on the remote-control charm button. This works under normal conditions because, you know, he could be behaving like the worst pig-headed, arrogant creep in the whole world, but provided he did it with charm I'd do anything for him.

But wanting a baby wasn't normal conditions.

Besides, I noticed a fundamental contradiction. His smiling lips said: 'Of *course* children would be wonderful, Julie – what's to stop us discussing it again in a year or two when you're more established in your career?'

But his eyes said: 'Julie, this isn't you speaking, it's your hormones: don't fuck up your life over a hormone.'

It was clear that Ronan was in no mood for a steamy lay in the soft folds of our marital bed, or even on the leather couch in full view of several innocent tropical fish. To him, 'steamy lay' meant one thing and one thing only: twenty-year-long child-rearing horror.

(Incredible the way sex can make a man so nervous.)

Undaunted, I slid up to him and started pressing a few buttons of my own. I slid my arms sexily (or so I thought) round his neck and made these purring noises, which normally worked when-ever I purred them. I pressed my hand under his shirt and started squeezing and massaging, and I buried my lips into the tight bristle under his jawbone.

But he drew back – ever so politely – escaped to the drinks cabinet and poured himself a brandy. He didn't feel like me right then. No problem, I told myself, I'm a reasonable person. I could make allowances for these embarrassingly unmanly displays of impotence.

'Julie.' He sighed heavily, examining his brandy glass. 'We're far too young to be doing ridiculous things like having babies.'

'Twenty-nine. The older we get the more ridiculous it will become.'

'We're professional people: we have an image to maintain. And I really don't want it soiled by a baby.'

I laughed.

'They consume time, energy, food, money,' he observed. 'They download on your peace of mind. They puke on carpets. They piss on armchairs. They do worse on car seats. They grin like clowns, they chew rugs. Babies bring disease, according to recent research. The whole thing is sordid.'

He emptied his glass, then extracted his silver cigarette case. After a series of deft movements the space around his head was billowing with smoke. Then he sauntered to the french windows and stood there gazing out to sea, indulging his Camel cigarette in that sophisticated *je ne sais quoi* way of his, a handsome figure silhouetted in his all-black trousers, jacket and polo-neck sweater against the deep-blue mid-summer evening sky, his gold Raymond Weil wristwatch glistening like a minia-ture sun on his dark-haired wrist. 'As Louis Armstrong once said,' he mused, 'we've got all the time in the world.'

'If he was singing about getting pregnant, then he had all the naivety in the world.'

'Come on, Julie, you know what having a child would do: it would tie us down. I'd lose my freedom. You'd lose your figure.'

'No man wants children until they arrive.'

'No man wants children *when* they arrive. Anyway, what do you expect? To have them delivered by taxi? Have you any idea what childbirth is like?'

'Yes.'

'I suggest you read up on it.'

'Books are your solution to everything.'

'Books could turn out to be an inexpensive method of contraception.'

'When you see its lovely pudgy face and tiny squashy fists you will fall in love with it.'

'Falling in love with a woman is quite enough, thank you.'

'It will change your life . . .'

'That's true.'

'. . . you'll adore it! You'll end up ignoring me. Besides, you can teach her everything you know.'

'I know nothing.'

Actually, he regards himself as a bit of an intellectual.

'You're sensitive to art and philosophy, Ronan. Don't deny it . . .'

'Yes, and I'm sure a baby would be thrilled to be introduced to Kant and chiaroscuro on its first day on earth.'

'Just think about it, Ronan, that's all I'm saying.'

'Fine, I'll think about it. Anyway' – he sighed – 'the holiday is booked. Go away for the week and enjoy yourselves.'

Yourselves?

'What do you mean "yourselves"?'

He told me he couldn't go himself: his dental appointments book was full up. I was to take a friend. 'That ball-busting friend of yours, for instance.'

'There's no need to talk about Sylvana like that.'

'Take a girls' week out: renew your friendship. Do you both the world of good. Think of it. Sauna and plunge pool, aromatherapy massage, reflexology, seaweed treatments, muck treatments, facials, electrolysis, manicures, exfoliants . . .'

'Of course. What more could a woman ask for?'

'You talk enough about needing to relax and destress.'

He's right, I do. 'But Ronan,' I purred, 'it's *you* I want to go with.'

'Sorry, Julie, but teeth come before love.'

He actually said that.

I figured Ronan was using the health farm idea as a tactical manoeuvre to make me drop this ludicrous egg-sperm creation thing. His theory was: baby blues are aggravated by stress overload, therefore they will be sedated by stress management. His ploy was this: send me away to be cured.

But I reasoned: go anyway. A chance to rediscover the sunny oasis of well-being trapped within that arid human wasteland called work. Destress, detox, depox. Read literature and sniff perfume samples from magazines. Eat abstemiously, but with plenty of liquor and conversation added. Concoct paybacks for all those people we love to hate, draft avoidance schemes for those we hate to love and bitch about the rest. Resort to the local bar and cackle till closing time like a couple of cauldron witches. On the more spiritual side, perhaps, experiment with yogic communion and, yes, muck treatments. Sleep like pigs in space, buy some new clothes, return home looking absolutely amazing.

And . . . get him pregnant.

Very simple, very basic, very effective.

He bent down, then, and kissed me on the forehead, assuring me that Sylvana and I would have a wonderful time together. 'She'll love it,' he offered, like he really cared about her welfare.

I reluctantly agreed. He smiled, thinking he'd won the day.

And now?

I know better.

He moved in his little whore while I was away. He swapped me for a few days' marital cost-benefit analysis. He imaginatively transformed her into his wife, comparing and contrasting at every turn. He even tried her out in my bed. If she turned out good, he'd dump me.

Very simple, very basic, very effective.

I go back inside and pull the thick wine decanter from the drinks cabinet. It weighs my arm down like a ball of lead. I could use the empty bottle of Jameson's instead, but although it might well be sufficiently sturdy to interface with one skull, it could splinter on the second and I don't want to create a mess of glass shards around the place. Bone I can take. But not glass.

I drop the solid stopper into my jacket pocket and I close the door of the drinks cabinet. I pause on my reflection in the glass.

I look horrendous.

My face is thin and bony as a scarecrow, pale as milk gone off. My mouth is vexed and stark, my eyes small shiny discs. I had my black shoulder-length hair trimmed and further darkened by the resident coiffeuse at the Cliff Castle Hotel. The red lipstick and purple eyeshadow make me look weird: two elongated canines and I'd be perfect.

Sylvana often tells me how beautiful I am. I often tell her how crazy she is. She frequently adds that 'even men think so' but I know she's only being ironic so I don't have to go and stab her.

Once in the bathroom, I stand in front of the mirror and wipe the ugly-looking smear tracks from my face: no point in resembling a crazed madwoman even if I feel like one. I refuse to let the bitch see that I'm upset, even though I will have no choice but to let her experience a little-known alternative use for crystal glass wine decanters: cranial removal. By the swimming pool.

I finish tending to my face. Good. I feel instantly better. I am going to make an impression now.

In someone's skull.

I go back out to the lounge to close the french windows.

Suddenly I stop dead.

On the floor, leaning semi-concealed against the side of the leather couch I spy a slim burgundy envelope case.

I pick up the case and place it on the coffee table. Inside are a fitted notepad, pens in pen holders, a mobile phone, a diary, a brochure of some sort, a tube of deep-red lipstick, a bottle of Issey Miyake eau de toilette and a packet of condoms. Unopened. Meaning that they are using ours.

Or using none.

There's just one newspaper: last Monday's. Unopened. Today is Thursday. What does that say?

I smash my fist down on the coffee table. A sharp pain runs up my inside arm but I don't care because I've just seen something. A sketch pad. I take it out. It's seven by five inches. On the first few pages there are a few detailed sketches of tropical marine fish. Did she sketch these from our aquarium? If so, how come there's one variety I've never seen before?

The next few pages feature sketches of a man. In one, he is reading a paper. In another he is smoking a cigarette with his legs crossed. This is Ronan. She has perfectly captured his elegant, effortless posture and his trademark sexuality: pensive and intense. In another sketch he is asleep in bed, a study of serenity.

She has grasped his proportionality exactly: tall but not too tall. Slim but not gangly. Head and shoulders in proportion to his body, legs and arms neither too short nor too long. His stylish clothes accentuate this architectonic harmony.

I pick up a final sketch of Ronan's face – a close-up this time. He could be watching TV. He is concentrated but relaxed. The large eyes, the long thin face, the long elegant nose, the slightly protruding but well-proportioned lips, the small chin, the high narrow forehead, the thin black receding hair, short thin sideburns, the perfect ears, the thick but neatly trimmed eyebrows, the clean-shaven, nostril-plucked neatness.

There are five nude sketches of Ronan. I stare at these for a long time. Then I replace them quickly, snap shut the sketch pad and fling it back into the case.

I pull out the brochure next. A travel brochure? Paris, where Ronan and I honeymooned. Ronan's favourite city.

Now I grab the diary and plunge through her private scribblings. A name. That's all I need. On the inside flap are scrawled addresses, numbers and short notes in blue, black, red and green ink. On the next page you get information on clothing sizes, birth stones and wedding anniversaries.

I flick a page. Metric conversion.

All I need is a name, a number. *Something.*

Recommended daily diet. This looks more interesting. 'Female, age bracket 23–28' is underlined in blue, as is the '68in.' part. She's five foot eight. I examine the calorie chart. She's scored an impressive two thousand calories per day.

14

I can feel my pulse steadily increasing.

Next page 'cocktails' and 'long drinks'. Then 'distances'. Then 'notes', which is covered again in barely legible scribbles in black, blue, red and green.

Then travel and currency information for countries around the world. Paris is underlined in green.

Then finally I get to the 'personal details'.

Everything is there.

Name, 'Nicole Summers'. Address, telephone number, mobile number. I scribble everything down on the back of my hand.

Replacing it all just as I found it and returning the envelope case to the floor, I stalk into the hall, grab my bag off the couch and leave the apartment, crystal glass wine decanter swinging in my hand like death in the air.

4

The warm sun slants on to my face as I walk through the car park. It's so bright today that I have my shades locked tight into my eyes.

When I reach my destination I place the decanter on the ground beside me and, like a drooling raptor, I glare hard at Ronan's pride and joy. His principal pleasure in life after sex.

I am talking about his car.

The Porsche is almost new. It's the first real sign of the accumulating wealth of his dental practice. I had the colour changed at the last minute from Ronan's preferred Sherwood green to pale yellow – coincidentally. We'd had an argument over money: I demanded that he put the car into joint ownership. As a reprisal, he made me contribute one grand to the purchase price. I got even by changing the colour. He was not happy.

It really *is* a wonderful machine, though.

Now I'm slamming the decanter stopper hard into the windscreen. I start counting to twelve. Twelve seconds later there are twelve lunar crater designs on the glass, patterned around a wide cavity in the centre.

15

Whew! This kind of manual labour takes it out of you.

Halting, I eye the decanter, a shining monument on the warm carbon tarmac, a jewel blistering with a billion sun sparkles. I'm saving it for later. For my two friends by the pool.

You should hear the crunching now.

Expertly, I'm working my way through left side window number one. These decanter stoppers are exceptionally good battering rams. They're terrific. To be recommended.

You know, it annoys me intensely to think that if a man is violent he is described as 'aggressive', whereas if a woman is violent she is merely 'hysterical'.

I will damn well be aggressive if I want to be.

I mean, what do you want me to be? A lady? Come on! Am I supposed to sit down with my husband at the breakfast table and discuss in a calm and appropriate manner the causes of his random sexual addiction? Or burst into tears? Or forgive his youthful, errant ways? Or slam the front door in a huff, suitcase in hand, and write frigid but tearful letters from Mother's pad? Not me.

I prefer to be the dragon he'll never forget.

In three tough blows, left side window number two disappears. The two right side windows go down. I seem to have more energy than there is window surface. In one single blow, the plastic sunroof surround cracks.

After a second short mid-afternoon break I take to the shiny yellow bonnet like a tiger in heat. I'm battering away at the soft metal until I'm swimming in an ocean of yellow paint dust.

The wing mirror takes a hit.

I think I've had enough now. Besides, I might be seen. I smooth down my trousers. I check my hair in the reflection of a nearby car window – there aren't any left in the Porsche to speak of.

How do I feel?

Terrific. *Alive*.

I pick the decanter off the tarmac and stride back through the car park towards a narrow path that leads past our apartment block to the swimming pool at the rear. I know I must look odd with the wine decanter and the scarecrow scowl, but you can't always look your best, can you?

This is where the fun begins.

Just as I reach the edge of the car park, a bright red BMW 318i screeches to a halt several inches in front of me, blocking my progress.

The tinted glass window rolls down.

It's Sylvana.

Sylvana is big, brash and impatient. She's stylish, rich and confident. She's incredibly generous to those she loves: with her crippled father, for instance, she's like an angel. (To those she hates she's a nightmare.)

She's as blunt as a Celtic gravestone. She'll tell you if you look like crap or if your make-up resembles muck veneered with poster paint.

She has just one genetic defect: she's pathologically incapable of taking shit from anyone. Especially men, which is one reason I love her so.

On men: dump them. With no second chances, because nobody needs even a first chance to prove who they are. A chance is just a licence to cause further hurt. Better to enjoy, use and abuse. Crush and consume the grape but spit out the pip. Rinse your mouth afterwards. Above all, don't commit if you want a varied and exciting life filled with pleasant surprises and odours. It's time, she says, we stopped craving to spend our whole lives with three-year-old automatic pilots.

People say she's a stuck-up dragon.

Jealousy – such a terrible burden.

How does one describe this truly weird and wonderful woman who is my best friend and whom I have adored since the days we used to rip off her mother's lipstick to smudge our faces, and paint our toes with her purple nail varnish?

It's like Sylvana was born with dogshit in her mouth but to her friends up close her breath smells like roses.

She has always been a supportive pal.

Or so I thought.

'I've decided to have a baby,' I told her just before lunch today, anticipating a supportive reaction.

We were sitting in the pleasant carpet-faded Gothic seventeenth-century drawing-room of the hotel to which Ronan banished me in order to spend time with his side shag.

I was tinkling away on a piano, eighteenth century by the feel of it, while Miss Impervious Herself sat nearby on a commodious nineteenth-century armchair, venting her sublimations on her favourite novel, *Interview with the Vampire*, which she regards as the greatest literary event of the twentieth century – carelessly omitting a whole range of interesting personalities from James Joyce to Salman Rushdie and a hailstorm of Nobel Laureates, but that's Sylvana for you.

'Did you hear what I just said?'

She acknowledged my query with a dead grunt.

'I'm going home today instead of Saturday.'

'Shush! I'm coming up to a good fang part.'

'You've already read that book three times.'

'Multiply that by two.'

I hit her with it again: 'I've decided to have a baby, Sylvana.'

This time she heard: I knew this because her eyeballs moved.

I'd just stopped playing the piano, so the atmosphere was weighed in favour of speech. Eventually her head followed her eyes and she spoke, frowning at me. 'Nice one, Julie.'

'I'm not joking.'

My voice was casual, but my pulse beat with annoyance. I had half expected her to say this was wonderful news. But no, she was behaving like I'd just betrayed her.

I felt her sunburning glare on my skin. I rebegan my battered rendition of Beethoven's *Pathetique* sonata. After a while I heard her voice slide over the piano sounds: was I actually going to have a baby, the voice politely inquired, or had I merely decided that I might *one day* have a baby?

Again I ceased playing. 'I've actually decided I'm going to. Starting tonight. It's the perfect time of month. Ronan won't guess a thing.'

My fingers were sweating on to the stilled piano keys.

Returning to her book, Sylvana calmly informed me that this was a totally natural phase I was going through.

I resumed my Beethoven, at once botching up the B–D minor

chord progression at the start of the fast passage. I struck the B chord again. Hard.

'This totally natural phase,' I intoned, 'as you call it, might well be issuing between my legs in nine months.'

Pause.

'Can I remind you of a few facts?' she said, still reading.

'Be my guest,' I hissed, tripping over some harrowing bars.

It was like Ronan all over again.

Now, I have never known a pair of people who disliked one another as instantly as Ronan and Sylvana. It was loathing at first sight. Their mutual antipathy is so intense that there is only one thing that could possible unite them: their baby philosophy.

To both, the thought of babies is akin to the taste of cyanide: they kill off life as you know it. A single hour in their company would quell a woman's maternal resolve for a generation.

Sylvana first started lecturing me on the subject when we were eleven. She's still doing it.

Let her waffle on, I told myself.

'You imagine, Julie, that having a baby is like helping yourself to a piece of cake.'

'It is like a piece of cake,' I coolly replied, making sure to avoid her *Interview with the Vampire* glare. 'One that will make my life sweet again.'

From the corner of my eye I espied my friend leaning forward in her armchair and placing her book down on a nearby table. 'There's just one problem, Julie: you have to *bake* the cake first. Baking is equivalent to agony. Would you like me to remind you of the details?'

No, I would not. Go away.

'I already know.'

'It's one of the most awful things that can happen to a woman.'

'Quite.'

'Julie, are you listening?'

'To Beethoven,' I replied, struck by a strong sense of déjà-vu.

While I mucked my way through the *Pathetique*, Sylvana proceeded to remind me that childbirth is like having a red-hot cannonball grow inside you, which simply refuses mercifully to explode and finish you off. She flung her standard childbirth lecture at me, containing samples on varicose veins, hyper-ventilation, contractions, bleeding, ripping, forceps delivery, strangulation. She told me that childbirth is a recipe for two days of agony, followed by two weeks of joy, followed by two decades of servitude, frustration, disappointment . . . and a fat, shapeless stomach.

'This is all very Ronan,' I replied, trying to conceal my flusterment behind the musical score.

Sylvana: 'Do you really believe all that well-intentioned advice, Julie? Candy-floss such as: "It will pop out in no time at all!" Or: "Controlled breathing will defeat all pain." Or: "Up to ten thousand babies are born daily; it can't be that bad."'

She paused for breath and continued: 'Guess why people concoct all this nonsense about painless childbirth: because they don't want you to panic. They lie to you because they "care" about you. But what kind of caring is it if they let you squirm on your hospital bed begging for the last rites?'

Sylvana is quite right.

'You're quite right, Sylvana,' I replied in between a G- and a D-major chord.

'Oh Julie,' she begged. 'At least *think* about it before you decide. Don't rush in like a fool without at least . . .'

I pointed out that I couldn't survive an hour of Sylvana's brutally honest friendship and remain a fool.

Her voice then became softer, sad almost. 'I tell people I'm child-free and proud. Not because I can't have children but because I don't want them. People think that if you don't want children there's something wrong with you. They say it's selfish, but how can you be selfish to beings that don't even exist?'

She awaited my considered reply.

'Sylvana, I've decided, okay? I'm perfectly well aware that I am heading for the most harrowing and crude and bloody disgusting experience of my life . . .'

Sylvana, open-mouthed: 'But the thought fills you with joy?'

'Precisely.'

She picked up her Anne Rice novel again, sat back in her seat and muttered, 'I don't understand you any more.'

I stopped playing.

I told her that I appreciated her concern, but that I had decided to surrender my existence to the torture chamber that is Mother Nature. I told her that pain comes, but then pain goes.

I told her I was going to have a baby because it was the right time career-wise, and anyway I was almost thirty and balding fast. And babies aren't much use to you when you're old and grey.

I readily conceded that a baby constituted – at a certain ontological, pre-linguistic level – a highly developed squawking, tearing, fast-food processing, puking and shitting machine. Nevertheless, I insisted that this highly developed squawking, tearing, fast-food processing, puking and shitting machine was the very entity that would in some inexplicable way bring me to the very source of meaning, fulfilment and love in my life.

Sylvana fell silent at this point. She must have sensed my seriousnesss of purpose. She tried to protest that I was just doing it because my mother was desperate to be a first-time grand-mother.

I calmly shook my head and hit her with it then: I told her I was doing it for our marriage. For love. For a wonderful new family.

'But Ronan doesn't want a baby,' she shot back, shrewdly but cruelly.

'They all say that.'

After that, Beethoven's *Pathetique* came to my fingers like a dream.

Ironic, isn't it?

God, I'm such an unbelievable fool.

5

Staring at me through her car window, Sylvana's caustic expression reads: *Well, I'm here now: what are you going to do about it?* 'You forgot something, darling,' she drawls, eyebrow curled.

'What?'

'The present you bought for Ronan: *Art and the Postmodern.*'

'Oh yes, that.'

It cost me sixty pounds.

'Now he'll be able to bore us interminably on the nature of postmodernism,' she says.

I look away.

'Julie, is something the matter?'

I look back. 'Can I have that book, please?'

'What are you doing with that decanter?'

'I'm throwing a party.'

She inspects me more closely. 'Has something –'

'Give me the book, Sylvana.'

She looks worried now. Without taking her eyes off me she passes a plastic bag through the window. I place the decanter on the ground and take the book, lifting it out of its bag. It is large and heavy. It is truly a beautiful book. The plates and illustrations are of the highest quality.

Modern art is one of Ronan's passions. If his father hadn't forced him to do dentistry he would certainly have studied art. At twenty-three, he joined his father's practice as an apprentice assistant, having studied anatomy, physiology, biochemistry, general medicine, endodontry, exodontry, orthodontry, pharmacology and a host of other tongue-entwining ologies.

When all he wanted to do was learn about art.

At twenty-four he left the apprenticeship and then, against his father's wishes, he headed for the Sorbonne in Paris, where he received a diploma in aesthetics and history of art two years later. Then at last he got real (and poor) and returned to set up his own dentistry practice, his father retiring and sending forward his former clients. I was one of his first patients.

One of his first casualties.

I open *Art and the Postmodern* halfway through: page 186.

Completely ignoring my friend's protestations, I start ripping out the leaves in chunks of five and six pages. I collect the twisted, loose sheaves in the same hand. I am careful not to drop any to the ground: it's important to respect other people's property.

Now there is a gap between pages 186 and 270. Quite a large

gap: my palm is stuffed with eighty shiny pages including two chapters devoted to Jacques Derrida and post-structuralism. This should increase the value of the book considerably.

I am being closely observed by my friend, I sense. But, luckily for her, she doesn't try to stop me. Perhaps she feels that this is somehow my prerogative? That it might even be good for me, therapeutically speaking?

'Julie, what are you doing?'

I glance down at her and put on this big frown. 'Do you require a further demonstration?'

'But that's for . . . Ronan.'

'*Was.*'

'But . . .'

Sylvana's forehead is creased helplessly, like a person in great pain.

'I'm amazed that you're so concerned about Ronan's property. It's not compulsory to like him, you know.'

'Julie – get in the car.' She reaches over and snaps open the passenger door.

'Why? Are you worried what the neighbours might think?'

My voice is shaking. Tears are welling up. '. . . I'm the one who has to bloody live here,' I sniff coarsely, 'with that bastard!'

Sylvana's eyebrows go right up. Her expression reads: what the hell is going on here? Of course, she can't know.

She clambers heavily out of her car, comes up to me and tries to coax the remains of the book out of my hands, but I grip it all the harder, animal-like.

She starts talking to me as if I am aged four. Normally I hate being treated like a baby, especially when Ronan does it. When Sylvana does it, though, I'm flummoxed.

I allow her to usher me into the passenger seat. I feel like a semi-reluctant geriatric must feel: resisting but realizing you've got no choice. Sylvana picks the wine decanter off the ground, dumps it on the back seat, gets in herself, drives to the nearest parking enclosure and jams on the handbrake.

She inspects me and informs me that my hands are bleeding.

Very, very gently she asks me what the hell is going on.

So I come clean.

23

I tell her that I just smashed up Ronan's car, which is presently lying in state in the next parking bay just over the low bush. Her face remains expressionless. She gets out of the car and walks to the corner of this section of the car park. She stands up on the stone border and peers. A second later her heels are snapping back towards me. I could be mistaken, but is that a suppressed smile I spy on her mug?

She gets in again. 'Was that you, Julie?' she asks in a clear, pleasant voice.

'It was.'

I swear I detect a glimmer of admiration in her eyes.

She asks me why I did that, so I tell her everything, trying my best to remain calm. She falls silent, then looks away. With a dark, forbidding grimace, she is analysing the situation, dissecting it into small pieces.

Just witnessing Sylvana turn bad-tempered on my behalf is in itself a supreme comfort. It's like she's transforming my problem into her own personal crusade. She is one of the greatest get-the-shit-off-your-chest friends I've ever had because she refuses to weep and flutter over the minutiae of your misery. No. Instead, she aquires this dark, brooding, apocalyptic expression on her mug like she's just discovered rat entrails in her burger and she's planning a secret hit against the manager.

This can only lead to good.

At last the oracle turns to me, her eyes gleaming diabolically, branding the air with one black-smoked word: *reprisal*. She wants me to confront husband and lover by the poolside.

Like I need to be told.

'The hose,' she says.

'What?'

Oh yes, the hose. Beside the pool is a hose used by the caretaker to wash down the stone slabs each day.

She explains what we are to do: we are both calmly to enter the pool area, grab the hose, point it at the two sunbathers, smile, twist the knob and windscreen-wipe them off the face of the planet. We will watch them dance and scream like a pair of rats drowning in their sunglasses.

24

Getting out of the car, she suggests that I might then give the woman a good smack across the cheek and warn her (pulling my well-practised vampire countenance, which she insists was inspired by Dracula, although in actual fact it was inspired by Hannibal Lecter) that if I ever see her ugly mug again I will tear it off, dry it in the sun, frame it and hang it over my mantelpiece.

I swing my arm to the back seat and grab the neck of the wine decanter. Then I hop out after her.

'What on earth is that for?' she inquires.

'To fill up with her brains,' I explain.

She says she's sympathetic to this approach, but in the same breath she calmly advises me to put it back down. I cannot understand the ridiculous logic that says: 'confront your adulterous spouse, yes, but take care to avoid aggravated assault.'

In the end, though, I replace the decanter in Sylvana's car. I hate being managed like this.

Empty-handed and dumb, I follow her to the pool along a narrow path located between our apartment block and the one next to us. She reminds me of a fearsome headmistress dragging me to her office for some discipline. Soon we connect with the pathway that leads to the pool. A six-foot-high hedge encloses the sizeable swimming-pool area. There is a small wooden gate set into the hedge.

Sylvana opens it. She is about to step through.

'Wait!' I whisper furiously, teetering on the brink.

'What?' she whispers back.

Confrontation.

This is not the right thing to do. I sense I am making a mistake. A mistake I will pay dearly for.

A mistake my mother made and paid dearly for.

'Sylvana, don't go in there!'

'Julie, if I have understood you correctly, they have both been using your bedlinen to get to know each other a whole lot better.'

But something is tugging away at me, telling me no.

'Come on,' she whispers seductively, smiling mischievously.

'No!' I counter.

25

The whole time she is whispering urgently at me to accompany her through the gate and be my husband's worst nightmare. She is assuring me that she will be with me every second of the way on this joyride to Ronan's ruination.

But I can't. I'm standing here making these crazy hand signals. Then my cellphone rings.

We stare into each other's eyes as if we've just been caught pilfering a safe full of banknotes.

6

'Hello there! You called, I believe?'

Cretin.

I don't reply.

I move surreptitiously to the left, hugging the hedge that conceals us. Sylvana follows me away from the wooden gate. I stop and peep through a tiny gap in the vegetation.

'Julie, are you there?'

I can just about make out the two of them. Still in their shades, skin textured like golden syrup, glistening like eels from sun lotion or water or sweat. Ronan is on his stomach, phone to ear. She's still on her back, casually reading her book, her long golden hair tossed over her shoulders. Her figure again. I can actually feel my fingers closing in round her neck and squeezing.

Sylvana is still inciting me to follow her into the pool enclosure and give Ronan an afternoon to cherish for the rest of his life.

But I resist.

'You're breaking up.'

'Hello, Ronan, where are you?'

'Where am I?'

Even before he opens his mouth I know what he is going to do. Before he utters so much as a word, something tells me that all is lost. Ronan is about to re-enact the haunted ghost of my past. He is about to lie.

I'm gripping the hedge, squashing and twisting sharp twigs in my hand. I thought I'd finished with it for ever. But no, my

26

family history has returned with a vengeance. For years it shackled me in a cage. Then I met Ronan and I believed that chapter of my life was closed.

Father's lies.

I was eight or nine when my mother first learnt about his mistress. He stepped into a car outside his workplace one day. There was a woman inside, only it wasn't Mother. She was in the taxi directly behind, wearing shades and a scarf, telling me to make myself scarce in the back seat.

She confronted him, but he made an art of evasion. The next six months were filled with demands from her and lies from him, although at the time neither she nor I recognized them as lies. The woman was a business contact: that was his excuse.

Mother so badly wanted to believe him. There were late-night bedroom arguments, early-morning breakfast rows. There were tears – always hers. There were pleadings for truth and reassurance – always her pleadings. There were angry remonstrations – always her anger. The broken glass issued from her own hand, the broken dreams were sourced in her heart alone.

Then, six weeks later, I saw Father with that woman again. I was, unknown to him, on a school trip to the Law Courts. He exited High Court number two holding her hand. He spotted me, placed her to one side, and came up to me. One minute later he'd sworn me to silence.

From then on I sat back, witnessing him spin around Mother his golden web of deceit, his silken tapestry of lies. I hated my secret knowledge. I hated Mother's attempts to discover the minutest signs of infidelity – searching his pockets for clues, smelling his clothes, analysing his habits. I could have told her everything she needed to know and I would have told her if only she'd asked me. I detested her weakness. I was repelled by the trust and faith she reposed in him, revolted by her belief that honesty and confrontation could cure infidelity.

All it did was alert him.

Hand him the advantage.

Her openness cost her a further wasted year of her life, until she was finally tipped off: he was seen again with the same woman. This time he was without excuse. She threw him out.

*

'You know where I am, Julie.'

'Where's that?'

'It's Thursday afternoon.'

'So you're still in your surgery?'

'Is it a problem?'

Sylvana is pressing her ear into the phone, her hair tickling the side of my face.

'On such a beautiful day?' I reply. 'You're crazy not to be spending it by the pool.'

'Some people have to work, honey, while their little wives play.'

'Husbands are allowed to play too.'

'Extracting teeth isn't much fun.'

I snatch out a branch from the middle of the hedge like some crazed anarchist type and I fling it on to the path beside me. That's better, I can see him now. As he speaks through his phone, he is surveying Miss Bosoms, who is still on her back sheltered from the sun by her book.

'You're extracting a tooth?'

'Yes.'

Pause.

'Is it sore?'

'Not my own tooth, Julie.'

'So because it's not your own, that means it's not sore?'

Pause.

'Well, if there's nothing else . . .'

'Is it the sixth molar?'

'Julie, have you been drinking?' He sighs, a reference to my slightly slurred consonants.

'Or the bottom left wisdom tooth?' I suggest.

I am trying his patience.

'It's okay, Ronan. Don't mind me. Go and extract her tooth.'

'Who says it's a she?'

'You mean you don't inspect the insides of women's mouths?'

'Men's mouths, women's mouths – they're all the same.'

'Do you kiss men?'

'Julie, I have to go.'

'Don't get your knickers in a twist, Ronan. I was merely checking up on you.'

There's a slight pause.

'What do you think I've been doing in your absence?' he quips. 'Laying some sexy blonde?'

We both watch as the Nicole woman raises her left arm and slaps him in jest. Grinning, he shields himself. She returns to her book. Sylvana, grim as death, blinklessly studies the scene.

I hit him with it: 'I'll be home in an hour.'

He jerks his body on to his side and flurries on to his behind, holding up his other hand as if telling Nicole not to move. 'I assume you're joking, Julie,' comes his calm voice.

'I'm not joking. The Cliff Castle Hotel was haunted.'

'Where are you now?' he snaps.

'On the motorway.'

He scrambles on to his feet.

'Is it a problem, Ronan?'

I smile crazily at Sylvana.

Now Nicole gets up like lightning. Her book falls to the ground. How inconsiderate of me, disturbing her pleasant afternoon read. She stuffs my towel into the yellow bag, arches her slender arms one by one and pokes them through a yellow T-shirt, a brief visual experience which aggravates me intensely.

'Where exactly are you?'

'We've just entered the western suburbs.'

He puts his hand over his mobile and says something to Nicole. She starts moving towards the wooden gate. Ronan tells me to hold on a minute, kneels down quickly and stuffs something into a bag. Presumably he is calculating that it will take me a minimum of one hour to get home, taking into account rush-hour traffic. He slips into a mustard-coloured T-shirt, then follows Nicole towards the gate, apparently deep in concentration, mobile phone to his ear. Sylvana and I pull back further round the bend as they approach.

'Aren't you thrilled, Ronan? Now we can have a few extra nights together.'

'Yes, it's wonderful,' he says.

He has caught up with Nicole now. Alongside him, she is almost as tall as he. She has a relaxed, graceful way of walking, though she tilts her head downwards. I wish she'd take off her shades. With shades off, you can measure the more abstract qualities such as intelligence and personality, if she has any.

They pass through the gate and head towards the car park.

'Look, Julie,' comes his voice again, 'why don't we have dinner in town together? Say, La Bohème's? We haven't done that for a while. You can park your car in town overnight and I'll drive both of us home in my Porsche.'

Pause.

'In your Porsche?'

'Yes.'

'I don't think that would be quite . . . feasible.'

He insists that it would be quite feasible.

I tell him it's a sweet thought but I'm a bit tired. He insists, so for the hell of it I promise to meet him at La Bohème's at six o'clock.

We say goodbye.

We both stalk them along the narrow pathway to the front of the block. They disappear through the main entrance and I make a beeline through the car park towards my green MG.

Sylvana: 'Where are you going?'

She's panting behind me. Sylvana was never the fittest.

'Never mind.'

'They've gone up to your apartment, Julie.'

'You don't say.'

She starts pleading with me now. To follow them upstairs on a seriously fun slash-and-burn jungle trip.

'No, Sylvana.'

'Julie, you must confront them. You're not thinking straight.'

Oh yes I am thinking straight.

I'm thinking: Nicole's address on the back of my hand. Cherbury Court, Sandymount, by the sea. I'm thinking: someone's house is about to get added to the trash list. I'm thinking: ice-pick. There's one in the picnic hamper in the boot of my car.

You can't get much straighter than an ice-pick.

When I get to my car I check to see if it's still there.

It's still there.

I circumvent a frowning Sylvana and get into the driving seat.

'Julie, where are you going?'

'See you later.'

She looks flabbergasted. 'Julie, they'll be gone when you get back. Now's your chance!'

'They're not going anywhere, Sylvana. Believe me.'

Fifteen seconds later I'm doing ninety down the coast road towards Cherbury Court.

7

I'd be lying if I told you tears weren't streaming down my face, melting deep ravines through my make-up.

But frankly, darling, who *gives* a shit.

I'm numb. Numb drunk. Dizzy. Reality is making strange shapes. Houses are pulling ugly faces at me. I swear that bent green postbox just gave me the finger. And I think that tree stuck out its tongue at me. I'm whizzing past out-of-focus telephone boxes and blurred parked cars and elastic garden walls. Shoe-shaped machines of varying colours are coming at me at various speeds.

Quite possibly, of course, I am hallucinating.

I slow down to seventy – not bad for a residential area.

And suddenly, from nowhere, I am seized by an image of Ronan and Judy the daughter we were going to have, our wonderful new family. I can see Judy walking between us, a lovely tiny person, giggling, holding our hands.

My eyes fill with a fresh wash of tears.

What did I do wrong?

Is it the sex?

The personality? Am I too boring? Smothering?

Do I annoy him? Slam him down, what with his bragged-up vanity and his lesser intellect?

Has it anything to do with my poor skin?

Or the fact that I'm nearly thirty?

Already I'm whizzing up the motorway through Blackrock. Dangerous driving gets you places quick. I'm doing seventy again. The lights at Blackrock College suddenly turn red. I slam on the brakes and almost scream into the back of this bloke in his forties whose silver 2000D Mercedes has been holding me up for the last half-minute in the outside lane with his pathetic sixty miles an hour.

I have been a naive idiot.

I always thought Ronan was different. I thought we saw the world through the same eyes, breathed the same air, shared the same skin. I thought he was refined. Honourable. Trustworthy.

I remember the first time I met him.

It was at a party. Sylvana and I had gone there with the express intention of getting laid – or so we said. I was twenty-six. Not having experienced that great primeval ape-to-ape thing since I'd attended the zoological enclosure frequently referred to as 'college', I was, let's say, moderately hungry for fresh banana. Poor deprived creature that I was in that impoverished five-year interregnum – the most I'd got from a man (apart from the usual insult veiled as casual interest) had been half a night of mouth-to-mouth fornication with one delicious piece of walking beef, followed by an ugly lip sore.

As soon as I set eyes on Ronan the first thing I said was: 'Jesus, Sylvana, look at that.'

'I prefer older men,' she replied with disdain.

Next, Ronan appeared with his large brown eyes and serious expression, smart, neat and professional-looking. He spoke to me in that earnest, respectful way of his, although he barely looked at Sylvana, which possibly didn't get them off to a great start.

Right away I wanted to play apes with him.

The music swirled its warm arms around us as we danced, surrounded by bodies, voices, dimmed lamps, shadows. I loved his lean, handsome designer face and his velvet-smooth sexy voice as he told me of his love for art, for music, for everything French, of his toleration for dentistry.

I was sold. Before falsely imprisoning him in one of the bedrooms upstairs, I flung him a few impressive details from my own curriculum vitae, including my 'no grade' in pass maths due in no small part to my original though unautographed doodles of horse-mounted Mexicans toting sombreros on the examination notebook.

To balance the picture a little, I also told him about my three years studying for my law degree, my two years in the King's Inns imagining what it would be like to be a barrister, followed by my apprenticeship to a Junior Counsel and my scramble for a piece of the rich personal-injuries pie. Within two years, I modestly informed him, I had fought and won so many cases that I could afford to buy a penthouse apartment in Temple Bar where I then resided.

Two hours later, our mouths were locked in mortal combat in the upstairs bedroom on top of two dozen coats, him trying to pull my clothes off and failing, and me trying to pull his clothes off and winning.

With Sylvana standing outside keeping guard.

Little did I know that this small foray was the crucible for marriage one year down the road.

I have managed to overtake the silver Mercedes. I'm so annoyed at him for purposely holding me up on the fast lane that I give him the vigorously-moving-up-and-down hand sign.

I swing to the right across the railway tracks and speed up along the strand road towards Sandymount, maintaining a fairly respectable sixty-eight.

I brought Ronan home to Mother some weeks later. Big mistake. She thought there was something 'less than fully transparent' about him. 'Is that all?' I wondered.

No, she replied, he was also conceited, opinionated and false. And 'irresponsible'. Had he not, after all, put his dentistry career on hold while he skipped off to Paris to study aesthetics and the history of art?

From that day on I felt I had to prove something to her. Ronan had turned into a kind of crusade.

We got married. We honeymooned in Paris, city of our dreams. He took me by the hand and led me through yellow streets adorned with ancient jewels; bright, sun-washed boulevards lined with trees and cheered by corner cafés with red awnings; high, dark alleyways with crooked shutters and slanting roofs; the scents of hot bread or *gaufres* or coffee.

We laughed and joked and conversed and planned for our future together in the bustling cafés, the elegant restaurants, the cobbled walkways, the museums and the parks of the city. And in the privacy of our bridal suite we shared the intimate secrets of life and love.

For once in my life I began to believe in something I never thought it possible for me to believe in.

Trust.

Passing the Martello Tower beside the wide expanse of Sandymount beach, I take the next left. I drive past Cherbury Court and park in the next street up. Climbing out of the car I immediately lose my balance, lurching over and practically ending up in handstand position. Post-Traumatic Whiskey Disorder.

I open the boot and extract the ice-pick from our picnic box, slide it into my pocket and start walking.

Trust.

Why did I trust Ronan? Simply because I fell in love with him? Because I adored his company? Because I married him? What sort of reasons are those to trust someone?

I squeeze my fingers hard against the sharp tip of the ice-pick. When I feel the pain cutting into me I squeeze even harder. I walk into Cherbury Court. A row of terraced two-storey red-brick houses with front doors painted in luxuriant reds and greens and blues. Narrow strips of garden. Railings in front, well-sheared hedges. Driveways with expensive-looking new cars. Classic middle-class territory.

Unevenly, I walk towards number two. On top of both gateposts are the stone heads of dogs. The narrow gravel driveway is empty. The front garden is neat and lush, enclosed by a clipped hedge and a row of conifers along the front wall. Curved flowerbeds, a small round pond with a fountain in the centre, a pretty bird stand topped by a wooden platform with enough room for, say, two blackbirds to have dinner together.

I approach the front door. On each side stands an evergreen plant in a heavy terracotta pot. Just above the door there hangs a small red octagonal disc with a round mirror in the middle and gold-embossed sign language at the edges. Must be to ward off evil spirits like me.

The front door has a stained-glass panel in the middle, with a picture of a red sailing boat in a blue sea under a yellow sky.

I ring the bell several times.

No one at home.

My fingers clasp the handle of the ice-pick.

Checking first over both my shoulders, I extract the weapon from my pocket and start smashing.

8

The metal blade bounces off the glass like a pencil.

I stop for breath. I smash again, but again it glances off the sailing boat. A quality sailing boat indeed.

There's no sound from inside. And there's no suspicious movement from outside. Me apart.

One more blow and the ice-pick goes straight through the middle of the tall red sail. Very functional ice-pick, this. I wait for the alarm to go off. It doesn't. So I stand on my toes and stick my arm through and open the latch.

The earthenware-tiled hallway at the bottom of the stairs is bright and warm. Just inside the front door is a bright orange curtain and to the right is a small wooden table. On top is a vase containing a two-foot-high jasmine plant. I break it in two like a stick of celery. Hanging on the wall above the table is a pretty watercolour depicting an empty beach with strong waves.

I hack into it, punching a hat-trick of holes into the canvas.

Directly in front of the door is the stairway. On my way into the main room, I hack off a wooden bannister. I pull and pull until it dislodges like a tooth. It falls to the floor. Would make great firewood.

I enter the sitting-room now, close the curtains and start smashing everything in sight. Whole minutes pass.

When I'm done I sit on the lemon-yellow couch, exhausted.

I survey the jungle of devastation around me.

It's like the aftermath of Gallipoli: there's a hole in the TV.

The two rhododendrons which flank the TV have been decapitated: large jurassic leaves lie scattered around the floor. The gold-framed mirror above the mantelpiece is distinguished by impressive Milky Way impressions. The small vase containing one red carnation, which once stood on this same mantelpiece, is nowhere to be seen, although the carnation itself is stuck to the sole of my left shoe. A golden wall light swings from a flex. Silverware and trinkets of all kinds lie strewn about the floor. The stone fireplace is flavoured by the stench of alcohol. Glass fragments sparkle across the room, and over there I spy this most elegant and lovely drinks cabinet. I seem to recall it recently had glass in it.

Anyone would think, looking at all this chaos around me, that I have not been exceptionally well brought-up.

I have – this is the exception.

In one corner I notice two orange porcelain ducks perched all alone on a narrow table. They remain completely untouched. I just didn't have the heart.

I am now in the process of observing the coffee table. Humiliated and glassless, it is lying on the floor alongside a scattering of magazines and books: *Cosmopolitan*, *Time*, *House and Home*, *Aromatherapy Journal*, *Amateur Gardening*, *DIY Home Repair Manual*, *Woodworker*.

She must be living with a man, then. A brother, perhaps? A flatmate? A partner? A husband?

There are some books too: *Buddhism* by Christmas Humphries, *The Road Less Travelled* by M. Scott Peck, *The Power of Positive Thinking* by Norman Vincent Peale, *How to Make Friends and Influence People* by you'll never guess, *How to Kill Your Husband and Get Away with It* by yours truly.

Most of these I have read. The great search for Meaning in this Life, to which my family history drove me, has not totally passed me by. Despite any recent impressions to the contrary.

Only one self-help book ever succeeded in majorly pissing me off. It was a paperback from America which suggested that when persons or things cause you annihilative anxieties (i.e. you want to kill or destroy them), you should attempt to focus positive thoughts on the entities in question. This supposedly frees up powerful psychological energies. I fed the book into the latest hi-tech paper shredder in the Law Library. I clogged up the machine bigtime, which I must say was a nicely ironic footnote on deblocking energies.

I lean over from the couch and pick up a pocket-sized book called *Feng Shui: transform your life with ancient Chinese wisdom*. It's full of photographs of rooms and gardens. The blurb says it's important to harness *chi* or energy in order to achieve peace and harmony in your home or office environment.

I have a real problem with this: how can a woman crave to live in harmony and communion with ancient Chinese wisdom and at the same time nonchalantly misappropriate husbands?

I pocket the booklet, get up and go over to the teak drinks cabinet on the off-chance that in this archaeological ruination of glass bottles there might still remain one unscathed. My optimism is rewarded: a small Cointreau bottle peeks from the corner of the cabinet, concealed by a fractured bottle of Martini.

While I am polluting my insides with the stuff, I notice these raggedy bloodstains on the armrest of the couch where I've just been sitting. I quickly examine my hands. Cuts everywhere. Serves her right.

I walk towards the only brittle object in the room which has survived my onslaught, bar the orange porcelain ducks and the orange Cointreau: the fish tank, which I have studiously ignored until now.

It's a stunning community aquarium, more beautiful even than our own. It contains a magnificent aquascape. On a gravel of coral chips and coral sand rises up a structure of pale tufa-rock boulders with crevices and caves, arches and terraces. There are a few light-green living rocks: that one there, for instance, is an Atlantic anemone, populated by an utterly mouth-watering invertebrate melange of tubeworms, fanworms and soft corals.

And the fish? They're just so cute. I bend down to look. The first one is having a little stroll. Possibly he's on a reconnaissance mission. I think I'll say hello.

Hello little *Hyphessobrycon erythrostigma!* How could they call you that? Your nickname is so much nicer: bleeding-heart tetra, what with the stabbed bloodshot look in your pretty eyes.

Oops! There is your cousin rounding the corner. Also, there's a lemon-peel angelfish or should I say, a *Pterophyllum scalare*, poking its nose into the glass in a fairly doomed attempt to make contact with me. That lemon-yellow colour again – it's a real obsession with her. Behind it flutters a yellow tang (the Latin escapes me) possibly on a food crusade. The tangs are great lettuce eaters, though they won't find too much lettuce in there right now.

Moving on to the right side of the tank, there's a game of rounders going on between this humbug damselfish, which resembles a zebra with fins and prefers bloodworms and shrimp for dinner, and several guppies.

That's when I spot the solitary tiger barb, an aggressive, revolting-looking fish with green and black scales, and a huge fanlike fin bearing red and black tiger markings. This woman is not great on aquatic politics. She ought to know that you should *never* mix the tiger barb with the guppy. Give them a day or two and they will be minus a fin or two.

On that point, lemon-peel angelfish eat newborn guppies for breakfast. What d'you bet I'll soon see a piranha cruising the joint waiting to pick up some floating breakfast?

Still. This is, truly, a marvellous aquatic tapestry.

My ice-pick seems to crash all by itself – effortlessly – into the glass, sending torrents of cold water over my legs and feet, and as I watch its life draining out before me I am totally unmoved to see a squad of fish sucking desperately against the drenched woodblock floor, fins flapping uselessly against their pale bellies. A guppy is trapped at the bottom of the tank, poor waterless, thankless thing.

God, I'm drunk! Drunk like a fish.

Leaving them there flippering on the floor, I exit the room, thinking: I have waved goodbye to what was once a self-image of decency and temperance. I am a destroyer. An anarchist. A hooligan. An Antichrist. A savage. An ogre. A Goth. A hag.

A terrorist, actually.

And it's giving me this warm, happy glow inside.

Upstairs, I enter a tidy lavender-smelling bedroom. There is a double bed, cosy and plump with pillows, with a man's shoes underneath the bed-end. The jilted husband?

On top of the built-in dressing-table is a magnolia plant, and a photograph of a woman and a man. It's her. She has the same long, wavy, golden hair. In the photo she's shy and feminine-looking, if slightly girly. She's got these large, sparkling eyes and a nice smile. She's got freckles and I know some people would call her cute. The man, certainly in his mid-thirties, is strong and wolf-like.

I ascend a narrow metal ladder to the attic. I penetrate the darkness above and flick on a nearby switch. It is a tiny cramped space, smelling strongly of timber, paint and white spirit. Just beneath the V-shaped rafters is an easel on its stand carrying an unfinished painting: a formless wash of colours splashed together like a patchwork quilt. There are paintbrushes lying on a fold-up table alongside paint tubes and palettes, and sticking out of jamjars. On the floor, perched against the brick partition wall, are a few dozen canvases and a few framed paintings.

I am heartened by the first painting: entitled *Foetus*. Its naivety beggars belief. This is funny. I have to call Sylvana.

When she answers, I tell her I'm in Nicole's home.

'Oh,' she says after a long pause, 'I was just wondering.'

'I'm in the attic, right?'

'Why not?'

'I'm staring at this painting . . .'

'She's an artist?'

'Could you please refrain from abusing language. Slobbering on canvas, Sylvana, does not constitute art. Now, this glorified muck, which I am presently holding in my hands, is supposed to represent a foetus, okay?'

'She's probably pregnant.'

'It is pinky red and has two tiny white blotches, which are supposed to be the hands, and a large round white blotch with a dark thing in the middle – that's supposed to be the head. Are you with me so far?'

'I'm with you.'

'Now this . . . *blob* – which is meant to be a foetus although it looks more like a shrimp – is surrounded by all this red stuff . . .'

'I like the symbolism,' she remarks.

She's trying to tease me.

I snatch up another canvas. On the back are scrawled the words *Wind and Water*. Wind and piss more like it.

'Julie,' she says in a more serious voice, 'I think you should leave now.'

A third canvas is more intriguing. It consists simply of eight small figures spaced randomly all over it. Each figure resembles a face: each is composed of patterns of parallel strokes like the ones I saw on that mirror thing hanging outside the front door.

I describe it to my friend.

'She clearly has talent,' Sylvana observes.

Cursing, I switch off my mobile and fling *Foetus* at the water tank, causing a dull booming sound. I now glare at each painting in turn, ranged along the wall, verbally tagging each one with a juicy linguistic crudity.

What if Sylvana has a point? What if the tart *does* have talent? What about those portrait sketches of Ronan? They worry me because they suggest (but no more than that) that she has something vaguely resembling a brain, and Ronan admires and respects women with brains.

I could destroy all this 'art' shite with one swipe. I could do it. I could take each painting in turn, apply a spoonful of white spirit and cause a small fire sensation.

But I don't.

Why not?

Because I have just heard the sound of a vehicle in the driveway.

I know I should be concerned, but I can't seem to find the energy. So I redescend the ladder at a fairly leisurely pace – probably the Cointreau.

I walk to the front bedroom and look out. Oh yes, I'm thinking, how interesting. There's a man out there in the front driveway, climbing out of a Land Rover. He reminds me a lot of the man in that photograph. Fancy that!

Calmly I descend the stairs.

You can hear his footsteps on the gravel.

I run out to the fitted kitchen and unlock the kitchen door into the garden, my eyes glancing off a magazine on the table. I stop and look again a second time. On the cover is this huge pink face of a grinning baby. It is entitled *Your Baby and You: help and advice through pregnancy, birth and early parenthood.*

She has a baby?

Sound of the front door opening.

Might as well steal the magazine too.

I grab it, shove open the back door, race down the garden and take a running jump for the top of the back garden wall but I more or less flatten my nose against the plaster so I try a running jump again. This time I scramble over and hit the ground head first. I'm in an alleyway. I pick myself up and run in any direction.

Wandering around the locality for at least a half-hour, drip-drunk, I eventually locate my MG. I realize I've been carrying the ice-pick the whole time, in full view. That's what you get when you pump alcohol into your bloodstream: stupid.

I lock myself inside the car, ignite, accelerate and zoom away like I have a whole squadron of police cars after me.

And maybe I do.

9

By the time I've driven back to our apartment complex at top speed, my bloodstained fingers are beginning to sting against the steering wheel. Evidence – that highly irritating disincentive to crime.

Catching a sudden glimpse of Ronan walking out of our condo, I pull the reins and screech into the nearest parking bay – one up from our own. He turns, but before he sees me I'm gone. He must be on his way into town to meet me in La Bohème's for six, dutiful husband that he is.

I pull into an empty parking space and switch off the engine. There he is, his head bobbing like a buoy over the hedge top as he approaches his vehicle. He stops. He is standing with his back to me in the far corner of the car park underneath a cherry tree whose leaves are the colour of violent purple.

He appears to be observing something. His Porsche, at a guess. I scroll down my window and wait, and watch and listen with a nice little fizzle of anticipation.

He is now circling a large object in a broad arc – very cautiously – like hunters circling a freshly slain lion. He is examining a large object, which I cannot imagine ever moving again. Now he's glancing around him with darting, suspicious movements, but there is no one in sight and although I'm sitting crouched in the only black MGF 1.8i in these suburbs, the poor man still doesn't see me.

He goes to the edge of the car park, beyond which lies a football pitch. On it a soccer match is being waged by teenagers wearing a colourful assortment of jerseys.

Now you can hear something that is sheer joyful music to the ears. It is a Vivaldi quartet awakening the buds of an Italian springtime. It is a Mozart aria cutting through the glassy air of Salzburg. It is a Debussy sonata filling your head with mystifying sadness as you tread the silent back alleys of Paris.

It is the sound of Ronan roaring.

I open the car door to improve the reception. He is screaming at those poor lads. The subject? His recently deceased Porsche. My heart goes out to him at this difficult time, for his soul is suffused with agony. What a horrible deed. What an appalling offence against his property.

My pining husband is still hurling accusations at those youngsters. They in turn are answering back, as is their constitutional right. You can hear their high-pitched voices pierce the air in stupefied rebuttal. The poor things. They who have taken time out to enjoy an innocent game of footie and thus in their own way to recreate the meaning of life. I regret having put them in this position, but there you are.

Ronan marches back to his car, utterly defeated-looking. He should lighten up and join the boys for a game of football; he'd know all about defeat then. A chimpanzee would make it to the first eleven sooner than Ronan.

Now he is leaning with both arms against the roof of his car, lamenting, head bowed, shoulders hunched, grief-struck as if someone has just died on him.

There's a term in ancient Greek, frequently on Ronan's lips whenever he rambles on about dramatic structure in Sophocles.

This is the term: tragedy.

How very appropriate.

Point of information: how will he get into town to meet me in La Bohème's? Will he take a taxi instead?

I'll ask him. Out comes my mobile. I input.

Out comes his own mobile, which he raises to his head. 'Oh, it's you,' he says.

'Jesus, don't sound so enthusiastic.'

'I'm not.'

'Am I calling at a bad time?'

'Where are you?'

'I'm going straight home: I don't feel like dining out tonight.' Creepy silence.

'What do you mean you're going straight home?'

'I mean: I'm going in the opposite direction to away.'

'Stop being a bloody idiot, Julie.'

'I apologize.'

Ronan is normally so composed, so soft-spoken. He prides himself on never raising his voice, on sublimating any annoyance through the cool channel of his so-called intellect.

'We made an arrangement,' he says.

'It's an argument, I grant you that.'

I pay him the courtesy of explaining that on account of the acidification of my digestive tract I just don't feel up to eating dinner in a restaurant tonight, and it suits me better to go home directly and await his return.

I hear this great sigh-heave. 'Julie, I've already arrived in town.'

'How did you manage that?'

'What?'

'So you're in town?'

'We had a date. I booked a table overlooking the canal.'

'How romantic.'

'They're doing Duck Provençale tonight.'

Has he any idea how ridiculous that sounds?

'That's romantic too, although not for the duck.'

'It's your favourite dish, Julie.'

How well he understands my weakness for quack-free Provençale-sauce-dunked duck.

'I'm sorry, Ronan. I have to go home.'

Pause.

'Jesus,' he says then, 'you're about as dependable as a . . .'

I know what he's thinking. He's thinking something disparaging about my hormonal system: I'm unreliable, unpredictable, liable to spontaneous bursts of scattiness, mercuriality, irresponsibility, insanity . . . cantankerosity? It's the usual put-down.

'. . . as a hysteric on . . . Prozac,' he concludes lamely.

'Ouch.'

'I can't respect people who fatuously cancel arrangements.'

I crave to tell him that I can't respect people who flaunt their marriage vows, but I refrain.

There's an ominous silence on the line.

'What's the matter with you today, Ronan? Is it the piles?'

Further portentous pause.

'If you must know, my car had a slight accident.'

'An accident.'

'Just now.'

'Where?'

'In our car park.'

'I thought you were in town?'

'I am.'

'I see. What happened?'

'Oh, it got a bit smashed up. Vandals. Just some thugs who couldn't handle the idea that some people work for a living and drive nice cars.'

I'm a vandal now. And a thug.

'What did they do?'

'Oh,' he says, minimizing, 'tossed a few bricks at it, that's all.'

Pause.

'Is that all?'

'It's enough.'

'Have you called the police?'

'They were on their tea break.'

'But the police work in shifts.'

'No, Julie, I didn't call the police. Nor do I intend to.'

I find this somewhat reassuring.

He starts complaining now: 'This would never have happened

44

but for the colour. I mean, green or blue or black would have been fine. But *yellow*? As it is, I feel like I'm Elton John driving this thing.'

Ronan is insinuating that his car was victimized because of its hilarious yellow visibility. And since I am the one who chose the yellow colour through a surreptitious last-minute change, I am somehow to blame for its being trashed.

It's a scandalous accusation. 'So you're saying that I'm responsible for having your car smashed.'

He tells me to stop being paranoid.

'*Paranoid*? Did I hear somebody use that word?'

'Relax, Julie.'

Everything stops for five seconds. 'Relax' is another word *nobody* uses in my presence.

'Okay, Julie. I'm sorry. Of course you're not responsible for what happened to my car. Now will you meet me in town?'

I'm not? Did I just hallucinate bashing in his car? Did I? God, I think I need therapy to remind me that I'm going sane.

'You actually think I'm paranoid, don't you?'

He softens his tone immediately and insists that we have a nice romantic meal together at La Bohème's. I interrogate him as to whether this means I am paranoid or I am not paranoid.

There's just this tremulous silence.

I inform him then that I wouldn't dream of inflicting a paranoid squid on him for dinner, that I've far too much respect for him to do such a thing.

'Julie,' he groans. 'Let's just meet in La Bohème's, okay?'

'One point, Ronan.'

'Yes.'

'Did you actually drive your trashed Porsche into town?'

He clears his throat. 'Yes, Julie.'

'It must have been painfully embarrassing.'

'Look, forget the car. Just meet me in town. Half-six. Okay?'

'Okay,' I lie.

He hangs up.

I see him disappearing behind a tall bush. I feel like a guardian angel peering over his shoulder.

Next thing I hear a car engine bursting into action, followed by an almighty revving and screeching of brakes, and suddenly this bright apparition flashes through the hedge to my left. There's more brake-screeching and tyre-wailing as the car stops abruptly at the main road, then the noise vanishes.

He should have more sense than to be embarrassing himself in public, driving a wreck like that.

But where is herself?

Is she still in the apartment? Cleaning up after the picnic?

I get out of my car, baby book and ice-pick under my arm. Psyching myself up to scalp her.

I'm glad I did that to his car, though.

Really, doing that stuff to his Porsche has turned out to be seriously good for my health.

In ancient Greek, I think that's called catharsis.

10

I still get that lemon scent, though it's more muted now.

'Where are you, you bitch?'

I slam shut the door of the apartment and flick on the hall light for some extra illumination, throw my reading material down on the banana couch and stand perfectly still, clasping my fingers around the hard, thin shaft of my weapon.

She's in here somewhere. I know it.

And she's mine.

The lemon-yellow Wonderbra is gone, of course. I fasten the chain across the door and draw the bolts across the top and bottom. I will make a Fort Knox out of my front entrance. Like a wildcat, she will scratch and scream and scrape, desperate to escape. While I calmly close in on her and proceed to staple her with my heels to the wood.

The kitchen. I check everywhere. Under the table. Under the sink. In the broom cupboard. Nothing.

On tiptoe, I pass through the second kitchen door, which leads into the lounge. I traverse the lounge and go through the second lounge door back into the hall, cross the hall and search our sleeping quarters. Under beds, in wardrobes, in the hot press, behind the bathroom door, on the narrow bedroom verandas.

But there's no sign of her anywhere. Not even inside our large dirty-clothes basket.

She must have left before Ronan.

The place is immaculate. It is clean and dust-free. The bathroom taps are shining. The hallway smells like a flaming pot-pourri. Ronan would never do this. *I* would never do this. It's crazy overkill.

His own *personal* grooming is meticulous: he has his shirts professionally ironed, the washing basket receives a daily draft of his underwear, he uses Aramis aftershave, he flosses his teeth nightly and on occasion I've even seen the gobshite pluck his eyebrows. But not *once* have I ever witnessed him lift a sweeping brush.

How is he going to explain this new Hoover-friendly personality implant of his? I can't wait to see what he dreams up.

Once back in the lounge, I pour myself a Cointreau. I notice the level has significantly diminished since I was last here, two hours ago. Ronan never drinks Cointreau. Only I drink Cointreau. Nicole has been guzzling it in the meantime, the greedy glut. And in somebody else's house! No respect.

I drench my gullet with a large burning gulp of the stuff. Suddenly I notice something peculiar. I can feel my body tense up like a tiger.

The french windows are slightly ajar.

She's outside on the balcony.

While I'm in town supposedly dining with Ronan, she's lounging around here, practising being Ronan's future wife.

Heart pounding, I clench my grip on the ice-pick. I proceed forward, but she's beyond my range of vision. She must be at the far end of the veranda. I'm going to push her off the balcony. By accident.

I swing the doors open, remaining inside. 'Get in here,' I snarl.

No reply. I'll try the sly approach: 'We can discuss this reasonably.'

Still no response.

'*Get in here you bitch!*' I'm snarling. '*You've been sleeping with my husband!*'

Still nothing.

'Have it your way.'

I burst out on to the balcony.

It's empty.

There's no one there. Just the white plastic table with two soiled wineglasses standing lonesomely on top.

I send the ice-pick crashing down on to the two glasses, scattering smithereens over the edge and down into the patio far below, and there's this screaming sound now and I'm vaguely aware of our neighbours sunbathing in the adjacent apartment block and my throat tightens up like I'm being throttled and there's this wet sensation filling my eyes and my nose and my windpipe right the way down to my heart and I lurch back into the lounge and stray like a ghost in no particular direction and I end up back out in the hall and my eyes fall on to the couch on to the baby booklet I'd forgotten all about and I go over to it and pick it up and stare at the huge pink grinning face of a baby with its mouth open and its tongue glistening and its beautiful grey eyes and its flecks of straw-coloured hair and its cute ears and the title *Your Baby and You* and suddenly I can feel my knees hitting the floor, and I can hear this unearthly wailing sound – as if it's coming from outside me – and everything I touch is wet and slippery and my knuckles are stuck hard into my eye sockets and I'm ordering myself to stop this ridiculous behaviour, I tell myself that I'm overreacting, that I've been drinking and I might even be hallucinating and now I'm having difficulty breathing and the only thing I can think of to take my mind off this terrible, terrible pain is the Jameson's and I'm begging someone, begging someone with all my heart, would someone please come and take it away . . .

11

Where am I?

In front of me is an ultramarine-blue wall with a familiar painting on it. It's a group of female nudes, with translucently blue skin. Their hair is long and their flesh is pink, orange and yellow. They have large bums. Mermaids stranded on the shoreline, perhaps, forced out of their primordial submarine hideaway. I know how they feel.

It's Cezanne, that much I know. But whose wall is this? Whose purple colour-washed pine floor? Whose large net curtains billowing gently in the infiltrating breeze?

I rub my eyes.

There's a noise of clinking cups in a nearby room. I try to get up from the comfortable fat couch I'm lying on, but my strength fails.

I've certainly been here before.

Over the mahogany mantelpiece opposite me to my left is another familiar print. The picture is of a pale-faced woman sitting on a chair, caressing the skull of what appears to be her dead husband.

Each to her own.

Suddenly it hits me: this can only be Sylvana's.

I stare at my watch and gasp: a quarter past midnight.

Everything floods back now, memory and anguish, and I collapse into the couch. It's as if I've just had a heart transplant. Only instead of going through the regular surgical channels, Ronan has ripped it out of my chest without permission and now both he and his side piece are playing football with it, kicking it happily from one to the other, so absorbed in their game they've forgotten it's a part of me.

I try to call out.

A familiar voice emanates from the kitchen. 'Have you returned to the land of the living, Julie?'

Yes, I seem to remember being drunk out of my brains while I detonated on the hallway floor, haemorrhaging tears.

'How did I get here?'

'I drove you in my car. You called me, remember?'

'No.'

'You were in bits.'

I want to die. I've had a rotten life.

Firstly, I was born.

Then I grew up. Grew up in the shadow of my parents' mutual trashing sessions, and spent my early teenage years trying to haul Mother from the emotional cesspit into which she fell, after she finally threw Father out. Me the quiet, unacknowledged partner throughout, the silent voice of suffering.

And it goes on: the unrelenting torment to which my life appears equivalent, with fleeting moments of solace in between, thanks to Sylvana and shopping. And whiskey. And chocolate. And Mother, when she's not in excavation mode down your neck.

But what about that card Ronan gave me a year and a half ago, on Valentine's Day? I remember the words he wrote: 'This is just to say that since I met you I haven't stopped loving you.'

What does that say?

When you handed it to me and saw me reading it, there were tears in your eyes, though you pretended to laugh it off. That says you meant it. And what about all the beautiful things you have given me? What about the twenty-four-carat gold bracelet you bought me for my last birthday? Surely that means something?

Hard heels click against the floor.

Sylvana strides in with steaming coffee and her favourite snack: Ryvita stacked with goat's cheese and peanuts, glued on with mayonnaise. She sits down on the couch, pressing against my thigh. She starts munching a peanut. 'So,' she says, flicking me her sly, you can't-fool-me look.

I know what she's thinking. 'So what?'

'How did the Cherbury Court thing go?'

What a funny way to phrase it. It's like saying: 'How did the money-laundering thing go?' or, 'How did the drug-heist thing go?' or, 'How did the tax-dodge thing go?' She makes it sound like I do this 'Cherbury Court thing' every day as a matter of boring routine. Jesus, what does she take me for?

'Oh, fine.'

'Meaning?'

'It was grand.'

'How did you get into the house?'

'Oh, you know . . . I got in.'

'That much we have established. But how?'

Like a sadistic dentist who enjoys pulling teeth, Sylvana gets a great kick trawling classified material out of me, and the more the procedure hurts the more she seems to enjoy it.

'You've nothing to be ashamed of.' She grins, chewing peanuts in that infuriatingly non-committal way of hers.

'I'm not ashamed.'

She's dying for a bit of juice to liven up her day. She would love to discover that I happened to spend part of my Thursday afternoon criminally lacerating an unknown citizen's living-room and leaving her fish world overbowled on the floor. But she's not getting any more out of me than is strictly necessary.

'You prowled around the back, didn't you, when no one was looking? You found an open door and sneaked through it like a thief.'

'You're making me out to be some sort of criminal.'

'A criminal?' she disdains. 'You wouldn't have the guts.'

'Actually,' I reply, irritation rising, 'I dislodged a glass panel in her front door.'

Silence, while she beams on me full force. 'Dislodged.'

'With an . . . implement. Only so I could reach through and open the latch.'

'Of course,' she replies. 'How practical.'

Now there's this slender guilt creeper crawling up my spine.

'I admit I don't do that sort of thing very often.'

'Using an implement to smash your way through front doors.'

'Yes, Sylvana.'

'That's breaking and entering, you know.'

'I don't necessarily feel good about it.'

'You don't.'

'In retrospect.'

Tilting her head, she looks at me like I'm a cute newborn puppy. 'She doesn't feel good about it,' she drawls. 'Well, my heart bleeds for you.'

'I . . . I was *hammered* . . .'

I'm well aware that alcohol is no defence in law.

'You mean,' she corrects, 'you were doing the hammering.'

'Ice-picking.' I correct her back.

Her eyes widen. 'You used an ice-pick to break in?'

'Sylvana,' I blurt impatiently, 'how else was I supposed to get

51

into her house after I practically caught her in the middle of shagging my husband?'

She picks up a few more peanuts from the tops of the snacks, pops them into her gob and starts munching. 'You could have tried ringing the bell,' she replies.

Why is she being such a cow?

'Julie, what you did is what the Indians used to do.'

'You're thinking of a hatchet, Sylvana.' I sigh. 'Indians didn't use ice-picks. They didn't inhabit de luxe apartments and drive down to the country on sunny weekends with their picnic hampers and iceboxes. The nearest north-pole analogy would be the Eskimos. Only Eskimos lived in igloos, not avenues, and besides . . .'

'You smashed her place up, didn't you?'

She's still chewing.

'What?'

'With the ice-pick.'

She gives me this rather sly look.

I laugh. 'Whatever gives you that idea?'

'Admit it.'

'I will admit no such thing.'

I'm not a good liar. Have to work on it.

'I know you have a terrible temper, Julie.'

'Don't be silly.'

'What about Ronan's car?'

'He deserved it.'

'Of course he did. Julie, for God's sake, you can tell me!'

'I'm sorry to disappoint you, Sylvana, but there's nothing to tell.'

She stands up.

'Where are you going?'

'I get the picture,' she says, stalking into the kitchen.

'What picture?'

'You went in there with your ice-pick, determined to get even with Ronan, full of these wonderfully ambitious redecoration schemes. But once inside you chickened out and stared at a few paintings instead, and called me because you were secretly shitting a brick.'

52

Why do I get the feeling that she's manipulating me? 'You think I was shitting a brick?'

'It's obvious,' she replies, her voice shrilling through the box-like acoustics of the kitchen. 'You left the house very, very quietly. And intact. The whole time thinking, God, if I get caught my law career is over.'

'You think so.'

'You probably told yourself it was Ronan's fault, not hers, so therefore it'd be wrong to damage her property. You slunk back out of there like a rabbit.'

From the kitchen comes the crinkly sound of Sylvana removing the plastic wrapper from a cigarette box.

'You obviously think I'm some sort of angel,' I call to her, slightly hot under the collar.

'You ran out of there, all wobbly and virtuous, leaving the place like a palace.'

I can hear the metallic cling of her cigarette lighter lid. Now there is silence, now the lid is clinked shut again. She reappears at the doorway, stares at an old photo of her father hung up on the adjacent wall and scrapes a mark off it with her thumbnail.

'You think I left the place like a palace?'

'I do.'

'If you must know, you bitch, I happened to turn that woman's living-room into downtown Baghdad.'

She moves around to another photograph, this time of her father as a young man, together with his first wife. 'Yes, yes,' she drones, bored. 'Of course you did.'

So I explain to Sylvana that I behaved like the Terminator in a china shop with no exit doors.

There's a slight gap, then she asks me to explain myself.

My friend was never one for obscure allusions. Abstractions have the effect of making her eyeballs roll uphill. She loves the explicit, the vivid. In short, Sylvana worships concrete.

'For example,' I clarify, putting my head back down on the armrest, 'I put a hole through the television with my foot.'

During a brief, shocked intermission in our dialogue, I do a little more boasting about all the wonderful and various activities I pursued in Nicole's living-room. I can hear Sylvana's shoes walk across the room towards me. We are now once more in eye contact.

'You *didn't*,' she says, her voice tainted by the merest whiff of admiration.

'Well, yes, I did,' I reply with a rejoining whiff of pride. 'I most certainly did.'

Now a deadly silence reigns in the room, interrupted only by the puffy sounds of her smoking as she stands there and quietly observes me. To shock her even further I confess that I also smashed her fish tank.

Dare I say it, but I'm beginning to enjoy myself.

'You could go to jail for that,' she says, her suspicious look slowly returning.

'Stop exaggerating,' says I, although I've a sneaky suspicion that that's exactly where people like me are put. 'Sylvana, stop looking at me like that. I was smashed out of my brains! I didn't intend to do it, I just . . .'

'That's right: someone forced you to do it at gunpoint.'

'It wasn't like that . . .'

'No. You *chose* to go. You enjoyed yourself. You had a ball.'

This is an inquisition. Sylvana is interrogating me. Why is she being such a cow? 'Well, now that you mention it, yes, I did have a ball.'

'Julie, you axe your way into a total stranger's house in the middle of the afternoon and you proceed to smash up her living-room . . .' her face is a monument to incredulity '. . . and you stand here and tell me you had *fun*?'

I don't have to lie here and take this. 'Yes, I had fun. It was *brilliant* fun. It was sheer one hundred per cent quality enjoyment. I was blissfully happy during that minute of my life.'

She smirks at me. 'But I thought you felt *bad* about it?'

I stand up. I walk straight out into her octagonal turquoise Ottoman empire hallway. 'I'm going home. I'll call you some time.'

I stop at the huge mirror with the thick grey metal frame where there stands a glass bowl full of bright-red tulips. I take one good look at myself.

This is what a jilted wife must look like: horrible.

No one understands what I am going through. You'd have expected Sylvana of all people to have some sympathy. But no.

As I open the door I'm hearing this strange panting noise.

I turn round.

I can see her through the door sitting on the edge of the couch, in a kind of convulsion. At first I'm curious about whether she has a medical condition she's kept to herself, but after a while I realize she's laughing at me.

She tries to stand up. She steadies herself on the armrest and totters through the sitting-room door and over to me. 'You're brilliant,' she says.

'W-what?'

'I never thought you'd have the guts to do anything like that.'

'You didn't?' says I, confused.

She gives me a sudden hug. She's giggling into my ear now like a crisp, deafening loudspeaker. I find myself deflating into a sigh of foolish relief.

'You should have seen yourself just now,' she says. 'You looked furious.'

She's hugging me, but I'm still very cross.

'I'd have done the same myself,' she cackles, 'or worse.'

'You're a bitch, Sylvana.'

'I know. Look, we'll write them a letter of apology. I'll compose it. "Dear Madam, we regret to inform you that on the recent occasion of the vandalization of your abode we made a slight error of judgement and we do hope that you will accept our humblest apologies . . ."'

Sylvana is doing the theatrical bit now. I fold my arms and stare at the door latch.

'". . . and in particular, we regret the destruction of your lovely fish tank, but, given the serious danger of carnivorous behaviour, we felt at the time that we had no other alternative."'

I refuse to smile, although I can feel myself softening.

'"But this is in no way to detract from the utter sorrow we feel that where once you had a drinks cabinet you now have a pile of glass."'

'Don't forget the summer alcohol collection,' I point out.

'"And we would like to offer our condolences in respect of

your summer alcohol collection, and over the fact that we are unable to provide compensation for the entirety of aforesaid damage and hence you will not require our address, but we will unhesitatingly remember you in our prayers."'

We're both laughing now – crying – into each other's hair.

When we've calmed down a little and are ensconced on the couch again, Sylvana picks up the plate of goat's cheese and peanut snacks and puts it on her lap, and we start eating ravenously. After a fair amount of rude noshing, she turns away and stares out of the window for some time. She only ever does this when there's something bothering her big time.

'Julie, you can't go back with him,' she says, eventually.

I just look down.

'Do you agree?'

'Maybe.'

'Why don't you move in with me?'

'I don't know. We'll see.'

'It's no problem.'

'Thanks, but not just yet.'

She gives me this crooked look, like I'm extraordinarily naive even to consider staying with Ronan after what he did. But I refuse to be Sylvana's filofax. I will not lie here and listen to her reorganize my life. Some good old-fashioned solace, that's all that's needed.

'So what are you going to do?' she says, munching peanuts.

'Let's drop this topic.'

'I won't let you destroy yourself.'

'I'm fine.'

'I can't respect women who turn themselves into victims.'

'You never liked Ronan anyway.'

She tweaks her left eyebrow sardonically. 'Funny that you're asking me to like him at this time.'

'He does happen to be my husband.'

'Not for long, I predict.'

'Sylvana, I don't want to hear any more, is that okay by you?'

My face is roughly four millimetres away from her nose at this point. I can feel her nasal breeze wafting against my upper lip. The aggravation is tugging away at my gut like a row of meat hooks.

In a smooth movement Sylvana closes both eyes and turns away from me like I don't exist. 'Fine.' She shrugs indifferently, blowing smoke out of the far corner of her mouth.

Sylvana is more stubborn than rubber. She really despises Ronan. She thinks he's pretentious and self-opinionated. Civil on the surface but secretly spiteful. I'll never forget the time she told him at a party, while contemptuously crunching crisps between her tiny, perfect teeth: 'There's something distinctly unlikeable about you.'

The one thing that would crown Sylvana's pleasure (and my pain) is for me to give him such a hard flying boot in the arse that he'll land in Antarctica and run out of heating oil. She has always wanted Ronan to be an adulterer. Why? Because then, she thinks, I'll kick him out.

Now, she figures, is her golden opportunity. 'I believe in telling the harsh truth, Julie,' she says after a while. 'I know his type. Too many of my friends have refused to listen to me in the past. And then when I turn out to be right, do they thank you? Not on your life, they drop you. A cigarette?'

Saying nothing, I accept one from her and she lights me up.

'I just want to wait,' I tell her.

'For what?'

'And see.'

'Oh, right, wait until some blinding virtue you never knew he had comes and smacks you in the face?'

'Sylvana, is this code for get lost? Because if you want, I'll go.' I'm sitting forward on the edge of my seat now, glaring at her.

'Have it your way,' she replies with indifference.

'I happen to love him. Is that okay?'

'That's fine.'

I take a long drag of my cigarette, then exhale a bucket-load of smoke at her. 'My marriage happens to be important to me.'

'Great.'

'In fact,' I continue, those meat hooks of aggravation still clutching my gut, 'it's so important to me that I might even consider forgetting Ronan's little flirtation.'

She takes the trouble actually to look in my direction. 'I know you're only joking.'

'I'm not joking, Sylvana,' I reply, standing up. 'Anyway, I have to go home now.'

'Julie, for God's sake, don't do anything rash . . .'

She stands up herself. I feel like I'm on a roll.

'We both know what men are like,' I tell her. 'When it comes to sex, they get a bit hysterical.'

'But . . .'

'He was just fooling around while I was away.'

She stares at me as if I've completely lost it. 'You don't really believe that.'

'Why not?' I inquire, walking away.

She follows me into the hall. I pull on my jacket.

'Julie, they were sunbathing together!'

'So?'

'She sketched him on a sketch pad – *nude*.'

'They say that can be quite erotic.'

I open the front door.

'Julie, this is more than just a three-night stand. They slept in your bed, for chrissake!'

'But that's what people do when they have flings: they sleep in beds together. Have you forgotten your own philosophy, Sylvana? How women, if they so choose, can turn men into sexual cripples? How if they weren't programmed to think with their cocks the human race would die out? How sex has nothing to do with love and everything with orgasm? How men conceive of sex as remote-control masturbation with zero emotional content? How kings do it, paupers do it and even American presidents do it?'

'Yes, I remember saying that but . . .'

'Just because he's had sex with another woman doesn't mean he's stopped loving me . . .'

'Oh Jesus, Julie, you're not thinking clearly. Come back . . .'

'Goodbye, Sylvana.'

I stride quickly through the lobby and pull open the main door of the building. She starts to follow me.

'You'll lock yourself out, Sylvana.'

'At least have a drink before you go . . . ?'

'Nice try, I'll call you soon.'

The lobby door slams behind me.

I must say, walking out on her like this feels so good.

Sylvana is absolutely brilliant. She is wise, she is clever, she is strong and beautiful and she's a fantastic friend.

But that doesn't mean she's right about Ronan.

Clarification: she's right about the fact that he's a stuck-up, two-timing, arrogant bastard with vanity as thick and immobile as a thousand-year-old oak tree, and it's perfectly understandable why she nurtures long-standing urges to drown him by hand in a septic tank.

But does that mean I should consider him toxic waste?

12

'I noticed your Porsche.'

I spread my husband a wide, jolly smile.

He looks up from the white leather couch in which he is relaxing – aggrieved and stressed out – with a book about Impressionist art balanced on one crossed leg. He's wearing a light-brown suit, a cream polo-neck sweater and light-brown perforated leather shoes.

Seeing him now properly for the first time since I went on holiday, I suddenly realize that there's something of the poseur about his handsomeness, something slightly disreputable and untrustworthy.

'It didn't look in the best of form,' I add.

He is glaring at me now. What a nice way to welcome me home. Nothing about my holiday. Nothing about missing me. No fuss-making. I don't expect a big red-carpet welcome: a nice smile would be enough. But no.

Since he doesn't reply, I decide I might as well indulge him in some small talk. 'Did you enjoy yourself while I was away?'

Still no reply. He is clearly in a rotten mood. Lesson: never expect perfection in a man whose car has just croaked.

And croaked it has: as I was parking my MG in the car park just now, I happened to pass the piece of banjaxed-looking junk that once went by the name of Porsche. It was lying in state, mourning under the sparkling light of the night lamp. Truly a sad sight.

'Where the hell *were* you?' he says.

'Haven't you heard? I was in the Cliff Castle Hotel.'

He just observes me.

'Aren't you going to ask me how I got on?'

'You stood me up, Julie.'

'Thursday is late-night shopping. I couldn't hold myself back. I craved some kinky lingerie in nice bright colours.'

He leans forward. 'So you were actually in town.'

'I was in town. Yes.'

'And you just didn't bother showing up at La Bohème's.'

'Kinky lingerie is a vital accessory, Ronan. You of all people should know that.'

He sits back in his seat once more. 'I assume *that* one was behind it.'

'Sylvana has a name.'

'That wouldn't surprise me.'

I smile insanely. 'What's that sweet scent, Ronan?'

It's not just the smouldering reek of tobacco. It's what it's attempting to blot out but not quite succeeding.

'Your mother was here this evening,' he replies.

'My mother smells sweet, but not that sweet.'

'You'd think she might have called in advance to warn me of her imminent approach. She just dropped in as if she owned the place.'

'Is it massage oil? I didn't know you practised self-massage.'

'I couldn't get rid of her. She plonked herself in front of the television for the whole evening. Her indiscretions never cease to amaze me . . .'

'You're the height of discretion, of course.' I laugh.

'The woman had the nerve to ask me when we were planning on having children. She seems to think that having lived sixty-five years has granted her immunity from proper social inter-course.'

'You'd know all about that.'

'I know not to be inquisitive.'

Ronan has experienced, in a fairly personal way, Mother's

antisocial elephant's foot. He assumes it's a lack of social sophistication on her part. Truth is, she gets a real kick out of aggravating him. On the Richter scale of animosity her toleration for my husband is roughly four.

Quite a healthy average, mind you, when set against Sylvana's permanent eight.

I start walking around the room now, making a big deal of sniffing the air. 'You still haven't told me what that smell is.'

'Tobacco, I'd say,' he arrogantly replies, exhaling a fresh cloud of blue smoke into the air above him.

'No, it's a fruity scent. Have you been wearing perfume?'

He continues reading.

'I won't tell anyone, I promise.'

He recrosses his legs.

'Or air-freshener?'

'Did you know,' he reports from his page, 'that French Impressionists in the eighteen-sixties drew inspiration from Japanese woodblock colour prints?'

This is his polite way of telling me to shut up.

'I was in the bedroom just now,' I sing.

'Is that a fact?'

'I see you changed the sheets,' I add.

I leave this hanging in the air. Although his face betrays nothing I can almost hear his mind unravel at the speed of light. He flips a page.

'I didn't notice any dirty sheets in the basket, though.'

This is fun.

Without looking up, he speaks very calmly: 'You broke our arrangement to meet in town and you're worried about some dirty sheets.'

'Where are they?'

'If you really want to know,' he says casually, 'I took them to the laundry.'

'*You*?'

He looks up. 'Precisely.'

'Any particular reason for this rare behaviour?'

Nothing.

'Which laundry?'

Pause.

'It hardly matters.'

'I'd like to know. I've got a bagful of washing myself.'

'I'll take it for you.'

'This is very impressive.'

'I feel like a drink,' he says.

Resting his cigar on the ashtray, he gets up and walks to the drinks cabinet. He pours himself a gin from the measure, uncaps the tonic with the bottle opener and empties it into the glass.

I wander in his direction, over to the aquarium. Our fish always look like they could do with being cheered up, although I doubt us humans have what it takes to make them roll around in the aisles. I bend down and try to attract their attention, tapping my fingernail against the glass. This causes some renewed aquatic flickering. I do so adore causing a sensation with my purple nail varnish.

I turn round again. 'Ronan . . .'

'I've had an unpleasant week, Julie. Could you give it a rest?'

He's had an unpleasant week.

I want to scream.

Why can't he be honest with me? I could put up with nearly anything provided he were honest with me. Oh please, God, make him stop lying over something we can work out.

I stalk over to the french windows and fling them open, stamp out on to the balcony and slam them behind me. I lean against the railing, staring out at the night, punctured by the solitary white lamp lights posted along the dark pier and seafront, wondering what I am going to do.

Why can't *I* be honest with *him*?

No. I must remain silent. I must. Mother was honest, to her detriment. What if he lies? Continues to lie to me?

I must calm down.

I must bide my time.

I will find out the truth.

Myself.

Friday, 17 June, morning

13

It's ten a.m. and I'm still at home.

I should be in the Law Library beating away briefs or schmoozing with creeps. Drafting statements of claim, even.

But I'm not.

Why?

I've been having a few thoughts over cornflakes, tea, toast and marmalade. While Ronan is safely out of the flat treating someone's root canal, I have been thinking: okay, we know that this was probably no more than a three-day fling. An aberration. A limited fornication edition. He was just playing around, at the mercy, poor thing, of his hormones.

But.

That doesn't exactly debar me from checking her out, does it?

This is why I have just lifted up the receiver and dialled Nicole's home number, having first double-checked that her name appeared in the phone directory.

As I'm crunching the last corner of marmalade-infested toast betwixt my canines, a man's deep voice answers: 'Yes.'

'Hello, could I speak to Nicole Summers, please?'

'Who are you?'

Everybody seems to be in a foul mood these days. At a guess, his spare parts are being poorly serviced at the moment.

'Excuse me,' I daringly reply, 'but who are you?'

'Harry. She's at work.'

'I don't actually have her work number.'

'Who's this?' he inquires less gruffly.

'It's just a friend.'

'And you don't know where she works?'

'We haven't met in a long time. Not since college.'

'She didn't go to college.'

63

Pause.

'I meant, not since *I* went to college.'

'Actually, she was at college.'

Further pause.

'Piano school,' he says with an edge.

So she *is* cultured.

'She was always interested in music,' I offer outrageously. 'Does she still play?'

'I sold her piano last week. She was always banging away at it. Never any peace. I do a lot of DIY. I couldn't hear myself hammering.'

He sold the piano. Lucky for the piano. How I'd love to have hacked away at the piano keys and the soundboard with my ice-pick, chopping through wood and wire.

'I suppose painting is a lot less noisy,' I remark.

'Except she *sings* while painting.'

I pay him the compliment of finding this comment funny and he seems to warm to me. Another innocent just like the rest.

'Does she still work for . . .' says I, fishing in an empty barrel.

'She's still in the travel business. She's in town these days. Recent transfer. Clearway Travel in Marlborough Street.'

I underscore this mentally. 'She was always interested in travel,' I say, hopelessly out of my depth.

'Still is. She was in Portugal this week.'

'Really? I saw her yesterday afternoon.'

'No, she flew back yesterday evening.'

'But I'm certain it was her. The long golden hair . . . everything about her. That's why I'm calling.'

'What was she wearing?'

'A cream-coloured suit and shoes, a white blouse, a lemon . . . er . . . shades.'

There's a long pause in the conversation at this point.

'Where did you see her?'

'By the canal.'

'What was she doing?'

'She was sitting on a bench.'

'So why didn't you go over and say hello?'

'She was with some guy.'

'Oh, she was.'

'Yes, she was sitting on top of him. They were moving around like a chainsaw. He looked like he was in serious pain. Are you her brother?'

No reply.

'I felt it would be wrong of me,' I add, 'to disturb her simply for old times' sake.'

There's still this pained silence.

'*Bitch*!' bursts out through the receiver.

I can't tell you how much this moral support means to me.

'I hope I haven't . . .'

'Describe the man to me.'

'I'm very sorry for being the bearer of such . . . sad tidings . . .'

'I want to meet you.'

'Oops! My hot chocolate is boiling over. I have to go. Goodbye.'

I press the red button.

I get showered, faced and dressed.

And drop into my car like speed.

On my way to Clearway Travel, I phone my mother.

She picks up. 'I'm busy,' she says at once.

Immediately I regret phoning her. She can be so moody. I make a daily habit of forgetting this, due to what she calls my 'generous forgiving nature'. The label has stuck. I really believe my mother endowed me with it years ago with a purpose: she knew she could devote her life to the unfettered pursuit of her greatest pleasure – grumpiness – and get away with it. Knowing I'd still love her.

I do my best to disguise the wobble in my voice. 'It's me.'

'It's me. *It's me*. Great introduction. You know, the world is full of people called me. And I'm lucky enough to know just about half of them . . .'

I let her rant on in that articulate voice of hers, roughened and deepened by her sixty-five years, so much so that with each passing year she sounds more and more like my late grandfather.

The problem is she thinks I view her as a hollow wooden charity box into which you dump your weekly dues and promptly forget for another week. Actually, I love her to bits.

'So, which me is it this time? If it's Bridie, you and John owe me five pounds for beating you at bridge. Or is it a different me? Is it the me who failed to clean behind the taps when I pay her handsomely at least to pretend she's a cleaner? Or the me who gave me a tea cosy for my birthday last March when she knew I wanted that bracelet? Or the me who conveniently forgot about me last Mother's Day? Would it be that me, perhaps?'

Let me point out at once that Mother was not always like this. I think that her separation from Father left a permanent imprint on her personality.

So I just keep my trap shut.

Some time passes.

'I was worried sick about you,' she says eventually.

She really is a dear.

'There was no need to be.' I sigh. 'I was with Sylvana.'

'I left a message on your phone at least twice.'

'Four times in total.'

Mother dislikes being teased when she's sulking.

'I promise to be a better daughter in future.' I laugh.

'I don't need your charity, Julie. If I need charity I'll ring up that organization that sends out smiling young people on minibuses to make friends with you. I'm not senile or helpless, you know.'

'Of course you're not helpless.'

'That's not funny, dear. The point is, I sensed something wasn't right with you.'

'I'm fine.'

'I even called round.'

'I know. Ronan told me.'

'I had to put up with that creeping Jesus for three whole hours.'

'Although it *is* his apartment.'

'You ought to tell him he can't treat his guests like that; it was so obvious he resented me watching his precious digital TV . . .'

'Of course he didn't.'

'. . . despite the fact that he was the one who plonked me in front of it in the first place to shut me up for the evening. And then what does he do?'

'What.'

'He goes to his bedroom to read a book for an hour, comes back out at nine o'clock and tells me he wants to see the news.'

'And?'

'And? I was watching something else.'

'But you always watch the news.'

'I was watching *Deconstructing Harry*.'

'But you hate Woody Allen.'

'Yes, but do you think I was going to let him saunter in like the pink panther and dictate my evening's pleasure? I point blank refused to switch over. I won't be bossed around by a brat with one or two manners. All my two friends agree. They think he's very odd.'

'All dentists are odd, Mother.'

'It's all that staring into people's mouths. It can't be good for a person's mental health.'

'Dental health.'

'Well? How was your holiday?'

'Fine.'

'Did you make any important decisions?'

I know what she means. 'I'm going to hold off having a baby for a while longer. I have to sort one or two things out first.'

'Such as?'

'Just one or two things.'

Very disapproving gap in the conversation at this point. Mother wants a baby even more than I do. My baby, to be precise.

'I admit you had me completely fooled,' she says at last.

'What do you mean?'

'You went ahead and let me buy a Mickey Mouse blanket for this wonderful child you told me you'd be having next spring.'

'Oh, Mother! You didn't go and buy a Mickey Mouse blanket.'

'I did.'

'Well, I'm sorry, you'll have to find an alternative use for it. Use it on your knees instead. Save on your winter heating bills.'

'Oh, I see: because I'm a stingy cow and prefer to freeze myself to death in my own house – that gives you the right to tell me you're planning children so that I get my hopes up and go and invest in a Mickey Mouse blanket?'

What can you say?

'It was the same with the pram,' she relentlessly pursues.

'Oh God! You didn't go and buy a pram.'

'I did.'

'Mother, whatever about the blanket, I never suggested you go out and buy a pram.'

'No. I suggested it for reasons of shrewd financial planning and you let me go ahead and have it delivered.'

'I told you not to.'

'Only because you think I can't afford it. I'm not poor: I have a valuable home and I'm selling it. I think I can afford a pram.'

'You're going on as if *you*'ll be the mother.'

'Haven't you heard? These days it's grandmothers who get landed with all the rearing.'

'Can we drop this subject now? For the time being you have a spare pram and I suggest that you use it as a shrubbery.'

I ask her if she's still thinking of selling her house. I ask her this because something has just occurred to me.

'I already told you I am. It gets bigger and colder each year. Either that or I'm getting smaller with age.'

'And warmer.'

'A small apartment is just what I need, with plenty of spare cash, which I can lavish on myself for a change.'

I fall silent for a moment.

'Mother?'

'What?' she snaps.

'I have a proposition.'

'Is he handsome?'

'I'd like you to move in here for a while.'

She doesn't reply for some time.

'I don't understand.'

'You just said you wanted to sell your house.'

'Yes . . .'

'Well, you can stay with us while you look for another place and avoid the worry over bridging finance.'

When she has partially recovered she says she couldn't possibly move in with us – even temporarily. And this from the

68

person who never ceases to complain that we never have time for her.

'I'm serious, Mother.'

'But you two lead busy lives.'

She really is a sweetie. 'Not so busy that we have no time for you.'

'Well, it's very thoughtful of you, love, but I don't know . . . I'd only make a nuisance of myself.'

I detect a sudden tearfulness in her voice.

'You're a young couple,' she continues. 'You have your own lives. I don't want to interfere.'

'But you don't.'

'Yes I do. I go on about you having children. I don't mean to, not really. Whatever you decide – you know I'm behind you.'

'I know,' I reply, my nostrils turning liquid.

'And I know I'm too harsh on Ronan.'

'I don't know.'

'Well, I am. It's just that I worry about you. I think of your father and what a sorry mess that whole thing was, and I think of young men these days and I suppose I just worry.'

'Well, don't.'

Suddenly I feel a pang of guilt. Why am I inviting Mother to stay? I know why. If I am to be honest, I'm doing it to torment Ronan. That is my primary motive. But Mother can benefit too, can't she?

'I want you to call your estate agent today to set the whole thing in motion. I don't see why you can't move in immediately.'

To her progressively weakening protests, I keep insisting. I tell her I'll be calling over to her place this evening around seven to help her pack a few suitcases.

She tells me that I am a wonderful daughter and she doesn't know what she'd do without me. And she says she doesn't really blame me for forgetting to send her a card last Mother's Day.

I end the call.

Mother is moving in. Ha!

I can't wait to tell Ronan the good news.

14

Marlborough Street.

Clearway Travel.

I've been peeping through the glass window into the interior of the premises for the last five minutes, in between travel posters announcing special deals to the Azores, the Caribbean, the Algarve and Prague. I don't know how much longer I can continue to find these posters fascinating without raising attention.

Your one is inside.

How different she looks during the day, without her shades, her lipstick, her bikini. Ronan should come here and have a good peep. She's like she was in that demure dressing-table photograph. Only a lot worse: she's got dark circles round her eyes (I can see them from here; they're like huge muddy hubcaps) and she looks rather depressed and exhausted.

In short, she's nothing much to write home about.

Course, that means nothing, as we women know. I myself am not much to write home about, although to judge by the amount of genital pestering I get, maleside – at work or in the middle of the traffic or walking down the street – you'd expect that a lot of pricks out there would simply die to put pen to paper. But then why should any positive self-image I might have depend on, let's face it, pricks?

Still, this woman needs to be, how shall I say . . . demythologized. Ronan should come here and take a close look through the glass. Demagicated women do wonders to stimulate male impotence. Imagine! A live flesh-and-blood woman with minimal cosmetics plus turn-offs such as spots and odours and feelings and spiritual wounds, and fears and hopes and insecurities: Ronan would run a mile if he guessed.

Option one: I could go in and glean something about her IQ or lack of it. I know Ronan: zero IQ in a Formula One Ride has the same effect on his libido as a quick plunge in an ice bath. Intelligent women, now – that's a different matter entirely. A high IQ and I swear Ronan would take her even if she looked like the Macgillicuddy Reeks in glasses.

I know my own husband: as soon as he gets tired of the sex he won't stay around for the personality because to him a woman without brainpower hasn't *got* personality. I mean, why do you think he married me? Because I'm able to give him shit and it sounds intelligent to him, but then anything with shit in it generally convinces him of intelligent personality and seduces him into acquiescence. Besides, hey, I'm a lawyer!

Nicole doesn't look like the kind of person who's got the backbone to give Ronan shit.

And anyway, travel agent is hardly the correct image for a man for whom snobbery is a mental illness.

Option two: I could go in and make a scene. Say, go right up to her and ram my arm down her throat and pull out her entrails by the roots and pin them to the notice board and tell her she needs to take a good look at herself.

Option three: I could just stand here and bitch. Always an insanely attractive option.

I extract my pack of fags and light one up. Bad for babies, I know, but there you are. I start dragging intensely.

What do I know about this woman anyway? Apart from the fact that she's an unscrupulous, immoral, sluttish lust-dog?

Watching her deal with a customer now, her face lights up and she looks suddenly prettier. She has so much hair that all you can see is an oval opening at the centre – her cute bunny-rabbit face. Her lips, I notice, are large and red. Ideal for phallic gastronomy.

She comes across as a bit of a blabbermouth. She's all smiles and shy expressions and profusions of helpfulness.

I mean, for God's sake, she's a travel agent.

I have to laugh. Travel agent. What do you bet she calls herself an excursion consultant? She's hardly board-of-directors material. Imagine! She lives out her days tapping on a keyboard, making bookings and phone calls, sending faxes, receiving e-mail, printing printouts, tidying files and smiling at customers. Oh, and brewing coffee.

Real glass-ceiling stuff.

Still, I'm worried. For a start, she paints. And she plays the piano. And she sings along. How cultivated! How civilized! How dignified! Doesn't go too well with the floozie-in-the-jacuzzi image. Even if according to her partner she does have this voice you'd rush to bury underneath a manhole.

I can see the two of them right now. In our lounge. Lights dimmed, crimson wine sparkling from two Waterford crystal glasses and the wine decanter with its as yet unchipped stopper. She, straddled across our coffee table geographically below my couch-engulfed husband, in a bikini bursting at the top like two Virgin balloons about to pop under the razor glares of Ronan's drooling eyeballs, blowing his preferred melody on his favoured instrument, exemplifying effective embouchure, excellent vibrato and perfect finger technique, he melting into the leather beneath him like a helpless whale.

It concerns me that in such romantic circumstances, IQ is frankly irrelevant.

Oh God! I want to die.

She stands up now. She goes in behind. Must be on coffee and biscuits duty.

I enter the premises. It is average to plush. I grab a few brochures big enough to hide my muggins behind and I sit myself down on this soft spring-attached seat with armrests to keep you from bouncing off.

Five minutes later Nicole comes out carrying a tray with three steaming mugs of coffee on it, which she distributes to her colleagues. Then she retakes her seat and presses a buzzer for the next customer.

She won't recognize me, I know, because Ronan removed all pictures of me from the apartment. But it's wise to take precautions so I keep the magazine in front of my head. I have it opened at Greece, Cyprus and Rhodes, where a woman with long blonde hair is posing neo-naked on the beach, her head juxtaposed beside an inset of the Acropolis.

I flip the page. There's a white Greek church with those Spanish-type bells on top. But there is no old woman emerging, as you'd expect, dressed in black; there's no local wedding procession, no patriarch with robes and a funny top hat. Instead there's this perfect West-European couple, the girl carrying a map and the guy in these ridiculous floral shorts (neither is carrying a camera – that's how subtle it is). They're so good-looking, though, it makes you wonder why they don't just advertise the models and leave out the scenery.

Gradually, I lower my brochure. The customer sitting immediately in front of the Nicole woman has just stood up. Nicole says goodbye to her and gives her a nice, friendly smile. She picks up the phone now. Straining my ears, I can make out her voice. It is soft and soothing. Like Wella shampoo. It is keen and friendly, and worried and interested, and can't do enough for you.

I am feeling more nervous now than ever.

She's the nicest three-day lay *I've* ever seen.

15

I'm sitting in my car across the road from Clearway Travel, waiting for her to come out for lunch.

Sure enough, at twelve thirty she emerges from a nearby alleyway, a tall, slender figure in a brown velvet jacket and a tan skirt, wearing shades even though it's overcast. What with the burgundy envelope case under her arm and the high heels tap-tap-tapping against the pavement, she reminds me of an accountant in drag.

This isn't sour grapes. I'm not afraid of being fair-minded about her. I'm not afraid of admitting that she has nice long legs and a pleasant face and a great head of hair, for such a slut.

I get out of my car and follow her up the street.

She disappears into a newsagents.

I stop at a shop window.

She comes back out a minute later with a copy of *Image* magazine under her arm. And she's got this lollipop stuck in her gob, which makes watching her a treat. She drags me through the city centre, down O'Connell Street, towards the bird-shatted black statue of Daniel O'Connell.

From a safe distance of one foot behind her I am trying to sniff out her brand of perfume. Such things tell a lot.

She stops suddenly to do some window shopping and I almost bump straight into her. I proceed past her and duck into a nearby porch. She is inspecting the posters of a competitor travel agency. Market research? This is impressive. And she the glorified coffee grinder.

A few minutes later she proceeds up the street past me and I fall into motion behind her again, still dying to locate the brand of perfume. I close in once again. I'm getting White Linen. No. Charlie? Hm, difficult one, that, when you're dealing with this end of the scale.

God, though, I am so tempted here and now to shove her off the pavement in the path of an oncoming CIE bus. And shadow Ronan to the funeral celebrations, surprising him over my Calvin Klein sunglasses with a graveside eyebrow smirk that reads: *this is just a warning.*

She turns her head to the right and I duck left. This is a dangerous business. I fall back. She leads me across O'Connell Bridge, thronged with tourists and prams, and mis-fed Dubliners. She muddles her way through the human blizzard, stopping and starting, and avoiding and hesitating, and moving forward by degrees.

A few minutes later we hit pedestrianized and busy Grafton Street. I'm on to my second cigarette. She leads me to the top of the street, through the gigantic entrance of Stephen's Green shopping centre on the corner, a huge rectangular edifice with three floors of absurdly white galleries, columns, arches and glass roofing that reminds you of a wedding cake.

She drags me through a succession of clothes shops. In the first, she dives head first into a loose lingerie bin, but the knickers and bras on offer are too cheap (decency-wise) for her liking – which is curious. In the second she gets into this conversation with the shop assistant about bra-strap rashes, while I contemplate nightdresses behind a nearby pillar. In the third she purchases black stockings, suspenders, panties and a few Wonder brassieres – not a drop of lemon-yellow in sight.

I follow her to a fourth clothes shop, where she buys a long dark-red dress with a diamond pattern sewn in gold. In an adjacent shoe shop she splurges on a pair of light-brown (Ronan's colour) knee-high leather boots.

Now she trawls me through the interior-decoration section of

Dunnes Stores. With cash she buys a white tablecloth and a medium-sized mirror, and several vases and a mantelpiece-type clock. I had no idea I destroyed her clock.

In a small furniture shop she delays for several minutes at the coffee table section, investigating some specials. Then she spends ten minutes in a television shop. This is getting to be fun. In a craft shop she buys a green silk batik scarf. Her eyes are green, if I remember correctly from the photograph.

Now she hauls me into a bookshop. She seems to know what she's looking for. From the non-fiction she chooses a book which I notice is entitled *Taking Better Care of Your Indoor Plants*. From the best-sellers, she grabs a Catherine Alliott, a Jackie Collins and an American paperback about how to get in touch with one's hidden powers. From the alternative section she picks up a book bearing the large letters in pink: *Feng Shui and Sacred Space*.

After making her biblio purchases with a credit card, she lugs me into this tiny, cluttered aromatherapy booth. It's so narrow that when she slips past me on the way out she brushes against my back, making me want to turn round and start a scrap.

One after the other, we ascend the escalator to the top of the shopping centre. She is burdened down by a lot of plastic bags. She reminds me of a well-to-do bag lady, only younger and in fashion. She goes straight into a jeweller's. With all her luggage.

I follow her in. There are eight or ten people inside this sleek, red-carpeted interior. She dumps her bags – apologetically – on the floor beside the entrance. Sophistication for you. She goes over and peers down into a glass cabinet with a Raymond Weil placard on top.

I move discreetly in her direction, pretending to be fascinated by the gold and silver chains in the glass cases to her left. I edge closer to her. The floozie's legs are so long, she must be at least two inches taller than me.

Still, what use is being tall when you're crippled?

I sniff. I can get her scent better inside. She smells rather good. Seems like it might be Happy. I slide behind her and pause to gaze into the same Raymond Weil case, sparkling with men's watches from Geneva, the most expensive in the shop at just under a thousand pounds.

How could she possibly afford those?

She leans down for a better look. I am observing her carefully.

Expensive-looking gold chain round her neck, dangling in the air as she bends over. Long aquiline nose. Not unlike Ronan's. Enragingly lineless eyes. Some freckles. The lips again. Next time I kiss Ronan I'll be kissing them too. Next time I kiss Ronan I'll be participating in a threesome germ orgy.

Suddenly she raises her head and smiles towards one of the assistants and she points towards the display with a carefully hand-crafted fingernail. 'Could I see this one, please?' she shyly asks in this sickly-sweet voice that tries to be full of girlie appeal.

While she's inspecting the watch on and off her wrist I move along, frowning deeply at some engagement rings.

'Do you have a nice box?' she wonders.

She's buying Harry a watch.

She's buying Harry a watch!

I was right! It was just a silly little fling.

Quietly I withdraw, flooded with relief.

Feeling ever so slightly foolish, I slip past Nicole's messy bundle of shopping bags by the door and leave the shop.

On the way I take out my mobile and dial Ronan's number.

I must see him. Now. I must go to his surgery, to prove to myself that everything is okay. To show him – in deeds rather than in words – that I forgive him his little fling. That I still love him. To remind him that I'm the one he loves.

'Julie, are you free for lunch?' is the first thing he says.

I can't believe I'm hearing this. He's just asked me out to lunch. And his voice is gentle and soft and kind, nothing like it was before. He feels guilty. He's trying to make up.

Okay, he played around.

But can he help being male?

We arrange to meet in Dalkey in the King's restaurant-bar.

'But how will you get there, Ronan, with your car . . . out of circulation?'

'I'll take a taxi.'

Sunstream beaming straight into my soul, I blissfully dance the remaining distance to my car, skipping along the beautiful litter-filled pavements of the city.

16

Ronan doesn't seem too bothered about the fact that I'm spooning chocolate chip ice cream straight into his mouth at this time. Actually, neither of us is batting an eyelid despite the fact that we're sitting plonk in the middle of a busy bar.

This is an excellent sign.

Also, since I arrived here at three Ronan has been kind and sensitive, and utterly fantastic with me.

'Anyway, how have you been?' he says nicely, suddenly peering into my eyes.

'Me?'

'Yes, you.'

'I've been fine,' I reply, lowering my head.

'Are you sure?'

I nod.

'You've been behaving strangely since you got back,' he says.

'How do you mean?' I ask, the Porsche suddenly flashing like a wailing police siren into my mind.

'Well, you haven't seemed yourself.'

'Haven't I?'

He knows I suspect something. He is worried about the Nicole thing and its implications for our marriage.

'Everything's fine, Ronan. If I've seemed a bit tired, or argumentative, don't mind me.'

Art and the Postmodern quadruple-flashes across my brain.

'Are you sure?' he inquires again.

He's looking for reassurance. He wants to know things are okay with me, so that we can get back to the ordinary business of our marriage and put this whole thing behind us. I put my hand over his.

'What happened . . . it'll be fine, Ronan. Really it will.'

He looks confused. 'What happened?' He frowns.

'It doesn't matter.' I stroke his hair. 'At all. Let's just forget about it.'

He sips his wine, staring at me. There's a hint of embarrassment. He must be so ashamed.

He plunges the eight-inch spoon into the bowl, scoops out a dollop of ice cream and feeds me with it. A waterfall of emotion gushes through me. I know it sounds sick, but I feel like I'm in eighth heaven: Häagen Dazs plus Ronan dispensing it, what more could a woman ask for?

'Oh, by the way, Julie, you were wondering about the sheets.'

'Oh yes, those. Forget about them.'

'I can explain what happened.'

'I don't want to know.'

'I'll tell you anyway.'

I put a finger up to his mouth. 'Ronan, will you excuse me for a second?'

Once in the loo, I call Mother.

But get her answering device instead.

'Mother, there's been a bit of a situation. Now I know you're going to kill me, but do you remember I phoned you this morning and sort of said you could come and stay with us for a while? Do you remember I said that? Well, there's . . . there's been a slight change of plan. Ronan's been acting up. Not over you. At all. Over something else and it's just that right now wouldn't be the right time . . . Mum I'm *really* sorry, would it be okay if we put it off . . . for a while? I'll call you later to explain.'

I punch out, unsure quite how I am going to explain.

Rejoining our table, I bend down and kiss Ronan tenderly on the mouth. His lips are soft and warm. We sit quietly together for some time. I just watch him finishing off the ice cream. As I observe him eating, chin in my hand, I'm beginning to notice a softer Ronan than earlier on, a more relaxed Ronan, a thoroughly nicer Ronan.

The sort of Ronan, actually, who would make a great father.

I can just see it.

Ronan and me and Judy our new baby, my wonderful little daughter. There she is, toddling into the lounge from the hall. Ronan and I are seated on the couch. She crawls over to me. I pick her up off the floor and give her a hug. Now her daddy takes her from me. Giggling, she starts playing piano with his cheeks, now she's chortling as Daddy rubs noses with her, now she's poking her tiny sweet fingers into his ears as he lifts her on to his shoulder.

This is how it will be. To Judy, Ronan will be the sun-god with aftershave. (How every man secretly wishes to be viewed.) He will be the hero of her universe. (I'll have to settle for best supporting actress.) He will have a direct impact on her intellectual formation, including reading *Rumpelstiltskin* and *Cinderella* and *The Three Billy Goats Gruff* at her bedside.

Of course, when Judy gets bigger we will have to move from our present apartment because, although there's a stunning sea view, babies can't play on balconies. Not if you want them to stay babies.

We'll buy a house with space for Judy to breathe and develop her creative potential with daisy chains and slug trains and hide-and-seek and muck formations. No prams or dolls, of course.

And when I and my other dinosaur half are old and withered, Judy will return to us all the care and affection we bestowed a thousandfold.

And Ronan will finally understand the true mystery of life: that what's important is not what lies in your groin – but in your heart.

'Julie?'

I exit from my daze.

'You're daydreaming again.'

I smile. 'What would you say to the following suggestion, Ronan?'

17

Half an hour later I am removing Ronan's shirt and tie and belt, while gnawing at the flesh around his neck. We are in the middle of the office attached to his dental surgery. It was the closest available emergency location.

He, needless to say, is doing something similar to me. 'This is incredible,' he gasps, blubbering his moist lips and tongue around the top of my brassiere.

'You get way too little practice,' I add, chewing his earlobe.

'You're so . . . caustic,' he says, wetting my bared shoulder.

'Like soda.'

'It turns me on.'

'That's nice for you.'

'I mean, it really turns me on.'

I check to see that he means it. And he really does mean it.

'Don't stop,' he gasps.

So I don't. He backs me on to the desk. Helplessly, I hang from his shoulders.

I love Ronan's smell. It's like no one else's. It's a comforting potion. It blanks out my mind. It's been a nightmare, this last day. And it's over now.

The bare skin on my neck is tingling under his six-hour bristle, his strong, hot, quickening breath. He's moving fast. Fingertips in his hair, I push him back a little, to slow him down. He comes up for air now, enclosing my lips in his.

When I open my eyes again they come to rest on a painting on the wall behind him. I haven't noticed it before. Must be a recent purchase. It's a picture of goldfish swimming in a large round bowl: eight in all. Some are red, some are green, others gold. It's a very beautiful colour combination. The background is of flowers and grass, which is not green, as you might expect, but a shade of dark-blue.

In a flood of shock, I realize that this must be Nicole's painting.

'Ronan, wait!'

But he is now gyrating his hips against me. Perspiration is trickling down his forehead. Eyes closed, jaw stiffened into what looks like a forced smile. Thrusting and squeezing and grunting. He is concentrating.

I could be anybody.

A woman with a body.

For all I know I could be Nicole.

I *am* Nicole.

'Ronan . . .'

'What's the matter?' He quickens his pace as if he's afraid I'll suddenly back out.

'Where did you get that painting?'

'What?'

'The painting.'

He doesn't answer. He quickens his pace a little more.

'Stop!' comes from inside me.

'Hold on.'

He's still ignoring me. He's straining and puffing like I'm being bench-pressed: short sharp bursts of air like a piston. He's completely taken over by this thing which is *me*. Eyes still closed. I am being enjoyed. Consumed.

My mobile rings.

His eyes pop open.

'Leave it!' he orders, suddenly still.

But I reach for my jacket. He resumes motion. I take out my mobile. The ring pierces out loud.

'Oh for God's sake!' he shouts, shoving against me with increased urgency.

I press the green button.

'Hello?'

'I got your message.'

It's Mother.

She doesn't sound at all in a good mood.

'It's not a good time,' I pant, straining to sound normal.

'Is it ever a good time?'

'Especially not now.'

'You young people are all the same. You think you were born on a magic carpet. You weren't. Someone had to go through torture to get you here, remember that.'

The whole time Ronan is consuming me like a hamburger and I won't bother telling you how crap it's making me feel.

'I'll call you back later.'

'And that's another thing, Julie, you used up half the tape. They didn't invent answering machines for monologues, you know.'

'I have to go.'

'Don't you dare hang up on me.'

'Goodbye.'

'I'm moving into your place tonight.'

I pull the mobile back up to my ear. '*What?*'

'Goodbye, Julie.'

She hangs up.

Ronan has upped the ante. Eyes shut, he's thrusting and thrashing about, face and forehead tensed.

'Ronan, stop!'

'Just a minute,' he groans.

'That was my mother.'

He flinches, but doesn't stop.

I drag his hands off my chest. He supports himself on my thighs instead, claws squeezing. He continues to pursue his objective – leaning and grunting as he relentlessly slams against me. I have angered him. He's butting and lunging and pelting me like a dog.

I put my hand up to his face and squeeze his cheeks. '*Ronan . . .*'

'I heard you,' he gasps, forehead dripping, eyes tightly shut.

'My mother is moving into our apartment tonight,' I blurt out.

He moves his head back from my squeezing fingers and continues hammering.

'Ronan, my mother . . .'

'Will you shut up about that stupid . . .'

But no. He doesn't complete the sentence.

He's just made his wisest decision ever.

'We'll put her in the guest room,' I yell.

He stops.

He glares at me. I have destroyed his pleasure. He curses. He pulls away and tucks himself in.

'Your *mother*,' he spits. 'Jesus!'

I rearrange myself. He turns to the office window. I feel dirty. Used. Compared. Rejected.

I angrily swipe away the tears before he sees.

I walk out of the room and slam the door to his surgery. I walk past the receptionist, eyes clinging to the main door. I leave the house and run down the steps. When I get to my MG I discover a yellow county council truck double-parked against it, blocking my exit. I begin cursing because I can't see the culprits anywhere.

I start knocking on doors neighbouring Ronan's building, looking for stray county council workers. No one has seen them. I'm getting worked up. I cross the road and call into a total of ten houses. I'm getting angrier and angrier at the people who open their doors to me but I don't care.

Nobody has seen them anywhere.

Hot, sticky and furious, I return to my car. On the way back I almost fall into a manhole.

I bend down and scream obscenities into its dark void.

A head emerges.

A man in this ridiculous yellow anorak thing climbs out of the hole like something from the *X-Files*. He gives me a grinning lecture about nice girls in fancy cars who use not very nice language.

I respond with a grinning lecture about dull county council employees attending public-relations training courses.

He gives me a filthy look like I've just called him a stupid asshole to his face, which of course I have.

'Look, will you please remove your pathetic truck.'

'All I'm saying, missus, is that . . .'

'I'm not here for a sermon,' I interrupt. 'That's why they invented the Mass. Just remove your piece of junk.'

Getting into his truck he says something under his breath to the effect that maybe I should go to Mass for being such a minge-bag.

I let it pass. Jerks aren't my responsibility.

With that cruel image of the fish painting emblazoned on my mind, I jump back into my freed-up car, slam the door shut, ignite, vroom crazily and career dangerously on to the main road, very nearly giving the county council waster the two fingers. Taking a first left, I head in the direction of Cherbury Court.

I can only think about one thing: disembowelling Nicole.

18

I have parked my MG in Cherbury Court, several houses up from number two. My purpose: to pay my respects to the living.

In common parlance that means she's dead.

I get out of the car and start walking. When I am just two

houses away from my destination, an apparition suddenly exits the gateway. It's her. I lower my head at once. She is walking towards me, head bowed, holding her hand over her mouth and nose, walking with slight unevenness. At once I am terrified by what I see.

Her hair is lank and wet, and tangled messily over her shoulders. She's holding a bloodstained handkerchief up to her nose. Her left eye is swollen and closed, her make-up is a mess, her lip is cut and enlarged, and blood is streaming over her jaw and dripping on to the pavement, marking a dispersed trail from her house. Her sheepskin jacket is stained with blood blotches. Her other arm is folded around her stomach as if she is in pain. She is stooping.

She passes me, as if painfully aware of my presence but too ashamed to look into the eye of a stranger.

Where is she going?

I approach her front gate and stop. My eye is caught by something bright on the ground. It's an earring. A silver oval ring about two inches in diameter. I pick it up. It's somehow familiar.

Nicole has stopped at a yellow Fiat Cinquecento not far from my own car. She is fumbling in her bag for her keys. Now she's piling out the contents of her bag on top of the short sloping bonnet. Make-up, small bottles, notebooks, pieces of paper, coins.

I go towards her. I don't care. I quicken my pace.

'Excuse me . . .' I shout, holding up the earring for her to see. 'Is this yours?'

She flashes a quick look towards me but then looks back down and continues to fumble for her key, only more desperately now. She finally takes out a bunch of keys, chooses the correct one and sticks it into the lock.

I go up to her, holding out her earring.

She opens the door.

With one hand on the rim of the door, her eyes meet mine. She is totally different from before, crushed-looking. Her good eye is wide open and pained, and streaked with mascara. Visible through strands of stuck-together hair is a bare pierced earlobe.

When she takes the earring from me I notice that her hands are trembling.

'They're lovely earrings,' I tell her.

I must be having a positive effect on her because she's starting to sob now – despite the fact that in her book I am a total alien.

My hand moves, as if by itself, on to her arm. 'You can't drive in that state.'

'I can't stay here. I'm going to a friend's.'

'A friend?'

She nods.

'Who is this friend?'

'Oh, he's just a friend.'

'Just a friend.'

She nods.

'Give me your keys, please.'

She stares at me.

I pick her things up from the bonnet and start stuffing them into her bag. Again I order her to hand me her keys.

She's perplexed, the poor thing. Weakened by my insistence, I coax the keys from her hand, hop into the driver's seat and start up the car. She's gaping down at me, her face frozen like there is not one slip of a doubt in her mind that I am a person who is at this very minute in the process of thieving her car. You do get a bit disorientated when you're bashed up.

'Get in. I'm taking you to hospital.'

'But I don't need to go to hospital.'

'Get in.'

'But I hate hospitals.'

I lean over and flick open the passenger door. She's still standing on the pavement, aghast, and her mouth is open like she's about to protest, but there's nothing coming out.

I insist and in no time at all she is sitting quietly in the seat beside me.

'I don't know what to say . . .' she mumbles.

'Don't mention it.'

'Are you from around here?'

I hand her a packet of posies.

'Around.'

'It's very good of you.' She sobs, just in time for a posie. 'But I don't want to go to hospital.'

Ignoring her, I pull out of Cherbury Court in this tiny box contraption. Could she not have got herself a decent-sized car? Oh, I forgot – she can't afford it: she's a travel agent.

'What's your name?' she whimpers.

I hesitate.

My name. She has a point. I must have a name.

'Blasted gears!' I curse, fiddling manically with the gearbox. 'They're a bit stiff.'

'There's no hurry,' she says, voice still shaking. 'I'm fine.'

'You're not that fine.'

I am beginning to ask myself what in the name of God I am doing driving her car.

A name. Janice? I don't know.

'Where's the nearest hospital?' I ask her.

She gives me some vague tearful directions to St Vincent's Hospital.

I pull out on to the coast road.

Mary? Too ordinary.

Florence? As in Florence Nightingale? No. Too charity-orientated. This is not about charity. It's about reckless improvisation. It's about opportunism. It's about sheer cricket-bat-headed craziness.

'Are you sure I take a right at the school?'

'No, it's a left, you're right.'

'You're confusing me now.'

'It's a left.' She nods earnestly. 'At the school.'

'Because a right turn and we'll get stuck in the middle of a beach.'

'What's your name?' she tentatively repeats, like I didn't hear her the first time.

Does she have to be so hung up on names? You'd think she'd have more important things to be thinking about while her face is falling apart. It's like she can't tune in to me unless I yield her a word – paralytic behaviour, if you want my honest opinion – but I suppose I must respect that.

'You can call me Julianne.'

She'll be after my address next.

She touches my arm. 'I'm Nicole.'

No shit.

'We'll be there soon,' I assure her.

'Thanks, Julianne.'

'So,' I begin, 'tell me more about your friend.'

'I'd better give him a call,' she moans.

She takes her mobile from her bag, presses a button and waits, head lowered.

'It's me.'

I steal a closer look at her. She is white-faced, quiet, simpering, uncertain. Her eyes are getting wet now and she's beginning to sob once more.

'He found out,' she whispers shakily. 'He tried to . . . to . . . drown me. No, no . . . in the bath . . . with . . . with the fish.'

Pause.

'He held my head down.'

The poor fish.

'Of *course* I didn't tell him,' she whimpers. 'No, I didn't . . . but he said that someone phoned him and said we were seen together by the canal. I don't remember us going to the canal. What are we going to do?'

She falls silent for a while, then resumes by telling him that a neighbour of hers is driving her specially to St Vincent's Hospital and that Harry is unaware of this fact. And could he possibly meet her there?

The friend seems to be hesitating. He appears to be tied up.

Now her voice starts squeaking and simpering, and she throws in a few loud sniffs for good measure. The woman is behaving like she's been knocked down by a truck.

'Please, Ronan.'

At the mention of Ronan's name I can't help the car going into a swerve. Nicole screams. We hit the kerb and are dragged along as if by a giant magnet for several seconds before I manage to pull back out towards the middle of the road into the path of an oncoming lorry. Nicole wails again. I scream at her to shut up, that everything's under control, although we're still heading straight for the lorry. It hoots, flashes, twists and veers up on to the pavement, and boots a Dublin City Millennium litter bin clean out of the way.

Everyone everywhere is beeping me and I'm just cursing back at the whole wide world, mouth as filthy as your local building site. I jam on the brakes and we end up in the middle of the road.

The beeping hasn't stopped, though. The fat-jowled, ugly driver of that truck is spitting saliva into the side window three inches from my face. Two words from him are enough to make my blood curdle; he has just mentioned something about a driving test. At this, I turn and shove him the middle finger where light bulbs do not fit. And accelerate, leaving him standing in the middle of the road shaking his fist, poor idiot.

Now I turn to face Nicole: 'WHAT A BLOODY AWFUL PIECE OF JUNK!'

'It's only just new,' she stammers.

'Oh, Jesus.'

I twist down the window until the car is filled with a hurricane.

'I'm sorry,' she mutters.

I raise my eyes to heaven.

It takes quite some time for me to cool down. It's not easy, because the truth of this whole goddamn thing is gradually dawning on me, the painful inexorable truth.

When I feel ready to converse civilly I turn to her: 'So. Who is this "friend" that you keep on automatic redial?'

'His name is Ronan.'

'I see.'

'Unfortunately he can't make it to the hospital before five.'

'Other commitments? Just when you need them, they go crap on you.'

'He's very good to me in other ways.'

'Oh Jesus, get me out of here,' I moan, pulling into the entrance of the hospital. 'Is this Ronan guy the one who gave you the earrings?'

'How did you guess?'

'It's written all over your face,' I reply, suddenly desolate.

'He got them in Paris,' she whispers, fingering her newly hung earring. 'In the Rue de Rivoli.'

I knew it. I knew I recognized them. I was with him in that jeweller's when he bought those earrings: it must have been when my back was turned. He'd offered me a first option on them and I told him they were beautiful but slightly too dangly for my liking. That was the last I saw of those earrings. Now I find they end up on Nicole's ears.

It's almost poetic.

There's no doubt, now.

Nicole is not a three-night stand.

I don't like to go on about it, but it feels as though my heart is about to break.

19

Why do I do things like this?

I've just parked the car in the hospital car park and, with my arm round her back, I have walked the shivering wreck into Casualty. A nurse takes one look at her and tells me she's not bad enough for in here. I reply that I think Nicole's wrist may be broken. Even if it is, she coldly informs us, it's not bad enough for in here.

I want to tell the cow I think she has a damaged liver and a ruptured spleen, and has swallowed a gobful of weedkiller out of a milkshake carton but I know what she'd say. Not bad enough for in here.

So I coax my new friend down a series of corridors to the out-patient department, reassuring her we're not good enough for Casualty, which brings the hint of a smile to her bruised lips.

Luckily the secretary can fit her in, although she might be in for a long wait. We take a seat on a plastic chair row in a waiting room with other casualties who look to me as if they've had a lot worse happen to them than a damaged liver and a ruptured spleen, and poisoned insides from a gobful of weedkiller.

There's broken ankles, legs, collarbones and wrists, burns, bruising, bandages and moanings, and an air of utter defeat about the place. And a wailing wall of children from one family who look as though they've been collectively food-poisoned.

Misery is hard to stare in the face, so after two minutes, I'm giddy already. I stand up and tell Nicole that I'm going in search of a coffee machine. I locate one at the end of a maze of corridors. I press the number four programme – white with double sugar – and a straight line of dark-grey liquid spurts down into the cup. At a guess, this is going to taste like something in the liquid-detergent line.

Still, it could hardly make me feel worse.

Carrying two cupfuls, I manage to get slightly lost on the return. But since I have left a continuous trail of coffee blobs on the floor – like Gretel without Hansel or bread – I don't have too much difficulty retracing my steps to the coffee machine, from where I take an alternative route.

I rejoin her a minute later. 'This is all I could get.'

'It's okay,' she replies. 'I like coffee.'

'I meant, I lost most of it on the way.'

But she is a profusing mess of gratitude.

We sit here in silent communion, sipping microchip Nescafé from our white plastic cups. I wonder if she's thinking what I'm thinking? Like, what the hell I am doing here?

The whole thing is so droll it's not funny. She and my husband are in love. It's almost hilarious. I should be finishing the job Harry began. I should be battering her to death with my fists.

Maybe then they'd admit her to Casualty.

She opens her swollen gob: 'It's really good of you to be staying here with me like this.'

'Not at all. I enjoy seeing people suffer.'

She laughs at this, a sudden spontaneous yelp, which makes her groan and crouch forward, and grab her midriff. I have discovered a weapon of pain infliction: humour.

'I wouldn't be anywhere else in the world,' I add.

While my buddy is groaning and chortling with the agony of laughter and generally getting a whole lot of shit off her chest plus a few fierce looks from some of the injured people in this band-aid purgatory, I raise my eyes to the tubular lighting. Wait till I tell Sylvana.

'Why did this have to happen?' she moans.

She starts rocking gently to and fro, head inclined downwards.

'Why *did* it happen?' I inquire suddenly.

She can't look at me. 'You don't want to know.'

'Yes, I do. Is it to do with the guy who gave you the earrings?'

Pause.

'Maybe . . .'

I can understand her point: who wants to admit their adultery to a person like me who gives the impression of being a decent and responsible member of civilized society? Answer: no one with any self-respect. That's principle for you: only ever admit your mortal failings to the equivalent of a scruffy hooligan.

'It's okay, Nicole, I won't judge you.' (From me, a simply amazing piece of reassurance.)

'Harry found out,' she mumbles, lowering her head. 'That's the man I've been living with.'

'Found out what?'

'You're going to think I'm awful . . .' She lowers her eyes.

'Try me.'

'I've been seeing a married man.'

'Hey! We have a marriage wrecker. Congratulations!'

'I feel awful about it.'

'Quite.'

'Are you married, Julianne?'

'No – I mean, yes.'

Hell, Julie, get a grip. Your wedding ring.

'I love my husband,' says I. 'He's irresistible. Do you find him irresistible?'

'Who?'

'The husband.'

'Yes, I do.' She nods helplessly.

'How long have you known him?'

'Since January. He came into the travel agency where I work, to book a holiday in Amsterdam for himself and his . . .'

'His wife?'

She nods. 'His wife – technically.'

'Oh, I see: technically.'

'He returned the following day to see me. He didn't even mention Amsterdam.'

I remember that weekend in Amsterdam. I remember that peculiar dreamy mood that fell over Ronan that weekend. Was I born naive and trusting? I really believed it was because we were having a lovely romantic weekend together – walking the canal cobblestones, boating and dining on the *Grachten*, strolling the Rijksmuseum, venerating the memorial of Anne Frank's house, nauseating at the thumb crushers and person sawers in the Torture Museum, sipping Tia Maria in Maxim's late-night piano bar and smoking dope in the tearooms.

I really believed that these things made him happy not just because he found them enjoyable in themselves, but because the two of us were enjoying them together. Now I understand his dreaminess: in fact, he spent the whole weekend fantasizing about this woman presently slurping acid coffee beside me.

'Then he rang me up and he just asked me out. I probably shouldn't have accepted.'

'Then why did you?'

She exhales deeply. 'I don't know. Harry was good to me, but I was going through a bad time when I met him. I don't love him any more. It was a mistake moving in with him. Ronan is different.'

The way she says 'Ronan', it's like she's imbuing him with this mystical hue.

'How is he so different?'

'He just is,' she says simply.

Romance: that's what it does to the brain. A couple of weeks in Ronan's company, believe me, and he turns into a fantasy-free zone.

'Explain.'

'He's a great communicator,' she says, almost nostalgically.

'You're joking!'

She eyes me, baffled.

'What man can communicate?' I say airily.

'He loves me,' she replies, turning away. 'That's all that matters.'

I'm sitting here, nodding away to myself. He loves himself. The poor woman. If she only knew.

'He loves your body, Nicole. Don't look at me like that. You do have a gorgeous body, you know.'

She shakes her head.

'With us it's not just *sex*.'

The way she pronounces the word, it's like sex is something subterranean and dirty. It's as if what goes on between her and Ronan transcends the commonality of carnal greed. It's as if stripping naked in my kitchen and sleeping with my husband in my bed has something indefinably noble about it.

'So what is it – if it's not just sex? Spiritual communion?'

'I just know he loves me.'

'How do you know?'

'He told me.'

This makes me immediately suspicious. 'Did you ask him?'

'I didn't have to.'

'What if he thought you were asking him and he said it to avoid complications?'

'Look, you've been really kind bringing me here like this.'

'Where were you when he told you?' I press.

'Why all the questions?' she moans.

'I'm just trying to find out if he's deceiving you too . . . I mean, as well as his wife.'

Sighs. 'He told me again yesterday.'

Pause.

'Where were you when he told you?'

'Does it matter?'

'Nicole, all I'm asking you is: were you wearing any clothes when he told you he loved you?'

'Maybe.'

'There's no maybe about it. Were you in bed with him when he told you, or were you not?'

All is still.

'Yes,' she eventually admits in a very weak voice. 'We were in bed together, but it was wonderful.'

I sit back. 'Doesn't count.'

'Of course it counts.'

I have offended her.

'It's his cock speaking, Nicole. And you ought to know that cocks are great liars: they will say anything to get their way.'

'But we'd finished making love. I remember because he

93

switched on his clock radio and this song came on and that's when he told me he loved me.'

I put on this horrified expression. 'Did you say *his* clock radio?'

'Yes.'

'Do you mean to say, Nicole, that you were actually making love to him in their marital bed?'

'She was away.'

'And that makes it right?'

She's pouting. 'He insisted I should stay,' she says in the spoilt manner of a young girl.

'Yes, but in another woman's bed? God, Nicole, what *are* you? You must feel really bad, breaking up a marriage like this.'

She starts crying. Oh, help me, Jesus.

Some minutes pass.

The crying is beginning to peter out. I glance over at her.

Her expression has turned into this vast, wet sulk. 'She's a cow,' she declares.

'Of course.'

'She doesn't deserve him.'

'Aha.'

'She's demanding.'

Demanding?

'Did he say why?' I wonder.

'You don't want to know.'

'I do. I do want to know!'

'She just sounds a bit unbalanced, that's all.'

'Unbalanced?'

'Oh . . .' she raises her eyes to heaven like she knows all there is to know about his wife and based on that she's not too impressed '. . . she's always pestering him about something or other.'

'Like what?'

'Oh, you know.' She waves her hand vaguely.

'*What*?'

'She nags him.'

I see. So I nag him. Anything else?

'I suppose she's possessive too, is she?'

'Yes. She tries to stop him going out. I don't know, she crushes him. She's the jealous type.'

94

That's a horrible lie! I have never tried to prevent Ronan going out. And anyway, even if I have – we're married, aren't we? It's not about jealousy: it's about responsibility and making a relationship work. Now the bastard's making out I'm the Grand Inquisitor and his little side munch is buying the story whole-sale.

'He said all that?'

She nods. 'I know you probably think I'm terrible to be giving out about her like this, because I'm not exactly in the right, I suppose . . .'

'Bloody hell.'

'. . . so I'll stop bitching.'

'Bitch, for God's sake. Bitch away.'

'It's not right.'

'I can take it.'

But she's clammed up. Her decision not to bitch straight to my face annoys me intensely. I want to grab her and knock her head against the hospital floor like a stubborn coconut, until she gives me a precise analysis of all the ways in which I constitute a bitch.

This isn't healthy.

I stand up. I don't think I can hold back the vomit much longer.

'I'd better go,' I mumble, moving away.

She calls after me. She tells me, guilty-looking, that I'm really kind. She adds that she finds me refreshingly frank. She thanks me for everything. She scribbles her phone number on a piece of paper and holds it out for me, smiling weakly, head tilted, hair falling down untidily over her shoulder. As she gazes at me I am unexpectedly struck by how beautiful are the eyelids and eyelashes of her good, open right eye.

Her expression, however, is one of profound sadness.

I fully accept that she may be going through hell. That she is human and that she has the capacity to feel all the painful emotions a human being can feel. But there are limits: my intestines simply can't take it any longer.

I grab the note from her and rush off round the corner and into the ladies where there's a queue, so rather than be civil and wait my turn and splurge it all out over the floor in front of everybody, I simply walk to one side and, nice and casual, I vomit into the sink.

20

I feel such a moron.

I'm standing in the flowerbed just outside Sylvana's ground-floor apartment, having squashed underfoot possibly a heather plant and definitely a hydrangea. I'm peering in through the living-room window at the blue mermaid painting and the wine-tinted couch. The room is empty.

But through the semi-open fly window you can hear this sizzling noise and smell what's being sizzled: rashers and sausages. Sylvana is in her kitchen, cooking.

I slide my back down along the wall, until my bum rests against the damp, fertilized muck. Now I sit among the flowers, equally squashed. A human thing such as me is way harder to unsquash than a plant, so the vegetation will just have to put up with it.

The damp feels like it's rising into me, sticking to me, percolating, spreading. But as I'm stewing here in my own juice I can't think what I care about any more.

I need to talk to Sylvana, to tell her that she was right about Ronan all along and that things are way more serious than I realized. But I can't bring myself to ring her doorbell to let her know I am here – I feel that foolish. I'm afraid that if I go in there, a miserable suffering circus, she will simply say (in not so many words), 'I told you so.'

And yet I'll have to tell her some time. She will wriggle it out of me eventually, just like she wriggled Cherbury Court out of me. She should have been a dentist like Ronan; she'd have been great with a pair of pliers.

So I take the mobile from my damp pocket and input her number. I can hear its shrill noise through the window just above my head. A few seconds later, I hear footsteps passing through the hard floor of her front room. Then they stop.

'Yes?' comes her voice.

'It's me.'

'What's new?'

'I met her.'

'Who?'

'Nicole. This afternoon.'

'You met her!' she shrieks through the window and my receiver. Getting Sylvana enthusiastic is, as a rule, like trying to explode a five-hundred-year-old oak tree with a gram of Semtex. But recent events have managed to dislodge her from her customary phlegmatic immobility.

'I bumped into her outside her house, bleeding.'

'Is this your poetic way of saying you beat the crap out of her?'

'No. Harry did it for me. In fact, he did such a good job I had to take her to the hospital.'

'Julie – you're speaking in riddles. Tell me what's going on.'

So I tell her what's been happening in considerable detail. At one point, I can hear Sylvana dragging a chair out from under a table and sitting down. I am in the process of making her evening come alive. 'She also told me all about myself,' I add.

'What did she say?'

I light up a cigarette to calm me down. 'Allegedly, I am a cow.'

Pause.

'Okay, but that's Nicole speaking, not Ronan.'

'You're crediting her with a brain, Sylv. Also, I am demanding.'

'I see.'

'Allegedly I am unbalanced.'

Silence.

'I mean,' says I, laughing despite myself, 'the cheek!'

Sylvana doesn't laugh, though. 'That creep has a nerve,' she hisses.

'I pester him.'

'You what?'

'I nag him. I crush him. I'm the jealous type.'

I can't stop myself; I let out a sob.

'Julie, listen to me, darling. None of that is true. I know you as well as anybody and . . .'

'Not as well as Ronan and it's true for him.'

'It's rubbish. Julie, where are you now?'

'Never mind.'

'Of course I mind. You're my friend. Where are you?'

'It's academic.'

'I'm worried about you. Will you come over to my place? No, on second thoughts, I'll come to you.'

'I suppose,' I sniff, 'you think I'm a danger on the roads?'

As Sylvana tries to reason with me, I'm getting this vague, bitter burning smell through the window. Her rashers and sausages are going to cauterize on the grill if she's not careful. Sylvana is so nose-dead you could stuff her head in an oven and she'd tell you she smelt roses.

'Julie, you shouldn't be alone.'

My friend is in serious danger of becoming well-meaning.

'What makes you think I'm alone?'

'Okay, then, will you promise that you'll . . .'

'I suggest you turn down your grill, Sylvana.'

'I'm sorry?'

'Do you want your grill to burn?'

Pause.

'How did you know I had the grill on?'

Good point.

'I heard it on the phone.'

'You couldn't have; my mobile isn't in the kitchen.'

More hesitation.

'Julie, where are you?'

Suddenly there's this loud knock on the window. She's seen me. I scramble to my feet, stub out my fag on her lovely white wall and chuck it on to the pretty but mangled-looking hydrangea plant beneath me. I emerge through the conifers past two women my own age who give me a good look. I start running. Sylvana has just burst out through the main door, shouting through her mobile for the whole neighbourhood to hear.

'Stop embarrassing me in public, Sylvana,' I address my mobile, breaking into a canter.

'Julie,' she pants into her phone. 'Come back.'

'No!'

I'm feeling this dreadful, heavy fatigue. I slow down to a walk. Forty feet behind me Sylvana is talking to me on the phone, brainwashing me, trying to persuade me that it's okay, that I'm her friend, and – most significantly – that she's sorry for the way she argued with me about Ronan earlier.

I stop.

And stand there on the pavement like an idiot. She comes up to me. I'm expecting to see a face brimming with determination and command in the face of my helplessness and tragedy. I should know Sylvana by now, but I don't. Nearly seventeen years as friends, but still she's no less alien to me than the little green people with bug eyes.

What I get from her is something totally different from what I expected. She looks urgent and troubled, like she's desperate to tell me something she's never told me before because she's never known how.

With total genuineness she says she's sorry for being insensitive, for making out she knew best how I should run my life. Her eyes are moist, something I've never seen before. She gently grabs me and strangely I don't resist. Instead, I find myself sobbing uncontrollably into her shoulder.

We get back to her place a whole five minutes later, me feeling closer to Sylvana than I've felt in my whole life.

The kitchen is a cloud of thick black smoke. She could have burnt the whole place down but she didn't care: she put me first. She complains about the sausages and rashers: they are brittle black bones on the grill. She complains about the black sediment everywhere. She complains about having to scour the grill with steel wool. She complains about being starved after her day at work.

Not once, though, does she complain about the stink.

We decide, on balance, it's best to dine out this evening.

21

Like so many males of his breed, Ronan finds it hard to express emotion by screaming, weeping, effing and blinding, teeth-gnashing, smashing plates, kicking, pulling hair, etc.

Odd things, men.

But I've just done something *real bad* and I'd be interested in seeing what effect it will have on his short-term personality, viewed on the ape scale.

Now what might this something be?

Told him he's an intellectually repressed womanizing creep? No.

Told him his erection looks like a half-cooked pork sausage? No.

Inquired after his receding hairline? No.

Asked him how his haemorrhoids are doing? No, none of these things.

What I've done is this: I've just moved my mother in.

Mother O'Connor is in the bathroom. More precisely, she is enjoying the cosy, bubbly luxury of our jacuzzi. She's had her tea and shortly will be going to bed; she does not wish to be in significant evidence when Ronan returns.

I've installed her suitcases in our second bedroom, which up to this evening has served as Ronan's study. The second major change in Ronan's living environment will be his TV monopoly, followed closely by his bathroom monopoly after my own bathroom monopoly. From now on he is going to share his toilet and toaster and jacuzzi and a host of other things with a woman half his size.

The only thing that will remain truly Ronan's will be his electric shaver.

And the food! Ronan has no idea what's coming. To put it all-encompassingly: Mother has a deep, caring, supportive relationship with fridges. Although he is familiar with her weakness for biscuits and tarts and sweet snacks, of all kinds, Ronan seriously underestimates her abominable lust for French cheeses and Danish pastries – his own personal favourites. Mother will, to Ronan's horror, come to represent food larceny on an unprecedented scale.

I can't wait to see his face when he returns.

Of course, what I really want to do is to punch Ronan and kick him and pull his hair out by the roots and scream at him and scrape my nails into his face until he comes away looking like a flayed indigenous Amazonian warthog.

Maybe then he'd tell me why he's doing this to me.

But I must not react. He must not suspect a thing.

There will be no confrontation. That much Sylvana and I agreed just now, over her pizza and my cannelloni supreme and our two bottles of Castle Ridge.

At long last I've got her over to my way of thinking.

She was most graceful about it.

While the mother of all wars is still in the middle of her long-life jacuzzi soak, Ronan troops in the front door soon after nine.

I'm sitting on the couch reading *Cosmo* when he strides into the lounge, consigning me to the planet of the unseen. He is agitated-looking, presumably because he's just visited Nicole, beaten up for love. He's carrying a large, fat, yellow, plastic bag.

'What's in the bag?' I wonder, idly scanning this trashy article about who really wears the trousers.

'I managed to pick up some fish,' he says, walking in.

'I hope you were wearing protection.'

Hold on, did he just say fish?

There's this rustic, brook-like sound of rushing water.

I look up. Ronan is pouring a ton of water from his plastic bag into our aquarium. And it's full of fish. I jump up and over.

'What the hell do you think you're doing?' I cry.

I almost add: *putting that bitch's fish in our community aquarium*? But I stop myself just in time.

I quietly explain to him that he should not put too many fish into the same fish tank or else some will get bitten due to the universal law of natural selection that says: 'Because I am hungry and we are competing for scarce resources and you are quite tasty and you are also smaller than me, it follows that you are mine for the eating. Now be a good little fish and swim into my jaws, please, while I eat you.'

'Oh, sorry.' He grins.

He peers into the tank as if he's expecting a decent naval battle to occur. But this is not how it works at all. It could take days for a fish to lose its fins to a companion's marauding teeth.

Heavy-hearted, I peer inside the tank myself.

Cavorting away in our aquarium – interspersed with our own puffers and triggerfishes and oldwives and our yellow-bellied devil – are now several additional items: two bleeding-heart tetras, two lemon-peel angelfish, one oriental sweetlips (which I used to think was a type of lipstick), the zebra-like humbug damselfish, the tiger barb with the green and black scales and the large tiger-like fin, and two guppies.

And there's one skunk-striped clownfish, which I don't recall seeing in her aquarium. It probably skulked behind a lump of coral when it saw me advance with the ice-pick.

Clearly, Harry returned home just in time to save them. In the absence of an aquarium, they were most likely dumped in the bath for a day. And they end up here: somehow, Nicole managed to pass them on to Ronan this evening.

'I never knew you liked fish, Ronan.'

'I love them.'

The lying creep! He has zero interest in fish. They don't go with the image. Fish might be aesthetically and chromatically interesting, but they definitely aren't cool.

'When did you get them?' I inquire, handing Ronan yet another opportunity to truth-twist.

'Oh,' he replies, 'after work. I chanced on an aquarium dealer and thought I'd buy a few.'

'Where was that?'

'I wasn't paying attention to the precise location. Not having my Porsche back from the panel beaters yet, I had to walk to the bus stop. And I bumped into an aquarist.'

'Did you say sorry?'

'They were going for a song.'

'They look a bit undernourished.'

He shrugs. 'I thought you'd be pleased.'

'I'm thrilled,' I reply dreamily, stroking his cheek with my index finger. 'Really.'

He backs away.

Me, the great big naive idiot. He has gallantly fostered these surviving tropical marine fish from his mistress. And simply offloaded them on to me. And I am supposed to do the decent, unselfish thing and give them a new and better life. Without a blip of protest.

'I'm sure they'll be fine,' he assures me.

'I don't think so. See our little baby yellow-bellied devil?'

'Yes.'

'Two to one it will not be here tomorrow morning.'

He just laughs. But of course, he has no comprehension of the fact that fish have feelings too. 'I'm going to bed,' he announces wearily.

'Mother's in the bathroom.'

Unsure whether to believe me, Ronan gives me this look and disappears swiftly out to the hallway to verify my story. It sounds like he's stopped outside the bathroom door. It's locked, but I can hear that humming jacuzzi sound from where I'm sitting.

He must be thinking this can be only one of two people: either it's Sylvana in there or it's my mother.

Please let it be Sylvana, he's secretly pleading.

For the first time in his life he's desperate for Sylvana to be not just in our apartment but in our jacuzzi. Because the alternative is too terrible to contemplate: that it has to be my mother who is in our jacuzzi. Because if she's in the jacuzzi, then she's certainly staying the night. And if she's staying the night, Ronan will have to be civil to her tomorrow at breakfast.

Soon he reappears at the doorway, ashen-faced. 'She can't stay here,' he croaks.

'She's an old lady.'

'Not old enough,' is his callous reply.

'If you can't find it in your cruel heart to be generous to an elderly citizen who also happens to be my mother, I'm not sure I want to stay married to you.'

He proceeds through the room and sits down on a leather armchair, grabbing last Sunday's paper from the coffee table.

'I have to *live* here,' he says, as if living here is a form of martyrdom.

Jerk.

I get up and go into the kitchen before I hit him, and make myself a cup of tea.

When I return he's left the room. I follow him through. Mother is still in the bathroom. Our bedroom is in darkness. I

103

push the door open gently. I can hear the sound of breathing from the pitch-black space where our bed is.

I pull the door to. Mother will have a relaxing, confrontation-free first night. And once she's in it will be impossible for him to get her out again.

One night gone, another several thousand to go.

He'll cope.

22

The apartment is quiet. It's three o'clock in the morning. Mum and Ronan are in their respective bedrooms, fast asleep. I'm in the lounge lying on the couch, gulping tequila, flicking through photo albums.

Ronan and me. At parties, with friends by the sea, in town. In some of the photos we're laughing, hanging on to each other. We did things like that, you know. Things ordinary married couples do: laugh, hug, hold hands, kiss. Then, the future was like a roll of film hidden in a gilded can clasped tightly under my arm, waiting to unfurl.

And now?

I turn my face downwards and bury it in the cushion, wrapping it hard around my ears. It feels like the light, the heat, has gone out of my life and all that's left for me to do is try to block it out completely.

But in this oblivion of red blackness behind my eyes, memories are now flooding through me and I can't get them out of my head. Good times together. The excitement of small things, when we first met. Sitting in a pub after an afternoon mountain jaunt, sharing a pizza, doing a crossword puzzle or going shopping together, walking by the sea in the late summer evenings, lying on our bed after making love and stroking his hairy chest as he switched on his CD player and proceeded to make love to the second most important devotion of his life: Chopin.

Paris. Walking with him, hand in hand in the Jardin du Luxembourg.

Our wedding day . . .

Mother.

I want to go into her room right now and tell her what has happened. She's been through it herself, she'd understand. She would listen carefully to me, offer constructive advice, she would build me up and make me whole again. She is my rock of strength and my fount of wisdom, my psychic sculptress and cosmetician. I can tell her anything. Well, almost anything.

But how can I tell her *this*? How can I go in there and admit to her face that she was right about him all along?

Besides, I want to protect her from pain. I want her to have a trouble-free old age. She might be a tough old bird, but still. Life has tired her out, her lined face bespeaks an oppressive past, she yearns for a future free of worry. Father is out of her life and only came back into it for a few hours to walk me up the aisle. She has her friends, her bridge, her walks, her knitting. Her television. Her concerts, her museums, her theatre. Her late-night blue movies, I suspect.

How can I tell her our marriage is floundering? How can I admit to her that the destructive years she endured with Father had not even the single redeeming feature of warning, of parable for the next generation? That not one shining spark of wisdom has been extracted by me from the bleak, carbonized ashes of her years of total breakdown?

I can't believe it, I just can't believe it. Ronan is doing exactly what Father did.

I want to smash every object in this apartment, because I know that every object in this house has her touch imprinted on to it like a black, indelible shadow.

I want to rip everything out. Every item of furniture, every inch of floor and wall. She has contaminated everything. I want our apartment to be just as it was when we first came here.

An empty shell.

Then, I wanted to fill it up with our dreams. Now, our dreams are poisoned. By everything she has touched, sat in, laid on. By everything she's seen, breathed upon, delighted in, wondered at, criticized . . .

Our dreams have turned into nightmares.

Once again this apartment is a barren shell. It is filled with cinders of promise, empty husks whose soul has fled like a spirit vanished from a corpse.

I grab an as yet unopened bottle of Bailey's Irish Cream from our drinks cabinet and pour myself a half-pint glass full of the stuff. I don't just consume it by way of a quiet sip. I guzzle and slurp and slobber and snort the medicine down my throat like I'm on a famine relief waiting list.

Until I can't drink any more.

There's still a quarter-glass left. I stride over to our newly blessed aquarium where a replenished variety of tropical fish aimlessly and eternally cavort. They don't have too much culinary variety in their lives, so let's not get a guilt complex about this.

I pour the remains of the Bailey's into the tank.

Thing is, right now they're getting an overload of variety. In a few short seconds it's like a thick rain cloud inside. Brewed as they are up to the gills in Bailey's Irish Cream, they are presently going catatonic.

This, I believe, is excellent *chi*.

Licking my chops, I go to the bottom of the bookcase and pull out our wedding video. I stick it on the VCR.

Ronan's face. It's like a detachable plate, a pleasant mask concealing something dark and alien.

I watch myself, moving gracefully beside him in my pale wedding dress, holding my bouquet, circling the church gardens, smiling up at him as we gracefully veer, under the guidance of the video operator, around the flowerbed, Ronan ambling with the golden walk of a god.

Next we are in the church. My father is leading me up the aisle. Ronan steps out to meet me and smiles as I take his arm. The witnesses gather, the priest mutters a few sentences to which I devoutly listen. Throughout a beautiful female voice is singing an old Celtic wedding chant to the accompaniment of strings, as Ronan and I utter the sacred words and ring each other's fingers with gold.

It was a perfect day. A cliché, I know, but it was the happiest day of my life.

I can only shrink in horror as I watch myself standing proudly and blissfully happy beside Ronan as if he is the central supporting column in my universe.

I am both struck and revolted by my own naivety.

And such a beautiful video.

I remove it from the VCR and fetch a small bottle of white spirit from underneath the kitchen sink. Then a box of matches from the drawer. I grab our largest frying pan and bring everything out to the balcony.

It is pitch-dark. The light of my life will soon burn brightly to extinguishment. I will be spotted by ships crossing the horizon. I will be just another of the thousand gleaming yellow city lights.

I throw the video on top of the frying pan and douse it with white spirit. I throw a match on it and the whole thing whooshes up into the air like a bonfire. It emits an acidic stench. I lean back and fan the flames with the lid. When they relapse I add more white spirit. Another minor whoosh. I lean back again and wait.

Soon there is little left but a piece of smouldering twisted black plastic whose dark smoke curls its way into my lungs, making me nauseous.

When the handle cools down I lift it up, poke the plastic until it rattles loose on the pan and fling the contents over the balcony down on top of somebody's patio. I know. I've no breeding.

I fetch our wedding album.

I stare at each photograph, stripping each one in turn from its transparent plastic cover. A dozen pictures of me and Ronan at the altar, pictures of us emerging from the church, people outside congratulating us including his friends from dentistry and two friends from Paris. Me alone in my wedding dress, me with my mother, Ronan with his fragile, adored mother whom he is so good to, me and Sylvana in her green dress, both families smiling obediently together, his family as a group, our family as a group and of course, Ronan and me standing blissfully in the limelight.

One by one, the flame sears through each picture, familiar faces and shapes and colours turning black in the bright blue and yellow fire.

The nicest photograph of all: we are both standing underneath a willow tree, kissing. Ronan looks so beautiful in his black suit. So smart, so handsome, so caring and sensitive.

I flick a match and watch the yellow flame catching the edge of this photograph. It flickers and spits through his face, and twists itself into a carbon parchment and tears through my memories like the sound of someone screaming as they witness their treasured love letter being ripped apart.

Twenty minutes later, the greatest day of my life lies in ashes: the charred ruins of my life with Ronan. I sweep everything into an old biscuit tin and drop it down the chute, entombing it like a coffin amid the rotten rubbish far below.

I fling the remainder of the tequila down my neck.

Now I stumble into the bedroom. Ronan is snoring, which makes me think that he couldn't care less that he might, in fact, be in the process of destroying my life.

I go back out and close the bedroom door behind me. I grab a blanket from the hot press, switch off the light and crash out on the couch, leaning my head against a hard leather cushion.

I have taken a stand. I have wiped out our wedding video and photographs. I have destroyed the most precious reminder of our love that there is. I have no idea if there are any negatives. There is only one video – that is irreversible.

What have I done?

Something tells me I've just done something very big.

23

'Either she goes or I go.'

Ronan has entered the kitchen for breakfast. His stark announcement is affably made, while withdrawing cornflakes from the press. He lets it hang in the air as if I'm supposed just to stand here and admire it.

He sits down at the table opposite me and sloshes the cornflakes into his bowl. Then he splashes in some milk. The piece of poison spoons the crunchy mush into his mouth and the thought strikes me: what did I ever see in him?

'So,' I reply, spreading low-fat marge on to a piece of Ryvita, 'when are you moving out?'

Motionless, he stares at his breakfast bowl. 'You mean, you're not going to try and stop me?'

'What for?'

'This is refreshing,' he approves, spooning in a second mouthful of cornflakes. 'I'm impressed.'

'At the thought that I can live without you?'

'I should think you'd survive pretty well with your mother,' he says indifferently, munching. He grins now. 'She's tougher than most men.'

He takes a sip of coffee, then reaches over to the sideboard for the newspaper. He must have popped out this morning to the shops while I was on the couch.

'And where would you go?' I ask him.

'Mm.'

This could mean anything. It's all in the intonation. Difficult one, that.

He's completely absorbed in an article now. He must have a lot of news to catch up on: jerking off with other women takes up valuable reading time. So I sit here, marginalized by a newspaper. His morning read is such an important ritual that I could be having a baby in here right this very minute and guess what he'd say? Could you lower the noise level, please, I'm reading.

This is why, on occasion, I smash plates. I find he pays attention best to the sound of breaking crockery. I consider smithereening crockery a primitive musical form. It mellows him, like all good music. But right now things are too serious to go reducing our pretty Arklow pottery collection.

'Where would you sleep, Ronan? The surgery? I suppose you could sleep on the desk. It's exceptionally comfortable, as I found out yesterday lunchtime.'

'It's all right,' he says, ignoring the reference.

'And what would you do for sex if I weren't around?'

He lowers his voice. 'I can live without it.'

'I suppose that explains the dearth for the last six months?'

'Sorry to disappoint you, darling,' he says in an agreeable manner, 'but I'm not in the mood.'

For what?

Oh, the bastard, I don't believe it.

I stand up and tear the paper out of his hands, bunch it up and stuff it into the garbage chute.

'Jesus, what's the bloody matter with you today?'

I have just defiled his very identity.

'Blame the hormones, dear,' I reply, gobbling half a banana in one go.

He leaves the kitchen with a scowl the length of a giraffe's gullet. I follow him into the living-room where I can have another go at him. He sits on the couch. This time without a newspaper to hide behind.

I take up position by the window, looking out into the slightly turbulent blue morning sea. Again the sky is a lovely blue and brilliant white clouds hitch-hike across the globe.

I give him a few minutes to calm down.

Then: 'Do I pester you, Ronan?'

Silence.

'Well? Do I nag you?'

His head moves towards me. 'What's all this about?'

110

'Answer me.'

'I'm sure we pester each other.'

Dead calm.

'So how do I pester you, then?'

He leans forward and picks up a book from the coffee table. Aristotle's *Poetics*, if you don't mind.

'You don't pester me, Julie.'

He opens it and starts reading.

'I see.'

'No more than any other woman.'

'So I'm like any other woman?'

'No, Julie. You certainly are *not* like any other woman.'

'Have you experience of any other women?'

'No.'

'So I might actually pester you more than other women?'

'Quite possibly,' he replies, after a brief spell of dumbness suggesting bewilderment.

'We're getting warmer.'

It's hard to know for sure if he is actually reading Aristotle or merely feigning to read Aristotle.

'Does it annoy you, for instance, when I interrupt your reading?'

He looks up at me, leaden patience on his brow. 'Now that you mention it, I do enjoy reading in peace.'

'Does it annoy you when I call you at work?'

'Only when I'm busy.'

'Like when you're extracting teeth on hot summer afternoons?'

Pause.

He lowers his eyes to his book once more. 'Precisely.'

'So it annoys you.'

'Julie, could we . . .'

'It annoys you.'

Glances up at me. 'Okay. You win. It annoys me.'

'And when my mother stays over. Does that annoy you?'

Exhales a huge breath. 'Well, *that* . . . annoys me. Yes.'

'We're communicating at last, Ronan. This is very healthy.'

He puts down the book on the table. 'I thought your period wasn't due for another two weeks.'

'That's a line of questioning I would not pursue if I were you.'

He picks up a copy of *Time* magazine instead.

'Do you think I'm possessive?'

He chucks down the magazine again, gets up and goes out to the balcony.

I follow him out for the next instalment of nagging. 'Well?'

'What?'

'I want to know if you think I'm possessive.'

'Well, yes,' he says, averting his eyes. 'Now that you mention it.'

'I see.'

I spread my vision around the blue bend of Dublin Bay. How lovely it is to live by the sea. You can actually hear the waves from here.

'How am I possessive?'

He's turns to me now. 'Julie, since you came back from your holiday on Thursday you've been making me feel like . . . like a rat.'

I turn to face him directly, my bum pressing against the railings. 'And how does a rat feel?'

'Cornered,' he replies, avoiding my gaze. 'I can't move in the apartment without feeling like an endangered species.'

'Rats aren't an endan—'

'Yes they are – in an apartment.'

'Do I endanger you? I do apologize. But I'm talking in general. Not just in the last few days.'

'In general you're fine.'

'Even in bed?'

'What?'

'Are you happy with the sex, Ronan?'

'Keep your voice down, our neighbours below will hear.'

'*Are you happy with the sex*?' I repeat in a raised voice.

'It's fine,' he whispers, grinding his jaw.

'If practically non-existent.'

'What do you want me to say?'

'Why are you perspiring?'

He takes a deep breath. I am seriously nagging him now. But is that not what I do? Is that not my speciality?

112

'I know why you're doing this,' he says, studying me with a cruel mouth. 'It's that thing about having children, isn't it?'

'Thing?'

'Ever since you've come back from the country you've been behaving oddly. You admitted as much yesterday.'

I turn back round and stare out to sea. Two seagulls are lolling and lounging overhead, crying and cackling, wide wings like surfboards cruising the breeze.

'This is about you wanting children, isn't it?'

It's not about me wanting children, actually. Athough now that he mentions it, I won't deny that having a child is a craving in my heart that is tearing away inside me. I don't deny that it's a longing and an emptiness, a scouring ache in my chest, a blockage in mid-stream craving to be freed.

I'm so sick of everything.

'You think this is about me wanting children?'

'Manifestly.'

'You *prick*!'

I'm gleaming at him like a death ray.

'Look, for God's sake, I'm not saying we can't *ever* have a child.'

'Liar.'

He grins suddenly. 'Is that alcohol I smell on your breath?'

He tries to put an arm round me. I forcibly shove him away and rush into the lounge, dart over to the aquarium and fling my weight against it as hard as I can.

The whole thing – pedestal plus fish tank – topples and crashes and splinters on to the marble floor, deluging the lounge with gallons of pouring water and shards of glass. And a panorama of colourful fish.

I fold my arms.

I'm becoming a dab hand with aquaria.

This is way, way better than Arklow pottery.

Ronan enters and proceeds to go ape. He's in and out of the kitchen. He's got a bucket and half a dozen tea towels. He's on his knees now, scraping around for survivors, dumping them into the empty bucket. Mouth agape, he shouts in a falsetto of panic what the hell is wrong with me. He needn't think I'm going to answer that particular question right now.

113

'Look what you've done!' he yells.

'So?'

Cool as can be, I stroll to the french windows and yet again admire our terrific bay view.

Ronan reruns into the kitchen and re-emerges with a mop this time, and starts mopping and mulching and squashing and squelching the water into the bucket with his fingers. He's shouting at me to grab a towel and make myself useful.

I smile at him – this is not woman's work.

My feet splash through the torrent as I saunter my lazy way through to the kitchen, grabbing his bucket as I pass. He yells again at me, wondering why I've just removed his bucket. I reply that dirty water and fish and broken glass don't mix. That he must care a great deal about fish if he's happy to let them suffocate in jagged shallow waters, their piscal pores clogged with floor dirt.

There are eight or ten poor darlings flippering helplessly away in the bottom of the bucket. By the tail, I extract the ones which Ronan brought home yesterday and drop them head first into the sink with a thud. In order of guest appearance: one skunk-striped clownfish, one oriental sweetlips and one lemon-peel angelfish. Barely a blip from any of them though I'll admit to spying a small flicker from the sweetlips. I now fill the bucket with water before the remainder kick it. Then I wrap the sink-dumped fish in a plastic bag and stuff it in the back of the fridge-freezer.

Ronan's roaring at me for the bucket. It's such a relief to witness him being human at last. I bring him the round metal bread bin instead – it's sure to leak. He's still thrashing about on the floor like a drowning rat (surely not extinct in de luxe apartments?), shouting and complaining, and panting like a dog. In short, seriously compromising his dignity.

Housework: this is the effect it has on them.

Mother appears.

In the doorway to the hall.

In her cream nightie.

I join her, folding my arms. She looks at me, I shrug and she looks away again.

We're just standing here, watching him pick up the remaining flippering fish and dump them into the leaky bread bin. Now he's soaking up the rest of the water with the mop and the drowned dishcloths, and squeezing them into same. Eventually he stops and turns round.

He sees Mother. She's smiling down at him.

'Oh, it's you,' he says, flushing.

'I never knew you were one to wash floors, Ronan,' she says. Silence.

'Whatever happened?' she presses.

'This is Julie's dramatic way of saying,' he pants, 'that she desperately craves a baby.'

Mother eyes me to see if it's true.

'That's a lie!' I shout.

'But I'm used to her,' he adds, mopping away. 'Julie has always been quite demonstrative.'

I glare down at him with all the venom I can muster and stride right out of the apartment, secretly wishing him as much ill as I can provide from this small, fragile heart of mine.

24

An hour later I make a silent re-entry into our apartment.

It's a fantastic day outside. I've just had a stroll along the west pier as it cuts into the smooth pool of Dublin Bay and arches around the huge harbour almost to join the tip of the east pier. I walked there and back, stamping my fury into the concrete and gravel and dog dirt underfoot. I rested on the low blue wooden bench, put my head back against the knobbly pier wall and soaked up the benign rays of the sun. For a solid twenty minutes my face burnt in this solar paradise.

If I have nothing else, at least I'll have a suntan.

Ronan has left and Mother is fast asleep in her bed, a cup of semi-drunk coffee on her bedside table. The fish tank pedestal has been righted on top of the gleaming marble floor. The tank itself, of course, has gone, the glass shards more than likely shoved down the kitchen rubbish chute. But where are the fish?

I go straight into the bathroom. And sure enough, the jacuzzi is full of colourful fish. Some swimming and some not so swimming. But all of them to all appearances alive, including five of the fish he got from Nicole.

I make a dive for the kitchen, extract the three fish from the freezer and dump them on the draining board. There's not a blip out of any of the little fatties as they lie there, cold, sodden, ogling and dead.

I grab a large glass bowl from one of the kitchen presses and place it beside our Moulinex mixer. From the drawer I extract a metal blade fixture and attach it to the pedestal inside the mixer.

Don't think about it, Julie, they're no longer alive.

First, the skunk-striped clownfish. It is orange-red in colour and has very pale fins. It's got a single white vertical stripe behind the eye, edged with black. Just like a skunk. You find these fish in Indonesia. Soon you'll find them in paste, manufactured courtesy of Julie Fitzgerald's Moulinex mixer.

The little bugger was a danger to life. A right little piranha. I saw it nipping away at one of our baby yellow-bellied devils earlier this morning. The clownfish eats only live food, whereas the devil – all the way from the East Indies – is a poor hen-pecked vegetarian.

The clownfish is just three inches long. It will easily fit in the mixer, though at an angle. I pick it up by the tail and dunk it into the food processor. Then I close down the lid on top of it and twist. I press the button. I can't stand that high-pitched, hoovering sound it makes so I leave the kitchen and stand in the hall for a minute.

What a day!

I've heard a lot of funny things recently.

But the funniest thing of all echoes in my eardrums like the laughter of a circus clown: *Ronan is a great communicator*.

Nicole would make you split your sides. Ronan the great communicator. The sensitive listener. The purveyor of meaning-ful human intercourse.

I know better.

Classic conversation with me: he pontificates and I ignore. Regularly he tries to lecture me on contemporary culture. It's way easier to ignore him than to disagree with him because then he's likely to shut up sooner and save you a trip to your bag for a paracetamol.

Sylvana is quite right when she says Ronan thinks he's God's gift. He really does imagine that the sun shines out of his arse. I promise you that I've been to places where he hasn't and I can quite definitely swear to you that the sun does not shine out of his arse, since his arse is just the same as anyone else's arse (as far as I'm aware) and he's just an ordinary guy who thinks he's extraordinary and manages to dupe me and others at times into believing that his arse is extra high in calories.

The heart is the organ that counts here. But Ronan doesn't seem to have one. In the centre of his chest pumps a stiff muscle of rubber.

I re-enter the kitchen, go over to the mixer and calmly observe my russet clownfish juice. This is going well so far. Next in line: the bright yellow lemon-peel angelfish, fairly straight from the Pacific Ocean. I pluck it off the tray by its tail, a heavy, greasy slob of a thing. I drop it into the mixer to join its ensouped cousin and press the button, and I race out to the hall where I again take up sentry duty, this time seated on the banana couch.

Let's hope Mother doesn't suddenly decide to wake up.

It really aggravates me, though, the suggestion that Ronan is a good communicator. Take the incident last November, for instance.

One Sunday he drove me up the mountains for an afternoon trip. I say 'he drove me' advisedly; he doesn't like it when I drive because firstly, he has this weird idea that I enjoy breaking the speed limit and secondly, he doesn't trust me not to take a wrong turn.

He took a wrong turn.

He opened out his map without stopping the car. He wrapped it right over the steering wheel. Did he once ask *me* to consult the map for him for safety's sake? He did not. He did not want to admit he required my help. Requiring my help is an admission of weakness. After all, it's an act of communication.

I said to him: 'Why don't you let me consult the map for you?'

This sensible suggestion of mine was intended to make the vehicle in which we were travelling safe from a state of enwrapment around stray roadside trees.

But he cut down my suggestion with a machete: 'No, Julie.'

His reasoning was simple: I required remedial classes in map reading to supplement my retarded spatial abilities. His way of describing this ailment is that I, like most women, was geometrically challenged. We were useless as a class, he said, when it came to lines and curves and angles and distances. He qualified this analysis by conceding that we were excellent at bends.

Going round them.

Here was an interesting concept, so I decided to pursue it further. I suppose I thought I'd get him to communicate.

I did, but not in the way I'd hoped. Actually, it ended up quite nasty.

'What's so critical about lines and curves and angles and distances?' I wondered mildly.

He gave me an incredulous sideways glance. 'The civilized world as we know it could not have been designed without lines and curves and angles and distances. Never mind constructed.'

'I get on quite well without them,' I retorted.

'How would you feel living, say, in a mud hut?'

Pause.

'Unlucky.'

'Exactly. You owe all your comforts to applied mathematics.'

I thought about this.

'Without lines and curves and angles and distances, Julie, your teeth would have fallen out by now.'

'Every woman's teeth would be equally rotten,' I pointed out. 'Not just mine. Therefore it wouldn't matter.'

'Without geometry and mathematics you'd be wearing adapted potato sacks and animal hides instead of designer labels.'

I made the point that as regards lines and curves and angles and distances, modern man has contributed precisely nothing to the single most important priority in Ronan's life after aesthetics.

'What's that?'

'Sexual pleasure.'

'Correction: modern man invented the condom.'

'Including the ones that burst.'

'He invented vibrators.'

'Thank heavens.'

'Don't lie.'

'Don't flatter yourself. I don't need a man to do it with. A vibrator is ten times more effective. Do you want proof?'

'You're warped.' He laughed.

'Actually, it's the vibrator that's warped.'

He considered this point, poker-faced. 'You're right, Julie. And what do you think accounts for the warp factor? Lines and curves and angles and distances. If you've ever bothered to inspect the design.'

'I have. Intimately.'

'They're all about engineering,' he prattled on, the condescending buffoon.

'They're also about multiple orgasms, something you're incapable of giving me.'

'Do you blame me?'

It was getting nasty.

But the point is: Ronan's sheer inability to communicate in a way that women prefer is so thorough, so determined, almost, that it infiltrates even the most intimate area of our lives. In the very place where he has the opportunity to do some really mind-blowing communication – the bedroom – he bungles it and it's all over in two minutes. When I actually think about it.

It's like a five-second confession: imagine you're just getting comfy in the confession box and you're about to reach the mortal-sin punchline and the priest suddenly stands up and walks out on you. Think how that would make you feel.

Still, for all his communicative neglect, Ronan seems to bond well with Nicole.

I go back into the kitchen and turn off the knob.

The smell is that soggy, raw odour you get from recently docked fishing boats.

The final fish to take a nosedive into my Moulinex is the truly lovely oriental sweetlips. It is dark brown and looks like it's just been covered in random round blobs of yellow paint. I chuck it into the mixer to join its fluid comrades. I switch on the button again and leave it for a minute. After this, I strain out any stray bits of skin or eyeball or fin with a fork.

Now I think I'll give my darlings one last shake-up together with a carton of cream. I pour in the cream and add a sprinkling of herbs. I press the button and wait a full minute, to ensure a proper merging of personality. Now I pour almost a pint of the much creamier fish booze into the glass bowl.

I must say, I feel a sense of achievement: we have here the basic, raw ingredients of my first fish mousseline, fine and lump-free as a soup.

I cover the bowl with plastic and put it in the fridge. If anyone discovers it I'll tell them I picked it up at the local deli.

I open all the windows and wash my hands with loo detergent from under the sink and dry them with half a roll of paper towelling.

Nauseated, I visit the bathroom. Sitting on the toilet lid, head hung low in my hands, I ponder the tragedy that is my marriage.

Trust.

It's like biting into a golden apple, trusting to its healthy, juicy goodness – and finding a worm crawling between your teeth.

Trust takes people as they are, sparing itself the effort of endless analysis and suspicion and doubt. But Ronan? His is a counterfeit generosity, a bogus sincerity, a fraudulent benevolence. Beneath the face of the man I thought I knew and understood lies a disease of deceit.

And it's making me sick to the gut.

I hear a door banging.

Feeling sordid, I stand up and flush my mouth with Listerine and wash and do up my face. In our bedroom, Ronan is lying on the bed with his hands behind his head. I must try to be normal.

'Afraid of bumping into my mother?'

'It's safest in here,' he replies.

I sit down on the chair by the open window through which you can hear the piercing summery noise of kids splashing and shouting in the swimming pool below.

'Is everything okay, Julie?' he says, with unexpected concern.

'I'm fine.'

'Are you sure?'

'Yes, Ronan,' I sing. 'Apart from the fish-tank episode, everything's fine.'

'That was a bit . . .' he begins.

'Extreme?'

'Yes.'

I don't reply.

'I never cared much for fish anyway,' he comments, yawning.

'Thank you for saying that.'

'They're in the jacuzzi.'

'I noticed. Thank you again.'

'I've phoned the dealer. I'll pick up another tank.'

The happy shrieking of the children in the pool is starting to dull my senses. I close my eyes. My eyelids are cold.

Ronan tells me he has to go to town for the afternoon.

I blink my eyes open again.

'I have to buy shoes,' he explains.

'Shoes.'

'Yes, my brown ones are wearing out. I thought I might have lunch in town, cruise the bookshops, buy new shoes—'

'Why don't we both go?' I interrupt.

'I enjoy browsing in bookshops,' he says.

'So do I.'

'Alone.' He smiles. 'I'm a bit odd that way.'

Paternalistic prat.

'Why don't I meet you later on then? We can both go shopping together.'

He stands up. 'I'd rather shop alone. Women are always making impractical suggestions about style and colour, and especially about price.'

'What women?'

'Women in general.'

It drives him bananas, he observes.

'Okay, then, why can't we meet after your bananas? I'd quite like a drink together, late afternoon . . .'

'Julie, I can't organize my life to fit exactly into your routine.'

'Did I just say something wrong?'

He gets up and leaves the room. I follow him out, sticking my foot in the front door to prevent him closing it behind him.

I gaze deeply into his large brown eyes. 'Where are you going?'

'I already told you,' he replies, staring into the space above my head.

There's a taut, static tug of war going between the two of us, standing on both sides of the door. Me trying to draw him in and him trying to shut me out.

What's the point?

I let him go. First, I extract a commitment from him to return here for seven so that we can spend the evening together like a proper married couple. Given that it is Saturday night.

Sighing, attempting to conceal his annoyance, he agrees.

It is, after all, proper form.

Once he's gone I fetch a small plastic fishbowl and a fishnet from the broom cupboard and bring them into the bathroom where I fill the bowl with water. I fish out Nicole's five surviving fish and drop them into the bowl. Not much room for them to do more than ogle each other like a quintet of stupid Sumo wrestlers. I place the bowl into a plastic bag and carry it down to my car, where I jam it behind the passenger seat to prevent capsize. I drive straight into the aquarist down the road and flog the lot for a ridiculously low twenty quid.

Then I call Nicole.

Yes, she confirms excitedly, she's meeting Ronan at four o'clock this afternoon. But would I like to meet up for a drink first? I'm very welcome to come out to her place for lunch.

If I'd like to.

This is it.

Now is the time to end it all.

25

I walk straight up the white gravel path of number two Cherbury Court and ring the doorbell. The new red stained-glass panel on the front door is pretty, though I must say I preferred the sailing boats. The door opens almost immediately. She's wearing a long red dress patterned with diamonds in sewn gold – the one she bought at the shopping centre yesterday.

She gives me such a pleasant smile that I feel this spontaneous blinding urge to throttle her.

She puts her hand on my upper arm, a gesture of shy welcome. I can feel myself deflating like a punctured lung. It's funny: when people are nice to you it's a mighty tough job being a bitch.

And it's even harder when in addition they possess face wounds that would make Frankenstein consider himself lucky. I mean, look at her! Her left eye is peeping out under a slight bulge, which is discoloured, as black eyes generally tend to be. Her thickly made-up face barely conceals heavy bruising.

Still and all, she doesn't exactly look miserable. She manages, in her hour of woe, to look more upbeat than beat up, and this combination, which borders on the side of happy, is managing to cause me intense irritation. I'm thinking: is there something I should know?

'It's really nice to see you again, Julianne.'

'Yes. How are you, Nicole,' I inquire, 'after your beating?'

First she's startled, then she shrugs. 'Life goes on, I suppose.'

What an odd way to view life, mere hours after mincemeat has been made of your visage.

'Nicole, there's something we have to talk about.'

I'm not in the least friendly.

'Oh?'

'Yes, about Ronan.'

Hearing this, Nicole smiles lovingly. She takes me by the arm and tries to usher me inside. I pull back violently.

'Julianne, is something the matter?'

'Where's Harry?'

She's frowning now, perplexed as a stranded walrus. 'He's gone out.'

'When's he coming back?'

'In about half an hour. Why?'

'Half an hour? Good. I can wait.'

'Julianne, are you . . .'

'I'm fine.'

'You seem . . .'

'I said I'm fine.'

When my gaze returns from the hedge to Nicole, she is staring right into my soul depths with something bordering on real concern: 'Is it . . . husband problems?'

'What did I just say?'

'I shouldn't ask,' she reverses, shaking her head.

'Oh, feel quite free to talk about my spouse.'

'I'm sorry.'

Unlike Sylvana, Nicole is not the sort to lever gossip out of you with a pickaxe. Nor is she the type to shove and kick to get her own way. 'What's his name?' she wonders nicely.

Names and addresses again.

'Shithead.'

Blank stare.

'He's not in the good books right now,' I explain. 'Is that okay?'

'I understand.' She nods vehemently.

Of course, it's not that Ronan is not in the good books. Put simply, I want to beat him to a pulp, but one doesn't admit these things in polite society.

'But apart from that he's in wonderful form.'

'That's good,' she replies, relieved.

'Yes, it's very good. He's shagging his mistress like nobody's business.'

Tragic face on her now. 'Oh, Julianne.'

I can't believe this: a canvas of sadness has just descended over her face. She really does look sorry for me. With kindness and sincerity she peers softly into my soul, while I stand here festering like gangrene in my own private marital cesspit.

Now I feel like crying. I am pathetic.

'Enough about me.' I sniff, looking around for something to distract my attention. My eyes come to rest on the octagonal disc hanging just above the front door over the porch. 'What's that?'

'It's a *Bagua* mirror. It's to ward off negative influences.'

Wasn't too effective in warding me off last Thursday.

'Before I hung it there,' she explains, 'I felt these disturbances every morning when I got up . . .'

'You have neighbour problems too?'

'No – I mean psychic disturbances. I've been told I'm quite sensitive to psychic phenomena. I figured it must be the hospital over there behind those houses across the street. When I put up the *Bagua* mirror the disturbances actually stopped.'

'I get the picture.'

'Hospitals create a lot of negative energy because of all the suffering. A prison would be the same. The *Fu* dogs help.'

'You keep dogs?'

'*Fu* dogs.' She giggles. 'On the gateposts, see?'

'You mean the stone dogs.'

'They're supposed to deter intruders.'

They too seriously failed in their duties.

'And they also stop energy leaking out of a house.'

'Whatever you're into.'

She opens the door wide for me to enter. I step up and in. The sun-drenched hallway has turned the curtain behind the front door into a bright orange flame. The atmosphere is warm and welcoming, from inside I can smell the burning of a scented candle: rose and gardenia, she informs me.

The missing bannister rail has been replaced, I notice. To my right, the painting which I triply dented has been removed and replaced by *Foetus*, stuck right in your face in the middle of her hallway. I lean over the small wooden table under the painting and inhale a new and younger jasmine plant with tiny yellow leaves.

'How pretty.'

'It's the plant of friendship,' says Nicole, eyeing me almost prayerfully.

'Isn't that nice.'

She shows me into the living-room. I halt at the door, flabbergasted.

The place is like new. It's almost exactly as it was before I got to work on it last Thursday evening. It is elegant and clean and neat. I look around for signs of my recent rampage.

But I can't find any. Was I hallucinating?

I move inside. Before long, I start to notice tiny differences. The drinks cabinet which I rendered into firewood has been replaced by one not quite identical. There's a new TV set. There are two dark-green-leaved rhododendron plants in ochre pots, one on each side of the television. I was seriously under the impression that I'd decapitated them.

Of course I did. These are new. Replaced in record time. She informs me that they are narcotic, which is of course of interest. She also points out that they absorb some of the *chi* that creates rheumatism. Why does she insist on taking for granted that I know what the hell she's talking about?

'What a lovely room.'

The phrase sticks in my throat like a chicken bone.

'Harry does all the work; I just come up with the colours. Colours are very important. They affect the way you ... you know, the spiritual side of life.'

'Do you paint?' says I, diverting my eyes to the repolished floor.

'I do my best,' she replies.

'Don't knock your talents.'

'I really love painting. I find it very uplifting.'

'I used to paint walls myself.'

Nicole stops suddenly. 'No, I mean, I paint pictures.'

'Do you use rollers?'

More confusion. 'No, I mean, I paint *paintings*, Julianne.'

'*Paintings*?' I just stare, like it's incredible she's chosen such a designation.

'You thought I meant painting walls?' She laughs. 'I never paint walls. Harry does that. I paint paintings. Up in the attic.'

'The madwoman in the attic.'

'In my spare time.'

I move past the mantelpiece, above which I notice something different: a new mirror.

'So,' I drawl, 'you're an artist.'

'I wouldn't say that. Maybe I'll show them to you some time?'

I remember the nudes in her sketch pad. 'That won't be necessary.'

I inspect the rest of the room. The dinner table is covered with a new white tablecloth. I'm tempted to look underneath for any dents. On the table lies the book I saw her purchase yesterday: *Feng Shui and Sacred Space*.

Sacred space. I love it.

There's a new glass coffee table in place of the old one – only less elaborate. On top of this there lies the same plethora of books and junk magazines I breezed through on Thursday evening last.

And the aquarium? It's disappeared completely. Pedestal and all. In the front right corner now stands a large chrysanthemum in a white square box.

You would never know I was here just two days ago. How did they manage to clear it up and paint everything so quickly? Two days: that's marathon cosmetics. The room is perfect. There may still be a slight odour of alcohol from the monsoon I created around the stone fireplace, but that piercing wine-vat smell has totally disappeared.

'There were bloodstains on the couch. I tried to remove them, but there are still traces left.'

'Did you stab Harry or something?'

She laughs, shaking her head, then quietly informs me that the room was ransacked last Thursday evening by intruders.

'You're joking.'

Me the great big innocent.

Sighing, she tells me she walked in the front door and everything lay in ruins before her eyes. I can just see it: Hannibal returning to a devastated Carthage.

'I was really upset,' she mourns. 'I mean, they didn't even steal anything. The only thing they took was a manual about babies and a small book on *Feng Shui*.'

I turn to admire the view of the front garden.

'They smashed our lovely coffee table and especially our antique drinks cabinet. There was glass and alcohol everywhere.'

'Flying cocktails?'

But there's no response from behind me.

She just doesn't get it, does she? She thinks her *Bagua* mirror and her *Fu* dogs will protect her.

There's one born every minute.

'Break-ins are a regular feature of modern life, Nicole,' I observe, concentrating on the robin redbreast poking about on top of the bird stand. 'One must take precautions. You need to double-lock your doors and bolt your windows . . . and of course, fortified glass is to be recommended.'

'I suppose so.'

'You keep a lovely garden.'

'They were probably just young gurriers.'

Suddenly, despite the depression weighing me down like leaden cannonballs, I want to burst out laughing. I very nearly do, as well. The poor gurriers have come in for quite a knocking recently. It's sheer prejudice, straight out of Ronan's mouth. It's like the vibe that goes: if you are, say, a travelling person then you're automatically a congenital kleptomaniac knifing rapist. It's so bizarre.

'Really, though, you have a lovely garden.'

'It's based on a Japanese design,' she says quietly.

'Tell me more.'

'Did you know that the Japanese were the first people in the world to cultivate a garden for aesthetic reasons alone?'

Aesthetic: where have I heard that word before?

'I wasn't aware of that.'

'They thought gardens were sacred places where you meditated and destressed. So when we first moved in I was careful to get the vibrations right, I made sure to have something from the element of fire – the lantern outside. And water – in the fountain. And metal – in the statue, and there's plenty of wood. I had it all done myself – Harry's not great on gardens. I made sure to have lots of curved shapes. Don't you love the bird house? Our hedges were evergreen, which was lucky. Deciduous hedges are inauspicious.'

'That's a point.'

I can hear her footsteps behind me and the doors of the drinks cabinet opening. She offers me a drink and I turn round. A black cat streaks across the floor, eyeing me with knowing menace. It's almost as if he spied me last Thursday evening, and it's making me nervous.

'Max, say hello to Julianne.'

'He wouldn't know me,' says I.

The cat glares at me accusingly.

Nicole pours herself a Cointreau. I tell her to pour me one of those. Handing me my drink, she shakes her head and sighs.

'Poor Max. He was affected, too. His box of cat biccies got soaked from all the bottles of alcohol thrown at the fireplace.'

'Don't tell me you fed him alcohol-soaked biscuits? No wonder he's behaving strangely.'

She laughs at this point. 'They destroyed your dinner, Max, pet. Aren't they animals?'

He should know.

Nicole bends down to feel him but he evades her long thin fingers, slinking back out of the room, leaving deadly vibes hanging in the ether.

I swing round to the garden again. Gardens. What can I ask her about gardens? I trawl for a relevant topic of conversation, but she beats me to it.

'We had an aquarium over there beside you.'

'A fish tank?'

'It was beautiful. They totally destroyed it. There was glass everywhere.'

'How could anyone do such a thing?'

'I know.'

'People have no respect any more.'

'We had a clownfish . . .'

A skunk-striped clownfish, she means.

'. . . and an oriental sweetlips, and a few yellow-bellied devils and –'

'What strange names.'

'When I came in they were lying all over the floor.'

She falls silent. I turn round again. A reverent, sad expression has overcome her. I can see that despite everything Nicole is essentially a good person.

'Do you know what Harry did?'

'No. What?'

'He stood on two of them. They were squashed like pancakes.'

'Fish cakes?'

Bad joke. Still, I can see her point. Although my personal record with fish would hardly qualify me as Honorary Secretary of the ISPCA, nevertheless I am not so cruel that I would actually stamp on the poor things. This was Harry losing his temper at beings a hundredth his size. I mean, how would you feel being trampled upon by King Kong's huge sweaty foot in the middle of Fifth Avenue? What an awful bully.

'Do you know what he did to the clownfish and the oriental sweetlips, after he stamped on them?'

'No.'

'I didn't want to say this, because every time I think of it it makes me so angry, but I will. He dropped them in boiling water.'

She looks furious.

I burst out laughing; I simply cannot help myself. I immediately apologize to her and try to explain that I'm only laughing because what she said reminded me of something I once did as a naughty child many years ago.

She looks like she thinks I'm making fun of her. 'Don't laugh, Julianne,' she pleads. 'They were in the pot, all puffed up like jelly. It was horrible. His excuse was that it saved him a trip to the fishmongers.'

'Some people seem to get a kick out of hurting poor defenceless creatures.'

'Harry refuses to buy another aquarium. He acted like it was my fault.'

Mournfully, she fetches a cloth from the fireplace. 'Basically' – she sighs, dusting the mantelpiece lethargically – 'he likes to make out I'm stupid.'

Nicole? Stupid?

'I wish you could meet him. You'd see what I mean.'

The idea that if I met Harry I would see what she meant irks me. Okay, she's proved her point that Harry is a bastard, but there are life alternatives open to her other than attempting to net Ronan for marriage: she could try moving out and getting her own place, and doing what many normal women do – meet single, unmarried men, for example.

'Will he be back soon?'

She consults her watch and nods. Then she throws her cloth back into the fireplace and slumps down on the edge of the couch next to the bloodstain. 'Ronan's great with fish,' she says mournfully, clasping her hands together in front of her.

'Excuse me?'

'He loves tropical fish.'

That's what she thinks. I know Ronan. Tropical fish bore him to tears. It's a typical strategy of his: he simply figured that flattering her fish was the M1 motorway into her knickers.

'I gave some of the surviving fish to Ronan,' she says.

'You think that's fair?'

Pause.

'It's the best chance they'll get,' she replies.

'I don't mean fair on the fish, Nicole. I mean fair on his wife.'

'But she loves tropical fish.'

'How do you know that?' I laugh.

'He said so.'

'I hope he's right. For the fishes' sake.'

'Oh God, don't say that.'

They're safe, I crave to tell her. In a glass bowl.

Me: 'She's a total saint to be fostering your fish like that.'

No reply.

'She sounds like a caring kind of person,' I add.

'Ronan told me he loved me again,' she says suddenly.

'Did he, now?'

She nods.

'He loved you.'

'He loves me.'

'When did he say that?'

'Last night. After you left me in the hospital he came in.'

'And he told you he loved you, in the hospital?'

'That's exactly what I'm saying, Julianne,' she pleads. 'Sex had nothing to do with it. He said that to me even though I looked the worst in the world . . . don't you see?'

I see. This is as bad as I'd thought.

She stands up and refills her glass with Cointreau. And I don't mean a simple measure. I mean bite-size. She's clearly addicted to the stuff. She refills my glass too, then sits down again and runs her fingers through her voluminous hair.

Suddenly she stiffens and becomes alert and rabbit-scared. She's heard something.

The door opens.

Nicole practically spits the next mouthful of Cointreau out

through her eyeballs. She attempts a speedy self-composition, then stares at the floor just as he enters the room.

I calmly turn my head for a full frontal close-up of her beater.

26

At once I can see why Nicole would fancy him.

He is stocky, firm-jawed, broad-foreheaded and good-looking. His sturdy nose locks into the thick bone of his eyebrows. He doesn't so much move across the room towards the drinks cabinet as pace. Like a leopard. He is commanding, uncompromising, territorial, shorter than Ronan, but physically strong. Very possibly, he's not too bright either.

I flash him my installation smile.

His expressionless, hard-shell blue eyes glance off me like a bullet off granite and lock on to the drinks cabinet towards which he's moving. What is it about them? I shiver involuntarily.

Nicole and I watch him as he pours himself a Boru vodka.

Now is my chance; it will be over in seconds.

Nicole's head is bowed in vulnerable humility. Submissiveness. Can I do it to her?

Yes, I can.

After all, has she not branded me a thieving hooligan? A pesterface spouse? A jealous neurotic? An unfit wife?

Oh, and another point: has she not tried to steal my husband? And I'm supposed to show her mercy?

I *can* do it: face her down, kick her in the teeth, shove her in the gutter and leave her for Harry. She deserves it.

He turns round and glares at Nicole.

'This is Julianne,' is her pathetic attempt to introduce me.

'How do you do,' he says ignoring me.

'How do you do,' I reply, trying my best to sound bored.

'I've been thinking about what happened,' he says to her, sipping.

'Harry – can we talk about that another time?'

He sniggers, swirling the vodka in his glass. 'Has Nicole told you about her fancy man?'

Nicole lowers her head.

'Are you talking to me?' I ask.

'No, I'm talking to the wall.'

'Slight problem.'

'What?'

'The wall's not responding. Seriously, though . . .'

He turns towards me.

'*Harry*!' Nicole beseeches. 'We already discussed that issue.'

'Did we?'

He's still staring at me.

'I already told you the truth,' she insists.

He turns back to her. 'The truth being?'

He's just used the gerundive, he can't be as thick as all that.

Nicole, begging: 'There *is* no one else.'

He swirls his vodka again, examining the glass fastidiously.

'There really isn't.'

Dear, dear – she's as bad as me for lies.

My heart is thumping like a monkey in my chest. Have I the heart to do this?

I have.

I turn to Nicole, suddenly ruthless, and open my mouth to speak.

I close it again.

I turn back to Harry, who is still examining his glass. And back to Nicole who is guiltily sipping her Cointreau as if it's stolen property, her frightened eyes flicking up and down at Harry's massive form, her slender fingers wrapped nervously round the stem of her glass.

I can't decide.

Suddenly he turns on me: 'Do I know you?'

I blush. 'Not at all. Why?'

'Your voice.'

'They tell me I speak like Demi Moore,' I reply, secretly shitting a condominium.

'Would you leave my house, please,' he says. Since he has addressed the floor, it's unclear whether this is meant for me or for Nicole. Or for both of us.

Nicole: 'How, how do you mean?'

'I've thought about this,' he says calmly, 'and I want you out of my house.'

Nicole: 'Who?'

'You.'

'Me?'

'You're not to be trusted.'

'But . . .'

'*Now*!'

Dear dear! It was so much more pleasant before Harry interrupted our little conversation about *Bagua* mirrors and *Fu* dogs, and rhododendrons and coffee tables, and the four elements and fish cakes, and Ronan's pitiable wife.

He points to the door. 'Out of my house, you two-timing bitch.'

She starts sobbing.

'There's no need to talk to her like that,' I suggest.

'I'll talk to that slut whatever way I like.'

'She's not a slut.'

I bite my lip. Did I just say that?

Harry is glaring at me now. 'Oh, she's not a slut, is she not?'

Nicole herself has no opinion on this fairly crucial point.

'Even if she is a slut,' I respond, 'she's not *your* slut.'

His head turns to me. He shouts: '*What do you think I hit her for? Jump-starting the car?*'

'Well, now, that's logical.'

'Julianne – *please* . . .' says Nicole.

Harry flushes. 'The two of you. Get out. You can make yourself useful and help her pack her bags.'

I will let him get away with this – just this once.

He turns and fills up his glass again. 'I want you both out in half an hour. Oh, and I want the rest of your stinking fish out of my bath.'

'But I have nowhere to put them.'

'They'll go down the toilet otherwise.'

A man after my own heart.

'But they'll die.'

'And I want your ridiculous canvases out of my attic.'

It's odd, the quarters from which you least expect moral support. He sniggers.

'What are you laughing at?' demands Nicole, offended.

'You hardly expect me to hold on to that shite,' he observes.

I feel like telling him that we are totally at one on that issue.

'Okay,' she says, mouth hardening. 'I'll go if you want me to.'

'And you can take that stupid cat with you. He gets on my nerves. Always slinking around the place following you as if you've done something wrong.'

This is amazing! He's paranoid, like myself. He's my very own soul-brother! We should suggest coffee some time. We agree on fish, on Nicole's painting, on Max. We've both been treated as asswipes from the same roll. Such a lot in common, it'd be a shame not to follow it up, to laugh a little together about life and its unexpected fate turns and quirky ironies.

One thing suddenly occurs to me, though.

What will Nicole do if she's kicked out? Where will she go? Some hostel for the homeless? I don't think so.

She will want to be with Ronan.

'Harry,' I begin, starting to panic again.

'What do *you* want?'

'I want to clarify something about this whole issue. I think it will help.'

'Help. Of course, you're the great Florence Nightingale.'

'I'm sorry?'

He sniggers at my etiquette. 'You, who've taken it upon yourself to pick sluts up off the road and bring them to hospital.'

I don't want to get sidetracked, but I'm afraid I can't help it.

'All it was, Harry,' says I, with the utmost charm, 'is that I was passing outside your house yesterday and I saw that Nicole was bleeding . . .'

'Your time's up,' he replies, pointing to the door behind me.

'. . . so I thought I'd stop to inquire after her health.'

'She can take care of herself.'

'I thought it best not to leave her semi-crippled on the pavement.'

'We have a real Mother Teresa here,' he jeers.

'No, just ordinary human decency.'

'Julianne,' Nicole whispers.

I admit it, I have this irreversible designer defect: it consists in the fact that, like Sylvana, I can't bear giving pricks the upper hand.

Harry is glaring at me now, rubbing his chin, though not as intelligently as Ronan is accustomed to rub his chin. Harry's gesture has something ill-mannered and stupid about it, completely lacking in Ronan's *savoir faire*.

'What was I supposed to do? Walk past her and say: "Is that blood I see dripping from your face? Are they bruises? How interesting! Well, have a nice day."'

He appears to be studying me with a measure of doubt. 'Harry, you deserve to know the truth about Nicole,' I say with perfect condescension, but he's too thick to pick up on it.

Nicole sits down suddenly on the couch, clasping herself like a tender wounded mammal. Through watery, anguished eyes she stares up at me, her apocalyptic face white as a sheet.

'I hardly know Nicole,' I begin. 'I met her yesterday for the first time. Being honest, she's not even my friend.'

I glance at her sunken, crushed posture.

'My own husband cheated on me. So I know what it feels like. It cuts you apart. I have no sympathy for women who do this and the last thing I'd want would be to protect them.'

Nicole is trembling like a tractor.

'I took Nicole to hospital yesterday because I saw her outside, injured. She was shaking and confused and in panic. She kept telling me she couldn't understand why someone would try to split you and her up like that. She insisted there was no other man. She was in such a state of shock she could hardly speak. People tell the truth in that state. I know you don't believe me, but it's true.'

He takes a sip of vodka.

Jesus, the things I have to do.

'Nicole told me she couldn't understand why you beat her like that, when you were the one she loved. Yes, that's right: she told me she loved you.'

Both Nicole and Harry stare at me with something approaching astonished bafflement.

'You're lying,' he says.

Lying. It's such fun! Being a barrister, I get a lot of practice. An important part of the technique is the following assurance. 'I know you don't believe me, but it's true.' Then you dive on to your king-size-bedded orgy of truth suppression and mass perjury, and have a whale of a time.

'I swear to you, Harry, on my mother's grave . . .' (She's not dead yet.) '. . . that I'm telling you God's honest truth . . .' (I haven't been to Mass in a while.) '. . . I really am.'

The atmosphere in the room is suddenly clogged up with extreme awkwardness.

'Nicole,' I command, 'did you not tell me yesterday in the hospital that you loved Harry?'

She lowers her head.

'*Didn't you?*'

She nods. She's got no choice.

Harry to Nicole: 'I don't believe you.'

Me: 'Tell him it's true, Nicole. Go on.'

Pause.

She looks up into his hard eyes, nods her head almost imperceptibly and affirms out loud that that is precisely what she told me.

Harry snorts phlegm up through his nostrils.

His way of saying that he is reconsidering events.

The room is a morgue of silence.

I open the door fully, step out and close it very, very quietly behind me.

I should demand top consultancy rates.

27

When I left Nicole's I came straight into town. I've been in Brown Thomas, doing what all jerked-on wives are supposed to do: purchasing strictly unnecessary merchandise.

More precisely, I've been on a revenge witch-hunt courtesy of Ronan's Mastercard, which I borrowed earlier from his wallet. I've been cunningly copying his signature, R. Fitzgerald, and I've had a terrific time: the lot came to just over one and a half thousand pounds.

I bought myself three pairs of black leather shoes, two pin-striped suits, a black leather jacket, jewellery including a new solid-gold watch strap (the metallic one I had gave me allergies), a floppy black hat I know I'll never use, new silk sheets, a new bathrobe and (believe it or not) a lemon-yellow Wonderbra to see if I get a response from him.

This time with matching knickers.

Having dumped the bags in the boot of my MG in the nearby car park, I am now on my second binge of the day. I am sitting in Bewley's café, lounging on one of its soft red-wine benches underneath a high stained-glass window and opposite a huge painting of white, blue and green surf, dunking my face into an enormous cup of cappuccino, eyeing my plate whereon reside a load of these utterly decadent cream cakes. There's a coffee éclair and a chocolate éclair with cream seeping out of them like two fat sidelong grins. Both as yet untouched. There's a strawberry cheesecake, already ransacked by my good self. And a chocolate fudge gateau, third-munched. Oh, and one caramel slice.

I called Sylvana but she informed me that she had a man by the balls and that it was the wrong time to let go, so could I perhaps call later. I was unclear whether she was at a business meeting or whether she was in bed, but I felt it best not to press the point at such a critical juncture in her life.

I could have called my other acquaintances for some succour and relief – and to help me with all these cakes, which I'll never manage on my own – but I have told nobody else about my marital indignities. Only Sylvana.

So what do I do? I call my mother.

'I'm only calling you, Mother, because I'm in Bewley's and I've bought more cakes than I can chew, and I was wondering if you'd care to join me.'

'What cakes?'

'So whether or not you decide to meet me in here depends on what cakes I bought.'

She grunts.

I tell her what I bought.

'You're bingeing,' she concludes and this from the woman for whom eating pastries is a religion.

'So?'

'It's a sign of depression.'

'Good.'

'Sorry, Julie, I can't meet you.'

'Would you have preferred a better selection of cakes?'

'It's not that. I'm expecting a delivery.'

'The fish tank?'

'No, it's my baby grand piano.'

I mull over the enormity of what she's just said. 'Mother, there's no room for a baby grand piano.'

'It's organized. There's no way I'm leaving it in the house for the new people: it's a valuable antique.'

'Mother, it's an ancient relic.'

'You learnt to play on it.'

'But it won't even fit through the door.'

'The men assured me it would. Sideways.'

'Ronan will have a fit.'

'Well, it's a pity about him.'

'He happens to co-own that apartment.'

'Then why has he been avoiding me like the plague all day? I go into the lounge, and he gets up and goes into the kitchen. I follow him into the kitchen and he slips back out to the lounge, or escapes me altogether to the bedroom. With him it's all artificial politeness. It's no wonder you find it hard to live with him, what with the fish tank episode, et cetera.'

'So you're moving in your piano to antagonize Ronan, is that it?'

'The point is, if he thinks he can survive in that apartment and pretend I don't exist, wait till he sees the piano.'

'Mother, I don't want to predict what's going to happen if you do this.'

Before she says 'goodbye, I love you so', she gives me strict instructions to carefully wrap the chocolate and the coffee éclairs (her personal favourites) in a separate tissue and bring them home to her. I am not to touch them, she says, because they'll make me break out in all kinds of nasty spots and I'll put on a stone in weight.

She hangs up without giving me a chance to defend myself.

I order another cappuccino.

I wrap the chocolate éclair in tissue and discreetly place it in one of my bags beneath the table. No one saw that.

While I'm waiting for nobody to arrive and keep me company, I just stare miserably at my other éclair. Things are going very badly indeed. I take a sip of coffee and I sit back in the warm comfort of the soft bench.

I stick my hand in my jacket pocket and pull out the booklet on *Feng Shui*. The one I coolly ripped off from Nicole's sitting-room. On each little page are scribbled a few lines of wisdom on a particular subject. There's a table of contents. I look up 'cats'.

According to the page on cats, they have the inner capacity to ward off harmful spirits. Also, they can counteract passive *yin* energy, which develops in your home when you're out all day at work. Fine. 'Jasmine'. She's right: jasmine is known as the plant of friendship. 'Magnolia': known to the Chinese as the secretly smiling flower, this plant increases a woman's beauty. Must try it some time.

'Colours': yellow. Yellow stimulates mental energy, and the expansion of wisdom and consciousness. Nothing about yellow on front doorknobs. It is appropriate, the booklet says, to paint the walls of your relationships area (?) or your children area (?) in yellow. Green represents harmony and peace to troubled minds. When mixed with red it can encourage travel. And jealousy.

'Money': be careful of it. Money has powerful energy, but it comes with the danger of taking you over completely when it's out of balance. A fast way of losing money, apparently, is to keep your toilet seat up. So there.

'Fish': very auspicious. Place a tank of lively guppies in the northern corner of your living-room and your career will come alive. Okay.

'*Feng Shui* in the bedroom': never sleep opposite a mirror – the reflections suggest the presence of a third party. How ironic. Ronan and I sleep opposite a mirror.

'The turtle exercise': sit down and close your eyes, let your chin drop to your chest. Inhale – slowly raising your head again – then exhale while tilting your head back.

Right now, I'm sitting in the middle of Bewley's crowded Oriental café, doing the turtle exercise with my eyes closed.

'Julianne, what are you doing?'

The cheerful voice makes my heart somersault.

It's Nicole.

She's in her red dress, out of breath, all smiles. Hurriedly I drop the *Feng Shui* booklet between my legs, close it and slide it surreptitiously into my bag beneath the table.

'I was just reading the Bible,' I reply, pushing the coffee éclair towards her. 'What on earth are *you* doing here, Nicole?'

'I'm meeting Ronan at four in Temple Bar. Isn't this an amazing coincidence? Julianne, I love the leather jacket.'

'I've just charged it to my husband's credit card, along with all these shoes and suits and things, and I also bought a lemon-yellow Wonderbra with matching knickers, just for the hell of it.'

Not a flicker from her. 'I've just bought a dress myself. Will I show it to you?'

'It's okay.'

'It's peach,' she insists hopefully.

'Charming. Enjoy your coffee éclair, Nicole.'

She sits down opposite me and starts picking at the éclair (Mother will be furious). After ordering a coffee from one of the waiters she turns to me all earnest, grave.

She says she realizes I just put myself on the line for her back there in front of Harry. She says she is extremely grateful to me for saving her life, and that owing to me, she no longer lives in danger of being thumped. Thank you so much, Julianne.

'You're welcome, by the way, Nicole . . .' I'm playing with my lower lip. 'I'd love to meet Ronan.'

'You would?'

'Yes. I was thinking: what about an introduction?'

'You mean, this afternoon?'

'It can't hurt.'

'I'd like that.' She smiles.

'I'm just curious to see what a jerk he is. Only joking.'

She tells me, in effect, that, at four o'clock she'll introduce me to my husband of two years' standing.

'Hands off, though.' She laughs. 'He's *mine*, okay?'

This is her concept of a joke, like.

'You have no idea, do you?'

'How do you mean?'

'Forget it.'

She flicks her hair back and takes another forkful of cake. She's beginning to look tired. She's lost the happy glow she had when I called up to her place earlier. That thing with Harry must have traumatized her, poor thing.

I take a bite from my own cream-orientated gunge, take several sips of my coffee and turn to her. 'Nicole, can I say something?'

She nods earnestly at me.

'You probably won't like this, but do you have any idea what you constitute in Ronan's eyes?'

'How do you mean?'

'To him you are just a sexual plaything.'

'I don't . . .'

'To Ronan you are merely an inflatable doll with a smile. A vibrator with a human face. He is just using you as his virility barometer.'

'Why are you saying all that, Jul—'

'You're just a *conquest*, Nicole.'

She quietly nibbles some titbits from her fork. I'm actually beginning to enjoy this.

'This isn't about sexual conquest.' She sulks.

'Face it, Nicole, you're no more than a mini-Everest.'

She flushes, sipping her just arrived coffee.

And most infuriatingly I add: 'Sad but true.'

'Ronan is not like other men,' she tries to explain.

'They never are.'

Again, I have to listen to a load of hogwash about how my wonderful husband is so different. She tells me that he's kind and gentle, and appreciative of her work as an artist, which of course makes me want to vomit recipe books wholesale.

'You'll see what I mean when you meet him at four.'

She goes quiet now.

'Look, Nicole, I don't see how you can continue to ignore

certain blatant facts: once upon a time he and his present wife actually went to the trouble of getting married in a church. In front of a priest and a congregation. In front of *God*, for chrissake! Think of this: he put a wedding ring on her finger and walked back down the aisle with her and took her on a honeymooon to . . . wherever, and he lived with her for a few years and is still living with her, no thanks to you, Nicole.'

'Have you any idea how all this is making me feel?'

'In the end he's only going to let you down. Like he did his own wife. Wait and see.'

She slams down her fork, leaving one small piece of éclair on the plate, and takes a sip of coffee. She waits a beat, then proceeds, as nicely as she can: 'Look, I know you're going through your own problems.'

'Stop right there, Nicole.'

'You were really kind,' she insists, 'taking me to hospital yesterday . . .'

'I didn't plan it like that.'

And I didn't. In actual fact I had planned to beat the crap clean out of her, but fate in its characteristically arrogant and unpredictable manner decided to jerk people around yet again and give the job to Harry instead.

'. . . and protecting me from Harry just now. You didn't have to do all that. You've been fantastic.'

'Dump him, Nicole.'

'But I'm in *love* with him, don't you see?'

'He's *using* you. For a bit of sex.'

'Is that what you think this is?' she pleads. 'A bit of sex?'

'Exactly.'

'If it's just a bit of sex, then why did he tell me this morning that his marriage was dead?'

Pause.

'He said that?'

'He phoned me after breakfast. His silly wife had been tormenting him again.'

'His marriage is dead.'

I mean, it seemed relatively alive to me this morning.

'That's what he said.'

'How dead is *dead*?'

She stands up, excusing herself and saying that it's nearly four o'clock, and she'd better 'pop' into the ladies with her plastic Brown Thomas bag to change into her new peach dress.

Oh, the joys!

Nicole is leading me up Dame Street to the Temple Bar area of town, a revamped cobblestone development housing the worst and the best excesses of humanity, from sculpture exhibition halls to institutions for getting pissed.

She's walking tall beside me in her vile new peach dress. She says Ronan has never kept her waiting. That he's a fantastic timekeeper.

'Has he considered working in aviation control?'

'He's great that way.'

I can't wait to see his face when we both walk in.

She tells me a little about him. Most of it a whole load of codswallop, like the bit about Ronan being a 'creative genius with words and images'. What can you say?

As we branch through a narrow side street to Temple Bar, she starts telling me that Ronan has offered to rent some studio space for her in the vicinity, which is full of artists' studios. She tells me that Ronan is loaded and he can well afford it, but that she hopes to be able to pay him back some time in the future if she makes a success of her painting.

'*If*,' says I, all sarky.

'There's something I haven't told you,' she replies.

'Go on.'

'I've had some good luck.'

'Pray tell.'

'Ronan received fantastic news about my main painting from Lucien Morel – he's an artists' agent Ronan knows from his time in Paris. They're going to exhibit it in the first week of September!'

'September?'

'Yes! And they want to see some more of my paintings. And apparently the art critic of *Le Monde* wants to meet me. Isn't that *incredible*!'

'What's the painting about?'

'It's called *Chi*.'

'Of course it is.'

I'm humming away to myself, wondering how Ronan will cope with his cardiac arrest when he sees me walking into the pub beside his nubile jerk-off.

'It's my best work,' she says. 'Ronan agreed to mind it for me in his surgery, in case Harry decided to fly into a rage and tear it up or something.'

I stop dead on the pavement and glare at her. 'Describe it to me.'

Surprised, she explains that it's a work in oils and features eight goldfish in different colours in a big bowl.

'I see.'

It's the picture hanging up in the surgery.

'The number eight symbolizes the *Bagua*. I painted each fish in different colours, to show that each is a source of *chi* but at the same time stands for something unique. The idea was based on the trigrams found on the *Bagua*. Trigrams are a kind of script using parallel lines. Each trigram stands for . . .'

'So this *Chi*, as you call it, is some sort of masterpiece?'

'I wouldn't call it that.' She laughs.

'So it's the best of a bad lot?'

She doesn't want to agree with this formulation either. 'I suppose it's my one really good painting.'

'The one on which your reputation depends.'

She nods. 'Ronan says it's got great possibilities, he says it's my real selling point.'

Can that cad ever keep his mouth shut?

'Anyway, as I was saying, each trigram stands for a thing. *Zhen*, for instance, stands for thunder, *Li* means fire and . . .'

I just switch off and let her drone on. We're approaching Temple Bar Square anyway, so my mind is on other things. The pub is located on the corner beside the barber's and the second-hand music store, near the narrow arched passageway that leads down to the quays. We've only about fifty metres to go.

'Also, he's taking me to Paris next week,' she says gaily.

I stop suddenly, alongside a bronze petalled lotus seat, presently being subjected to rigorous and loud intellectual scrutiny by a group of US tourists. 'What did you just say, Nicole?'

She's beginning to look apprehensive. 'Nothing.'

'Did you just say he's taking you to Paris?'

'It's for my art.'

I am completely flattened. 'When?'

'Next Tuesday. There's a late-afternoon flight. Look, I know you don't approve of the situation I'm in with Ronan . . .'

'Holy Christ.'

'Are you sure you don't want to meet him some other time?'

'I don't believe this.'

'But it's a fantastic opportunity, Julianne. I have to go.'

This is serious. This is critical. They are closer than I thought. She could become a famous artist. And where will that leave me? A mere barrister? She could be rich. And me? On impoverishment rations of fifty grand a year.

This is catastrophic.

I know that Ronan is at worst just a transient prick pedlar who leeches on to female soft tissue until spray time. But with art and glamour and wealth thrown in? Why, I haven't a stinking hope in hell.

If I go in there now I could force him to a spontaneous decision. I could risk everything.

I grab her by the arm and pull her to the right into the arched passageway leading to the river. We stop and I lay into her, my voice reverberating against the enclosing walls. I'm spewing out a torrent of exhortation, pleading with her generally to see sense and to devote her life to independence and autonomy, and responsible adulthood.

And what does she do?

She turns all soft and sympathetic on me. 'Julianne, you've been wonderful, you really have. It was wrong of me to burden you with Ronan. I wasn't considering your feelings, especially since this isn't an easy time for you, with your own husband.'

She touches the back of my hand affectionately and smiles at me sincerely, and says she's really glad we met just now and that we must get together again soon.

I want to cudgel her.

'But I'd really better go or else I'll be late for Ronan.'

'Go,' says I bitterly, turning away.

She smiles like I'm suffering from some hormone-related deficiency syndrome but since she's a woman herself she can fully relate to that. She apologizes and thanks me for some reason, and gives a small wave and whispers goodbye in a caring, sing-song way as if nothing has happened.

She retreats back up the alleyway towards Temple Bar Square, leaving me alone in this hellish windswept void.

I drive home by the sea. There's a thick band of sombre cloud hovering over the now dark bay. Thin speckles of drizzle flock against the windscreen. I let them fall without switching on the wipers. I prefer to view the world right now as a distorted chaos.

So.

My marriage is dead.

And he's taking her to Paris.

Well, at least I know where I stand.

I am weary. Too weary for anger.

Now thick raindrops are splashing against the glass. I leave off the wipers. The cars that pass me are just vague, ghostly shapes and I know I am putting my life and other people's lives in danger by the fact that my visibility is no better than a snowed-up television, but bothering takes far too much effort.

So I keep driving on and on in the direction of home, although that's the last place where I want to go right now, and it's only after my wing mirror snaps against an oncoming car that I get the fright of my life and flick on the windscreen wipers again. They cut through the opaque windscreen water wall and there opens out a shining wet road in front of me, bleary, miserable and grey.

Still, at least I kept my trap shut.

I have kept the advantage. If you can call it that.

She was right about one thing though: *Chi* does have great possibilities.

Chi is history.

28

Opening the front door, I've got the strange sensation that I've just walked into someone else's apartment.

Apart from the vague odour of dead fish, there's this old, chunky, tinkly, gargley, bolloxed-music-saloon sound coming from our lounge.

It's the sound of a piano.

Bizet, I think.

A few feet further on, guess who I spy through the lounge door?

Mother is sitting behind this shining black monstrosity – way too big for the room and for her, and as jarringly incongruous as a giant slag heap stuck in the middle of a desert of snow.

She's perched on a familiar, worn piano stool, her reading glasses crooked on her nose, her head bobbing up and down like a buoy as she reads from the score.

'I don't believe this.'

The music crashes to a halt. She looks up, surprised. 'Oh, it's you, dear.'

I am speechless. 'You *didn't* . . .'

'I had to pay the delivery men one hundred and fifty pounds. It's extortion.'

'I don't believe it.'

'Yes, I should have got another quote.'

'Mother, I didn't think you were serious.'

'I'm not, dear; I am known for my terrifying sense of humour.'

'I can't believe you actually had this piano delivered.'

'Well, then have a look at the dents by the front door.'

'Ronan will have a fit.'

'And we must give him all the support he needs.'

'Oh, God!'

I'm circling the baby grand like Ronan recently circled his Porsche – but with a great deal more difficulty, considering the thing has taken up nearly half the lounge and has sucked away any available walk space like a giant vacuum cleaner.

The dining-table and chairs have gone. Mother informs me that the table is being temporarily stored in our bedroom in a folded-up state, and the Victorian dining-chairs are stacked up in her new bedroom, but it's no problem: they're ideal as an elongated shoe rack.

'I've sold my house,' she explains. 'The purchaser didn't just want the house. He wanted everything. Carpets, curtains, furniture, even the antiquated lawnmower which I'm in two minds about. Everything except the piano. He said his favourite daughter died last year and apparently she used to play piano. He couldn't bear the sight of this thing in my drawing-room. I had to give him a handkerchief. It's awfully sad, isn't it?'

'You're changing the subject.'

'Also, it's very valuable.'

'What am I going to tell . . . ?'

'A piano brings a lot of possibilities to a household.'

'None of them good.'

She laughs the way she used to laugh when I was young and sulkful.

But maybe she's right? Maybe there is a bright side? After all, this will drive Ronan stark, stripping, internally haemorrhaging crazy, will it not? Surely that's a point to be borne in mind?

I mean, why should I consider Ronan's feelings here? Has he considered mine? He's forking a woman behind my back. And me? What great injustice have I committed? Hijacked his precious living-room space via an old grand piano?

Not very grim in the total scale of things.

Besides, look at her.

She's the picture of total bliss.

I shouldn't be so harsh.

Five minutes later – at seven on the dot – the front door opens. Mother scurries daintily into the kitchen out of harm's way, mischievous grin on her face. Ronan is about to discover something significant and she does not want to be around for the celebrations.

The front door bangs shut. Shoe steps in the hall. The rustle of

plastic. He deposits something large on top of the banana couch.
He sees me.

'Did you have an exciting afternoon?' I wonder.

There's this rumple of coats being hung up.

'What's that fishy smell?' he says.

'Well, did you get any?'

Pause.

'Any what?'

'Shoes.'

'Yes, I'm wearing them,' he replies. 'Were you cooking fish?'

'What's in the package, Ronan?'

'A fish tank, what else.'

Mother is peering through a crack in the kitchen door.
Grinning at me. She's in an excellent mood. Clearly delighted
she's got her grand piano. But also excited at the prospects
offered up by the next few minutes of life on earth.

The cloakroom door closes again and Ronan sits down on the
banana couch and removes two shiny new brown shoes. Then
he gets up and picks his package off the couch and approaches
the lounge. I lower my eyes to my magazine. His footsteps cease.
I assume he's reached the doorway.

Perhaps his eyes are delaying on the short black dress and
black shoes I purchased this morning? Or on my nicely arranged
hair? Or on my stunningly landscaped face?

Or perhaps he's noticed something else.

'Julie. What is that?'

First I look up, then following his gaze I very very slowly
glance over my shoulder towards the baby grand. 'Oh, *that*? Well
. . . it's got five letters.'

There's this barely audible click. We both glance towards the
kitchen door. Mother dear has just closed it. She's very discreet
that way. Very unobtrusive.

Ronan speaks again from his stationary doorway position,
inhaling deeply under the weight of the fish tank. 'What's it
doing here, Julie?'

'I won it in a raffle.'

Bad news has to be broken gradually.

He rushes in now with his heavy glass load, places it clumsily

150

on the pedestal and flips off the packing. There's silence behind me. I wonder if he'll recognize the piano?

'It's nice, isn't it?'

Now there's this squeaking sound: it creaks like lightning through the night sky of my memories. It's the sound of the piano lid being raised. Mother is privileged to possess a piano which, when you raise the lid, sounds like a coffin-opening party in *The Evil Dead*. I remember it so well.

'You won it in a raffle?'

'Yes indeed.'

'I'd recognize this piece of junk anywhere, Julie. It belongs to your mother.'

Guess who walks through the kitchen door just then.

Mum is great. She really is. She has Ronan by the balls. She's performing this charm assault on him that would make Michelle Pfeiffer look like Splodge.

The stages of her crafty, highly skilled technique are as follows:

1 *Warm smile: 'Hello, Ronan!'*
2 *Diversionary tactics: 'That's a lovely new fish tank you got.' She goes over to admire.*
3 *Blaming me: 'You should have let Julie buy it; after all, she was the one who broke it.'*
4 *Humble apology: 'Oh, by the way, Ronan, I'm sorry about the piano. I know it's taking up a terrible amount of space . . .'*
5 *Feigned recognition of authority: '. . . but if it's all right with you . . .'*
6 *Lies and conspiracy: '. . . I'll keep it here for just a few days until we sell it off again.'*

Old women, as we know, get away with murder.

Ronan is barely reassured. He just stands there, hands on his hips, exhaling deeply. He makes some face-saving, humorous comment about how the lounge in its present colour scheme reminds him of Carolan's Irish Cream.

Then he goes out and takes a shower, and prepares himself for dinner at La Bohème's, which he booked for the two of us to shut me up.

'He's right about one thing, though,' Mother says when we have the room once more to ourselves.

'What?'

'That smell.'

'Yes,' I reply, lowering my eyes to my magazine. 'I had no idea salmon would smell like that.'

'You were cooking salmon?'

'Yes, a kind of mousseline.' She grins, but in a way that makes me highly apprehensive.

My mother brought me up to be a good Christian and a good animal lover. Good Christians and good animal lovers don't do what I did to those tropical marine fish. Dead or alive.

'Oh, and by the way, Julie.'

'Mm?'

'Where are all the missing fish?'

When I look up I can see her smiling, bespectacled eyes boring into me over the top of her magazine. They are dazzling me with suspicion.

I stand up at once and leave the room.

29

And here we are at La Bohème's.

Ronan is formal and quiet and distant. For his starter, he's eating breaded mushrooms with yoghurt sauce, a fairly vile combination in my book. I'm just sitting here slivering lemony smoked salmon into my principal orifice, feeling a bit wicked over the fish.

We eat in silence.

Whenever we dine out he rarely speaks during the first third of his meal. His excuse is that eating is a form of work and he can't do two things at once. The truth, however, is that conversing with wives is a form of work. Mistresses, now, that's a different matter entirely.

In time our *escalopes de veau* (Ronan) and roast duck with

orange sauce (*moi*) arrive. It's not before his eighth bite into his escalopes that Ronan is ready for his speciality: communication.

'So . . .' he begins.

'Comma.'

'How is your duck?'

'Hysterical.'

He chuckles to himself.

'Ronan.'

'Mm?'

'When are you taking your summer leave?'

He clears his throat after a delayed spell of munching, wine-sipping and glass replacement.

'Some time between mid-August and mid-September.'

'Possibly early September?'

'Yes, why?'

'No reason. I just thought it'd be nice to go back to Corfu.'

'Corfu?' he says. 'Why not? It's lovely in August.'

'Do you remember our holiday there?'

We reminisce a little about the heat, the long, winding paths down to the beach on which locals on mules sold us cheap wine, the sunsets over the sea, Sotiris's restaurant in the evenings, the music and dancing, one dance where a waiter rotated on his haunches, swinging a table from his teeth.

'Behaviour like that can dislodge one's fillings,' he observes.

We talk about the women dressed in black from head to toe, the tiny whitewashed terraced houses and alleyways, the strange language, the way we used to pick figs from the fig trees behind the beach . . .

'It was so . . . authentic.' I sigh.

'If you exclude the *Sunday Times*.'

I laugh despite myself.

He breaks off and butters a small piece of breadroll and pops it into his mouth. 'I'd go back for the feta cheese alone.'

'The baclavas.'

'The swordfish, the *vino mavro* . . .'

'That was a bit sharp, Ronan.'

'What? The wine?' He grins. 'Remember the orange brandy?'

'The ouzo – after that I remembered nothing.'

'The baked Gruyère: not bad considering it wasn't French.'

'The lobster. Ugh!'

'The brain: a rare delicacy,' he says.

'Only in your head is brain a delicacy, Ronan.'

'Very good, Julie.'

'The mosquitoes . . .'

He frowns. 'What sauce did they come with?'

'Seriously, though, they drove me insane.'

'The thing about mosquitoes,' he begins, slicing his veal, 'is that those insects are highly gifted. Telepathic. You know, people think that they attack only when you switch the light off. They don't: they wait until you've stopped thinking about them. Then they pounce. They're even more cunning than spiders.'

'They were huge. Like bluebottles suspended in mid-air.'

'Not unlike yourself, Julie, they are partial to big epidermal booze-ups.'

'Anyway,' I remind him, ignoring this, 'we got our revenge.'

'Yes, although our host wasn't too happy with the red dots all over the wallpaper.'

'I wasn't too happy with them all over my body.'

'And he wasn't too pleased with our squeaking bed either.'

'How were we to know he was sleeping in the room beneath?'

'You could hear him snoring.'

'That's true. But we never got up to anything *until* he started snoring.'

'You forget, Julie, that he had a wife.'

'Don't remind me. The one with the whiskers.'

'Do you remember the bed?'

'Hard and bristly,' I reply.

'It nearly gave me a slipped disc.'

I pause at this point.

'We know why.'

Ronan laughs. 'I seem to remember once getting a leg stuck in the cast-iron bed-end.'

Kinky sex again. You just can't get him off it.

'We're talking Greek Orthodox, Ronan. Those beds were designed like that for a reason.'

For the first time in months I have just made Ronan choke on his food.

An excellent sign for the future.

'Ronan, I want us to go back there.'

'Sounds good to me.'

'I was thinking . . . the first week in September.'

'What's wrong with August?' He doesn't catch my gaze. He lifts up his wineglass instead.

'A friend of Sylvana's has an apartment in Pelekas but it's booked up in August. And I have to be back at work for the second week of September.'

'Leave it with me.'

'No. We have to grab it while it's there. I want to go in early September, Ronan.'

He frowns at my insistence. 'I may have something on that week.'

'Such as?'

'But I'll get back to you on it, as soon as I can.'

Restrained, I sip my Châteauneuf. 'By the way, I've booked the theatre.'

'What's on?'

'*Salome*. You adore Oscar Wilde.'

'Great. When for?'

'Next Tuesday evening.'

While I am forking duck into my gob I notice from the corner of my eye that Ronan's wineglass has halted in mid-air.

'But what's wrong with next Saturday?'

We normally go on Saturdays.

'There's a girls' night out next Saturday.'

'What's wrong with the following Saturday?' he complains.

'The production ends this weekend.'

I know because I checked.

He does not look pleased.

'Ronan, the point is: what is wrong with next Tuesday?'

'Actually, there's a problem.'

'What?'

'There's a conference in Paris next Tuesday.'

'Is that what you call it.'

'It's a dentistry conference. I forgot to tell you about it.'

'Aha.'

'It's on an important topic: *pyorrhoea alveolaris*.'

Whenever you feel horny and crave a dirty weekend, invent a conference abroad. Trouble is, he's been to dentistry conferences, aesthetics conventions, philosophy colloquia, art appreciation courses all over Europe. Where does that leave me?

'Why don't we both go?'

He shakes his head.

'Why not? While you're at the conference I'll go shopping.'

'It's awkward: I'm staying with French friends in La Défense.'

'I'm sure there'd be room for me in the bed.'

'They only have a couch.'

'I don't mind.'

'If I remember correctly, it's a bit small. Even for one.'

'So we'll stay at the Hotel Pierre, then. We're not poor.'

'I must go easy,' he says, replacing his glass. 'The Porsche repairs have made one or two inroads into my vast fortune.'

'I hope you're not overspending. You know how expensive it can be, buying for two.'

I can almost hear a ton of scaffolding suddenly collapse inside his brain. I sip my wine in perfect innocence. His cheekbones are beginning to glow. I throw him a wicked grin. 'I mean – for you and me.'

He laughs, refilling my glass. 'I thought you were on to me.'

I want to scream at him once and for all. I want to purge it from my system because it's driving me crazy and I don't know how much longer I can keep up the charade.

But I must remain calm.

He, after all, is calm.

I rest my chin on my joined fingers and gaze nostalgically out of the window into the blushing evening. This section of the restaurant overlooks the canal, on the far side of which is a row of trees overhanging the bank. The treetops spike the clear but darkening golden sky like a thousand scissor tips.

I gulp down some sparkling water. I lean forward. 'What's your opinion of adultery, Ronan?'

Pause.

'What's brought this on?'

'I just wanted your opinion. It's for a feasibility study I'm doing.'

He grins. 'Adultery is underrated.'

'I see.'

'Seriously though, there's one thing all women should understand about men.' He pats his mouth with his napkin. 'To most
married men, a mistress is no more than a remote-control
pleasure device.'

I glance at the table next to us. 'You mean, the wife has a
remote prospect of controlling her husband's pleasure?'

'No, Julie. I'm referring to the convoluted world of male
sexuality.'

He takes a French roll from the basket, breaks it in half and
starts to chew, although he's already finished his meal. 'A
mistress is simply an extension of male fantasy,' he explains.

'I admit it hadn't occurred to me.'

'Male fantasy life is intrinsically adulterous. It's back to
genetics – man the hunter, the warrior, the adventurer, the
guardian, the protector of women.'

'What a quaint way to view life.'

'What I'm trying to say is that adultery is a mental state.'

'Although a bed comes in quite useful too.'

He chews on his roll. 'Beds are overrated.'

'You prefer desks, then.'

'Desks, tables, chairs . . . With the *mind* . . .' he points to his
head, where he imagines his mind to be located '. . . with the
mind, any position is feasible. It's all about imagination. The
poetics of the possible. The point is, every man is guilty even
before he has a so-called affair.'

'So-called.'

'It's just a word.'

I want so badly, so desperately for Ronan to stop putting on
this act. I want him so badly just to be himself, to hide nothing,
to come clean. If only he did that I would be the best wife he
could ever have. I would never nag him again. I would never
question him again. Even my genetically encoded pestering
response would shrivel up and die.

A waitress approaches with a dessert menu. Ronan shuns it
and orders two coffees instead. She disappears.

I suddenly grab his hand on the table and hold it down.

157

'Ronan, I know there's something on your mind. I know there is. I know it's bothering you. Look at me, I'm talking to you. You know I love you, I knew from the first second I laid my eyes on you that we'd be together. We're so good together, everything is going so well: our careers, our home, we have fun . . . we've got so much ahead of us. I just, I just . . .'

He eyes me as if I am unclean. 'I haven't an idea what you're talking about.'

I am imploring him. Beseeching him. Appealing to every nerve fibre in his being that flickers in response to vulnerability, pity and humiliation. But he's frozen up like an igloo.

'Please, Ronan, tell me what's on your mind.'

'There's nothing on my mind, for God's sake.'

'Don't do this to me,' I plead.

'Well, I mean, if I had a notion what all this was about.'

He's testing me.

But I can't tell him. I can't. I cannot beg him to be honest. I cannot beg him to be loyal. I will not beg him to be faithful, to be true. I will not beg him to love me. If he doesn't want to love me the way I deserve to be loved, I will not force him. It must come from him.

'Ronan, whatever you've done it means nothing any more. There's just the two of us now.'

'You think I'm having an affair, don't you?'

'Ronan, please don't lie to me. That's all I ask you. Don't lie to me. Because if you do, everything will change. And there will be no going back. I mean it.'

'You think I'm having an affair.' He laughs, like I'm a fool.

'I don't know.'

'Yes, you do. You actually think I'm seeing someone.' He's incredulous, contemptuous.

I can't believe he's doing this to me. I just can't believe it. 'I didn't say that.'

'You implied it.'

'Well, is it true?'

'There you go again.'

'Well, is it?'

He shrugs and says in a bored voice: 'It's just your female insecurity.'

It's unbearable.

'Please!'

'Julie . . .'

'Please, Ronan . . .'

'You're pestering me.'

Dead silence.

He rearranges his napkin on his lap. The girl brings our coffees. Before she's even put mine down in front of me, I stand up and walk out through the restaurant.

He doesn't try to follow. At the doorway, when I look back, he is calmly sipping his coffee.

Once outside, I call Sylvana to instruct her to make up a spare bed.

30

The name Mr Ronan Fitzgerald BA BDent SC is written in gold lettering on a plaque (good word, for a dentist), next to an assortment of less elegant-looking plaques for general practitioners and a chiropodist. His surgery is straight through at the bottom rear of the building, an extension built out into the garden to accommodate four rooms: the main surgery, the office, the kitchen and the bathroom, which is equipped with a built-in shower.

Using a key he gave me a long time ago, I let myself in through the main door and into Ronan's rooms. The smell hits me as I knew it would. That dentist's disinfectant odour. That minty Listerine scent you get from guys in the Law Library who figure that if they wash their gullets with the stuff they stand a better chance of a free screw.

I lock the door behind me.

Dentists. They've brought me such pain in life. They've burst my gums, picked my teeth, drilled and ravaged my nerves, pliered out my molars and snurgled my saliva. I've never liked them.

It's a miracle I married one.

In here is where we had our third date ever. He clearly wanted to impress me by professionally penetrating the putridest recesses of my teeth. I don't know why I agreed to the privilege of a free consultation. I must have imagined he'd look sexy in his white coat.

He showed me into this acid-smelling torture chamber and made it all so very accessible, explaining to me the function of each little device in a relaxed though impersonal manner, me standing here the whole time dying to ride him on the chaise longue. But instead, he sat me on the chaise and flipped on this white face mask like he was afraid of catching something. Then, eyes poking like brown bulbs over his mask, he stuck into my mouth these cold metal implements which made these percussive sounds against my teeth. With his spatula he prodded me, frowning and silent, in the most barren, unromantic places imaginable.

Basically, I was forgotten.

Making me hold the saliva Hoover in my mouth, he syringed my interior cheek and filled my fourth left molar. He was silent until the end of the procedure when he told me to spit, which cascaded me into a whirlpool of anaesthetized, dribbling giggles. Not once did he smile: he was the total professional.

I figured he needed to be loosened up a little. So before we left the building for a light lunch, I pinned him to the door, tore off his shirt, undid his belt, trousers – everything. And I practically raped him.

He's been filling my cavities ever since.

I'm in his office now, staring at his pine desk, checking to see if there are any marks from Friday lunchtime. Buckle scratches, or ring scrapes, or bracelet marks, or suchlike. Nothing. It might never have happened. Things look so normal: his blotting pad, his phone and fax machine, his new computer and printer, his filing cabinet.

I turn to Nicole's painting on the wall. I've just noticed something I didn't see before. On the bottom right-hand side, marked in tiny letters, is the title of the painting.

Chi.

Ignoring this minor disturbance for the moment, I rifle through the three drawers of his desk. In the top drawer are contained recent receipts, acknowledgements, invoices in respect of goods delivered, dispatched, ordered.

In the second drawer are brochures from the Dental Health Association advertising upcoming conferences, exchanges, lectures. As well as brochures and leaflets containing information on new products, new technologies, new medications, new manuals.

For such an aesthete, all this garbage must kill him.

In the third drawer, alongside cards from patients of his, invitations and newspaper clippings concerning a local dentistry malpractice suit, I find a photo of Nicole. She is smiling appealingly straight at the camera, head tilted, wearing a thick white woollen polo-neck with a long yellow scarf draped round her neck and hanging down by her side.

I want to take the photo and smudge it in dogshit.

But no. It gets carefully replaced.

Turning to the filing cabinet, I pull out the second drawer and separate the files at 'M'. I finger through the 'M's meticulously. Immediately I find what I'm looking for. I pull out a letter, signed 'Lucien Morel', Ronan's former aesthetics lecturer at the Sorbonne. Careless boy.

It is dated 5 June. It is addressed to this surgery. It is in English. Crap English, but English none the less.

> *Galerie Richelieu*
> *47 rue des Ecoles*
> *75005 Paris*

Dear Ronan,   *5 June*

It is with profound delight that I take this opportunity to inform you that Georges (Lafayette) has arranged an exhibition of the work of the delightful Mademoiselle Summers. It will be for the beginning of September next and it will be in respect of her highly original oeuvre entitled Chi. *Your photographic representations of her three oeuvres entitled* Foetus, Umbilical Rope *and* Discarded Clothes *elicited some interest, but it is* Chi *which has caused a burst of lightning to emit from the sky.*

Georges is keen to arrange a further meeting with the artist some time in the coming weeks, in order to view these three aforementioned works with a view to possible inclusion in the September exhibition. There will be naturally exhibition charges and my own lesser commission, but I feel that there may be in this country considerable interest in Mademoiselle Summers's work and that the Lafayette Galleries are the perfect platform on which to launch her career in the direction of every success.

If you on behalf of Mademoiselle Summers are agreeable to

considering the possibility of sale of Chi, then this is something which I believe might be a fruitful theme for discussion.

I beg you to contact me at your convenience at the above number in the Sorbonne where I can be mostly found in order that we might arrange a date in June when you might both be able to travel here with the ultimate objective of organizing a programme of exhibitions for your client's oeuvre. So far, Tuesday, 21 June would be a convenient date for me, so if this is appropriate for you also, please let me know as soon as possible.

Please accept my most affectionate and distinguished respects,
Lucien Morel

I replace the letter, close the filing cabinet and sink into the chair beneath his desk.

Tuesday, 21 June. Mid-summer.

I just sit here in perfect silence for a long, long time, listening to the rumble of passing cars outside, tyres slashing and splashing, and splicing through the wetness of today's roads.

Raising my eyes, I stare for a long time at Nicole's colourful goldfish painting. Ronan's passport into the art world. The picture that has the capacity to transform his life. Nicole's life.

My life.

I, on the other hand, have the capacity to transform its life.

I lift the painting from its nail and carry it into the kitchen, dropping it flat on the table.

Not having eaten yet today, I open the fridge.

It's full of food. Either his secretary or Nicole herself was shopping. There's everything a starving human could ask for: cheese slices, butter, eggs, apple tart, bread, yoghurt, a pecan pie. I slice open a carton of diet peach yoghurt and pour its cold dairyness down my throat.

This gives me instant relief.

With the bread-knife I cut myself a slice of pecan pie.

Five gobfuls later and it's gone.

Jesus, I'm ravenous.

The bread. The cheese. The butter.

I'm thinking: I'd kill for cheese on toast.

I take two slices of bread from the pack, make two slices of toast, cover them in swimming butter, hack off two chunks of orange cheddar and implant them on the toast. Finally, I place them under the grill and switch on the mains, then turn up the knob.

Under the sink I discover an unopened six-pack of Budweiser. I tear one off and snap the ring and start drinking. I sit down at the table on a cold wooden chair and finish off the can. I contemplate *Chi*, lying in front of me. I have to admit that it makes me furiously angry and jealous that the people who count regard Nicole's 'work' as 'highly original'.

The sharp smell of grilling cheddar is making me salivate.

I guzzle some more beer.

Chi.

I hold up the painting, at the end of outstretched arms to see what all the fuss was about.

No. I just can't see it. Either I'm a philistine or I'm blind.

Or else it's truly crap.

Try holding it upside down.

Ah, that looks better already.

I drop the painting and grab the grill before my cheese on toast catches fire. The black edges are fuming with thick smoke. But the golden centres are saved. I shake them on to a plate and start munching into the rubbery cheddar, melting into my teeth. I spring open a third can of Budweiser.

Before the can rehits the table I get this blinding flash of light in my brain. I stand up.

Using a tape-measure I spotted in the cutlery drawer, I measure the painting along its shortest edge. Fifteen inches across. Fine.

Now I'm holding the tape-measure across the mouth of the grill.

Seventeen inches.

I shove it in and turn up the heat.

Sitting back down again, hands behind my head, I calmly observe the industrious toasting process of Ronan's grill going full speed ahead. There is inside my digestive tract a thickening, sickening sensation fraught with excitement and dread.

I could have done far worse. There's a lot of expensive

equipment in this surgery: the dental chair, made in Hong Kong, the cost of a second-hand MG to replace; the white robot-limb light fixed to the ceiling, the cost of a holiday for two in Barbados; the X-ray apparatus, the cost of a holiday time-share for a decade; the lotions and potions and mirrors and instruments and glass cabinets; the ornate spit fountain.

With the sledgehammer lying lazily under the sink? Ronan is a lucky man. I am doing him an enormous favour by in effect burning an extra-large slice of toast on the grill.

I am also saving his marriage.

A loud siren blasts off in my ear. The smoke alarm. I jump up and rip it off the wall, shove it on the table and banjax it several times with the lump hammer until it behaves itself. Then I beat my way through black smoke and caustic stench, and pull the painting from the grill and dump it on the draining board beside it.

A terrible beauty is born.

I carry the blackened remains through the surgery, leaving a trail of black smoke hanging in its wake. In his office I attach it once more to the wall, ensuring it's hung crooked.

I stand back to survey my richly allusive reinterpretation of Nicole's masterpiece.

I could feel guilty, but I don't.

You see, it's not enough metaphorically to kick my bastard husband in the teeth. I've been doing this for at least sixty hours, but like a stubborn mule he has failed to respond to the suggestive power inherent in the act. Hence, he's deprived me of the immense satisfaction you normally get from kicking bastard husbands in the teeth.

No: I have been driven to redefining radically that which lies closest to his heart.

Chi is no more.

Before I leave, I survey the state of the kitchen. A plate with crumbs and melted butter, three cans of Budweiser and the yoghurt carton. There's no point in clearing it away. Ronan will never associate the food with me. He will simply assume that Harry built up an appetite watching *Chi* smoulder.

Harry the psycho. When Ronan walks in first thing tomorrow morning, the poor boy will be shitting a colosseum.

Before I leave I grab the hammer and put a hole through the window adjoining the back door, then unlock it.

I leave the surgery the way I came in, double-locking it behind me.

I'm on the top of the bus going back to Sylvana's place, now, and we're purring along the blustery coastline. The only trace of the recent rainstorm lies on the glistening wet pavements. It is bright once again after the downpour, and I've decided to put on my cool tinted and totally seductive Calvin Kleins.

Every window is down, but still it's too hot. Warm air mixed with salty sea smells is billowing through the bus messing up my dream hairstyle, but what woman can have it all?

As I watch the glorious, dangerous blue of the sea stretching clear to the taut wire of the horizon, I am overcome by a pervading sense of peace. I think back on this last hour. It has been eventful.

And deeply pleasurable.

Once more I have hope in life.

In fact, I am quite unable to stop smiling. I'm getting one or two looks from these scruffy louts who are making me feel like an illegal alien from outer space. You feel such a prat on a bus when you're smiling and the rest of the world is glum.

Seriously, though, I am filled with such an unutterably profound sense of satisfaction after my evening's entertainment that I want this feeling to go on for ever.

31

I'm roasting in a tiny pool of sunlight, seated outside Renaldo's café only five minutes' walk from home.

Overhead is a wash of bright-leafed lime trees, sweeping gently in the welcome cool breeze and speckling the pavement with dapples of yellow confetti from the dazzling sun above. Through the leaves the sky is a fluttering blue-green. Opposite is the ferry terminal whose shiny white façade is lined by palm trees in huge boxes – imported. The pier stretches out into the sparkling sun and sea, yellow as a banana in the bright glare. At the end of the pier is the lighthouse one mile out. It seems like it's just resting on the hazy blue water.

It's one of those days where you want to say: if only Ronan were here to share it with me.

Instead, I get to share it with Nicole.

How did this happen, you ask?

She rang me this lunchtime. I was in a café at the time, adjacent to the Law Library, overdosing on espresso and caramel slices, experiencing repeated surges of pleasure as I visualized Ronan walk into his surgery this very morning, only to discover his recently combusted *Chi* hanging from the wall to cool.

He must be furious, I was thinking.

These fond thoughts were going through my head when my cellular phone suddenly pealed like a spiked javelin into the middle of the small café, and naturally every luncher in the place turns round and glares at me like we're living in some sort of mobile-free zone.

I picked up. It was Nicole.

I asked her how she was, in an utterly uninterested voice. Unfortunately, she told me. She was all: 'Hi, Julianne. I feel so great. What a wonderful world. I'm so happy! I'm overcoming my neuroses and insecurities, and it's all down to the most amazing man you'd ever meet and oh I'm so lucky, oh, I know you don't like me going on about it, but I've just got to share my happiness with someone – will you meet me today, Julianne? Please!'

I was sorely tempted to make one from a list of nasty sarcastic comments, including the expression 'you rat-turd' or a near equivalent. But was there any point? Things were working out in my favour anyway, so why waste energy getting upset?

'I've nothing to lose,' I replied.

'Great!'

We arranged to meet at five at a location of my choice.

So here I am, sitting at a coffee table just a few hundred yards down the road from where we live. Sipping a nerve-racking roast from Chile, so dark and strong it's sure to be loaded with cancer, which is precisely why I love it so.

You know, the South Americans are so good on coffee they must be the most wide-awake folk on earth. I dread to think what the males are like, though: Latin men are hyper enough as it is without mind-blowing caffeine to turn them hog-wild.

I order a slice of ricotta cake. Sheer confectionate orgasm. And thus do I squat, rocking gently to and fro on the two teetering hind hooves of my white plastic chair, listening to the ebb and flow of the sea wash one minute away, gently fingering the fading seconds of my eternal summer, before Nicole arrives and tells me something happy to put me in a bad mood.

She arrives half an hour late, just when I was on the point of ordering a second slice of ricotta. She's carrying this large box thing. Reminds me a bit of Ronan with the new fish tank. She's wearing this foolish pineapple smile that I want to tear off her face like a bumper sticker.

She gives me an unexpected little hug and tumbles her ramshackle apologies and excuses down on top of me for being late. She puts down her large rectangular object. It's got these plastic bars. I now see what it contains: it's a small, furry, black animal with tiny, piercing, evil eyes.

'Nicole,' says I, pointing. 'What is that . . . *thing* doing here?'

She sits down. 'Julianne . . . I've got a little . . . favour to ask you.'

'No way.'

'But I haven't even asked you yet.'

'Nicole, you bring your cat here, in a box, and you tell me you have a favour to ask of me and you think I can't guess what it is?'

'Okay,' she says, disappointed. 'I won't ask.'

Plastering over her hurt, she bravely orders two cappuccinos from a nearby waitress. It doesn't occur to her that I might prefer, say, a moccha. Sour grapes.

She bends down and starts fiddling with the clasps of the box. 'Poor Max,' she gushes, lifting him out of his cell like a soggy black sweater. 'Come and join us.'

Actually, I'd rather Max did not come and join us for a cappuccino. Cats and cappuccinos don't mix (not even extra-milky cappuccino). Besides, this particular cat makes me nervous. The runt knows things about me.

'Isn't he beautiful?' says Nicole, gently but firmly nestling the miniature panther on her lap like a baby.

'No, he's ugly and vicious, and I don't want him near me.'

She looks at me, confused for a second, then she laughs it off. She thinks I'm just being 'Julianne'.

'You're not ugly, Max, are you, pet?'

'Oh yes he is. And vicious and smelly and horrid.'

'That's not true. You're a wonderful cat, aren't you?'

Max purrs; he has no problem whatever with this hard sell.

'You're a darling,' she googles, kissing the mutt.

'Don't forget relativity, Nicole. If he were bigger than you you wouldn't be cradling him like a baby. You'd be nursing a huge bite in your jugular.'

'Miaow,' agrees Max.

'See? He's a natural-born killer. You should rename him Saddam.'

'Poor thing,' she sympathizes.

'Anyway, Nicole, what on earth are you doing wandering down the street with a cat box?'

She just keeps stroking her fur pot with the evil eye. 'I've done as you suggested,' she says quietly.

169

'What?'

'I've left Harry.'

I lower my chair on to the floor. 'But I didn't tell you to leave Harry.'

'You told me I should be more independent-minded and autonomous. I've thought a lot about that.'

'Yes, but I didn't mean for you to leave him.'

'Julianne, he beat me up!'

'Yes . . .' I falter. 'But is that a good reason to leave anybody?'

'Anyway, I've moved out now. While Harry was at work I packed four suitcases and as many canvases from the attic as I could fit into my Fiat Cinquecento.'

'You're moving into your Fiat Cinquecento.'

'I don't know where I'm going yet,' she says weepily.

'What about your job?' I ask, determined to avoid the topic of my hospitality.

'I'm not going back to the travel agency; I can't afford to bump into Harry again. He's dangerous. If he finds me he'll kill me.'

'I bet all this was Ronan's idea.'

She denies it. 'Ronan said he'd support me in my decision.'

'With money?'

She shakes her head guiltily. 'He's already been too generous. He gave me a credit card and made me an authorised user.'

'Is that a fact? And how much have you spent on it so far?'

'A few thousand pounds only.'

'Only?'

I'm gasping away like a fried rasher. I slump back in my chair, remembering the watch she bought in the jeweller's. I wonder how Ronan would feel if he realized he indirectly subsidized a watch for Harry, to the tune of one grand.

'It's a lot,' she says ruefully. 'I admit it.'

'I'd love to see his reaction when he finds out.'

Our cappuccinos arrive.

Nicole sits back in silence until the waiter slips the bill under the ashtray and leaves. When he's gone, she sits forward again. 'Anyway, I'll be able to pay him back,' she says urgently. 'If Paris works out.'

'You mean if *Chi* works out.'

'Exactly.'

I laugh out loud.

'Why are you laughing?'

'Dream on,' I mumble, sipping my cappuccino.

She sips her own coffee. 'I didn't tell you that Ronan met the *Irish Times* art critic.'

'Oh?' says I, yawning.

'Yes. They met this morning in Café Rio's.'

Panic.

'But I thought he was in his surgery this morning?'

'He's taken the day off to prepare for Paris. He won't be going back to work until Thursday.'

The burning effigy of *Chi* is shrieking in my inner ear like a siren, screaming to be noticed. Now Ronan won't get to see it until Thursday morning.

I take ten slow, deep breaths to calm me down. Change of plan. 'You know, Nicole, what with all this talk about *Chi*, you have me curious.'

'Do I?'

'You must show it to me some time.'

'I'd like that.'

'I mean, it seems to have created a bit of a storm.'

'I'd love to think so,' she smiles modestly.

'So I wouldn't mind seeing it.'

She nods. 'I'm sure I could show it to you some time.'

'Like what about now?'

She looks at me. 'Now?'

I sip my cooling coffee. 'Why not?'

'But it's in Ronan's surgery.'

'So?'

'I . . .'

'Would it be a problem?'

'Well, he did give me a key . . .'

'So let's go now.'

'Are you serious?'

'Very.'

Three minutes later the three of us (including the cat) are

171

squeezed into Nicole's stuffed-up-to-the-gills yellow Fiat Cinque-cento. There's only just enough room in the front seat. I have the Max box on my knees. Though I'm trying to ignore him, I sense the cat's eyes crawling up my neck through the bars just five inches away. He doesn't trust me. He's quite right not to.

Nicole is all happy again, now that I've decided to engage *Chi* with this sudden overwhelming burst of interest. '*Chi* is my personal favourite,' she says. 'It means a lot to me: it's my only really symbolic painting. I think Ronan was secretly impressed – although he never says so openly. That's why it'd be nice to have your opinion about it.'

'That won't be a problem.'

'Are you sure you don't mind me bringing you to his surgery?'

'Why should I mind?'

'I don't know, it's just that I know you don't really approve . . .'

I say nothing.

She looks over at me and smiles wistfully. 'I know things haven't been easy between you and your husband,' she says.

'Whatever.'

'Do you want to talk about it?'

'No.'

'No problem,' she says, narrowly missing the kerb.

'Nicole, could you try to drive without jerking?'

'Sorry. Anyway, if there's anything I can do to help . . . I have some experience with men. I've been in a lot of relationships.' She suddenly smiles weakly. 'Which probably means I'm the worst person in the world to be giving advice.'

'No comment.'

'But one thing that helps, I find, is to discover something you truly like doing, away from him. If you have that, it means you have something which is all your own and nobody else can interfere. And you don't even have to tell him what you're doing. Also, men really seem to like it when you at least pretend to be independent . . .'

'Nicole, could we perhaps change the subject?'

'I know I go on a bit.' She sighs, bashing into the car behind us as she reverses into a space near Ronan's surgery.

It's after six, so the receptionist who knows me will certainly have gone home. We shut Max up in the car on his own, his sneaky eyes shining like black pebbles in the sunlight.

The two of us head off to the surgery, side by side.

32

We're standing in the office annexed to Ronan's surgery, staring at *Chi* hanging crooked on the wall.

Nicole is shaking uncontrollably.

Her knuckles are clenched into her white face, she's ogling *Chi* in wet-eyed disbelief, like she's just discovered the fresh tomb of a loved one encased in the wall. She's trying to tell me what must have happened, but she's choking her words, they're coming out in gasps.

I'm getting scared. 'Nicole . . . are you okay?'

I never said I was good in an emergency.

She's beginning to suck in these huge gulps of air. I'm telling her to come inside and sit down in the kitchen, that I'll make her a cup of coffee.

Like, stupidly, I'm supposed to know there's a kitchenette.

But she's impervious. In fact, she's hyperventilating. She falls back against the desk, grasps it with one hand, holds her other hand against her chest, gasps for breath, crying, make-up streaking down her face.

I have my arm round her now, I'm telling her to calm down, that it'll be okay. Nicole is shaking her head, she's saying no, no, something to the effect that it will not be okay, that this is going to ruin her, that Ronan will be devastated.

I lean over and grab several of Ronan's posies for her and she takes them and holds on to them for dear life. She's trying to get the words out, but it's like they're blocked, like there's an expanding balloon of air inside her chest squeezing out the words in short, whispered, unintelligible gasps.

I'm getting upset myself. I don't believe it, there are tears in my own eyes now. I have to get her out of here. I lower my hand to the small of her back and gently urge her to stand up from the desk, which she does. I support her as I lead her out of Ronan's office. She strains her neck backwards towards her *Chi*, as if to reassure herself that her worst nightmare has come true.

I push her through to the kitchen and put her sitting at the table and I put the kettle on and, while we're waiting for it to boil, I'm standing with my back to her, staring at it, with Nicole sobbing quietly behind me. Oh Jesus . . . oh God, what have I done to her?

I make her a mug of tea, laced with milk and sugar. I make it too full, though: her hands are shaking so much that her mug is clattering against the hard surface and in record time there's this small tea lagoon shimmering like jelly on the table surface, expanding like a blister. As she sips I rest my hand lightly on her shoulder.

Soon she begins to calm down a little. She's still shaking, but now it's more a period of calm followed by a nervous shudder, followed by a longer period of calm followed by a slightly briefer nervous shudder.

'What are you going to do?' I ask her after some time.

'It's his wife,' she croaks.

'What?'

'His wife did that.'

Pause.

'How can you be so sure?'

'Who else could have done it? She must have found out. Now she knows about me and Ronan.'

Sniff sniff.

'I doubt his wife would have done a thing like that.'

'It would be just like her. You don't know what she did on Saturday.'

'What?'

'Ronan told me that she smashed their fish tank and all the fish went all over the place. Including the ones I gave him.'

'That's unfortunate.'

'She's a psychopath.'

I shrug. 'Yes, in all likelihood she's a bit of a head case. But still, does that mean she did this to the painting? I mean . . .' I point at the back door to the garden '. . . did you see the hole in that window over there?'

She turns to look at the kitchen door to the garden, the one I smashed a hole in. 'What does that prove?'

'It proves that there was a break-in. It was hardly his wife: she's bound to have a spare key. No. I'd say it was Harry. He probably followed you at some stage.'

This suggestion of mine is made in a casual tone of voice.

'Harry would have smashed the whole surgery. I know him.'

I cocked up. I bloody cocked up. I could have taken the lump hammer and turned Ronan's surgery into a bombsite. Then it would have been Harry. But no, because I show laudable restraint and spare his surgery, I end up the culprit. It's most unfair.

'You'd better call Ronan to tell him,' I suggest, ultra-sly.

She makes a quick movement and pulls out her mobile. She presses a number. Then she suddenly presses off. 'I can't.' She shakes her head, eyes closed.

'Why not?'

'It might wreck the whole deal.'

'Of course it will wreck the whole deal, Nicole – that's the whole point.'

She starts wailing now.

'So you must tell him. You can't let him go to Paris and negotiate for you over *Chi* when it doesn't exist any more. You'll make a liar of him.'

'Thanks for being so wonderfully optimistic.' She weeps.

'I'm only being practical.'

'I can't just wreck the whole deal.'

'But what does it matter, Nicole? Isn't love the important thing? Surely Ronan will understand? He loves you, doesn't he?'

'I don't know,' she moans.

'Call him.'

'I can't . . .'

She gets up and runs from the kitchenette. 'We must go to Paris. We must. I'll tell him about this when we return. We still have the other paintings. They're my only hope.'

I've driven Nicole and a baleful-looking Max to a B&B in Dalkey, into which she has just booked herself by mobile phone.

While she's checking in with the large, discreet, smiling lady of the house, I open the cat box in the car as requested by Nicole and viciously shake Max out on to the front seat like he's a rattlesnake. After some impressive soft-landing techniques and oily cat gymnastics, Max rights himself and pounces over the headrest on to the luggage in the back seat, from which relatively safe location he bares his teeth at me. In fact, it's such a foul grimace, so filled with humming evil and baleful nastiness, that it makes you think this cat has a serious problem with trust. There's some latent repression going on, I sense, and it's quite clear this cat requires immediate counselling.

I slam the door, making Max jump. I enter the B&B and make my way up the stairs to Nicole's room at the top rear of the house, case in hand.

It's a twin room. I can't help imagining whom she's twinning with. Or perhaps it's the only room available. It's pretty with its frilly silvery duvets, its white bedside tables and white dressing-table with a vase of red carnations on top, and its silver floral mirror and the jolly blue curtains on the slanted roof window.

She sits down beside a little table by the window and presses the knob of the small electric kettle. Then she slumps her jawline into the palms of her hands and sits quietly, rocking gently in her seat.

I walk to the window and stare at the scenic view of Dalkey Island a few hundred metres over the greyish, choppy sea. It is hilly and green, and dominated by its round, squat Martello Tower.

We don't speak. The kettle comes to the boil and together we make two cups of tea. She thanks me sadly when I offer her a tiny cream container. She looks totally juiced up, like she did when I took her to hospital, only worse, if you subtract the face, which is showing signs of healing.

I sip my PG Tips in silence. Me sitting on the outer bed crumpling the nice fluffy duvet surface, Nicole on the chair with her legs crossed, cupping the teacup in her palm. Her make-up is still blotched but she doesn't seem to care. She's in a daze, gazing towards the open window, adrift-looking, raftlike.

Her cup is still full; it must be going cool.

Suddenly she turns towards me and starts to say something but doesn't succeed, then she bursts into tears.

I put down my cup, go over to her, kneel down beside her, put my arm round her and tell her not to worry, that it'll all work out for the best in the end. And I actually believe this to be true. Without Ronan. She is lovely in her own way – surely she will find happiness in life?

'I'm sorry,' she burbles, grabbing my hand, her face caved in and crumpled like a piece of wrinkled dough.

'It's okay,' I assure her.

She's sniffing a lot. 'I know you mean well, Julianne, but it's not really okay.'

Saying this seems to calm her somewhat.

'But what's not okay? What's the matter?'

She starts telling me about her life.

She says, in effect, that it has been for years one unmitigated relationship *Titanic* after another. 'I've been dumped more times than a bin,' she mourns.

'You mustn't say those things about yourself.'

'Harry would have dumped me if I hadn't done it first.'

'You don't know that.'

'I do, Julianne. It's the story of my life.'

Sometimes, she says, she thinks Ronan likes her more for her body than for herself. She actually says that. She says she's been far too trusting of men in the past. She doesn't know if she can really trust Ronan, but she loves him like she's never loved another man before.

She says she doesn't know how she ended up with Harry. She says she wasted four years of her life with him. That he treated her abysmally. He gradually made her drop her old friends one by one. He dumped on her in public, and she cooked and cleaned and gardened for him in private.

But it went deeper: she couldn't remember the number of times he threatened to feed the contents of her aquarium to Max. Not out of any particular love for Max, naturally, but to save on catfood. At other times, he would enjoy sharing his boot with the cat's visage.

His boot cruelly extended to include her: he constantly

criticized her piano playing and her singing, and generally told her that she was no good. And if all this resulted in him losing his temper, his solution was simply to hit her.

'How,' she wonders, 'is a person supposed to live with that?'

'It can't have been easy, Nicole.'

Nicole bites her lip and nods tightly, and her face crumples up into a fresh paroxysm. There's something so lost and troubled about her that my heart almost hurts.

'Why is my life such a mess?' she asks, sobbing.

'But there's . . . good things in your life . . .'

'I can't see any.'

'What about . . .'

'What?'

Her car? But it's only a car.

Her cat? No, she wants to dump Max on someone else.

Ronan? Yes, it appears that the best thing in her life right now is Ronan. QED: her life must indeed be a relentlessly wet and slimy muck pit.

'You've got great virtues, Nicole.'

'I don't see how.'

'It's clear for all to see – you have an attractive personality.'

'Oh God, I know what *that* means.'

'I don't mean that, Nicole. I happen to know for a fact that men would find you very attractive.'

Pause.

'What makes you think I'm . . . attractive?' she says, blinking curiously at me.

Incredible. This new phenomenon in my husband's life has me singing her praises like she's the greatest motherfucking babe in the universe.

'Trust me on that.'

But she shakes her head. 'I don't think I am.'

This self-deprecation actually annoys me. I hate it when women run themselves down like this, even if it's true.

I turn away. 'I mean, Ronan thinks you are.'

'You're the only one I can tell about Ronan. I don't trust my father or my stepmother or my friends enough to tell them. They wouldn't understand. I've told one of my brothers all right, the one who lives in Amsterdam – that's Joel. He's really lovely, but it's here I need him.'

She sips her tea, which must be cold by now, but she appears not to notice because she immediately takes another sip – more of a gulp if you ask me – as if she's suddenly discovered a great thirst.

I take out my cigarettes.

She's got no one. Except me.

And Ronan.

Great.

Talk about being burdened on all sides. I'm a grief sponge on the one hand and a dumpee wife on the other.

Fantastic.

I offer her a fag but she makes a big fuss of declining on *Feng Shui* grounds. I let this social howler pass, lighting myself a cigarette and spewing a funnel-load of smoke into the room.

'Almost from the day Ronan walked into the travel agency, my life changed,' she recounts. 'I painted *Chi* just a fortnight after we met. It's as if I discovered my true vocation only after meeting him. *Chi* was like a celebration of the two of us. It was really special to me, can you understand that, Julianne?'

'Yes.' I sigh. 'I understand.'

'And now it's gone for ever,' she says, in a fresh wash of tears.

I take a deep, deep painful drag of my cigarette. 'Couldn't you paint another *Chi*?'

Pause.

'I don't know. Maybe.'

'Of course you could!'

'It would never be the same. All the emotions I had at the time, the love I had for Ronan, all that was in the painting. You can't repeat that.'

'I'm sorry, Nicole, I really am.'

And strangely, I mean it.

'It's not your fault.' She sniffs.

I try to smile at her, then I stand up, go over to the kettle and press the knob. 'I wish you didn't have to stay here, Nicole.'

'So do I.'

'I'd put you up in my place . . .'

179

'No. Honestly.'

'. . . it's just that my husband might not . . . approve.'

'I understand.'

'I'm not sure you do.'

'Really, Julianne, I'll be fine.'

She gets up suddenly, saying that she can't bear leaving Max outside in the car just because of an old house rule.

When she returns with the cat box a short while later she places it on the floor. 'You must be hungry, pet,' she says to him. 'I have some cat biccies in my bag. Isn't that good!'

She starts unscrewing the lid.

She bends down and whispers loving words to Max, just as a mother would to her child. 'Give me the cat box, Nicole,' I blurt out.

She looks up from her crouching position. 'How do you mean?'

'I've changed my mind.'

'But . . .'

'You don't really think they'll allow this cat to sleep in here?'

'But Julianne . . .'

'Give it to me.'

'He can always sleep in my car,' she suggests weakly.

'Look, Nicole, everything I said about cats was a lie. I love cats. I really do: they're gentle, fun-loving, sensitive, nurturing creatures. They make people happy. And Max? I *especially* love Max. Give me the box.'

Now she is laughing in huge, grateful, helpless gulps. I stand up and transfer the box to beside the door. She doesn't resist. She asks me about three hundred times if I am sure. Three hundred times I repeat to her that yes, I am sure. Her mouth is trembling. She says no one has ever been as kind as this to her before.

We're leaning on the window ledge together, staring out to sea. It's just wide enough for two. In front of us are two cups of coffee brewed from sachets. Nicole is sipping hers industriously, while it's still hot.

I suppose we fall into a bit of a daze, staring out at the green island which rises rockily up to the Martello Tower and descends again at a more gradual incline into the sea to the left, which has turned from a greyish blue to a greenish yellow. The sky, for its part, has lost its clouds. The left side of the stone tower is tinged with yellow-pinky paint light, foreshadowing the coming sunset.

After a while she perks up a little. 'Did you know that a cat brings good *fung shway*?' she says.

'What?'

'Having a cat is good *fung shway*. Don't you know what that is?'

'It rings a bell.'

She stares at me like I've never heard of the Spice Girls. She cannot believe that *fung shway* merely rings a bell. She spells it. Ah, she means *Feng Shui*. I tell her yes, I've heard of it. I make the point that spelling should always attempt to mirror speech and after a brief pause, during which she affects her lovable but very brain-dead expression, she goes on to explain that this *fung shway*, as she calls it, has to do with *chi* – the hidden flow of energy pertaining to everything in the universe, which she says we need to 'go with and not against'.

She also says that was the whole point of *Chi*, the painting. 'I know some people think all this is naive,' she says sadly. 'But I don't think so. For instance when I first took up *Feng Shui* I bought two mandarin ducks. If you keep them on a table in the south-west corner of your house, they are supposed to bring romance back into your life. Just four months later I met Ronan.'

She shrugs as if she's just stated an obvious universal truth. I simply nod and sip away at my coffee and stare out at the island.

Now she gives a few examples of *chi*, reminding me of the *Bagua* mirror, the *Fu* dogs, the harmonious arrangement of her living-room and garden. She explains how *chi* affects the most intimate details of our lives. She speaks of the energy that flows from the moon and regulates menstrual cycles, about the energy that flows from the planets when they form certain configurations, causing whales to beach themselves and insects to behave erratically and birds to migrate.

This woman is utterly unbalanced. A moment ago she was an

181

emotional wreck. Now she's all enthusiastic again. In the space of two minutes. Talk about giddy.

'This *chi* can come from living things, too,' she goes on. 'We absorb the energy of animals around us. For instance, if you have a tortoise in your house, you could be in danger of becoming sluggish and lethargic yourself.'

'No objection to becoming a tortoise at the moment.'

'And if you have fish, they pass on a very vibrant energy.'

'I think I'll give fish a miss.'

'Cats represent really positive *Feng Shui*. Really boundless energy. They . . .'

'So let me get this right.' I frown. 'By handing me your cat, you're doing *me* a favour?'

'I'm only saying.'

She slaps me playfully on the arm and laughs heartily, this woman of a thousand moods, this girl with a weathervane flitting about in her soul.

Over towards Dublin Bay you can see dozens of sailing boats riding the breeze like a molten rainbow. You can smell the iodine seaweed from here, hear the gentle lick of the water on the brown-clad rocks at the end of the long garden of the guest house.

'Isn't it beautiful?' says Nicole.

I nod.

I feel jaded. Dead beat.

I feel like a tortoise.

I close my eyes and try to concentrate on the sea air dancing gently through the corridors of my face. It makes a nice change from the good old dustbin air of the city. It blows like the low melody of a pipe, which I inhale deeply.

Neither of us feels the need to speak.

I open my eyes to a pale-blue, misty sky and a blue-green water channel ripped and torn by currents. Nicole has left the windowsill and has started to unpack her bags. In the background is the sound of Max scratching away in his cat box. Nicole has started chatting away to me again about her life, her lover and her *Feng Shui* – and I'm listening to her every word and I'm thinking, what the hell am I doing here?

Two days ago I fantasized about bludgeoning Nicole.
Then we meet and she tells me the story of her life.
And what do I do?
I agree to look after her cat.

33

I'm back home, if you'll pardon the expression, awaiting Ronan's return. Plan: to manipulate him into stopping by his surgery this evening.

Mother is out at bridge. She rang me at the Law Library this morning while I was in court seeking an adjournment for a personal-injuries case. I'd forgotten to switch off my mobile: it screamed through the courtroom, which was so stuffed up with barristers I couldn't move to the exit. Basically she rang me to tell me it was time for another man in her life and there were a few nice married men in her bridge class. I had no option but to punch her out, even before I had a chance to say hello.

That woman.

Alone I am, therefore, once again, with surely the most spiteful quadruped known to man. He is crouched at the far end of the short kitchen table, ignoring me, chomping away on Nicole's 'cat biccies' and quaffing milk from the plate. My diet lies at the other end of the scale altogether: pineapple wedges. I'm sucking them from an idle fork at the opposite side of the table. Every so often the miniature raptor emerges from his milk for a breather, his eyes sauntering insolently around the room, having for some reason decided that I am a total irrelevance.

Before this tragic twist with Ronan, the only living creature that ever succeeded in making me feel totally ignored was the cat. At this time, Max is making me feel like a tube of yellow-pack toothpaste.

Thank you for your time, Max.

Down again goes the head for some more milk.

And up again.

I am once again ignored.

Sylvana pops in unannounced. Entering the kitchen, she steels

Max a power gaze of hatred. He jumps from table to floor and retreats to the skirting boards, cowering.

Sylvana, of course, is not the sort of person you can ignore.

'Whose is *that*?' she inquires in her normal imperious tone.

I don't feel particularly comfortable telling her whose is the cat, so I start preparing a snack on the draining board. It's Sylvana's favourite again: cheese and peanuts glued with mayonnaise on to Ryvita crackers.

She repeats her question.

'Oh, it's just a neighbour's cat.'

'Why are you blushing, Julie?'

'How much mayonnaise do you like on your Ryvita?'

'Why are you—'

'It's Nicole's cat, okay?'

There's this creepy silence behind me.

I start humming, sprinkling sesame seeds over the snacks.

'What the *hell* are you doing with Nicole's cat?'

'She gave it to me.'

'Pardon?'

'She rang me. She was desperate to meet me because she'd just finished with Harry. She had nowhere else to go except to a dingy B&B, where cats are against the rules.'

'I see. You took pity on her.'

'I did not.'

'You pitied her, so you took her cat.'

'I wanted to take care of Max, so I offered.'

'You the great lover of wildlife.'

'Correct.'

There's a deep sigh behind me.

'Sylvana, I like cats, okay?'

She inquires whether that's why I've imposed a ban on my sister-in-law visiting, the one who brings her cat with her wherever she goes.

'This cat is different.'

'Aha.'

'Max is special.'

'What if Ronan recognizes him?'

'He's cat blind.'

In a very quiet voice, Sylvana wonders why I am dragging myself through the dogshit. She wants to know what my agenda is, meeting Nicole like this and taking her cat.

I turn round to my friend. 'I'll be fine. You're going on as if Nicole is some sort of monster. She's not so bad.'

She erupts when I say this. So I turn back round to my snacks and for want of something better to do I sprinkle on a few more sesame seeds. 'She's no threat any more,' I explain. 'When Ronan discovers what happened to *Chi* in his surgery he'll just dump her.'

'What happened to *Chi*?'

'I burnt it. It's unrecognizable.'

By the time I've finished recounting the details to her she's calmed down a little. 'Nicole is convinced that *chi* brought them both together and now that I've burnt *Chi* – the painting – she thinks it has to pull them apart.'

Sylvana makes a disreputable sound behind me. 'She's one of those.'

'One of what?'

'She's a *Feng Shui* junkie.' (She pronounces it *fung shway*.)

I shrug, feeling a strange resistance creep up inside me. 'I suppose you could call her that.'

'This chasing after alternative forms of comfort. Why can't people just grow up?'

'I've nothing against people seeking happiness.'

'Through *chi*?' she scoffs.

'Whatever.'

'She's pathetic. Why can't you see it?'

'She's just herself.'

'You do realize, Julie, that you are actually defending the woman who is presently bonking your husband.'

'Presently, she's sitting in a B&B in Dalkey like a sweet-smelling dump site. Alone.'

'As far as you know.'

She's trying to get me to admit something again. I don't even want to know, so I just bring the plate over to the table and tell her to enjoy her favourite snacks. I then inform her that I'm having a bath and I just walk out.

*

185

I'm soaking away in the jacuzzi, up to my neck in scented froth, bubbling and burbling away. I brought in my gigantic mid-Eighties ghetto-blaster, which has become something of a design classic with its chrome surfaces and bulky knobs and twin cassette deck and wide trunk handle to elevate it to the top of your shoulder and jaunt down Grafton Street in your shades and your tigerskin boots, and your chopstick-short black miniskirt.

Just to get my mind off things, I'm listening to Fatboy Slim telling us about doing something revolting in heaven, which I won't go into right now.

Sylvana bursts through the door.

She plies her way through the steam haze, wielding my cellphone and a wry face. 'It's her.'

'Mother?'

'That Nicole one.'

I eye the phone like it's a dead rat. I stick out my dripping, soapy hand and take it from her. She leaves.

'Yes?'

'Julianne!'

'What.'

'I just called to say hi!'

'Hi.'

'Is it a bad time?'

'Not at all. It's just that I'm in a hot bath, covered with lemon shower gel and there's shampoo foam stuffed in my ears, nose and throat.'

Pause.

She laughs like a soprano into the phone, then apologizes profusely for ringing at this inappropriate time, begging my forgiveness and wondering if she should call back later instead.

There's something so naive, almost, in her response that I calm down a bit and tell her to wait just a second. I put down the phone on a ledge and spray my head with water from the nozzle, and try to wash the shampoo out of my eyes and my aural canal.

Then I grab the phone again and lie back down in the bath until the warm water massages its fingers over my shoulders. 'Did Ronan call?'

'Yes.'

'When?'

'Just now, from his car.'

'Are you seeing him tonight?'

'No, he said he has to put in time with his wife tonight.'

'He makes marriage sound like purgatory.'

'She's a terrible drain on him. He's so unrelaxed at the moment.'

'Did you tell him about *Chi*?'

'I couldn't.'

'So Paris is still on?'

She doesn't reply.

'Is it?'

'We're going tomorrow morning,' she says quietly, as if she's just told me something gruesome.

'Don't go.'

'What do you mean?'

'Don't get on that plane with him, Nicole.'

'But . . .'

'Are you superstitious?'

'I suppose I am but . . .'

'I dreamt something would happen, Nicole. Something bad.'

Silence.

'What?'

'There was a plane crash.'

'Really?'

'I dreamt I was in this big, empty house with nothing in it but a TV. I was looking for Max everywhere because it was feeding time and naturally the last place I checked was the TV room. Eventually I found him sitting in front of the telly watching a news bulletin. There were pictures of a wrecked aeroplane fuselage. The interesting part was this.'

'What?'

'Max was whining.'

'Are you serious?'

'Absolutely. The way cats do when they lose a loved one. I'm telling you . . .'

'How *is* Max, anyway?'

187

'Nicole, I forbid you to go to Paris.'

'But . . .'

'You do realize that we are surrounded by spiritual forces.'

'I agree with that.'

'I mean, you believe in *Feng Shui*, don't you?' Believe it or not, I pronounce it *fung shway*.

'Of course I do.'

'And you accept that planes are bad *Feng Shui*?'

'How do you mean?'

Yes. How *do* I mean? I scour my memory of the *Feng Shui* book I recently skimmed. Plenty about cats and fish and colours and plants. Nothing about planes, though.

'Look, Nicole. I'm psychic: I get these vibes. Visions. I've a really bad feeling about this flight. Don't play dice with death.'

'God, you really have me worried now.'

'It's in the family,' I bullshit on. 'My mother was a medium.'

'Oh, no!'

'So I know what I'm talking about.'

'But . . .' she stalls, 'what if . . . what if the plane doesn't crash and Ronan manages to clinch a deal for my other paintings – then I know I'll be thinking, you silly thing, you should have gone after all.'

'I'll tell your family,' I add, perfectly maliciously. 'I'll call your father's home and tell them you're going out with a married man. I'll tell Harry where Ronan works . . . I'll tell his wife . . . I'll . . .'

Now I have her laughing hysterically.

She probably thinks I've been out on a binge.

'That's what I love about you.' She chuckles. 'You're so funny. I wish I knew more people like you.'

I do not reply.

'Julianne? Are you there . . . ?'

I still do not reply.

'It's not that I don't appreciate what you're saying . . .'

'Don't go to Paris, Nicole; 747s have had a bad run recently.'

'I know that you probably think I'm stupid and foolish . . .'

'Did I say that?'

'. . . but I'll just have to put my life in the hands of . . . God . . .'

'God. You speak of *God*?'

'Fate. I have to go to Paris, Julianne. I've no choice.'

She's pleading with me for understanding.

Angrily, I switch off the phone and drop it on to the floor, and turn on my tummy and sink to the bottom of the bath and hold myself underwater like a tropical marine fish, balefully beholding the murky grey. It's hard to cry down here, it's hard to feel sad when you're swallowed up by warm water. What a nice way this would be to die.

I lie like this for a minute, until my chest begins to burst. I force myself to stay down. Now there's this strange garbled sound, which reminds me of the noise a cellphone makes.

My heart makes this skipping, lurching movement and I rise up like the great Leviathan, and the edges of my body are awash with waterfalls. Panting like a beach dog, I stretch my dripping arm down to the floor and pick up my phone again and collapse back into the bathtub, exhausted.

I input the phone and scream: *'Look, I'm sick to death of you! What the hell do you want now?'*

Pause.

'Have you been drinking again, Julie?'

It's Mother.

34

The front door bangs.

Seconds later Mother appears in the kitchen where Sylvana and I are seated. Ignoring me, she passes through to the sink and washes her hands. I observe her in silence.

'That was a nice way to talk to your mother,' she says.

When she turns round again to dry her hands, she's wearing this mischievous smile, which proves she actually enjoyed being shouted at like that.

'Just think of it, Sylvana,' she says. 'You ring your own daughter to say you'll be a bit late, and she tells you she's sick to death of you.'

Sylvana giggles. 'How did the bridge go, Gertrude?'

189

'She doesn't go there for the bridge, Sylvana.'

'No,' Mother confirms, taking a packet of chocolate Hobnobs from her shopping bag, cutting the top with a sharp knife and putting one in her mouth. 'I go for the men.'

She puts on the kettle.

'Anyone nice today?' I ask her.

'Yes, but they're all single.'

'Why should that be a problem?'

'Married men are much more fun,' she replies.

'I love your mother,' cackles Sylvana.

'You don't know her like I do.'

'Anyway, Julie, where have you been?' inquires Mother, munching her cookie. 'I haven't seen you since Saturday last.'

'I'm fine, thanks,' I reply, grinning at my friend.

'I didn't ask you how you were, I asked you where you were.'

'Like I told you, I've been staying with Sylvana. There's this guy she's trying to shake off and she wants me to stay over with her because she thinks I will repel him.'

Mother: 'Now there's a vote of confidence.'

'Anyway, I'm fine,' I lie.

'You're feeling better after your bath, then?'

'Somewhat.'

'And I presume His Lordship will be home soon?' she asks, pouring boiling water into the pot and carrying it over to the table and sitting down.

'So I'm told.'

'He's been behaving strangely for the last few days,' she says, pouring out the tea.

Sylvana: 'The last few days?'

'I don't think he wants me staying here.'

'That's only because you steal his Danish pastries,' I observe.

'He has this terrible long expression on him. He's very humourless at the moment.'

'It's a genetic character trait, Gertrude.'

'And now that the piano is here, he seems to want to play it whenever I watch TV. He does it to annoy me, I know he does . . .'

I'm laughing at this point. Sylvana isn't.

'He thinks he's musical. You should hear him on Chopin. He destroys the poor man, if the Master only suspected.'

'He acquired the Chopin disease in Paris,' I say. 'It's endemic.'

'Well, it's certainly not contagious.'

'Chopin,' mocks Sylvana. 'God! Who does he think he *is*? I mean, what's his *problem*?'

Mother grins happily at us. 'Am I stirring it up? I love living here. There's so much variety.'

She announces that it's spaghetti for everyone, including Ronan whenever he returns. She fills a huge cauldron with water and puts it on the hob, turns on the switch, then takes out the spaghetti, the tomato puree and a tub of Parmesan cheese from the press, and puts them on the sideboard. 'There's something all women should know,' she intones.

'What's that, Gertrude?'

'There are three remedies for unhappiness. Eating well.'

She pulls out a fistful of spaghetti.

'And . . . ?' prods Sylvana.

'Sleeping well.'

She falls silent.

'Yes, Mother?'

She breaks the fistful of spaghetti in half, then turns round to address us.

'And castrating him,' she says.

Right now, Sylvana has forgotten the meaning of self-control.

One hour later Ronan walks in the door.

'You're just in time for some supper, Ronan,' says Mother.

'Thank you – I'm fine,' he says, defridging a beer, butting the door shut with his knee in a movement that tries to be cool and actually succeeds.

'It's spaghetti and a special sauce, although I'm sure the girls would prefer tomato puree – it's more slimming. Sit down there beside Julie.'

'Well, if there's enough to spare.'

Ronan always has to be the gentleman. 'So, you've joined us?' he says in Sylvana's general direction, as he sits down.

My friend's visage, right now, constitutes one glowing high-lighted text. It reads: you're such an asshole you'd need a forest of trees to wipe you off the face of the earth.

Sylvana: 'Seems more like you've joined *us*.'

'We're getting daring.' He grins. 'Is life treating you well?'

'Wonderful.'

'How is your nice little business coming along?'

Neither of us has bothered explaining to him that Sylvana no longer owns and runs a single Whole-Self Shop. No, she owns and runs a chain of them, which is now receiving valuable international orders. Basically, she's about to be a millionaire. And when Ronan discovers the fact, she wants to be there to watch his face fall at the bad news.

'How's your decay-prevention business?' she counters mildly.

'Superb. And the dieting?'

He slides a murky eye over her figure before returning it to base.

'Shut up, Ronan.'

He mulls this over, as if I've just made an interesting point.

Why can a woman be attractive only if she's slim? Sylvana is extremely attractive. Why else would men (mostly rich and older) be tripping over one another's spare tyres to get near her? She's so popular with the foul sex that she's ended up being a kind of fly-swatter on automatic pilot.

'And how's the love life treating you, Ronan?' she returns, smirking as she chews an ageing Ryvita snack.

Beaming, he revolves his head over to me. 'Sylvana wants to know how you've been treating me, darling.'

'Exceedingly well, I think.'

'How are you, anyway?'

'Non-existent.'

'Where have you been these last few nights?'

'Wherever,' I reply, eyeing my friend.

He butters his bread, pokes it into his mouth and slowly bites.

Mother has taken a bowl of pasta from the oven. Now she produces another bowl: a familiar glass one. As soon as she removes the tin foil, a strange scent hits my nostrils. This must be the pasta mix Mother was referring to. It has a distinctly fishy smell.

It doesn't take me too long to realize what it is.

Without a word I stand up, leave the kitchen and go into the lounge and pace up and down for a few minutes, every so often glancing over at the aquarium.

Mother has been baking Tropical Marine Fish Mousseline.

I didn't intend for this to happen. Not really. Oh Jesus.

Is Mother doing this in full knowledge? Coolly aware that the mousseline planted by myself in a bowl in the fridge originated in our aquarium and took a slight deviation via our Moulinex mixer?

If so, her hatred of Ronan must be *Slavic*.

Or perhaps she did it in all innocence?

Either way, do I go in and raise the alarm?

At this late stage?

I go back inside and sit down and keep my mouth shut.

Mother opens the window and begins stirring the contents of the glass bowl. I am so glad I strained out the eyes and the fins and unwanted pieces of bone. You can choke on shit like that.

Ronan is watching Mother, curious about what's on offer. I can tell he's going to ask her something about it.

'Ronan, dear?'

'Yes?'

'I think I might have left my bracelet in your surgery that time.'

'What time was this?'

'You know . . . *that* time.'

'Oh' – he grins – '*that* time.'

Sylvana raises her eyes sarcastically.

'And I really need it for tomorrow.'

'Yes, well I'm sure it's still there.'

'Perhaps you could drop me round later to pick it up?'

'If you like,' he says, shrugging. 'Or you can go yourself. You have your own key. Whichever.'

True. I can go later myself. And report back to him anything unusual I might happen to have seen.

'Can I ask what the recipe is, Gertrude?' he inquires.

'When are you going to Paris, Ronan?' I interrupt, pouring into his glass from a bottle of Châteauneuf.

There's this slight jolt in the kitchen.

'Tomorrow afternoon,' he replies, composed.

'Well, I hope it goes well.'

While Sylvana's expression is mutating, Ronan is sitting there downing his wine, in excellent form, content in the assumption that I'm not going to plague him over Paris.

Sylvana: 'Some tooth conference you're attending, is it?'

'That would be one way to describe it.'

'The spaghetti is ready, children,' Mother announces.

'I could eat a horse.' He brightens.

'You'll wish you had,' I mutter.

Now she turns the spaghetti pot upside down and drains the water into the sink. She forks three heaps of steaming spaghetti into three bowls and I offer Ronan some more baguette, and suddenly Mother shrieks and my heart jolts and we all look up.

Standing on top of the kitchen surface, poking its claws into the fish bowl is a large black cat. Mother yells at the poor crud, who is intent on getting an honest bite of fish. Max darts his head back like a snake, motionless and startled – but his paw is still in the fish bowl. She shakes her apron at him and he scarpers.

Mother: 'Where did that come from?'

'It's Sylvana's,' I reply.

My friend observes me coldly.

Ronan is concentrated on Max, who is now licking his paw on the floor by the cooker. If he's seen this cat before, it's clearly not registering. But then, he was never a great animal-watcher.

'Does it have a name?' Mother wonders.

'Well, Sylvana?' I grin.

'Prudence,' she replies, kicking me under the table.

'What a wonderful name,' says Mother.

Ronan: 'I assume Prudence will be accompanying Sylvana home tonight?'

'No, Ronan.' I hope Prudence drives him batty. I hope the quadruped moults on to his trousers. I hope it licks his scented, shower-gelled toes as he sleeps. I hope it salivates over his cornflakes as he's reading his paper. I could train it to poo on his postmodern art books. That would be good. That would be symbolic. Such excellent taste, for a cat.

'Sorry about the cat, Gertrude,' says Sylvana. 'I'm completely unable to control her.'

'It's a he,' corrects Mother.

'These days sex doesn't matter,' says Ronan drily.

Sylvana: 'Unless you're married.'

Mother: 'Isn't he beautiful? His fur is black like a piano.'

We watch the spectacle of Mother lovingly caressing the creature on the ground, with Max putting his whole neck and upper torso into the plying movement of her hand. 'Lucky Sylvana,' she says.

'There's some cat food under the sink, Mother.'

Mother fills a bowl with cat munchies. The split second the bowl hits the ground, Max homes in.

'You've brought him up very well, Sylvana,' says I evilly.

Ronan: 'Never trust a cat.'

Sylvana: 'Or a man.'

'Is our dinner ready yet, Mother?'

Mother carries over three bowls of spaghetti, one for each of us. She herself is abstaining. Then she fetches the fish sauce. 'The puree is in another dish, for you girls.'

She appears to be steering us away from the fishpaste.

'Yes,' I say. 'I'm in the mood for tomato puree tonight.'

Sylvana: 'Me too.'

If only she knew.

I get up and fetch the heated dish of puree and the canister of Parmesan. Mother now pours several ladlefuls of the grey gunge on to Ronan's bowl of spaghetti, Sylvana watching with distaste.

Mother returns to the sink with the half-empty bowl of mousseline. She advises us all to eat up otherwise it'll go cold. I blot out my spaghetti with puree.

Ronan stares at his dinner, scratching his head. 'This looks . . . interesting.'

'He means that as a compliment, Mother.'

'I know.'

'Is this the Delia Smith recipe you were talking about, Julie?'

'Yes,' I reply, nervous. 'It's an old Mediterranean thing.'

'It's salmon mousseline,' says Mother, scrubbing some pans. 'Try some Parmesan; that should take the bite out of it.'

Salmon mousseline? Where did she get that idea?

He lowers his head to sniff. He raises it again and asks me to pass him the Parmesan.

I pass it to him and he sprinkles it over his dish.

I watch him, fascinated.

Sylvana senses something is going on, but doesn't know quite what. She's frowning at me like a crumpled sheet, searching helplessly for clues that might explain the strange, secretive vibe she's getting from me.

And so, to help her out, while Ronan's head is tilted down in his fish dish and Mother's back is turned, I start performing this swimming, breaststroke motion over the table for her benefit and then I point at his dish.

She frowns at me doubly deeply. I need to find a more effective way of helping Sylvana to mentally associate tropical marine fish with the marine slurry Ronan is on the point of shovelling into his gob.

So now I pretend to be a proper fish. While doing the breaststroke, I loll my head from side to side, ogle my eyes and open and close my gob in that cute brain-free way that fish have when they're just being themselves. And I point at his dish.

She is as lost as ever.

I draw a fish in the air with my fingers. She's nodding: she's with me so far. Now I pluck the imaginary fish clean out of the air and place it in my mouth, and I close my mouth and pretend to chew, shutting my eyes as if I'm in seventh heaven; then I open my eyes again and point like daggers at Ronan's dinner.

But she still doesn't get it.

She's shrugging, nodding, having figured out the part about Ronan eating fish. But their precise origin still eludes her. This is incredibly frustrating for me: I want her to share in the sheer pleasure, which has now begun in earnest to spread like creamy Mitchelstown butter all over my being, as I observe Ronan placing the first squiggly mouthful of spaghetti and fish mousseline in his mouth.

The kitchen is in perfect silence. So silent that you can hear the sound of Ronan's horse-like chomping as he eats. Sylvana's eyes are flickering like an iguana from Ronan to me and back to him. Mother is bemusedly observing the proceedings from the sink, drying plates with a dish towel.

Ronan looks up suddenly. 'Is something the matter?' he wonders.

Sylvana and I simultaneously avert our eyes.

Mother turns back round and starts making a real racket cleaning pots and pans in the sink. 'How is your dinner, Ronan?' she asks.

'It's . . .'

'No complaints, Ronan. Mother made it specially.'

He screws up his mouth, looks over at me as if I've just committed an act of sabotage against him, then he lowers his head again to study the contents of his plate. After a while he decides to twirl another load of gooey spaghetti around his fork.

I can't bear Sylvana not to know what's happening. I pick up the nearby *TV Times* and open it at the crossword page.

'Right, Sylvana. Test out your brainpower. Two across: "Walks softly". Five letters.'

'Treads,' says Sylvana.

'Creeps,' offers Ronan.

'Crawls,' suggests Mother, still crashing away at the sink.

'It depends on two down: "Receptacle for fish". Eight letters.'

'Fish tank,' says Mother.

'Aquarium,' offers Ronan.

'*That's it!*' I shout.

'Although,' he volunteers, 'it could be both.'

'Try three down then: "Moulinex". Five letters.'

'Moulinex?' says Ronan, entwining a further load of spaghetti on to his fork. 'That's a brand name, isn't it?'

'Hm . . .'

He chews away at this mouthful too, with a slight grimace. Mother is still making a lot of noise with the pots and pans.

'Don't they do mixers?' suggests Sylvana, slightly frustrated by my abstruse references.

'Mixer. Yes. That's five letters.'

I pretend to write in 'mixer'.

When Ronan descends for his fourth mouthful I make all manner of faces at Sylvana while repeating the word 'mixer' out loud several times, as if absent-mindedly, and all the while I am pointing at Ronan's dish. She clearly thinks I'm crazy. She looks again at me. I am gleaming meaningfully back at her. Then she studies Ronan's dish and looks back at me again, and I do a quick breaststroke motion, and now there seems to be a slight alteration in her countenance and she suddenly gets up and leaves the room through the door to the hall behind Ronan.

With her hand over her mouth.

'What's wrong with her?' says Ronan, attempting his fifth mouthful.

'She's not feeling great today,' I explain, quickly breaking some baguette and clumsily applying butter. 'You shouldn't be so harsh on her.'

'Oh, Sylvana and I – we understand each other.'

I've got bat ears, but I swear to God I honestly cannot tell whether that heightened acoustic noise in the bathroom is Sylvana laughing her heart out or puking her guts up.

Mother, returning to the table with a cup of tea and some cream crackers on a plate: 'Well, guess what I did today?'

'What?' asks Ronan.

'I went to see my friend. She lives just down the road.'

She smiles brightly, as if she's just announced she's won a trip for two to Lanzarote.

'Really?' Ronan is doing his best to be polite and discover an interesting angle on old ladies who meet their friends in the afternoon. I mean, what do old ladies do when they're together? Plan tax dodges? Plot bank robberies? Hardly likely. 'Did you go for a walk?' he wonders, trying to chew his sixth mouthful.

Well, that's true, you do see them out walking on occasion.

'No,' she answers. 'We chatted for a while over afternoon tea.'

Ronan nods – no surprises there. That's an image he can connect with. They probably did a spot of knitting too, but of course he's too polite to ask.

Sylvana returns now, big wide grin on her face.

'And then,' Mother goes on, 'I returned and watched a video.'

Ronan is impressed. Like he regards technology in the hands of the aged as something of a good omen. 'You watched a video,' he repeats, nodding.

'You could say that.'

'Anything interesting?'

'You want to know the plot?' says Mother drily. 'Well, it didn't take me long to grasp it: it was the story of a man and a woman dead keen to show the world the uses to which greenhouses can be put. Apart from watering the tomatoes.'

Ronan asks Mother to be more specific.

'It was about a man and a woman doing things to each other, things they didn't need clothes to do them with. You know the sort of thing. A film dedicated to grunting and naked bodies.'

Ronan chokes on something. An escaped fish fin, probably.

'Mother,' says I, frowning, 'are you saying you went down to the video store and rented a porn movie?'

'It's a free country,' says Sylvana.

'Is that what you both think of me? Do you really think I went into the video store and walked up to the counter and said, "Excuse me, young man, I like the look of that video on the shelf entitled *Whip Chick* and is there a reduction for old-age pensioners?"'

Sylvana cackles with delight.

'Then where did you get that video?' I insist.

She gets up, goes over to the cooker, grabs the bowl of mousseline, returns to the table and ladles another large spoonful over my husband's spaghetti.

'No, really, Gertrude, I . . .'

'I insist, Ronan. It's nourishing.'

He succumbs.

She offers Sylvana a final half-spoon of the fish sauce, saying that she doesn't want any leftovers tonight.

'Thanks awfully, Gertrude, but I seem to have lost my appetite.'

'Mother! Tell me where you got that video.'

Mother to Ronan, as she sits down: 'Will I tell her?'

I turn to my husband who I suddenly realize is blushing like a cooked crushed tomato. 'Don't tell me it's *yours*?' I gasp.

Deafening silence.

'In actual fact,' continues Mother, 'I felt something sharp sticking into my back the first night I slept here.'

Sylvana is laughing out loud now. And she's not stopping.

'What were you thinking of, Ronan?'

He tries to shrug it off. I glare at him, but he's begun to eat his meal very quickly now, trying not to look too discomfited.

'You've gone all red, Ronan,' observes Sylvana once she's ceased giggling.

'What's it to you?'

'Is it fun, watching steamy video sex?'

'Steamy sex is nothing to be ashamed of,' he says in that utterly reasonable tone of voice.

'Then why do you look so ashamed?' inquires Sylvana. 'Do you make a habit of indulging in it?'

He laughs. 'I happen to be married.'

He's weakening.

'All the more reason to be ashamed,' she replies.

This is getting good.

'I'm not ashamed of being married, are you, Julie?'

'Ask me next week.'

Just think: me and the two closest people in the world to me have embarked on this joint venture to crucify my husband to the dinner table.

And Mother, simultaneously, is in the process of poisoning the poor bastard.

It's a most unexpected bonus.

35

When Mother leaves the room to get ready for bed, Ronan is enduring the last remnants of his fish pasta.

Sylvana and I glance at one another.

And we let rip.

'Did you enjoy your fish puree, Ronan?' says I.

'Tell your mother it was excellent.'

'You're a brave man,' observes Sylvana.

He hesitates for a second, then continues his fork motions. 'It's not that bad.'

'You don't have to be polite,' I tell him.

Suddenly Sylvana reaches over to Ronan and pretends to pluck something from his jacket. 'A hair,' she announces, making a flicking motion with her fingers over the floor.

'*A hair*?' I echo.

'It's blonde.' She grins.

'What's her name, Ronan?'

I rest my chin on my knuckles and turn to face him, with an air of infuriatingly suggestive expectation.

'That hair strand could belong to anyone,' he says, unruffled.

'Oo!' squeals Sylvana. 'He gets around.'

He's now gobbling the remainder of his meal like there's an invisible finish line, like he can't get it down him quickly enough.

'Do you both mind if I eat this delicious meal in peace?'

Sylvana winks at me.

Me: 'It's rude to speak with your mouth full.'

'At least I speak through my mouth.'

He jerks his head towards Sylvana.

'Is that what you call it?' is Sylvana's deft reply, which sends me into a sudden spasm of giggles.

'Don't mind him, Sylvana, he's just annoyed because you found a blonde hair on his shoulder.'

'Your implication is a little extravagant, Julie.'

'Then why do you look so pissed-off, honey?'

'It suits him.'

'And speaking of extravagant implications, what is a porn video entitled *Whip Chick* doing underneath my mother's mattress?'

'More to the point: what's your mother doing on *top* of it?'

'Sleeping, like most people do on mattresses.'

Sylvana, grinning: 'Don't be naive, Julie.'

Ronan: 'Well, she can sleep somewhere else.'

'Sylvana, is there a Society for the Protection of Old Folk?'

'He'll be old himself some day.'

'But not overweight,' he cuts in.

'And bald,' Sylvana adds, ignoring the slur. 'Soon he'll be buying hats to keep the draught out. And impotent, too. Can you imagine the freedom, Julie? In a mere thirty to forty years' time most of our male peers will be failing miserably in that area. Not even *Whip Chick* will be enough to bring it back.'

It's not easy to maintain one's composure when Sylvana gets going like this.

'But why the video, Ronan? Was it to spice up our sex life?'

He just looks at me.

'It's not such a strange question, Ronan. After all, your whole horizon is sex.'

'Is that a problem?' he tries to joke.

'You'll start making mistakes.'

'Like what? Leaving porn videos underneath mattresses?'

'No. I mean real mistakes . . .'

Like the kind of mistake I'd hoped he might make with me.

Sylvana: 'Don't worry, Julie; no man travels without a condom these days. It's called estate planning.'

'This is pathetic,' he says, rising suddenly to his feet.

Sylvana is roasting him over the fire. Before last Thursday I wouldn't have allowed her. Now I don't give a damn. It's great.

He brings his bowl over to the sink and just leaves it there. He expects Mother to pay for her keep by washing his dirty dishes. He glares, I mean furiously, at poor Max who has never lifted so much as a paw against him.

He exits the room without another word.

Sylvana and I light up and congratulate ourselves on a job well done.

'He actually finished his meal too,' I observe after a while. 'It can't have been that bad.'

'Then again,' muses Sylvana, 'there's no objective reason why fish cooked straight from the sea should be any tastier than fish cooked straight from your aquarium.'

She has a point. Sylvana can be so balanced and judicious at times.

'I agree. I mean, fish is fish, isn't it?'

'Can I ask you one thing, Julie?'

'Feel free,' I reply, exhaling cigarette smoke.

'Does your mother know where the mousseline originated?'

'That's what's worrying me, Sylv.'

'Perhaps she imagines you purchased it at the deli.'

'Yes, but why on earth would I buy raw fish guts at the deli? Besides, they don't sell raw fish guts at delis.'

'This is true,' she replies, sinking into a smoker's pose, nodding as if I've just made an interesting point, say, about foreign-exchange rates.

'Mother must guess where it came from. I just can't believe she did that, Sylvana.'

'Although you're the one who actually went ahead and liquidized them in the first place.'

'Yes. So?'

'With the intention of feeding it to him in any case.'

'So?'

'I think you're brilliant.'

We burst out laughing and she sits back in her chair.

'I only wish you'd let him know what he's just eaten.'

And in a way, it does seem a crying shame that Ronan gets to leave the kitchen without so much as a clue that there is cargo of tropical marine life presently swimming through his intestinal corridors, in a rather devolved form.

Hers is an attractive proposition. But how would I break the news to him? How does explain such a thing? How does one choose the words? How does one convey the images? I couldn't keep a straight face.

'No, Sylvana . . .'

I take a drag of my fag before I add: 'Always allow a decent delay before the punchline.'

36

Ten minutes later I go into the lounge. I'm expecting Ronan to be in fairly poor spirits after our joint whipping session.

He is.

He's standing with his back to me, arms crossed, glaring through the french windows at heavy, purple-streaked rain clouds, black fumes visibly smoking from his body.

For the first time I notice that Ronan is wearing a wine jacket with his mustard-coloured polo-neck sweater and trousers. An unusual blunder for him: wine and mustard definitely don't mix.

'What,' he says calmly, 'the hell was that all about?'

He doesn't even bother turning round.

To avoid illuminating my husband as to what the hell that was all about, I continue past the couch until I hit the aquarium. I then lean over and start counting our slightly depleted fish stocks. Just watching them would make you dreamy. My remaining swimmering darlings – the originals – are gleamering loverly and lappily in the gleen, brubbily waterlight.

He repeats the question, using the same word pattern.

'What was all what about, Ronan?'

I can hear him pacing up and down behind me.

'What was all that bullshit, Julie?' he shoots.

'I thought it was fish mousseline.'

'Cut the crap. You're still hung up on that affair business, aren't you? You're the lawyer; you present evidence when you make a charge. So where's your evidence?'

Does he really expect me to tell him what I know? Does he truly want me to put his mind at ease? To put him on notice of the evidence against him, to concede him the advantage, to carte blanche my auto-erasure?

Not a chance.

'I'm not hung up on your affair at all,' says I into the fish tank.

'What's your problem, then?'

'You want to know what the problem is?'

He waits.

I turn round. 'Okay, Ronan. I'll come clean.'

Standing in the middle of the room with his hands in his pockets, he stares at the floor. He's listening. For once in his life.

'Those colours just don't go,' I tell him, striding towards the french windows.

'What?'

'You know very well that mustard and wine don't match. They make you look like a circus clown, Ronan . . .'

I swear I just heard muffled laughter from the kitchen.

'. . . and I will not be married to a circus clown.'

'This is pathetic.'

'Oh, lighten up, Ronan. Debung your arse. We were just having a bit of fun with you over that pathetic video. That's all.'

'The two of you were behaving like a couple of witches over a bubbling cauldron.'

I laugh out loud at the pinpoint accuracy of his metaphor. Stuff like this puts you in good spirits. I can't wait for him to learn about *Chi* later on tonight when I return from his surgery.

He goes over to the aquarium and leans against it, flushed with annoyance. He stands there for a while. Uh-oh. He seems to have noticed something. Something tells me he's going to begin a discussion about entities, which unbeknown to him are presently digesting in his upper to middle intestines.

He scratches the underside of his chin and straightens himself. 'Julie.'

'What?'

'Where are the fish?'

'In the aquarium.'

'You know what I mean.'

'No, Ronan, I don't know what you mean. The fish are in the fish tank. I can see them with my own eyes.'

'I'm talking about the fish I bought last Friday.'

'You bought fish on a Friday?' I eye him aghast. 'You do realize, Ronan, that it's against Canon Law to buy fish on a Friday? Or should that be meat . . .'

'Julie,' he says in the voice of a terminally patient school-teacher. 'What did you do with them?'

'They went missing,' I shoot back.

'Where?'

'I don't . . . really think you want to know.'

'Did you return them to the aquarist?'

'All but three of them.'

'All but three of them.'

'Yes.'

When he recovers from this he starts feeling his neck. 'What about those three? Where are they?'

'I flushed them down the toilet.'

He starts pacing again. He's stroking his chin. He's mulling this over as he walks. 'You flushed them . . . down the toilet?'

'Pre-cise-ly.'

'Makes sense,' he replies, as if I've just discovered a highly practical method of deblocking the sewage pipes.

'They don't mind,' I assure him. 'They'll have enjoyed their swim.'

'In the excrement?'

'They'll find some clear spaces.'

He nods, then bows his head. He looks like he's biting the knuckle of his index finger, concentrating. 'It sounds like PMT.'

Now he's pacing around like a Hollywood impression of a courtroom lawyer.

'Come on, Ronan, fish don't suffer from PMT.'

'You, Julie. *You*. You've gone completely . . . hormonal.'

Me? Hormonal? Hardly! What I did was gory, perhaps, but not hormonal. Sociopathic maybe, but certainly not hormonal.

It's time to defend what sanity I have left. 'You know as well as I do that adding those extra fish last Friday threatened the existing ones.'

'Did you really flush them down the toilet, Julie?'

'Yes.'

'I quite liked them, you know.'

'You enjoyed them, did you?'

'As a matter of fact I did.'

'It gives me great pleasure to hear that, Ronan.'

'You killed off aesthetic objects, Julie. Just like that.'

'They weren't objects, you idiot. They were alive.'

'They were beautiful.'

Amazing. He bought them three days ago and already he's nostalgic.

'But of course, when it comes to aesthetic appreciation, you clearly have none.'

I think about this for a few seconds. 'I agree.'

It's game, set and match to Ronan. He is absolutely right. On the scale of aesthetic appreciation I lay claim to pure zero. One only has to remember the art book I bought him and what I did with it.

His arms are straight as buttresses against the aquarium as he peers inside at all the free space. Suddenly I notice something expose itself underneath the edge of his jacket sleeve. I get a huge shock when I realize what it is. It's that gold Raymond Weil watch, the one that managed to cost nearly one grand.

I dart over to him and pull up the sleeve. 'Ronan, where did you get that watch?'

He freezes. He glances at his new Raymond Weil. Gold. Simple face.

'I bought it.'

'Did you really?'

'Yes. It's second-hand. Not that expensive.'

I survey my husband with disgust.

I am staring into the eyes of the man who only two years ago asked me to marry him, who told me he loved me, led me up the aisle, promised to be faithful, found and furnished a wonderful apartment for us to begin our new life together.

I am staring into the rotten soul of the man who recently told Nicole that he loved her, that I nag and pester him, that our marriage is dead. The man who scooped her off her feet in order to market her paintings in Paris.

I am staring into the heart of the man whom I am supposed to trust above all others. But what does he do? He attempts to tangle me in riddles of lies.

And now?

I find him wearing her expensive watch before my very eyes.

He's flaunted Nicole in front of me – that was bad enough. He's slept with her in our spousal bed. That's worse, although I wasn't at home at the time.

But this?

It's almost as if he's laughing at me right to my face.

How much am I supposed to take?

I storm into the kitchen, grab Sylvana by the arm, haul her out of the apartment, shove her in my MG and drive her straight to Ronan's surgery.

Standing in witness to *Chi*, Sylvana is suitably impressed.

So impressed, in fact, that she makes an immediate offer for the painting. However, I politely decline her offer as being derisorily low, reminding her that the value of an artwork lies in proportion to its archetypal, underived uniqueness. And I calmly point out to her that this *Chi* masterpiece hanging incinerated on the wall is unrivalled as an artistic experience because it is telling us something important about nihilism in the late postmodern era.

Sylvana strokes her chin as if she's beginning to be duly impressed by my reasoning.

'Where would we hang it?' I giggle.

Sylvana suggests my cloakroom.

I suggest her toilet for thematic reasons.

When it comes to art, Sylvana and I are notoriously incompatible. She seems to appreciate clashing colours and of course she has an aversion to subtle meanings. For example, if a painting has red in it and the room has red in it then in her book it's okay to hang the painting in the room. Now I'm not saying that Sylvana has to be a culture fruitie like Ronan, but on her theory you'd easily end up with, say, Caravaggio's *Last Supper* hanging over your bed because it matches the curtains, while you're not very reverently munching your partner underneath the sheets.

We exit the surgery and say goodbye, Sylvana ordering me to call her after I've broken the gospel to Ronan.

When I get back home he's not there. I assume he's defuming himself on the moonlit pier, as husbands are wont to do; you know, furiously walking off their frustration at being wrong.

When I walk into the kitchen there's a letter on the table with my name written on the envelope. The fun evaporates like a ghost. I tear it open.

> *Julie, I've changed my mind about Paris. I'm going tonight instead. Perhaps in the meantime you'll manage to work out your frustrations. R.*

I dash to the phone in the hall and call him. He's powered off. I call Nicole. She too is powered off.

Furious, I race back down to my car. Sylvana will know what to do. She will tell me to dump him for ever.

And you know, maybe this time I might just listen.

Tuesday, 21 June, evening

37

Sylvana and I, flattened out on our sunloungers on the roof of my new penthouse apartment under a cerulean blue sky.

We're all but naked-assed, besmirched in Ambre Solaire gunk, slotted with waspish black UV-protected shades to negate the sun God sent us this day in a blinding blaze of glory, beating down upon us like a deafening cymbal roll.

There's not a cloud in sight, it's a smelting, sweltering, glorious, almost vindictive mid-summer heat.

That doesn't mean I don't feel suicidal: let's just get that clear.

On the other hand, nor do I have any immediate plans to descend the spiral staircase of my new apartment and slash my wrists in the bathtub. I want a halfway-decent suntan first.

'Have some more champagne,' she suggests, holding out the bottle for me.

'No thanks, Sylv,' I reply. 'I'll stick to the banana milkshake: it's cooler.'

Another reason I decline the champagne is that in this heat it tastes like radiator water in mid-winter, with bubbles.

Talk about a house-warming. It's a penthouse meltdown.

Champagne.

She bought it specially for me. It's her present to celebrate my new-found freedom. She thinks I have irrevocably decided to dump Ronan from my life. Why else, she reasons, would I go to the trouble of renting a new apartment using funds from the sale of my husband's Porsche? She simply cannot understand why any wife, having pulled off such an outrageous feat, might subsequently decide to return home.

She did inquire at one point whether this apartment was merely a ploy to win Ronan back. Of course I denied it vehemently. Returning reluctantly to her *House and Home*, she announced she was relieved that I had decided henceforth to debar myself from future marital enslavement.

With my straw, I suck my banana shake in a most ignorant and gross fashion. I must try to forget Ronan. I must simply soak up the sun and Sylvana's company, and try to pretend I've never met him. Here, there are no reminders.

'Ladies,' Sylvana drawls, 'don't suck milkshakes.'

'You needn't lecture *me* about sucking things, Sylv.'

Unfortunately, in my hour of woe, Sylvana takes this as a cue to initiate one of her favourite conversations. 'Did you know, Julie, that Polynesian women are prohibited from eating bananas for certain clearly defined cultural reasons?'

I think about this for a sec.

'Sylvana, what am I supposed to do with that interesting piece of information?'

'What I'm trying to say, Julie, is that now you will no longer have him to service you, you may wish to turn your attention to something more, well, mechanical.'

'What could be more mechanical than a man?'

'You know what I mean.'

Truth is, Sylvana is obsessed by those plastic bedtime bananas with mobile heads and batteried bodies. She's always telling me she'll lend me her buzzing implement whenever I get lonely. I generally reply that I am perfectly fulfilled by my electric toothbrush.

'The little mechanic without overalls that you speak of, Sylvana, has a few serious flaws.'

'Go on. Annoy me.'

'It is constitutionally incapable of buying you flowers, or calling you on your birthday, or bringing you on trips, or telling you I love you.'

'The one I purchased in New Orleans last year told me he was crazy about me.'

'Yes, but that's why you purchased it.'

'Well, I figured it might have other things going for it as well. Considering the box's assurance that it vibrated at a frequency of five hundred megaherz.'

'Surely, Sylvana, if men are an irrelevancy, then their substitute is doubly so?'

210

I yawn lazily under the absurd heat.

'Listen, honey,' she says, raising her shades from her nose. 'We're talking here of a man without a brain, without sweaty armpits, germs, smells. Without balls. Writhing helplessly, so to speak, in the palm of your hand.'

'You should go into tele-sales.'

'Thank you.'

Her shades slot back on to her nose and she collapses again on her chaise. Just to annoy her, I continue rudely to suck my banana shake.

'Julie, I appreciate that your banana milkshake is phallus in glacier form, but could you perhaps lower the distortion level?'

I grab the bottle of factor twenty Ambre Solaire, photostable, hypoallergenic, anti Uva-Uvb, anti cell-ageing, water-resistant, active moisturizing, Laboratoires Garnier, Paris – talk about overkill – splurge a pool of white puree into my palm and start rubbing it on my left arm.

'Julie?'

'What?'

'I never thought you'd do it.'

'Do what?'

'Move place.'

'*I* never thought I'd do it.'

'Permanently.'

'Quite.'

I splurge the cream on to my right arm now, then my neck and chest, belly, face, legs, feet, toes. In four minutes flat I'm waxed yet again up to the eyeballs like a globule of succulent tar. When I'm finished, Sylvana takes the bottle from me and starts smearing it on to her own arms and shoulders. I sit back, close my eyes and try again to forget.

Now you can hear her sunlounger creaking under the weight as she stretches over to the fruit bowl containing an assortment of fresh cherries, grapes, sundried tomatoes and Belgian choco- lates, which when I last checked were bleeding on their black paper trays into dark molten puddles. Now you can hear the sounds of Sylvana munching something.

I open my eyes again. 'Remember, Sylvana, this place is a secret, okay?'

It would be so humiliating if the world got to find out that I'd moved out of home, only to do a U-turn and move back in again.

'Right. But you do plan on staying here, don't you?'

'I'm not ready to let the world know,' I reply evasively.

The world.

I dread the thought of work tomorrow. Only in the Law Library will I have to face the questioning glances, the narcotic female stares, the intrusive requests after my health. If someone dares to ask me if I am okay, I swear I will steal a judge's hammer and murder them with it.

Here in my 'new apartment', at least, I can put the world into brackets. I am incognito. Safe. My hideaway, north of the city, is discovery-proof. I will not be bothered on the street or in the supermarket. No nosy inquiries about my marriage. No one to stick their pincers into me and tug at the weak, bruised, bulbous parts of myself. I can think in peace. Get myself back into working order in peace. Fortify myself against him.

For war.

I dread the thought of Mother. She is so inquisitive she should be locked in solitary. There's only so much stretching her curiosity can take before her discreet wonderments turn into hellish interrogations. How to deal with her?

'Don't let the world know, then, for the moment. And whatever you do, don't see that woman again, promise?'

'Okay.'

'Just forget about everything, Julie, and soak up the sun.'

'Sylvana.'

'Yes?'

'I love you.'

I close my eyes again.

And yet even she doesn't really understand. No one really understands. Nicole now. She's probably the only one who comes close to grasping what it's like to feel the way I'm feeling right now. There's something touchingly pathetic about that.

I am alone. When Sylvana leaves tonight – and she will leave if I have to force her to – I will be even more alone.

There doesn't seem to be much meaning in things any more.

Life seems like a barren wasteland. A dark, stinking pit. An ocean bereft of shorelines.

If there is a God, why did he create love when it causes such pain?

38

In the last thirteen hours, things have happened in my life that most respectable people would regard as scandalous. Things that would make men tremble to the roots of their toes. Things that would make *me* tremble to the roots of my toes if it weren't for the nail varnish.

But let me tell you about my new apartment first.

I fell in love with it at first sight, even though it was just supposed to be a holding cell.

A superb, recent, fully furnished three-bedroom penthouse apartment with a delightful roof garden. South-facing balconies, accessed off the main bedroom and the living-room, affording fine views over the adjacent park. Finished to a very high standard internally, the decor is fresh and bright, and features warm Scandinavian oak flooring throughout. Electric storage heating, cable television, 1200 square feet approx., accessed via security gates, containing good car-parking facilities. Excellent local shopping centres; churches, schools and transport systems easily accessible . . .

The estate agent whom I seduced into subservience showed me through a small square hallway with three doors leading to three separate areas: one to the fitted kitchen on the left, one to the bedrooms and bathroom straight ahead (this is where the spiral staircase to the roof is located) and one to the lounge to the right, a long rectangular room with the all-important french windows plus shutters, French-style. He took me out to the balcony.

The park is a hidden oasis of tranquillity, centred by a lake frequented by swans and surrounded by a band of assorted rare trees: Spanish chestnuts, African cypresses, giant redwoods, Douglas firs, Scots pines, Ilchester oaks . . . and a swathe of illustrious rhododendrons . . .

Narcotic, isn't that what Nicole said about rhododendrons?

It's like this.

I was annoyed.

Here's what happened.

As soon as I discovered that Ronan was heading for Paris last night, I dashed to Sylvana's, screeched and stamped about the place for five minutes, then phoned Nicole's B&B. The lady of the house told me she would be gone for two nights, but didn't say where she was going. After screeching and stamping about a little more, Sylvana gave me a cup of hot milk with honey and put me into her spare, queen-size bed. I am certain she laced it with sedatives.

This morning I called Nicole again from Sylvana's.

She was thrilled to hear from me. Her voice was full of it. 'Guess where I am!'

'I haven't a bloody clue.'

Pause.

'Julianne, we're in Paris!' she squeaked, all excited.

'God love you.'

'Ronan's in the en suite just a few feet away. Would you like a phone intro?'

'I don't think so.'

I was pacing up and down Sylvana's sitting-room, manic and directionless as a crab, goofed on Jakartan espresso.

'Ronan came over to the B&B late last night and told me to pack a bag, and while I was in the middle of doing that we sort of made love, then he went downstairs and paid the landlady and . . .'

'Does she charge much for the service?'

Pause.

'Only about twenty pounds. It's expensive, but it is a lovely B&B and anyway Ronan can afford it. Oh, Julianne, I adore Paris. There's a view outside our window of the Tuileries gardens just across Rue de Rivoli, beside the Louvre . . .'

'Rue de Rivoli.'

'Yes, that's where he bought me those earrings, do you remember? And then the River Seine – you can just about make out the stone walls of the river bank. You can even see Pont Alexandre III from here. The light is amazing – it's incredibly bright, it's so bright it's almost white – can you imagine that? As I'm speaking I'm looking at the Eiffel Tower over to the right, going all the way up like a huge tree trunk. I wish I could paint this view, Julianne, but I didn't bring my canvas or materials. Ronan's not in a great mood after last night. I think he's furious with his wife.'

'Did you tell him about *Chi*?'

'No, but they had an argument. He actually called her a bitch. To my face! I couldn't believe it. He really doesn't love her; it's clear to me now, Julianne. I told him I wanted to move to Paris. I'm really excited. It's as if . . .'

I pressed off and tried to call Ronan then. But as usual he was suffering from cellphone erectile dysfunction.

I went home.

Mother was still in bed. When I went to the kitchen for a Danish and coffee I bumped the door into something semi-soft. It was Max beside a bowl of cat food. This time he was not ignoring me. Purring dangerously at the far kitchen door, the sniggering feline viper looked in the mood to scrape my eyes out and use them to play marbles with.

I made a dive for him.

He did a U-turn underneath the kitchen table and escaped between my feet, out through the kitchen door in a flash. I mounted a search. He was hiding beneath the banana couch in the hall. I flushed him out with a cushion. He sprang into the living-room. He took a running dive and slithered up the side of the fish tank, snarling like a starved rat, clinging to the glass edge with two sharp-clawed paws. One was now inside, digging fruitlessly away at water. The fish were going berserk.

I ran at him, thinking how dare you harm those poor fish.

I flokked him with one of the white leather cushions, sending the water in the tank up in thuds against the glass. Max scattered. After I finished counting the fish and establishing that

215

they were all present and correct, I again searched for Max. Everywhere. Under the couch, armchairs, in the fireplace. He had to be in here because the door to the kitchen was closed, as were the french windows.

But where?

At last I spotted him seated with royal indifference on top of the grand piano. Or should I say, Max was seated inside the piano, making these scraping noises against the strings as he licked tropical marine water off his wet paws. He was positioned just beneath the huge pear-shaped piano lid, looming above him like a guillotine.

A guillotine suspended, as it were, by a matchstick.

One push of the finger, I was thinking, and the lid would crash down on the little squid as he smiled, slicing him through the tight mesh of music wire. There would be a resounding crash, some deft scattering of silent dust, perhaps a slight strangulating squeak from our furry friend, and finally an aural-friendly reverberative chasm of minor fifths and demented sevenths.

I moved in for the kill.

I laid my index finger against the lever when suddenly Mother walked in, wearing my tartan pyjamas.

She asked me what I was doing.

'Mother, could you please tell me what you are doing in my pyjamas?'

'Don't pretend you like them.'

'I wear them.'

'What's the matter, Julie? You're rather pale-looking.'

'I was just . . . admiring the internal workings of this baby grand.'

'Babies again.' She smiled.

She approached the piano. She didn't notice Max because of the angle. She sat herself down on the piano stool and started laying into poor old Schubert, quite unaware of the fact that she'd just sent Max into spasm to avoid getting his paws belted by the hammers.

He hopped on to the floor, twirled round a few times, then settled down on his bum and started to re-lick himself, happy to be on terra firma once more, sporting this familiar look of cat contentment, which I find so easy to despise.

When Mother was not looking I closed in on Max, grabbed him like a rug by the back of the neck, hauled him from the floor, carried him out to the veranda, shut him in the cat box in case he fell off the veranda, and closed the french windows again. And clapped the dust off my hands, satisfied.

I dashed into the bedroom, packed a large suitcase in five minutes flat, stole a Valium from Mother's private collection in our bathroom, popped it into my mouth and felt calmer at once, slid out of the apartment, dived down to the car park and commandeered Ronan's Porsche, and it was with a sense of driving purpose that I screeched through suburbia in a yellow blaze track of smoke to my estate agent, a roaring spitfire across the city.

Six hours later I handed my estate agent one month's deposit and two months' rent – three grand in total. I got the cash from the sale of the Porsche to a service-station crook I knew well from a recent Circuit Court prosecution.

The rest I blew on a fantastic day out at the shops.

'What you need is an image change,' Sylvana advised as we waited in the seating area of Toni&Guy.

'I haven't got an image to change,' I replied. 'So what am I doing sitting here?'

'Rubbish,' she countered. 'You're a stunning sex bomb, Julie.'

'I know: I explode whenever a man goes near me.'

She advised me to have my hair cut short. That men these days loved women with short hair. I protested that at this low ebb in my life I'd rather not make my hair the pretext for male fantasies.

'And keep it black. Black is seductive and mysterious and . . . dangerous.'

'Of course, I'll be like a sex bomb, then.'

'Primed to go off at the rate of ten creeps a minute.'

So I just sat there with my eyes closed and let the guy cut my hair short and darken it by a few degrees (like you can darken black). When I opened my eyes again I discovered with horror that I was shorn like a sheep. I ran out of there crying.

Sylvana found the whole thing most amusing. She led me into one of her own Whole-Self outlets and re-emerged with a bag full of soaps and shampoos and conditioners and aromatherapy oils. All for me.

While I was at it, the fancy grabbed me to purchase eight thick candles – recommended by the *Feng Shui* booklet I'd swiped from Nicole's place. Sylvana asked me if I was planning for a blackout in my new place so I just told her yes. To shut her up.

Finally, we took a standard deviation to purchase lipstick, mascara and foundation. To her credit, Sylvana succeeded in drumming up some enthusiasm in me.

I was equipped, at last, with my new identity.

On the way back to my new place, we hopped out at a local supermarket and bought provisions, most crucially milk, coffee, bread, butter, jam, bottled water and enough bananas to turn us into overnight baboons. In the drinks section we got a bottle of brandy, naturally, and Sylvana insisted on buying champagne. The most expensive in stock.

We were back just in time for the potted-plants delivery man: Sylvana's idea for my new roof garden. The bloke managed to put a dent in the landing wall with a rectangular earthenware pot. Not a squeak of apology out of him. It's hard to credit it – the man just shuffled in and out of my new apartment, leaving his personality on the wall. Every time I look at that dent, there'll be a blundering male in the flat with me.

One good thing, though: the same blunderbus banged his head as he was ducking through the low roof exit – presumably because his vision was impaired by the begonia he was carrying. He grunted – and then, believe it or not, he apologized. Either to himself or the begonia, I can't be sure, but at least he apologized.

After he left, with his foul breath and his BO issues and his baggage-smashing installation techniques, we both unloaded the car and filled up the kitchen presses and made up my new bed with fresh-scented sheets that Sylvana had thoughtfully purchased for me, along with duvet, pillows and pillowcases.

I was set up in my new 'home'.

We stripped, togged out, grabbed our Ambre Solaire and our champagne, our magazines, our shades, our radio and our new chaises, and a fruit bowl sprayed with cherries and Belgian chocolates.

And we headed up here to bake.

It's half-seven, now, and there's no sign of us moving yet. The heat is still raw, blistering down on our skin like acid. I'm baking away like a scone in the oven. My head is leant back against oblivion, my eyes closed beneath my Calvin Kleins and that hazy, lazy, dazy sensation is just about holding back the teetering frontiers of forlornness.

I look over at Sylvana.

That icon of humorous disdain and playful contempt, the woman without whom I might now be dead, is enclosed behind a pair of shades the size of conjoined badminton rackets, letting it all hang out like a bulging basket of autumn fruits barely covered by a skimpy napkin.

I needed Sylvana to tell me I was young and pretty. I needed her to tell me I was intelligent and smart. I needed her to tell me I was sexy, and warm and generous. I needed her to tell me I was strong and independent and self-reliant and self-confident. I needed her to tell me I was talented, lovable, good to be with. I needed her to tell me I had a great, happy future ahead of me. I even needed her to tell me that my dream of having a daughter will one day come true.

And you know what?

She told me all those things today.

She even told me I was beautiful.

'Sylvana?'

'Yes.'

'Never mind.'

Pause.

'Sylvana?'

'What?'

'What am I going to say to my mother?'

Shading her eyes with the side of her hand, she concentrates on me for a few moments: 'Say nothing for the moment, Julie,' she says kindly. 'Just tell her you're staying with me because you and Ronan are sorting out a few problems. You need your own sanctuary for now. And when the time is right – when you're happier in your own mind about things – you can break it gently to her.'

What the hell am I doing here?

I tell Sylvana that I'm scared. She says she knows, and she assures me that no matter what happens she'll be there for me if and when I need her. She's so earnest and sincere and free of any trace of sarcasm or irony when she says this that for the first time I really think I might make it through this nightmare.

39

It's strange, the quiet.

It's after ten p.m. I am exhausted. Apart from the gentle breathing of wind from the park, the world seems as still and silent as death.

Sylvana has left. I didn't really want her to go, but I refuse to be a burden on anyone so I insisted. I'm standing on the roof garden, surrounded by my potted plants, clutching the white railing and peering out at the trees round the lake. They seem to be whispering restlessly to one another while the diminishing light of day strains the colour from things and reduces them to a dusty greyish-green.

Alone.

It's cool now. I shiver.

I tread down the dark spiral staircase to the living quarters below. Without turning on the light, I enter my bedroom, my movements scratching against the bare walls. I sit on the bed, staring through the window into the dusk above the trees in the park.

I like the dusk. I like it when the receding daylight fills a room with itself, spreading its pervasive natural rhythms into the space. That's why I have the electric light off. A room is more lonesome under a solitary lit bulb.

I can still hear the sounds of birds through a slit in the window, chirping themselves to sleep, unaware that I too seek a piece of the stuff of life they seek, that every living thing must seek.

I lie against the pillow. Its clean edges wrap around my hair. Crisp, clean duvet, pillowcases, sheets never before used. The flat newness of linen that has not yet seen washing detergent.

The only sound I can hear is of me breathing.

What now?

They're in Paris now.

Dining in a restaurant, probably. I can see them together under a low-hung, dim-lit light. Nicole with cleavage and an armful of clinking bangles, dangly earrings dancing from her ears, her beautiful hair combed down to the table, fluttering and giggling and laughing with Ronan.

And he, well-dressed, talking easily about aesthetics from Kant to Heidegger, unthreatened by the quality of Nicole's intellect, able to do or say anything because he knows Nicole will not judge him, oppose him, cease to make herself available to him.

In about an hour from now – because Ronan does not favour late nights – they will taxi back to their hotel. No. Two hours: Paris is an hour ahead. And there they will share a guilt-free bed in the anonymity of a foreign city. Make love and then fall asleep, Nicole on Ronan's chest.

Then I'll be free to fall asleep.

I let my shoes fall off my feet on to the floor and I push my legs under the duvet. I am colder than I realized. I pull the duvet over me and lie on my back, frost fingers biting against warmed palms. Then I twist off my wedding ring and put it on my bedside table. I consider whether or not to get up and flush it down the toilet, but I'm too exhausted.

Love!

Do I still go on believing in it?

I used to think it was like a secret garden, hidden amid the sharp corners of an urban landscape, concealed until the appointed hour when you and your lover met. A beautiful place where happiness and laughter and trust and friendship and respect and comfort could all be found, and much more besides. And you sought out this garden of your birthright because you believed in it, because someone had been there and had brought back news of its wonders, because you believed that in this garden you would discover not just one thing you needed but everything you needed, because you believed that when you found it and sank into its enfolding arms, the abraded pieces of your life would soften and melt into a soft light, a halo illumining everything in its path, and you would become like the vanishing cracks of a crossword puzzle, melting into bliss.

Is this such a naive dream?

40

I'm in the Law Library staring over my desk into a giant square space where wooden bookshelves containing ancient law reports line the high walls, where brown desks overflow with documents, where barristers in suits or in the court-ready mantle of wig and gown shout into cellphones, study at their desks, flit in and out or congregate in small groups, and all around is the murmur of voices well-spoken or keen to be well-spoken, broken by the occasional curt blast of names over the PA.

I'm trying my best to concentrate on a statement of claim concerning a dubious action against Dublin Corporation where the plaintiff (a local drunk according to my solicitor) alleges he fell into a badly flagged hole near Sandymount Green. If the award is made, it could keep him in booze for the rest of his life. Just think.

I don't feel like this, but if I don't keep up with the work I'm afraid my solicitors will stop sending me their briefs.

I'm depressed.

For reasons which you can, at this stage, imagine. But I'm depressed for another reason: because I have committed a particularly dumb mid-summer blunder. I went home just now and I discovered Max on the balcony.

Dead.

Nearby are a number of younger barristers who strut around like they are soon to be top-earning senior counsel – but in actual fact most of them are working for less than a dishwasher's wages. They get round this acute difficulty through various potential-enhancement mechanisms: posture, accent, mannerism, hairstyle, garment, head-tilt, or speech content touching on private wealth, vocation, relative in the business, insinuation. Another effective solution is simply not to hang around and be seen in a state of well-dressed unemployment, waiting for cash to arrive in the form of briefs, which may or may not hit their postboxes depending on whether or not solicitors choose to regard them as non-existent entities.

I've got a thudding headache, and my heart feels like it's got a knife stuck in it and I can't pull it out. I should be in bed, but I've too much to do. I also have a drink-driving case to prepare for next week, a statement of defence to dictate into my Sony for my secretary on the panel, mail to open . . .

I hate people today.

What do you bet someone will come right up to me and say hello? There's so many sociable people in the place I swear it'll drive me to early retirement.

On a sudden crazy impulse I grab my mobile and input. Seconds later I hear Ronan's voice and this screeching noise in the background. 'Where are you?' I demand.

'I'm outside Dublin airport, about to get into a taxi. I can barely hear you, Julie, with that aeroplane.'

'Are you alone?'

'Sorry?'

Of course he's not alone.

'*Scumbag*,' I shout.

'Sorry, Julie, could you speak up?'

'So you've decided to come home? What makes you think I've worked out my frustrations?'

Slight pause.

'Oh yes, the note.'

The screeching background noise dies down.

'How are you anyway?' he asks, fatigued-sounding.

'Terrific,' I reply. 'I've just rented an apartment.'

'I didn't know you were getting into real estate.'

'I'm not getting into it: I'm using some of it.'

A car door slams in the background. Must be the taxi door. Now two further slamming noises. Must be the cabbie's car door. And Nicole's car door.

'You're using, are you?'

'I'm presently residing in a new apartment.'

'Presently.'

'I've moved out,' I snap.

Through the mobile you can hear what sounds like a bus rumbling to a halt.

'That's interesting,' he says finally.

'Interesting.'

'That's wonderful for you, Julie, what do you want me to say? Congratulations!'

I grit my teeth until my neck hurts.

I look up. On the bench, three desks up from me is a female barrister tuning into my conversation: she's leaning right over in my direction, her head in her palm, pretending to read some papers.

'Is that all you can say?' I whisper.

'What do you want me to say?'

I punch off, stand up and walk straight out of the Law Library, through the corridors and atrium of the Four Courts and out to the River Liffey across the road where I fill my lungs with its vaguely dietary reek. I sit down on the low wall and stare into the giant green moving snake.

My phone rings. It's Sylvana. Inquiring as to my health.

'I feel terrific, thank you. Truly marvellous.'

'Good.'

'Except for one thing.'

'What?'

'The cat.'

'What cat?'

'Max.'

'Prudence, you mean.'

'Max.'

'What about Max, Julie?'

'He died.'

She fails to reply.

'I knew you'd react like this.'

'Did I react? Tell me some more.'

So I tell all.

I returned home this lunchtime in order to free Max from his cage. On the way home I bought him several tins of the best cat-food brand I could find, with a choice of flavours from salmon to beef to tuna to rabbit to turkey. He had gone without food and water for close on thirty hours and I felt that the least he deserved was a banquet.

I twisted open the knob on the french windows, guilt-rotten. I stepped out on to the veranda and approached the cat box, apprehensive on account of there being no sound from within.

I opened the lid.

I understood immediately what had happened: Max had fried in sunlight all day yesterday and all this morning. In brief, he'd died of heat exhaustion.

I was devastated.

Although there was anguish, too: I now had a body to get rid of.

'She deserved it,' Sylvana declares, after a brief hiatus.

'Who? Nicole?'

'The cat.'

'It's a he.'

'Okay, he deserved it.'

'He did nothing wrong, Sylvana. He was just a cat.'

'He was Nicole's cat,' she argues.

'So what you're really saying is that *Nicole* deserved it?'

'Okay, Julie.' She sighs. 'Have it your way.'

'I will. Nicole deserved it, but the cat himself did nothing wrong to deserve death in the cat box on my veranda.'

Redrawing of breath. 'What do you want me to say? That you are a malicious, bloodthirsty animal slayer?'

I consider this interesting and peculiarly valid point. 'Yes, Sylvana. I'd like it if you said that.'

'Anyway, where is it now?'

'He has a name.'

'Prudence.'

'Max.'

'Max. Where is Max?'

'Still on my balcony, in the cat box.'

'What are you going to do with it?'

'With him, Sylvana, with *him*.'

'No Julie: it. It is dead, remember? What are you going to do with *it*?'

'I thought you might have some ideas, Sylvana.'

'You want want me to dispose of the body?'

'Are you offering?'

'When's your next garbage collection?'

I don't believe I'm hearing this. 'You really do think Max is garbage, don't you?'

'I do.'

'What am I going to tell Nicole?'

'Don't beat about the bush. Tell her you suffocated the cat. Tell her you crucified it. On purpose.'

'You actually believe that, don't you?'

'Julie, will you calm down, it's only a cat.'

I raise my eyes from the green water of the Liffey and focus on the Ha'penny Bridge way downriver, curve-spanning the channel like a delicate ice-cream wafer.

'You think I suffocated the cat on purpose.'

I can feel tears coming on.

'Julie, you're not yourself. We should meet.'

'I'm *not* myself,' I wail. 'I feel like I'm going nuts! Why are you laughing?'

'Of course you're not going nuts. You're one of the most balanced people I know.'

'You're crazy.'

'I mean it.'

She's behaving like I'm some kind of saint who missed her vocation. Yes, a saint who smashes and steals and ends wildlives, but a saint none the less.

Problem is, she never smashed a living-room in her life. She never ice-picked a Porsche, tore up an art book, liquidized a squadron of tropical fish, stole a car or induced heat suffocation in a cat.

QED: she's in no position to grasp depravity.

So I end the call, with the footnote that she's not to worry about me, or feel responsible for me, or imagine that she has to come to me and hold my hand.

I replace my phone in my pocket and start walking, hunched, along the exhaust-choked quay, towards the statue of the Great Liberator. As I walk, I press my phone for messages. There are six. Everybody wants me, it seems.

I'm a crazo and I'm in demand.

My solicitor with another brief; a colleague from work; the estate agent with a highly reassuring titbit about the heating system in my new apartment being banjaxed but not to worry because 'it's not a problem'.

Mother. She's commanding me to call her back at once because she's worried about me. And I should try to consider the feelings of a frail old lady for a change. To quote.

Ronan, with a grouchy message informing me that he's just arrived home from the airport and is wondering where his famous Porsche is.

And finally – guess who?

With the following message, spoken, I must admit, in a voice that has a lovely, cheery, hesitant, humorous lilt to it: 'Julianne . . . em . . . you're not there so I'm just leaving a message, if that's okay, em, did you get cut off yesterday when you called me in Paris? You seemed a bit upset . . . anyway, just to say I'm back in Dublin now and, if you want to give me a call some time, that'd be great, em, we could even meet up or something . . . anyway, I'll sign off now, Julianne. See you soon. Bye!'

41

Why do I put myself through this?

Nicole just picks up the phone and tells me she wants to meet me and what do I do? I come buzzing after her like a dragonfly after a turd.

As I wait for her, I'm sitting here on Dun Laoghaire pier on a hot bench drenched in sunlight, facing into the blue bay bend of Sandycove, a gentle breeze tugging at my earlobes, the sun a warm facecloth on my countenance.

Of course, she's late as usual. Half an hour late. It makes the agony worse. It makes it feel like I'm dying for Ronan, thirsting for him. Pining and yearning for him. Craving him like I haven't savaged a bar of Bournville in months. Spluttering and gasping for him.

And of course I am. It's so woefully pathetic it's undignified.

I mean, I still haven't reduced my wedding ring to a sprangle under a lump hammer. What does that say?

This is what I should have done instead: I should have sent Max's remains by overnight parcel delivery to Nicole's B&B (there's nothing in the rule book about keeping dead cats in B&Bs). With a short regret note attached. And had my mobile number changed.

(Besides, a balcony is no place for a cat. The stink is already beginning to escape despite the old tarpaulin I hauled over it. I can only hope and pray Mother does not go out to the veranda to test her fear of heights.)

Here she is at last.

She's in a light-blue sweater and white trousers. She's wearing shades and her trademark fragile smile. Her hair seems even more golden than before. She looks relaxed and well.

She sits down beside me and crosses her legs over her conjoined hands so that they are squeezed in between. She apologizes for being so late. Then she smiles warmly and thanks me for seeing her at such short notice. After we get over the unnecessary formalities I go straight for the jugular.

'Actually,' she replies, staring out to sea as if there's something on her mind, 'it started on a bad note.'

'Don't stop there.'

'We were invited to dinner by Lucien Morel yesterday evening in his apartment near the Jardin du Luxembourg. He's that art dealer who lectured Ronan in aesthetics at the Sorbonne. It's his former university in the centre of Paris . . .'

Yes yes yes I know. It's where Ronan went for two years. It gave him an appreciation for art, and posing, and bullshitting, and generally damaged his personality.

'He was flirting with Lucien Morel's girlfriend behind my back – she's an art critic with the *Parisien* newapaper.'

'How awful.'

'It really was. I was in the main room with Lucien who was

telling me about opportunities in the Parisian art world – of course I didn't have the guts to tell him about what happened to *Chi* – when suddenly his phone went off and I went out into the kitchen, and I saw them together. I can't even remember her name . . .'

'I'm sure he can't either.'

'. . . they were in the kitchen by the window and he had his fingers inside the bra-strap on her shoulder.'

'Maybe it was hurting her?'

Nicole is staring wildly at me, as if I should be somehow horrified by her recent predicament. 'I went straight back into the living-room, Julianne. It was so humiliating.'

'Dump him.'

'As it turns out, we made up.'

She tells me that from eleven o'clock on Tuesday night to ten o'clock the following morning they made 'love' three times.

I can just see it. The two of them doing sixty-niners on a pair of cheap French flannel sheets in an expensive hotel room in central Paris at two in the morning, experimenting with options from a variegated oriental menu of positions from which my husband finally chooses one, highly compatible with the survival of the species.

'Nicole, I don't want to be rude but I'd rather not hear about your sexual exploits with Ronan. Talk about something else. Tell me what Morel thought about your other paintings.'

'Well . . . I don't want to boast . . .' she says.

'Oh, boast away.'

'Well' – she hesitates – 'he said he personally loved them.'

'He was being polite.'

'Julianne . . .'

'Either that or he was trying to get into your knickers.'

Noticeable gap in the conversation here. I ask her what the art critic of the *Parisien* thought of her other work.

'She's just a hack.' She sulks. 'She knows nothing about art.'

'Jesus, would you listen to the modesty.'

It's Ronan's fault, of course, putting these pretentious ideas into her squashy head.

'I wasn't going to say this, but Lucien told me he thinks he may have found a buyer for the painting entitled *Foetus*.'

This whacks me on the head. 'You're joking me.'

'I'm serious.'

'How did you manage to pull off that freak occurrence?'

Nicole frowns uncomprehendingly. 'Julianne, did I say something to annoy you?'

I shut up now and let her whine. She tells me she wishes I wouldn't imply she wasn't capable of it, because it's bad for her self-confidence.

She's being assertive for once in her life. That's a positive development, even if it's over painting endeavours that would make a three-year-old doodler look like Picasso. I saw that stuff up in her attic. I saw it all. 'Art'! Are we on the same planet here or what? I mean, are we even *talking* about the same planet?

'Anyway,' she adds after a short pause, 'I don't really believe I'm as good as everyone says.'

Oh Jesus get me out of here.

I stand up abruptly and we start walking in silence along the pier, the harbour water to our left shimmering in the reflected light of the sky. Yachts loll about in the wide basin, the same ones you can see and hear from our apartment, gathered like variously flavoured triangular lollipops, tinkling notes in the light wind blow.

After a while she tells me that she made three resolutions while she was in Paris. The first, she says, is that she wants to live in that fabulous city. Ronan says he's also tempted to live there. He said that going back was a reminder.

'Of what?'

'The first time he fell in love.'

'With his wife?' I shoot back.

'No.' She sighs. 'A Frenchwoman.'

I am a hopeless romantic idiot. I really believed I was the first person Ronan fell in love with. And why did I believe this? Because Ronan told me I was.

I have to get home. Where I can crawl on all fours to my private waste-paper basket and chuck myself in.

But she doesn't give me a minute.

'My second resolution is that I've decided to become a *Feng Shui* consultant.'

I turn my head away and look at the colourful boats.

'I mean,' she clarifies, 'in my spare time.'

'And that's supposed to make it okay?'

'It's very big in Paris,' she says.

'Yes, well with a population of up to eight million . . .'

This seems to confuse her. 'No. I mean *Feng Shui* is big in Paris.'

'Oh, I see what you mean.'

'We were in a bookshop in Boul Mich, as Ronan calls it. It had loads of books on *Feng Shui*. Ronan translated from some of the introductions, because my French isn't perfect. I bought one book called *Feng Shui et le Bonheur*. That means—'

'I know what it means.'

'His French is fantastic.'

'It's not bad.'

'Sorry?'

'French is an interesting language.'

'He said that *Feng Shui* could be seen as an aesthetic moment in the course of the great Hegelian Dialectic towards the Absolute.'

I'm staring at her now, searching for bye-bye-brain signs.

But suddenly she bursts out laughing at the ridiculousness of it. 'He can be so silly!' she shrieks, unable to stop giggling.

'He's an absolute jerk,' I reply.

'But he thought my *Feng Shui* idea was a good one. He said I could advertise my services in the papers and magazines. I already have a mobile phone so I'm set up. The idea is that you go into other people's houses and for a small fee you give them—'

'What's your third resolution?' I rudely interrupt.

Recovering her dislocated centre of gravity, Nicole tells me she's come up with this plan. She says she has decided to repaint *Chi*.

I look away.

Then I look back.

'What the hell do you mean?'

'I mean—'

'I thought *Chi* was over? Finito? How can you repaint something that's dead?'

'I was thinking of repainting *Chi* from the professional photograph I had taken of it. It's the perfect solution. I know Ronan will agree when he finds out.'

'You mean, you're going to pass off a copy as the original.'

She doesn't approve of my choice of words. 'I'm going to paint another original.'

'Another original? Nicole, it's a bit late in the day to be laying into the Law of Non-Contradiction, considering it's been around since the ancient Greeks.'

'It was your idea,' she's urging me.

'What?'

'Don't you remember what you told me in the B&B, after we both returned from Ronan's surgery that time?'

'What did I tell you?'

'You said I could always repaint *Chi*!'

'*I did not*!'

'Those were your exact words.'

I swallow hard, inwardly punching myself.

I say nothing. Just stare ahead and keep on walking in silence until we reach the main road. I tell her I have to go home now and that I will call her some time, which theoretically means never.

'Are you sure . . . ?' she says uncertainly.

'About what part?'

'Are you sure you don't want a coffee or anything?'

I look out towards the picturesque bay of Sandycove. What *is* it about her when she speaks in that dejected voice and pulls that unhappy, lamenting face? It's so annoying. Each time she does it makes me want to stop hating her. 'Why? Do *you* want a coffee?'

'Oh, it was just an idea . . .'

I make a show of consulting my watch.

'You have your own things to do, Julianne. It's fine . . .'

I hate this. I hate being undecided. I like to have things straight down the line. How can I stand here and feel sorry for this woman?

But that mournful, lost, irretrievable expression on her mug is eating my heart out: she really does want me to accompany her

233

somewhere for a coffee and chat, and yet the last thing she wants to do is pressure me. This happens to be something I like about her. She doesn't insist. She leaves you free. She doesn't try to manipulate.

This makes it far harder to refuse.

'I don't know,' says I, weakened. 'Where would you suggest?'

'We could try Renaldo's.'

'Full marks for originality.'

She laughs, and I'm almost ashamed to admit it but when she laughs in that gay and childlike way she has about her, my heart lightens up as if a leaden plate has just been lifted off.

'I'll walk you to your car, Nicole, and decide on the way.'

As we walk, Nicole places her hand momentarily on my shoulder. I throw her a glance, with her long, golden-blonde hair and her pale, slightly freckled skin and the soft eyes behind her shades, and it's very strange, but the familiarity of her hand on my shoulder just now felt oddly natural.

'I went home to my father this morning just after breakfast,' she says suddenly. 'It was the first time I've been home in four years.'

'So long?'

She nods appreciatively. 'My father and my stepmother were both in the kitchen. I told him I was sorry for barging in like this but that I needed to come home for a few days because Harry and I had split up and I had nowhere else to go apart from an old B&B.

'My stepmother said what's wrong with the B&B – isn't the standard of B&Bs very high these days? I said it was very expensive and I didn't have a lot of money. My father started shouting at me then, accusing me of looking for money. I could smell the drink on his breath. My stepmother said I was just like my mother, that I had a nerve barging in looking for money and accommodation after everything that happened . . .'

We're walking along the coast road, the sun momentarily hidden behind a cloud, the air brushing warm against my skin. Nicole is effortlessly exposing her private life to me. Am I missing something here?

'What happened?'

234

'I was caught with Harry sleeping in my bedroom, several years previously. I put him on the floor in my room only because I knew my stepmother would have had a fit if I put him on the couch downstairs. And I couldn't let him walk home in the dark after the rave, with all the drink he'd taken. Anyway, she just walked into the bedroom at seven o'clock the following morning. She must have seen his jacket downstairs, I mean, it wasn't as if I was trying to hide him. She went and woke Father up and when they both came back Harry was just putting on his shoes and she told Father that she found the two of us sleeping together. I told him that wasn't true. He threw us out. He told me never to come back. It's just what she wanted.'

As an afterthought, Nicole adds that it didn't help that Harry referred to her father (to his face) as a 'drunken old fart' mere seconds after the latter had called her a 'little whore'.

'It's so obvious he thought I was a slut.' She laughs weakly.

She just leaves this hanging, like I'm supposed to object.

I don't.

'I think he'd been drinking again,' she says. 'I don't know, I think he must have been very unhappy.'

'Nicole,' I point out, 'some people are simply evil.'

'I suppose my mother's death must have affected him.'

'Nicole, he was a bad father. Can you say that? On a count to three . . . one . . .'

'Okay, he was a bad father, I suppose.'

'What do you mean, you suppose? He made your life a misery. He was a creep. Why can't you say it?'

Feebly, she laughs.

'Go on, say it!'

'He was a creep, is that better?'

'Nicole are you totally incapable of being angry?'

After a few minutes she resumes her story: 'Harry was marvellous, to give him his due. He really helped me through that time. We both moved into a flat and soon after that I got a job as a travel agent. I know it wasn't exactly the best job in the world. I was just doing basic secretarial stuff . . .'

She gives me a vulnerable look. 'You don't exactly have to be a genius to do that.'

'Well, I don't know.'

We've just arrived at her yellow Fiat Cinquecento in the car park overlooking the old Dun Laoghaire baths. She invites me to sit in.

Since I have nothing better to do, I sit in.

'Guess how I bought this Fiat?'

'How?'

She removes the steering-wheel lock.

'By giving piano lessons,' she replies.

'You play piano?' says I, reddening.

'I love the piano. It's one of the things I missed most when I left home. But when Harry and I moved into Cherbury Court we bought an upright, so I could play to my heart's content. Harry didn't like it, though. He gave it away to charity a fortnight ago because he said it got on his nerves.'

I thought he told me he sold it?

'He said he hated all the noise. Imagine! He thought Chopin was noise. He was really good in so many ways, but when it came to things like refinement and culture and art he was completely . . .'

'Sorry, Nicole, did you just say you played Chopin?'

'I try. I only started on Chopin recently.'

Of course she did: she only met Ronan recently.

'Chopin drives me round the bend,' I tell her.

'Really?'

'Yes,' I reply, starting to feel very shitty again. 'It's all the lines and curves and angles and distances.'

She nods slowly, as if trying to figure out what I mean. 'Do you play piano, Julianne?'

I hearken back to the Cliff Castle Hotel living-room, where I seem to remember wading my way through Beethoven's *Pathetique* while Sylvana breezed through her vampire book. 'I was never much good.'

'I'm sure that's not true. Can you play by ear?'

'I normally use my hands.'

'Playing piano makes you feel so much at peace. There's harmony in music. Will I tell you what I think?'

'What?'

'I believe that harmony is the secret to happiness.'

'So do I.'

And I do.

'And yet it's so hard to find,' she says.

Especially if you're a tropical marine fish.

Or a cat.

'Our minds are in terrible disarray,' she explains. 'You know, we're being constantly bombarded by information on all sides, distracted by deadlines and plans and timetables. Everything is about control. We control time, we control people, every aspect of our lives is controlled so that we seem to have so little of everything and yet the world is such a huge place with plenty of wonderful things for everyone.'

'You're right.' I find myself agreeing.

'Constantly we're being told that you won't be happy until you achieve your goals in life, some time in the future . . .'

She seems really keen for me to understand her point of view.

'But that's ridiculous.' She laughs. 'It's like in this huge effort to get happy we forget how to *be* happy.'

I think of how happy I used to be with Ronan.

'I mean, harmony is really simple,' she goes on. 'It's all about freeing up energy for living. The Buddhists teach us that harmony comes from not constantly striving after things. Have you heard of the doctrine of non-attachment? The Buddhists say you can achieve Nirvana if you stop being so caught up with the things of this world.'

Ronan and Nicole will find Nirvana together. And when they discover that it's not all it's made out to be they will, at Ronan's instigation, hurriedly become non-attached. For me, of course, it will already be over.

She's gazing through her open side window, across the bay towards Howth, melancholy. 'Love,' she says faintly. 'That's the most important thing.'

Love.

I turn my head and start gazing out of my own window at the round tower in the distance where James Joyce once stayed, perched atop the elevated, jutting peninsula at Sandycove.

Time passes and we talk about everything under the sun:

Hollywood stars, the Lotto, facials, a health farm she's been told about, sex scandals in politics, men, the travel business and whether there are any bargain-basement penthouse apartments going at the moment in Figi.

Max gets a mention too. He has a habit of turning up at awkward moments. She asks after his health. Rather than replying that he hasn't got any left, I simply tell her that he has been giving no trouble, which is perfectly true: cats cease giving trouble when they're dead. She offers to pay for the cat food but I won't have it.

We talk on and on, it seems: her family (again), war, holiday moments, whether low-fat yoghurt makes you fatter than you already are, a TV programme she recently saw about a person who wanted to be neither male nor female nor neutral but all three, the constitutional ban on discrimination on grounds of sex, race, creed, colour – a pet topic of mine.

She soon cops on to the fact that I'm some sort of lawyer.

But she's discreet and unprying, which I also like about her. So it's not hard to steer her clear of the topic of myself. When you think about it, all she knows about me is that my name is Julianne and my address is 'just around the corner from you'. But it doesn't seem to bother her unduly.

When it's time for me to go home, Nicole offers me a lift. I decline, saying my car is not far away.

She then hesitates, like there's something on her mind.

'What is it, Nicole?'

'Oh, nothing.'

'What is it?'

'I was just thinking.'

'Well?'

'Would you like to come back to the B&B for a cup of coffee?'

'Well . . . it's nice of you to ask . . .'

'It's not very exciting, I know.'

'It's not that. I just . . .'

'Oh, do come round, Julianne!' she urges, sensing weakness. 'We could even go for a walk on Killiney beach nearby, it's lovely in the evenings now. A lot of people go there.'

She's like an old college friend, full of naive gaiety.

'What about Ronan?' I ask her doubtfully.

'We won't be meeting tonight. Besides, he'd always call first.'

She knows him better than I do.

I feel all grotty again, real squashed like a heap of dung. 'I'd better go, Nicole.'

'It's okay – you've probably got other things on.'

'That's the whole point: I haven't.'

'Well then, if . . .'

'Look,' I say, 'maybe I'll drop round later . . .'

She nods to herself. 'Whatever,' she says, unable to hide her disappointment. It's so obvious she'd like me to come with her and keep her company.

I pull myself out of the car, slam the door and bend down to peer through the window of the Fiat and try to smile at her, but I can't.

I walk away then.

42

When I get back to my new apartment I turn on my phone and check it for messages to see who cares about me.

Not one single message. No one cares.

I call Mother.

No reply. Probably out with her bridge toyboys.

I turn it off again.

A fog of silence encloses me as I stand in the middle of my new hall. I can hear nothing except the distant rumble of cars. I walk over to the balcony and peer through the window at the beautiful park below.

Turning again, I notice something new and colourful on the dinner table. From Sylvana's royal-blue glass vase sprouts a bunch of red, pink and white carnations. She must have been in here this afternoon (she insisted on having a key). She came specially and filled the vase with flowers. She didn't have to do that.

She bought the two beautiful thick sheepskin rugs for me as well. She spotted them in the shop, and she insisted. She could have got a cheap rug. But no. She had to get the best for me. The potted plants. She organized it all herself. She has turned my roof garden into a botanic paradise. She's been fantastic. She's been here for me, she's listened to me, she's given me constructive advice. I don't know how I can ever repay her.

She wants me to make this my home.

But how can I make this my home?

I don't even know what I'm doing here. Trying to hurt Ronan's feelings? His response was: 'congratulations'. The bastard congratulated me.

Bright mid-evening sunset rays are bouncing off the small lake, projecting a shaking tremolo of colour on to the ceiling. Through my hand-shaded eyes I glimpse a darkening panoply of rich green. I open the french windows and you can hear the soft, dense hiss of nature, the occasional lonesome chirp of a bird or quack of a duck.

I take out my phone and input Sylvana's number. I wait. It starts ringing. Then suddenly for no reason I press 'off'. I collapse on to the sofa, gripped by a panic of emptiness, a tight knot of longing for Ronan.

How can I stay here, a foreign body amid all these pieces of bare, dead furniture? I can't make them come alive. Not even Sylvana can help to make them come alive. Even her beautiful flowers, the most alive thing here, look artificial. I can't make anything come alive without Ronan. I can't make *myself* come alive without Ronan.

It's dead in here. Empty. Lifeless. Like a museum. I'm looking at articles of furniture once sat in, eaten on, used by former owners or tenants, waiting for me to pour life back into them once again. But what life have I got without Ronan?

How can I sit here in this couch in this room, in those armchairs, at that table and feel that this is *me*, that this is *my* life? That's what Sylvana wants me to do, but I just can't. I should be with Ronan this very minute.

He told her our marriage is dead.

A lever snaps inside me and suddenly I find myself lying curled up on the couch with my head in my arms, and the dam has burst now and I can't stop crying. Ronan is the most important person in the world to me. My eyes are clenched closed but I can't get him out of my head. We're dancing, yes, we're dancing, but close together and he's holding me tight and I'm leaning on his shoulder kissing his neck, adoring his masculine scent and we're dancing, dancing away and there's music and it's just the two of us, and another bout of tears erupts inside because I'm scared that everything between Ronan and me rests on one thing and one thing alone.

Delusion.

He congratulated me.

I can't stay here. Why am I here? Moving in here to make a point? To frighten him? It won't work. It's ridiculous. It's a bad joke. It will only push him further away.

I must call him. I don't know what I'm going to say to him but I must call him. I pick up the mobile off the sofa and switch it on. I input his number. It's ringing. I am suddenly and strangely filled with hope. People make mistakes. People can forgive. Why be so hard-hearted? His real voice answers.

'Ronan. It's me. Julie.'

I'm wiping my face, trying desperately not to sob.

'Ronan, do you remember I was telling you about that apartment which I said I was staying in . . . ?'

'Where's my bloody Porsche?'

It's the way he just spoke to me.

I was paralysed, unable to answer. I held the phone away from my ear. He ground out my name several times, unsure if I was still on the line, his voice thin and harsh, scraping like a chisel against rock. He demanded his Porsche back. I could have responded, but I was unable, I was afraid. He hung up.

I'm sitting in my MG, parked on the kerb outside the front entrance of Nicole's B&B, staring down the sloping driveway to the front door.

Her yellow car is in the tarmacadamed front garden. I've just turned off the ignition and opened my door, but I haven't got out yet, although my right foot is on the road. It's waiting for my left foot to join it but there's no sign yet of that eventuality. Like a moron, I stay like this for over a minute. Normally I'm a decisive person.

I pull my foot back in again. I pull the door shut.

But I don't restart the car.

I stare up the road towards Sorrento Park and the Victorian terrace overlooking Killiney Bay, where Mother said she'd love to end up. Only problem is that Dalkey is a hilly place and when you get to her age you have to consider stuff like hills and walking up them, so her idea is not entirely practicable.

I just stare through the open window at the cold purple clouds above, the sun casting a golden-pink light on the faces of passing strollers.

One couple passes by. They seem content. A black Labrador follows behind, poking his nose into the backs of the woman's knees, melancholy, craving attention. The woman has her arm tucked round her partner's back and she is smiling. The poor dog is being ignored.

I get out of the car and shut the door without bothering to lock it. I pass through the gateposts. I crunch down the gravel towards the faded white front entrance.

Nicole.

How can a person so let down by life still have such native confidence in people? Such optimism in the face of misfortune? How can she still love beauty as she does, after everything that's happened to her? I can hear her voice, singing lightly in my head, appealing as a tinkly bell.

She believes in trust.

I can see her, by the window in her room, staring out to sea, longing to leave unhappiness behind and find joy with the man she loves. Alone, surrounded by her luggage.

How can I hate her?

I am at the doorstep of the B&B, staring at the bell, unsure. Turning round again, I notice it is almost dark. I can't decide. I turn round again to face the door. I push the door and surprisingly it opens. I hesitate.

Then I walk in. I pass the small office on the right, but the lady is not there; the sliding panel is shut. Quietly I ascend the stairs. The place is in darkness. Wiry television sounds spiral from a thin yellow strip of light at the bottom of one door. From another room reverberate the bass sounds of muffled voices. I go to the top of the house where Nicole's is.

I knock.

There's no sound. Before knocking again I put my ear to the door. There's just the low murmur of the TV. Now I hear some movement inside. She's probably in her en suite.

I delay a few minutes and listen. She's all alone. Her father and stepmother resent her. Her favourite brother is in Amsterdam. She has no family. She's never spoken to me about any other friends she might have. She's just finished a four-year relationship with a man who abused her. She's putting all her hopes in a man I know won't stick with her.

After several minutes I raise my knuckles to the door once more. I am about to knock when suddenly I hear this giggling. There's a man's voice now. I stand for another minute listening, paralysed. Until I am sure there can be no doubt.

I steal away until I reach the bend in the landing where I pause to listen again. I can hear only the scraping noise of televisions and the muffled sound of voices.

I run down the stairs and out of the front door.

43

It's eleven o'clock and I'm still in bed. I know this is going to be one day when I order the world to go shove it where light beacons do not fit.

I have an unexpected appearance in court scheduled for today. I'm cancelling. My Senior Counsel can go dance. I'll ring in sick. More appropriately, perhaps, I'll ring in mental.

Fact is, I'm due a break from work. It's important, sporadically, to give one's misery some good, quality time.

I knew I heard something.

I sit bolt upright in my bed.

There's a noise in the hall.

'Jesus, Sylvana! You gave me a fright.'

She walks in carrying a large paper bag, her haughty face locked into fierce alliance with me against mankind.

I drop back down on the pillow like a stone.

'Keep your hair on, Julie. Here – look what I've brought you.'

She opens her paper bag beneath my jaw. She's brought me some doughnuts and Danishes and coffee. She's a dear. I plump up the pillows behind me, and she hands me a paper plate and shakes a Danish on to it, followed by some stray pecan nuts, and she passes me a cup of cool coffee and I start to guzzle and slurp – even before she's made herself comfortable at the end of my bed and starts to guzzle and slurp herself.

She's a sweetie. She could have got me almond Danishes, or the chocolate or the strawberry Danishes, but she didn't. She could even have got me those disgusting raspberry muffins which remind me of the vile doughnuts they used to make (and probably still make in certain quarters) with that rasping crimson chemical ointment in the middle that smells like wart remover and tastes like varnish – and you're supposed to believe it's crushed straight from the juicy strawberry.

244

But no – she got me pecan plaits.

Stuff like that matters.

But why has she come, I wonder?

Gossip, I bet. She wants to hear if I've been stupid, and gone and contacted members of a prohibited list.

And the Danishes? The sweetener. The tongue loosener. This is the danger of Danish pastries: they leave you open to subtle forms of abuse.

'Julie,' she says at last, grimly. 'We have a problem.'

I look up at her, my cheeks full of Danish junk.

'Ronan called me just now. He was inquiring about his car.'

'He's neurotic about that Porsche.' I munch.

'He assumed you might have an idea what happened to it.'

'What a ridiculous assumption.'

Sylvana likes it when I'm like this.

'He told me he's calling round to my place later. If his Porsche is not there he wants you to be there instead.'

'His penis substitute.'

'What will I tell him?'

'I'll go home and sort it out.'

'Don't go back there, Julie; I really don't think you should see him.'

I grab a doughnut. When I glance at her to check if she thinks I'm being incredibly greedy, I find her frowning at the magnolia plant I bought yesterday.

She turns back to me. 'What's a plant doing on your dressing-table?'

'It's supposed to make a woman more beautiful.'

'Oh, don't tell me.'

'What?'

'*Feng Shui*.'

'Well, yes.'

'You're turning into a *Feng Shui* hippie. All those candles you got as well. They're not for a blackout at all, are they? I worry.'

'I happen to have a booklet on the subject handy.'

'You'll end up like her if you're not careful.'

'Like how?'

'She has a screw loose.'

245

'I don't know.'

I turn towards the window. I sense her eyes latching on to me.

'Do you think otherwise, Julie?'

I can feel myself reddening. 'Well . . .' I begin, sipping my coffee. 'She's not . . . exactly . . . a *bad* person in her own right . . . as such . . .'

I sip my coffee again.

'Do I still detect a note of sympathy for her case?'

'You do not.'

I start nibbling a second doughnut. I don't want this conversation right now. Even if I am grateful to be in the middle of guzzling most of Sylvana's breakfast.

'You just said "as such".'

'I met her yesterday.'

She turns her head and smiles into the distance with mute forbearance, as if she's wondering what I'll tell her next.

'She called me,' I insist.

'And that makes it okay.'

'She just needed someone to talk to. She's all messed up. She's been badly hurt.'

'She's a bitch, even if she's a saint compared with him.'

'It's not really her I blame.'

'Julie, you're not well.'

'Don't be ridiculous. Anyway, I only wanted to find out . . . information.'

'You plan to go back to Ronan, don't you?'

'Now what do *you* think?'

She says I must stick by my decision to embrace my new life and my new apartment and my new freedom. She advises me to do all the things I insisted Nicole should do. She forbids me to see either of them again. She says she's more than happy to mediate for me, regarding the Porsche.

I have to get out of here.

I reach for my mobile and input for messages. Ronan has left one, at nine o'clock this morning, informing me that he is currently in a taxi on his way to the surgery. (Is he about to discover a new angle on *Chi*, at long last?) He says that this is simply 'not acceptable' because one, he's going to be late for his

246

patients and two, he already has a car and he would like to know what the hell I have done with it.

The poor boy is chauffeur-driven to work and he's complaining.

There's a message from Mother, left this morning an hour after Ronan's. She's commanding me to come home and sort out my husband who has suddenly returned from work in dangerously 'Cyclopic' form. And if I don't come home now and bail her out, she threatens, I could be putting my own tropical marine fish in danger of liquefaction. She actually says that! She can be so droll.

I throw the bedclothes off me and jump on to the floor.

'Where are you going?' demands Sylvana.

'Home,' I reply.

'But why do you . . . ?'

'Because I have nothing but the highest regard for tropical marine fish.'

'What do you mean?'

'Madeleine Albright wants to see me.'

44

When I get home, Mother is in the kitchen manipulating sausages and rashers on the grill with a wooden spoon. She looks funny in her green apron and long light-blue dressing-gown and the huge pink furry Teletubby slippers I got her as a joke last Mother's Day but one, not guessing she'd actually wear them.

'He's inside,' she says, flipping the contents of the grill on to a plate.

'I guessed. How is he?'

'I bumped into him this morning,' she says. 'He got up a little earlier because he had to take a taxi to work.'

'Did he say anything?'

'He muttered something all right. I wouldn't swear to it, but it sounded strikingly like "good morning".'

'So he's still tormenting you.'

'He returned from work just now, for whatever reason. I passed him in the hall. He didn't even look at me. He went straight into his bedroom and shut the door. I'm convinced it's male hormones.'

It's *Chi*, that's what it is.

She puts the mixed grill down on the table in front of me.

'Mother, I've just had a huge breakfast with Sylvana.'

'What did you have?' she asks accusingly.

'Three Danish pastries and coffee.'

'Dear God, child, you've never lost your innocence. Sit down there, now, and eat some proper food.'

Grudgingly, I sit down and pick up my knife and fork.

'But what are you going to have?'

'Toast.'

'But you made this grill for yourself.'

'Motherhood, Julie, is all about sacrifice.'

Stony silence.

'What are you saying? That I should be a mother?'

'No, Julie. I'm saying that I am your mother and you haven't been home in three days, and I know something's wrong between you and Ronan. Now I realize that it's none of my business and I don't wish to pry.'

Translation: I do wish to pry because it is all of my business.

'Can we talk about it later?'

'I hope you're not planning on separating.'

I cease sawing a rasher in half and look up at her amazed. 'Why?'

'Because,' she eyes me with a strange glint, 'I refuse to live here on my own with him.'

'We're just having an argument. Sometimes it's healthy to take a short break away from your spouse.'

'I wouldn't blame you. Even Prudence dislikes him.'

'Prudence has extraordinary psychic powers,' I observe, rougeing at this mention of the cat.

What I will do is this: finish my breakfast and slip out and nab the cat box from under the tarpaulin and wrap it in a black bin bag and steal it out of the apartment for disposal, before she or Ronan gets wind of it, literally.

'Oh, by the way, Julie,' she says, as if reading my mind. 'Where *is* Prudence? I haven't seen him anywhere.'

'Oh . . .'

'Have you seen him?'

I have indeed seen Prudence. He's out on the balcony, decomposing.

I jump up to shove a slice of bread in the toaster. Mother is difficult to lie to, mere inches away. Three metres' distance and you stand a better chance.

'Don't worry about the cat, Mother. I got rid of him.'

She's nodding now. 'How did you do it?'

'Mother, I got rid of the cat in the sense that I handed it back to its rightful owner.'

'You don't really think I bought that story.'

'What story?'

'That Sylvana owns Prudence.'

'Of course she does.'

'Then how come she didn't know the cat's sex?'

'Can we just forget this conversation?'

I pour her more tea.

A second later Ronan walks in the door.

45

He leans against the wall, arms folded, glaring at me through eyes cold and scathing.

I know what this is about.

This is about *Chi*.

'So it's come to this, Julie,' he says.

'Is something wrong?' I wonder, casually buttering some toast.

'You're back early, Ronan,' chirps Mother. 'Had you no dental appointments today?'

'I had my secretary cancel them.'

'Are you not feeling well?' she asks.

He turns to me: 'Julie, let's talk about this inside.'

'Don't mind little old me,' says Mother, determined not to miss an opportunity like this.

'It's not you, Gertrude, it's just that—'

'That's okay, then,' she interrupts, pouring out a cup of tea. 'Sit down, here's a cup of tea.'

'No thanks.'

She gives it to me instead.

'Thank you, Mother.'

'You're welcome, dear.'

'Julie, my Porsche is missing,' he snaps. 'Where is it?'

'What makes you think I took it?'

'A few reasons.' He pauses, glancing at Mother. 'For one thing, you obviously imagine I've been seeing another woman.'

'Ah,' I observe. 'Motive.'

Mother chuckles to herself, stirring sugar into her tea. When Mother chuckles like this I read it as a warning signal. I do not want Ronan to see her dark side. There are dimensions to her personality he hasn't even dreamt about.

'Ronan, your car has obviously been stolen.'

'Obviously.'

'I think you should call the police,' I cunningly add.

'Against my wife?'

I look up at him, feigning amazement. 'You don't seriously think I stole your car?'

'Confiscated, borrowed, hid . . . it's all the same.'

'Only a non-lawyer could say something like that.'

'Well? Did you?'

'I most certainly did not steal your car.'

I *sold* it: important technical difference here.

Mother: 'Ronan – don't be at Julie. She's had a hard week.'

Ronan makes this sound: not quite a snigger, not quite a sigh.

'I'd never have suspected her – but for one thing.'

'What?'

I am insanely curious, flipping through my microchip memory, certain that I did not carelessly deposit so much as one microbe of evidence connecting me to the evil deed.

'Yesterday I was rooting in the kitchen press,' he begins.

'As husbands tend to do,' is my little filler.

'And I discovered the stopper of our wine decanter.'

Christ, the wine decanter. Sometimes my mind works even more quickly than I give it credit for. Like brilliant lightning, I flash back at him, '*Really?*'

'It had bits of yellow paint stuck to it.'

I swallow.

He eyes me inquisitorially, sucking away my defences like a monster octopus.

'How on earth did they get there?'

'I'll tell you how they got there: somebody used the stopper to smash my Porsche last Thursday evening in the car park.'

'*And you think it was me?*' I cry.

I am utterly incredulous now, frowning at Mother, shrugging in bafflement, my whole being a pious offering to integrity, a shamelessly poker-faced bonanza of moral rectitude. Right now, in other words, I'm playing a blinder. I am that desperate for Mother to think of me as a well-behaved, well-raised little daughter.

And Ronan knows it. 'You look surprised, Julie.' He smiles.

I hate him. He sees through me. 'I thought the gurriers did that to your car?'

'Gurriers *did* do it, only not the ones I thought.'

'I'll thank you not to refer to my daughter as a gurrier; I think I brought her up exceptionally well.'

'Yes you did, Mother,' I reassure her, secretly wondering what she would think of me if she actually knew what I did to cars and art books and living-rooms and paintings and living things, and things in between like bucket-suffocating tropical fish.

'But there's something else,' he resumes, stroking his chin.

This reminds me of the headmistress going through my annual school report. 'What now?'

'Somebody recently penetrated my surgery.'

'Penetrated,' I comment, taking a panic bite of toast. 'A good word.'

'Have you anything to say about that?'

'Certainly wasn't me.'

'You're lying,' he says with contempt.

'You're right; lying is wrong.'

'Children! What happened in your surgery, Ronan? Was there a robbery?'

I pour myself some more tea, splashing, trembling.

'The intruder grilled cheese on toast.'

He examines me with limpid eyes.

Smirking.

Real-time brick-shitting panic now. They found the cheese-on-toast remains I left in the surgery kitchen. But what makes them think it wasn't Harry?

I glance at Mother, shrugging helplessly at her.

'That doesn't seem such a terrible crime to me, Ronan,' she says.

Me (tentatively): 'I dare say the thief was hungry.'

He straightens up, leaning back further, and strokes his chin some more. 'Certain people are not into cheese on toast . . .' he says mysteriously.

'This is true,' says I.

He adds: 'And certain people *are*.'

Oh, I get it. He must be referring to Harry. Harry must detest cheese. This crosses him off the suspect list. Me – I adore cheese on toast.

They're on to me.

'Stop being so abstruse, Ronan.'

But he ignores me. 'Furthermore, toasted cheese was not all the intruder grilled.'

Whatever can he mean?

Again, I glance at Mother, perplexed.

'Do you remember the painting in my office, Julie?' he asks.

'Which one?'

'There was only one.'

'Oh, you mean that lovely one of the goldfish.'

'You think it was lovely.'

Pause.

'Well . . . it was interesting anyway. I feel sure it had a hidden meaning, even if I could never detect it.'

'Would you like to know what happened to it?'

'I'd love to.'

'The so-called intruder burnt it under the grill.'

Right now, I'm pouring Mother some tea, although her cup is already full. It seems to be a law of nature: when you're in dire straits, you run out of decent options.

'He burnt it under the grill?'

I eye Mother and she eyes me.

'It was a valuable painting, Julie.'

'Maybe that was its hidden meaning.'

'Doesn't it strike you as a slightly strange thing for your average intruder to do to a painting?'

'You get all types out there.'

Mother: 'Perhaps the gurrier in question ran out of toast?'

I can't help it: I explode in uproarious laughter. Immediately I apologize for my inappropriate reaction and offer my sympathies in respect of the sad loss of his dear artwork.

'I don't know you any more, Julie,' says Ronan, darkening.

'Try spending more time at home,' I reply.

He's not smiling.

'Oh, don't be such a stick-in-the-mud,' Mother teases.

'She destroyed a work of art!' he yells.

'There's no need to accuse my daughter of vandalism.'

'Thank you, Mother.'

I mean, it's a scandalous accusation.

'Also, she destroyed the equipment in my surgery.'

Staring out of the window, he patiently awaits my reaction.

Mother looks at me.

I look at Ronan. 'What did you just say?'

He gives a calm, graphic account of how the spit fountain in his dental surgery is presently lying in shards all over the floor, along with the former glass cabinet. He recounts how the mechanical-arm light has been pulled asunder, the dental chair has been cut into strips with its insides scattered all over the floor and most of the contents of his filing cabinet have been torn into pieces. The damage he estimates at fifteen thousand pounds.

'Shall I go on, Julie?'

I stand up furiously, eyeballing him in total shocked silence. 'You're lying!' I shout.

'It's true.'

Harry.

It's the only possible explanation. He must have followed Nicole to the surgery. Or discovered an address, or a name and he traced it to the surgery. He entered via the damaged back door.

Who else could it have been? It makes perfect sense. But not to them: Harry does not eat cheese on toast.

Just my luck.

'I swear to God, Ronan, I did not do that to your surgery. I swear on my grandmother's grave, I swear on . . .'

Mother: 'It's okay, Julie. Sit down.'

I sit down, numb.

'I believe you,' she adds.

'Well, that's no surprise,' says Ronan contemptuously.

'You watch your lip, mister. I'm her mother, and I'm not going to stand here and let you bully her.'

'Bully?' he says, laughing briefly. 'Haven't you heard what she did to the fish, Gertrude?'

Mother is turning white with anger. 'Don't call me Gertrude.'

'Mrs O'Connor.'

'She already knows,' I reply, watching her nervously.

'Did your exemplary daughter tell you that she flushed the fish down the toilet?'

'That's enough now,' she warns him, 'if you know what's good for you.'

'They were flushed down the toilet. Julie told me herself.'

'No, they weren't,' she replies, paling.

'Fine.'

'They were flushed down your *gob*.'

'I don't think there's any need to pursue this,' I say.

Ronan is frowning now.

'No, Gertrude – Mrs O'Connor – please, do go on.'

'Mother . . .'

'Did you notice anything strange about your pasta last Monday evening, Ronan?' she says stiffly.

I put my hands up to stop her but it's too late.

Funereal silence.

The kitchen is a graveyard of soundlessness. Ronan's face looks like a tomb. It is pale and morbid and shell-shocked. He is speechless as a gagged mummy. He is beginning to understand things about me and Mother that he never before suspected.

Oh God.

She gets up and goes to the sink, turns on the tap, squeezes in some Fairy liquid and starts scrubbing some cutlery, klakking it noisily on to the draining board.

I start pleading: 'Ronan, the fish were already dead. Don't you remember? You put them in the bucket where they suffocated without any water. What was the point in letting them go to waste?'

His countenance registers negative feedback.

'The recipe was straight out of Delia Smith,' I urge.

He starts nodding to himself. 'I'm beginning to understand.'

'Ronan, it was authentic cuisine . . .'

'With a totally tropical taste,' Mother adds, drying the dishes via our Eiffel Tower dishcloth.

Ronan is still sporting his recently crucified expression, his face a damp grey Turin shroud of woe.

His head turns very very slowly towards Mother. His mouth stiffens, and he nods again. 'I get the picture.'

'Ronan . . .'

'One of you actually put the dead fish in the mixer . . . "Moulinex" – now I get it . . .'

'It was me who did it,' I urge.

'It was me, Julie,' warns Mother, turning to me, trying to cover for me.

'Mother, I'm the one who pasted the fish, have you got that?'

Like, that's an order.

No way is she going down for me.

Ronan: 'And then your mother poured it on my pasta.'

'You're a quick learner,' she remarks.

'That's sick.'

Mother: 'Were you ill?'

'This is totally insane.'

'They kill fish every day,' she says. 'A few more won't matter.'

'There's a psychiatric term for this kind of behaviour.'

'Leave Julie alone. She's a very good person.'

'Do you think so?'

She rises to her full height: 'Yes, I do.'

'Then you haven't heard what she did to Sylvana's cat?'

Silence. While I die inside.

I was just about to get rid of it. Oh God, Jesus, he must have seen it under the tarpaulin.

'What cat?' Mother demands.

'The dead cat out on the balcony.'

'Are you talking about Prudence?'

'Yes.'

Mother loved that cat. Now I'm really scared.

'Oh, don't get me wrong,' mocks the swine. 'I don't mind; I never had much time for cats. It's just the smell I object to.'

I burst out crying.

Mother takes five small sharp steps up to Ronan and slaps him hard on the face.

Now he's holding his left cheek, aghast, like it's just been branded. He's glaring at her, enraged. Sweat bubbles have appeared on his forehead.

'You're just a low-life,' she spits at him.

Silence.

'I'd appreciate it if you left our apartment now.'

She's glaring at him, her face shiny-white as steel. 'You're a bad person.'

'Okay.' He shrugs.

'You're a no-good *wanker*.'

'I'm a wanker. No problem.'

The technical meaning of the w-word has escaped all of her sixty-odd years on the planet. Mother. You can't take her anywhere. You can't even take her home.

'You're a tomcat – you just can't keep it to yourself, can you? You've been out with another woman. *You're a shameful adulterer*.'

Hold on. How does she know that? Did Sylvana tell her?

Suddenly, everything makes sense. The pasta sauce. In the normal course of events, pouring that fishpaste on to his spaghetti would be a crazily unhinged thing for someone to do, even for Mother. But not if she did it because she thought Ronan was cheating.

'I'm an adulterer. Is this what Julie told you?' he inquires.

She looks furious.

'Don't mind him, Mother; he's not worth it.'

'God knows what lice you're bringing back home. I'm not an angel myself, but, my God, from the very start I knew you were bad blood.'

'I think it's time for you to go now, Gertrude.'

Ronan snaps out his cellphone and his wallet. He flips out a card, calls a taxi company and orders a taxi.

'Mother is staying here, Ronan.'

'I'll go, Julie,' she says. 'I can stay with Bridie while you sort out your differences.'

'You'll do no such thing.'

I stand up and start ushering her out of the kitchen. I wish she hadn't started this; strictly, it has nothing to do with her.

She flings her apron at me (as if I've just insulted her) and nails him to the wall with a hard glare. Stalking out of the kitchen, she slams the door behind her, leaving both of us ogling the disapparition.

Ronan with this big red mark on his cheek.

46

He's leaning on the kitchen sink with his back to me now, staring out of the window towards the apartment block to the rear.

'You're both cracked.'

'Mother's right about you,' I shoot back.

'It must be something in the genes.'

'Mother and I are respectable people: we don't wear jeans.'

'Respectable? Do respectable people do what you pair of madwomen did to those tropical fish?'

'They were already dead.'

'Do respectable people smash cars and . . .'

'Do respectable people have affairs?'

'So you don't deny it, then?' he suggests.

'So *you* don't deny it, do you?

'I admit that . . .'

He stops.

'Go on.'

'. . . I've played around . . .'

He said it.

'Who is she, then?'

'It's in the past.'

'She's dead?'

'No. She's still alive, as far as I'm aware.'

'What's her name?'

He turns round. 'You've changed, Julie. Instead of coming straight out with it, you've kept quiet. You've been sly. You've gone behind the scenes and spied on me and collected information. You've been a bitch.'

'When a man is sly he's a fox. When it's a woman she's a bitch.'

'You destroyed my dental surgery, among other things.'

'I swear I didn't do that.'

'Of course you didn't. And my Porsche. You smashed that too and removed it to some secret location. The painting . . . the list goes on and on.'

'Listen to him! Making himself out to be some sort of sanitized martyr. You're the one who had an affair.'

'I want to know where you put my car.'

I sit down and pour myself some tea. Unfortunately there's no more than a thimbleful left in the pot. I look up, straight at him. 'I am being honest when I tell you, Ronan, that I have not the slightest clue where your car is.'

He doesn't believe me. 'I can't live like this,' he blurts out.

'Like what?'

'Like this.'

'Like an adulterer? I'm glad to hear it.'

'How do I put this . . . ?' He scratches his crown. 'I think that I've . . .'

'What?'

No reply.

'You think you've what?'

'Nothing,' he answers, pacing the small area in front of the sink.

'Fallen in love?'

He stops pacing. 'I wasn't going to say that.'

'Oh, I see. You think you've fallen out of love.'

He starts pacing again. 'You said it, not me.'

'Have you any guts, Ronan?'

'Okay – yes.'

'Yes what? You have guts?'

He sighs.

'I see: Ronan has fallen out of love. Strange for someone who doesn't know the meaning of the word. For you, love is just a

258

snooker pocket. Something you fall into if you're lucky. And like a snooker pocket it leaves you the same before and after: empty.'

'Excellent metaphor.'

'You've no conception of trust. Of loyalty. You have no conception of caring. Of sacrifice . . .'

'I know what I feel.'

'Size 36D tits?'

He stops as if I've just shot him. 'How did you know that?' he demands, as if he owned them.

He's asking me how I knew his piece of history wears size 36D tits. It's a fair question. So I tell him. About everything except my liaison with Nicole. I tell him that I returned from holiday to an empty apartment last Thursday and found their clothes scattered all over the kitchen floor. I tell him about the lemon-yellow Wonderbra on the doorknob and in passing I throw in the fact of his being a total moronic idiot for getting caught.

He paces around a bit, pinching his nose, thinking. 'How did you link her to the painting?'

'You're determined to make me admit I burnt that painting.'

'Well, did you?'

'Of course I did, you thickhead.'

'How did you know it was her painting?'

I pause. 'I didn't. I just wanted to destroy something you liked.'

'I see.' He sighs, appearing relieved.

'A work of art,' I mock. 'That painting was *brutal*.'

He tells me I clearly have no appreciation for art. I tell him not to be such a stuck-up prat. He replies that he's not saying anything radical here: people who grill paintings, he explains, clearly have no appreciation for art. I accuse him of putting the cart before the horse and he boomerangs that at least he doesn't put the *art* before the horse, and I slam back that not only is he suffering from personality failure, hair failure and marriage failure, but to cap it all, sense-of-humour failure as well.

'Still,' says I, 'at least we're communicating.'

'Honestly, for once.'

'Says the consummate liar. The whole Cliff Castle Hotel idea. What a joke. You just wanted to try that woman out in our bed.'

'She wasn't in our bed.'

'You know, Ronan, lying has become so inbred with you that to stop would require surgery. Your pathetic attempt to short-circuit me at La Bohème's last Thursday evening. Guess where I was? In the car park, Ronan! Watching you ogle your ridiculous banjaxed Porsche. God love your innocence.'

He eyes me sternly.

'And that whole circus you made up about the laundry! How could you do it to me, Ronan? Do you feel good about it? Did it even occur to you that, gosh, perhaps I'm being a bit of a shit here?'

He shrugs. 'We all make mistakes.'

'Like hell we do!'

'On a scale of one to ten, I think car-smashing and destroying paintings scores higher.'

'He's moralizing, for a change.'

'Besides destroying my means of livelihood.'

'Ronan, I told you that was not me. It was probably that woman's partner.'

'Julie.'

'What?'

'We made a mistake.'

'How?'

'We just . . . made a mistake.'

'Oh, I see. You mean getting married was a mistake.'

He looks away.

I approach him. 'Well? Answer me. Tell me that getting married was a mistake.'

Please don't think I'm particularly trying to hold on to him. I'm not. I'm just determined to make him suffer.

'Go on, say it.'

'What's the point? You'll only go berserk.'

'Say it, shithead!'

He starts pacing now, colour high, nerves frazzled, asking the kitchen floor whether I want my mother to hear us or not.

'Say it!'

'Maybe it was, okay?'

Now I can hear the clock ticking.

I point towards the bedroom with a strong, raised arm. 'If that's how you feel, then why don't you pack your bags? I mean it. Go now. I won't stop you.'

'You want me to pack my bags.'

He's daring me.

'If you think our marriage was a mistake.'

'Hold on. Did you just say you wanted me to pack my bags?'

'Wash your ears, you thick piece of dogshit. I'm talking about you having the guts to take a decision about your future.'

'You're a part of this too,' says the coward.

'Why, how thoughtful of you.'

'If you want me to go I'll go.'

I walk up to him and smack him hard across the face.

Shock. Twice in five minutes. This time his dental eyes gleam with fury.

He storms out. I slam the door after him shouting 'good riddance'. I start pacing the kitchen like a starved jaguar, trying to resist grabbing a bowl or a pot and hurling it against something stainless.

The doorbell goes.

That's the taximan. I go out to the hall, pass the bathroom where Mother is and storm into the bedroom. Ronan is bending over a huge suitcase opened out on the bed, flinging clothes in.

'You can send the taxi back. Mother is not going anywhere.'

'You're right, she's not.'

'What do you mean?'

'I am.'

He zips up his suitcase and hauls it off the bed.

'Where are you going?' says I more faintly.

'It doesn't matter. Goodbye, Julie.'

He walks straight into the hall, opens the front door and slams it behind him.

Crying, I shout after him and follow him out, down eight flights of steps in pursuit. But by the time I reach the sunlit car park his taxi has disappeared.

That's the last straw.

I can't stand it any longer.

I am going to get them both together.

I dive on to the balcony, grab the box containing Max's

decomposing body and shove it into a black bin bag. I tear out of the apartment and down into my car, where I hurl it in the boot. Then I get in and start the car, skid out and head in the direction of Nicole's B&B.

I call her on the way. When she answers she's all happiness and jollity. Really chuffed to hear from me.

'Has Ronan called you yet?' I pant.

'No, he hasn't . . .' she says. 'Why?'

'I have to see you Nicole. Now! You're not to make any appointments. You're seeing *me*, is that clear? Where are you now?'

'I'm just leaving the B&B. I'd love to, Julianne, but . . .'

'Stay where you are. I'll be there in ten minutes.'

47

She's waiting for me at five minutes to midday, standing at the gate in front of her B&B, holding a black artist's canvas case under her arm. She's wearing a pair of light-brown knee-high leather boots (the ones I saw her buy in town), a colour-coordinating tan miniskirt, a light-lemon-yellow sweater. Around her neck is a gold chain. She seems to have added orange highlights to her golden hair, which drapes in long curls round her shoulders and back.

When I see her with those long, tanned, sexy legs of hers – beaming heartfully at me – it gets so underneath my skin that I want to bite my tongue off.

Instead, I buzz down the window and smile nicely.

'It's lovely to see you, Julianne.'

She strokes the side of my car with her right hand like it's some kind of cat substitute. It's sort of ironic to think that Max lies just a few feet behind me, in another world. 'It's an amazing car.'

'Yes. And it's green. One of your favourite colours.'

'Is it yours?'

'It's my granny's. Nicole – something's come up. I need you to come over to my place.'

She pulls this pained face. 'I'd love to. But the thing is, I'm being photographed this afternoon for my new career and I have to get my hair done . . .'

'It's urgent.'

'It's just that Ronan arranged the photo session himself and I can't let him down.'

I gape at her. 'What does *he* know about photography?'

'He's actually very professional. He took some photos of us in Paris on Tuesday and I've just had them developed. They're in my bag . . . do you want to see them?'

'At my place.'

'Oh, Julianne! I wish I could, but I have to meet him at the zoo at three.'

'You're joking.'

But she's not. 'There's a lovely aquarium there. He said it would be a nice publicity gimmick to shoot me standing next to the tropical fish. What do you think?'

I stare straight ahead. 'He's right. You'd look hilarious.'

'And that's why I have to get my hair done first.'

She's feeling it now like it's some sort of live animal.

'Nicole, come out to my place. Invite Ronan. Seriously! I'd love to meet him. Invite him for lunch. We can do a nice French salad with avocado and mango. I'm sure he'd like that.'

'He loves avocado and mango, but I don't know . . .'

'And then you can go to the zoo where you both belong.'

She laughs a lot at this.

When she recovers she asks me why I want her to come out to my place precisely now and not some other time.

'It's Max,' I reply, looking away.

'Max? Is he okay?'

'He's not in great form, Nicole. I think he's been sick. I can't guarantee his health any more. You need to come over and check him out.'

This gets her concerned. She wants to know more. She starts firing these questions at me about what he's been eating, whether he's been allowed to roam, whether there were any chemicals etc. he might have had access to.

I make up this whole pile of bull about me having spotted Max chewing vegetation in my neighbours' roof garden just feet away from an open-top cannister of weedkiller.

Now Nicole looks dangerously worried.

'And when you're there you could always give me one of those *Feng Shui* consultations. We need one badly.'

She is torn. Ripped apart, in an anguished dilemma of indecision. On the one side you've got Max plus *Feng Shui* consultation. On the other you've got hair. How on earth is one supposed to choose?

In a sudden flash she agrees to a brief visit.

Brief is all I need. It's all I need to lock her out on the balcony, get Ronan over and sort out the issue once and for all. With Sylvana, perhaps, hidden in the background.

'Should we go in your MG?' she says, excited now.

Thinking about it, I realize this is not such a good idea. I'm worried about this stink in the boot, percolating through the crevices in the back seat. I'm not saying Nicole would recognize the scent: after all, Max alive is a totally different smell from Max dead. But I'm just a bit afraid she'll start interrogating me about whether I left the boot open and, say, a hedgehog accidentally hopped in and set up camp for the night. It would be just like her to think up an angle like that on hedgehogs.

'Look, I've a better idea: you take your car and I'll take mine.'

'All right.'

'Just follow me.'

On the way to my new penthouse apartment, I pull up behind a yellow skip on the side of the road. Nicole stops just behind me. I get out and open the boot. Thankfully, Nicole does not get out. I lift out the bin-bag-enclosed cat box, carry it over and dump it into the skip.

I get back in and drive off.

Nicole resumes following me.

When she sees my new apartment she throws a wobbly. 'It's lovely here, Julianne. Your hallway is a real confluence of energies.'

'Thank you.'

'Max is so lucky.'

'Yes.'

'I wonder where he is?'

'That's a nice gold necklace you're wearing, Nicole.'

'Ronan gave it to me.'

She starts giving me a potted history of the chain Ronan bought her, where he got it, where they were when he gave it to her, but I just walk into the lounge, leaving her in the hall talking about Ronan and when she's finished that, prattling on about what a nice harmonious atmosphere there is in my new apartment and how the glass doors into the kitchen and lounge make the place lovely and bright.

I begin uncorking a bottle of brandy from the drinks cabinet.

Still in the hall, she points out that the spiral staircase leading upwards from the bedroom passageway is a lovely design, but in *Feng Shui* terms it is 'counterindicated because of the way it chokes and represses the energies of a house'.

It's not that I particularly disagree with this fascinating piece of information, it's just that I'm really not in the mood. I pour a triple brandy to calm myself down.

'There's very little clutter,' she continues from the hall. 'That's good. Clutter makes you feel all blocked; it stops the flow.'

'Aha.'

'Some chrysanthemums would be lovely,' she says, walking in. 'They bring laughter and peace to a house.'

I start sipping. Why did I have to mention that thing about a *Feng Shui* consultation? I should have just told her Max was making these odd choking noises and left it at that. Let's hope she doesn't accidentally wander into my bedroom. If she catches sight of that magnolia plant I'll never shut her up.

'Do you intend to keep the walls white, Julianne?'

I don't bother answering. I can't get it out of my mind that Ronan has, for the last several months, been laying Nicole like a dual carriageway.

She explains that colour is an important cure: different colour combinations can affect your health as well as your mood – as we all know from the colour of the clothes we wear.

'White is the colour of innocence and openness,' she infinitely ad-nauseates. 'It can make it hard for you to have definite opinions because it opens up too many possibilities.'

'I have no problem having opinions, Nicole. The only problem is when other people disagree with them. What can I get you? Cointreau? I got in a new bottle; some person drained the last one on me.'

She wonders if I have any fruit juice, saying that she's into the 'healthy option'.

'I'm afraid we don't carry healthy options here.' I stick my hand inside the cabinet and grab the Cointreau. 'We only stock stuff that seriously damages your health.'

I know I shouldn't be drinking brandy. But I'm wary of resolutions to give up alcohol, or anything else (sex, drugs, glue, et cetera) that has the obvious capacity to keep you alive.

I pour her the drink and hand it to her. She accepts it without a word.

'Could I ask you a favour, Nicole?'

Nicole raises her eyebrows and sits forward in her seat, fixing on me a serious gaze.

'I want you to keep my address to yourself. There are certain people I don't want knowing about this place. Relations. Friends. The parish priest, even. I'm keeping my husband in hiding, you see.'

At once she appears to see my dilemma.

'Can you promise me you won't tell a soul?'

'I promise,' she says with an almost ridiculous sincerity that reads *I would never dream of betraying a secret uttered to me in confidence.*

Still, I don't trust her. So I go on to clarify what I mean. I do this because I am seriously worried about what 'I promise I won't tell a soul' is generally taken to mean: 'I promise I won't tell a soul, except my partner, Orla, Hugh, Mixer, Freddie, Sandra, Bernice, Donal, my sisters, my mother, my grand-aunt, my colleagues, the women at the gym, John the gardener who is very discreet, let's see . . . Mabel who works as secretary at the chiropractors, not forgetting the librarian at Deansgrange who reads literature and therefore is hostile to idle gossip, and finally the new curate from Nigeria who wouldn't have anyone to gossip to anyway – all of whose soulful discretion is beyond reproach.'

I now explain to her in broad outline what I personally mean by 'I promise I won't tell a soul'.

266

I get across to her the general idea that betrayal of the location of this secret residence of mine will result in me taking personal charge of her flaying, but only after her tongue is ripped from its roots and dropped gently into the tropical waters of the zoo aquarium, to be used as nutrition for its rare somnambular fish.

She seems a bit taken aback.

'The point is, Nicole, can I trust you? Not even to tell Ronan, for example?'

'Of course you can.' She frowns severely. 'I won't tell a soul.'

I sip my brandy.

Concerned, she asks if everything is okay with me.

'Well . . . I do happen to have one or two marital problems.'

'I know you do,' she says kindly. 'I don't suppose you want to talk about it?'

'No.'

'I never even asked his name.'

'Helmut.'

Silence.

'Oh, that's . . .'

'Please don't say it's a nice name, Nicole.'

'It's . . . foreign, is it?'

'Yes. Anyway, we're just having an ongoing . . .'

She nods reverentially. 'It can't be easy.'

'. . . an ongoing difference of opinion: Helmut wants to buy an aquarium. I don't. I don't think I'd make a great carer of fish.'

'Of course you would, Julianne,' she strenuously objects. 'Goldfish are no trouble at all. They stimulate really healthy *chi*. Did you know that whatever is happening in your life is reflected in your fish tank? For instance, if your fish go all slow and dopey it means that in your own life you are becoming lethargic or . . .'

The woman is unstoppable.

'. . . and if they start eating each other,' she adds with laughable earnestness, 'it's a sign that there's too much stress in your life.'

Hold on a second.

'Surely if they start eating each other, Nicole, it's a sign that there's too much stress in *their* life? Or even that they're, like, hungry?'

She laughs, in a nice, innocent way, almost as if nothing I say can put her off. 'Fish also represent money and marital happiness,' she confidently asserts. 'A fish tank would do the world of good for your relationship with your husband. I'm serious.'

'That I doubt.'

'It's true. Really.'

'Ronan has a fish tank, hasn't he?'

She nods, puzzled.

'Well, if a fish tank is so good for marriages, how come he says his marriage is over?'

But she blindly continues, as if inoculated against common sense: 'It's not just marital happiness; an aquarium can also improve your finances.'

'Nicole, can we perhaps change the subject?'

But she insists.

If you place a fish tank in the career area, she harps on, it can have an incredibly positive effect on the amount of money in your bank account. She explains what the 'career area' is. The floor plan of any dwelling is divided up into nine traditional areas, for instance, career, wealth, fame, relationship, health, knowledge . . .

'And children,' she adds with a vulnerable look.

'Children.'

She nods, moist-eyed for some reason, then goes back out into the hall, saying she'll show me the 'career area'. I follow her out.

'Most of the energy in the house comes through the front door so the career area is always found here. It represents your vocation, your life path.'

'That's something I wasn't aware of.'

'Your life path is like a river. Water is a strong element. All this means that you should have fish near the entrance – over here, for example . . .'

She puts her hand on the low bookcase, but I return to the lounge, tired already. She follows me back inside.

'Seriously, Julianne, you should get an aquarium. It would be really good for your marriage. Even if it were just one fish.'

'Are you suggesting a threesome?'

'How do you mean?'

'Me, Helmut and a clownfish.'

She grins. 'It could be your new seabed.'

I actually burst out laughing at this.

I exit through the french windows, mentally noting that the key is in the handle. She follows me out to the balcony.

She erupts.

She is enraptured by the view of the park. Enchanted by the colours, the flowers, the trees, the bright water with the white swans and their slender S-shaped necks, the lemon-lime grass, the red-brick wall bordering the park to the right, the red roofs, the large blue basin of the sky . . .

'I have to paint this.'

'I'm sorry?'

'Julianne,' she says, almost out of breath, 'I have to paint this. It's like paradise.'

'You want to paint my park?'

'Would it be okay? My canvas and easel are down in my car.'

'You want to make a pirate copy of my beautiful park?'

'Julianne.' She turns to me again.

'What?'

'I have an even better idea.'

'What?'

'You don't have to agree to this if you don't want to – you'll probably think it's crazy.'

She gives me this timid gazelle look first.

'Go on.'

'What would you say if I began my painting of *Chi* up here? For the inspiration?'

I avert my eyes to the park, chewing my cheek. She thinks I will be happy to stand here and watch her as she masterstrokes a *Chi* replica on to her canvas, and uses it as a basis for getting rich quick and laid by Ronan even quicker.

'You're asking me if you can paint *Chi*. Is that right? Here on my balcony?'

'*Please!*' she pleads.

'But what about your hair?'

'It can wait,' she says, begging.

'But a copy will never be the same as the original.'

'I could always try.'

I extract a packet of John Player Blue from the inside pocket of my new black jacket – to give me something to do as insurance against going crazy. I pull out a cigarette and poke it into my mouth, locate a box of matches and light up, one hundred per cent certain that *Feng Shui* flip-outs like her ought to be lecturing me right at this moment about how bad nicotine is for world harmony.

Thinking about her request, though, does it really matter what she paints on my damn balcony as long as I get to lock her out and set up a rendezvous in the next hour or so with her principal kick?

'Well, I can see you're serious,' I tell her, waving out the match and flicking it over the balcony.

'Would your husband mind terribly?'

'He'd be amused.'

48

Nicole is a woman of great charms, as we've seen.

She's managed to persuade me to stand here like some unemployed waster holding aloft a large colour photo of *Chi* for her to paint.

The . . . artist herself is in white overalls. Her eyes are darting constantly from the photo to the canvas, which she has pinned to a tall wooden easel. On a small table next to the window are a line of brushes and paint canisters, and pegs and paper, and a bottle of white spirit. Her new painting is beginning to reveal the shadowy forms of eight fish in a pattern analogous to the original *Chi*. She says it won't be perfect, but adds that since her French contacts appear to be more interested in her 'impressionistic style', the fact that it will be only an approximation to the original should not be catastrophic.

So there she is, jabbing her brush into the palette in her left hand like she's on speed, making countless deft marks on the canvas, though you'd imagine she'd take greater care, considering she's having a go at fooling the whole Parisian art world into believing that *Chi* number one never actually ended its days inside a grill.

Two details: Nicole has this permanent frown stuck on her brow and she's constantly chewing her lip.

But a more interesting aspect of her work mode is this: as she paints she is unable to keep her mouth shut. Her conversation, as usual, is like the contents of a Christmas stocking: varied, colourful and full of surprises.

After a while, though, as you might expect, she touches down once again in *Feng Shui* fantasyland, so I've started giving off these please-stop-boring-me smoke signals.

Nicole heaves this big sigh.

'What?' I say.

'Oh, nothing . . . it's just that the sun has moved.'

She dabs the brush into the blue paint and – following the photo carefully – she starts to paint grass clumps in the background. In blue. I feel like pointing out to her, naive twit that she is, that grass does not generally come in blue. But I have a real horror that she'll start quoting Ronan's expressionist theories at me.

Again, she dabs her brush into the blue.

Angrily this time.

'There *is* something the matter, Nicole.'

'You won't believe this, Julianne.'

'Try me.'

'Guess what Ronan's wife did.'

'What?'

'Painting these fish reminded me just now.'

'What did she do?'

'She killed half the fish in their aquarium.'

'He told you that, did he?'

'Yes.'

Filthy liar. They were already dead. More or less.

'And you'll never guess how she killed them.'

'How?'

'She put them in the electric mixer and switched on the power.'

'I hope she remembered to put on the lid.'

'She turned the lovely fish into sauce,' she says bitterly.

'It must have made lovely sauce, so,' I cheekily reply, taking a puff of my fag (I will use outmoded eighties language if I want to).

271

She returns to her painting. 'She has no respect for wildlife.'

'Fish aren't wildlife,' I reply, taking another drag of my fag.

She jabs her brush aggressively into the palette and starts humming, as if to rise above my tiresomely flippant commentary. Her brush is flicking across the canvas, making scraping, scratching noises. Now she stops and stares at it. She doesn't look too pleased with what she sees.

'Ronan was at dinner with his wife and her mother and a friend last Monday night. Do you know what the mother did?'

'What?'

'She poured the fish sauce on to his spaghetti.'

'You're joking.'

'I'm serious.'

'Well, I'd imagine that was bad *Feng Shui*.'

Her mouth has turned hard and obstinate all of a sudden.

'And did he actually go ahead and eat it?' I ask her, suppressing a grin.

'He wasn't to know. The wife and her mother disguised the taste with lots of herbs and spices.'

'Cuisine is all about disguise.'

She stares at me with a look of puzzled vexation, her brush pointing towards the sky. She's clearly upset that anyone could do that to her darling Ronan.

'So what do you think of *that*?' she says.

I take a drag and look away. 'Hilarious.'

'They could have poisoned him, Julianne!'

'Don't be ridiculous: fish is fish. Don't be distracted by the outer design.'

From the corner of my eye I can see that she's still got her brush stuck upwards in the air, which probably means she's still staring hard at me. I'm clearly not giving this issue the seriousness it deserves.

'Your paintbrush is going dry, Nicole.'

She returns to her painting.

'I mean, to *do* that,' she declares. 'Her mother must be a madwoman. Ronan thinks it runs in the family.'

I laugh uproariously. 'Is that what he said?'

'Yes. Ronan says her mother is a real . . .'

272

I turn my head and stare at her now. 'A real what?'

'She interferes a lot.'

'A real what? A real bitch? Is that what he said?'

'A real old bag. I'm only quoting him.'

'What a nice way to talk about your own mother-in-law.'

'She's vindictive,' Nicole protests.

'I suppose that's where her daughter gets it from.'

'That's what he says.'

'Yes, well, as we already know,' says I with resignation, 'the wife is off her rocker.'

'But she *is*,' she protests.

It's beginning to aggravate me, watching her indulge her favourite pastime as she stands there calmly laying into me.

'And of course.' She sulks. 'That's not all she did.'

'What now?' I sigh.

'Ronan has come to the conclusion that it was her who destroyed *Chi*. He was in a terrible state when he rang me from his surgery, over an hour ago, and told me. I pretended not to know anything about it. He said she also destroyed his surgery with a sledge hammer.'

'A small finishing touch.'

'So what do you think of that?'

'Tragic.'

'She ate cheese on toast, which proves it was her.'

'Have you any idea how idiotic that sounds?'

'Ronan said she was spying on us in the apartment; that's how she found out.'

'It's her apartment, Nicole.'

'It's despicable. Also she is the one who smashed his brand-new Porsche to bits last week. And now she's stolen it.'

I can feel her annoyance peeling away on the surface of my skin. I should really call Sylvana at work; it's not right that she should have to miss this. So I draw out my cellphone from my pocket, careful not to burn my jacket with my cigarette. I am about to dial her number when Nicole interrupts.

'Julianne, I can't believe anyone would do all those things.'

'No, but then you don't know her.'

'I certainly don't.'

'I mean, you don't even know her name.'

Pause.

'Her name's Julie, but Ronan never talks about her.'

'Unless it's to criticize her.'

'She's deranged.'

She pokes her brush hard into the palette, raises it, flicks her hair back and daubs it (the brush, that is) on to the canvas.

I take a drag.

I'm deranged now – important qualitative difference here. We're on to a totally different level.

'I put a lot of work into *Chi*,' she explains in a hurt voice. 'It had great potential. It's really upsetting that I have to do this. I thought it was going well, but now I'm not so sure.'

'No comment.'

'I can't believe she actually burnt it under the grill.'

'I wonder if she added Worcester sauce.'

'Julianne!' she cries. 'She burnt my painting. It was really close to my heart.'

'How sad for you,' I reply, raising my eyes to heaven for indulgence.

'I can't believe you're being like this!'

I admit I'm being an absolute and total signed-up scumbag. I blow smoke straight into her face.

She is about to burst into tears.

'Okay, Nicole. I admit that your painting *Chi* is probably more than just . . . I don't know, a mixed grill, but for chrissake she only did it because she was under the impression that the painter was screwing her husband.'

Everything stops.

Nicole is standing there staring at me like a mannequin, mouth open, my words hanging in the air between us like a nasty odour, a droplet of bright-blue paint quivering at the edge of her brush, threatening any time to plop off and plunge down on to my clean balcony floor.

I input Sylvana's number.

It's ringing.

Nicole turns away suddenly. She stares at her canvas, a look of Eva Peron on her mouth.

'Nicole, I've a suggestion to make about your painting. You see your grass there? Would you not think of trying some, like, green?'

No reply.

'It's only a suggestion.'

She's still staring hard at her 'art'.

Sylvana replies.

'Hello, it's me, Julianne. Want a laugh?'

Nicole slams her palette hard down on the table, splashing speckles of blue and red and yellow and black paint on to the window. Why do I bother entertaining people like this when they're going to splodge up my apartment on me?

'What's all that noise, Julie?' says the phone.

Nicole slaps down the brush, rubs her hands fiercely on a cloth, pulls off her white overall, bunches it up and flings it down on the tiles with a light thud, then proceeds to unclip the canvas from the easel. She rolls it up.

'Well,' I reply to Sylvana, 'I have someone here in the process of losing her temper.'

'I'm coming over.'

'Yes, I think that would be a good idea,' I reply.

Suddenly Nicole stalks angrily through the french windows with her canvas, her footsteps snapping through the living-room and through my marvellous *Feng Shui* hallway, at which point the footsteps stop abruptly and she roars 'You cow!' just like that.

There's a nasty, gut-wrenching suspense in the air.

'Julie, are you still there?' says Sylvana in my ear.

Suddenly I remember something: wasn't I supposed to lock Nicole out on the balcony?

In a panic I run after her, shouting that there's something I'd like to talk to her about if she'd care to come back in and I think it might be of considerable interest to her.

But the front door slams with a crack that resounds throughout the hollow-sounding apartment. I pull it open and fling my head over the bannister: 'Come back!'

'I'm never going back there again,' she warbles, her voice spiralling up through the distorted acoustics of the stairwell, the clipped snaps of her shoes expanding into a pattering reverb.

'Where are you going?' I shout.

She advises me to go to hell.

'God, you hurt my feelings!' I yell back at her, following her downstairs.

Now she bellows something back at me, her refracted utterance containing the words 'never', 'such' and 'bitch'.

I'm supposed to fill in the missing gaps.

'Don't you want to see Max again?' I roar, nice and cruel, taking two steps at a time.

The lobby door bangs.

Bitch.

Suddenly I hear this squeak. It's coming from the mobile I'm still holding in my hand. It's Sylvana. I forgot all about her.

'What was that all about?' grinds her voice through the receiver.

'Sylvana.'

'What?'

'Do you like zoos?'

49

Sylvana? Like zoos?

Why, she should have been born in one. She goes ape every time I mention the word. She goes camel. She goes *hippopotamic*. She's not always the cut-you-dead-rational woman you suspected.

So I just mention the word 'zoo'. Her response?

Unexpectedly, she sighs. 'I do so adore watching animals belch and scramble and defecate,' she dreamily laments.

'Yes, it's just your sort of place.'

'And of course it's important now and then to renew the link with your forefathers.'

'Yours, maybe.'

'But why, Julie, are you asking me if I like zoos? You're well acquainted with my special romantic relationship with zoos.'

'I'm inviting you to the zoo this afternoon. Just meet me there at one thirty, okay?'

'Is this to do with Ronan?' she inquires suspiciously.

She drags it out of me. When I tell her that I intend to trap Ronan in the zoo today at three while he's photographing Nicole beside a giant fish tank, there's this scary hush.

'I thought you'd left him, Julie,' she says eventually.

'I have,' I lie, uncertain.

'Then why would you want to confront him?'

'I want to humiliate him.'

Sylvana is not fully content with my explanation, but since she realizes that I am going to do my own thing anyway – plus she doesn't want to miss a piece of the action – she finally decides to jump on the bandwagon. She wants to be there, she says, to witness Ronan's final disgrace.

We hit the zoo by one thirty. Nicole's car is nowhere to be seen. Presumably she is getting her hair done. We decide to park Sylvana's d BMW close to the perimeter wall, as much out of sight as possible.

'We have over an hour to ourselves,' says Sylvana, 'so we might as well enjoy the animals.'

'Right you are.'

Nothing like a few armpit-scratching baboons to lift the spirits.

Within minutes we're walking through the narrow pass between the giraffe and camel enclosures.

Right in front of us – blocking our path – is this peacock with a shiny blue neck and a brown-plumed behind, and a wide fan sweep of feathers. It's twirling round in a hissing, slow-motion dance, fluttering its huge blue bubble-design fantail.

Sylvana, nervous: 'He's coming on to one of us.'

'I think it's you.'

The bird squawks at us. Interpreting this as a communication worth bearing in mind for our personal safety, we swiftly retreat.

Still in a snot, the piece of colourful poultry draws its huge tail into what looks like a long bushy dust broom, and totters down the embankment bordering the path, traverses the ditch, hops up on to a wall and starts waddling painstakingly across the giraffe enclosure. For there to be a peacock in the giraffe enclosure was clearly not part of the zoo plan. Either the bird is lost or it's manoeuvring a sly short-cut.

One of the brittle giraffe creatures has sauntered lazily over to investigate us, curious specimens of life that we are. We get self-conscious, though, and wander to the other side of the path where these two camels await us. The nearer one, Alf, has a black face with a white snout. He's chewing away like he's been chewing for the last decade and he's happy enough to continue chewing for another. His head and neck form one thick column of brown beard. He's got long, effeminate eyelashes and a mop of red-brown hair over his ears, which according to the blurb protects him from Asian sandstorms, not that he'll bump into too many of those in these parts.

He eyes us scathingly. We are lesser vermin. His partner, Matilda, is lying down and who could blame her? There's not much for them to do around here except chew their own regurgitations, swing their tails and indifferently watch the rooks help themselves to their significant (and clearly tasty) droppings.

'Lovely,' is Sylvana's summation.

'It's unfair the way they lock up these animals. They should be out in the wild, doing what they've been doing for thousands of years – roaming around, rearing their young . . .'

'Killing,' she adds.

'Playing. I wouldn't mind setting them free.'

'Fine by me as long as you give me advance warning.'

She points to the cheetah in the next enclosure, pacing up and down like a growling sentry on hunger duty. 'Don't do anything silly, Julie. I'm opening a new shop next week. My champagne openings are generally more successful with two legs.'

'Don't worry,' I reply, 'they're well enough fed as it is. The keepers feed them thawed fish, apparently, and they have a good diet of chopped fruit and veg.'

'I suppose they use a Moulinex mixer,' is her slightly unnecessary comment.

The phone rings. Walking towards the hippo enclosure, I input. It's Nicole.

Sylvana puts her ear to the piece.

'It's you again,' I begin.

'Julianne, I just called to say I'm . . .'

'Has Ronan been in touch?'

'No. Julianne – look, I'm sorry about earlier on . . .'

'Yes, I seem to remember you calling me a bitch.'

'I didn't. I didn't call you that.'

'And you called me a cow if I remember correctly.'

Pause.

'I didn't mean to call you that.'

'You meant to call me a heifer, then.'

'No, I . . . I wasn't myself. I thought you were criticizing my painting even though I know you weren't . . .'

'It's the last thing I would do.'

'I know why you're annoyed with me and I don't blame you: because you think it's wrong to be going out with a married man, because your husband went out with a married woman, because you don't want me to end up hurting myself, I don't know . . . and I admit . . . I know it's wrong.'

'Hallelujah!'

'But what I've been trying to tell you all along, Julianne, is that no one I've ever met in my life ever gave me the confidence to go ahead and do what I was good at, and now for the first time I am so close to success. I mean, my stepmother kept telling me I was no good at art and even my brothers used to laugh at my paintings. That's only because my father did that and they didn't know any better. Harry was almost as bad: he nearly stopped me painting altogether. It's not that he hated art per se – he was just allergic to the smell of paint . . .'

'Like cheese.'

'So I had to have the attic converted so that I could paint there instead.'

'Nicole, you're taking up valuable phone time.'

'I know you have to go, Julianne. All I'm saying is – when you're in love, you just can't help it. Think how you would feel if you fell in love with a man who happened to be married.'

I think about this.

She's right.

Love is the bottom line, the baseline of reality. Like a golden paintbrush, it gilds everything it touches. It is a light that bathes all the dark corners of a room in itself. When it is present, there are no shadows, there is no wrong. When there is love, adultery is meaningless.

Love is such a coward that I know I would forgive Ronan if he showed me some decent remorse, some truth.

She tells me she called back to my apartment but I'd left. I tell her I'm in the zoo.

She can't believe I'm in the zoo. She reminds me that this is where she's meeting Ronan at three. She thinks it's wonderful that I am here. It doesn't seem to occur to her that the reason I'm here is directly connected with herself.

'Will you still be there at three?'

'Yes, I'll be very much here at three.'

'Are you with Helmut?'

'I'm with a friend.'

'I'll introduce you both to Ronan then, if you like.'

'Nicole – I wouldn't miss it for the world.'

At two ten, while Sylvana and I are staring into the flabby pink mouth of a hippopotamus called Linda, we glimpse Nicole walking slowly up the path, arms folded and head tilted down, her countenance sad but illuminated, almost, like a halo. She's still in her lemon-yellow sweater and tan miniskirt, and light-brown knee-high leather boots. Her photo session costume. Her hair looks darker from this distance.

'Remember, Sylv, I'm Julianne. What are we going to call you?'

'I don't know,' she says. 'Sonya or Marylyn or Roxanne or something romantic like that. Just don't call me Kimberly or Lavender or Lysandra. Or Labia for that matter . . .'

'Now there's an idea.'

'. . . or Imelda, as I've been called on occasion.'

I smile at this rather apt reference to Imelda Marcos.

We turn to face Nicole just as she's walking up to us. She's done something to her face and hair, presumably for the photo session, though I can't tell what.

I do the introductions. The second I baptize my friend Imelda, she gives me daggers – the real, diamond-studded, Arabian Nights, death thrust variety.

'So you're Nicole.' She glares sarcastically.

Nodding and smiling warmly, Nicole offers her soft hand to Sylvana, who latches on to it coldly.

'It's lovely to meet you, Imelda,' says Nicole.

'That's nice.'

Sylvana does not let go of the hand. Nicole's smile is beginning to fade into this forced loony expression. When she gets her hand back she tries to think of nice things to say about the weather, just to keep the show on the road.

'I believe your friend is taking some photographs of you beside some fish,' Sylvana remarks condescendingly.

'Yes,' Nicole replies, a bit deflated.

There's a slight tension in the air, so I turn the conversation to the hippo beside us, a great hunk of flesh chomping away at the edge of a great basin. 'Nicole – meet Linda.'

We all lean on the concrete edge of the basin. Nicole takes to the monster with delight. The hippo's massive, blubber-leathery back is almost covered with dirty grey water. She's got this great hunk of a head rested on the concrete side of the pool just inches away from our faces and you want to see it: her Fred Flintstone jaw alone is the size of an articulated-lorry tyre. Short bristles thick as straw spike out of the jaw (you need a make-over, Linda, and you'd better lose some of that cellulite fast) and she's got two nostrils which every so often spout what looks like smoke into the air, and the whole time she's chortling her lips and grunting, and making obnoxiously ugly farting sounds with her slobbering, masticating chops.

'She's lovely,' marvels Nicole.

Sylvana: 'We should sign her into a beauty pageant.'

Now she's opening her mouth. Linda, that is. It's a huge pinky white mass of flab. The teeth. They're as large as horns. And they're brown-stained like she's been cultivating a secret nicotine addiction. Something huge and heavy just flicked out of the thing's mouth and back in, fast as a lizard. It was her tongue. She closes her mouth again.

'What a vile creature,' says I.

'Leave Linda alone,' says Sylvana. 'She's a perfect peach.'

Nicole is still fawning over her. She is mollycoddling a hippo. She's behaving like she's just seen a baby wrapped in a pink blanket instead of a mammoth slab of fat, wet, slimy, jurassic junk.

All the kids gathered around us are now chanting, 'Linda, open your mouth! Linda, open your mouth!'

We decide it's time to head off for a coffee, taking in the shop on the way. When we get inside Nicole and I spend a fair amount of time feeling and stroking and touching some odour-free wildlife: the synthetic-furry variety.

Sylvana, who has no interest in furry creatures, queues up for a map of the zoo – she likes to be in control of her environment – then she goes off to the ladies across the way. While she's away, Nicole buys a few things from the girl, then comes over to me and takes something out of a paper bag and hands it to me. It's a simple white rabbit attached to a keyring.

'Look what I got you,' she says, lowering her head.

'It's a rabbit.' I laugh, taken aback.

'Rabbits represent happy relationships and warmth. It's auspicious to keep the rabbit in the relationship area.'

'Thank you, Nicole.'

'Also, the rabbit belongs to the wood element.'

Sylvana reappears with her new map.

'Look what Nicole gave me, Imelda.'

She looks.

'It belongs to the wood element,' I explain to my friend.

Only her eyebrows move.

Nicole removes something else from her paper bag: it's a squashy plastic brown hippopotamus with a wide, highly evil grin. Smiling, she assures us that she will name it Linda and hang it from the rear-view mirror of her Fiat.

Very quietly, Sylvana observes Nicole as if unsure what to make of her. Noticing this, Nicole throws me a quick glance for moral support, ever so slightly embarrassed.

I'm beginning to feel tugs of sadness for her again.

She has just given a person she now regards as her firm friend – me – a present of a rabbit keyring. She has taken the risk, unusual considering I hardly know her, of opening herself up to me despite not knowing my name, my address, my background, my history.

Let's face it, Nicole is so ignorant about me that she makes these kind inquiries after Helmut's health.

She has such hope and optimism. It's horrible to have to snatch it away from her even as I place this token of her friendship – her cute rabbit – in my pocket. She has literally no idea that in under an hour her wonderful life with Ronan will come crashing to an end.

How could you feel anything other than sorry for the pathetic creature?

50

Sylvana has such a tough, calmly obliterating personality that she would not melt if you inserted her into a microwave oven and turned the knob to ninety minutes on full power.

It is to Nicole's credit, therefore, that a mere ten minutes after we sit down in the zoo café – with our chemical diarrhoea referred to by the menu as 'nutty Brazilian coffee' – she has succeeded in using her poor-little-me charm to transform Sylvana into a grovelling amoeba.

Sylvana has caved in: she is telling Nicole all about herself.

I've just opted out. Sitting back in my chair, I'm smoking John Player Blues in packets of ten because they ran out of twenties. I'm staring out of the window at the heads of distant giraffes, trying to tell the males from the females.

But I am unable fully to tune out of their conversation. Somewhere in the rear of my mind I am aware of Sylvana recounting animated stories to Nicole about her father. Right now she's telling her how difficult it has become to accompany the old man to the theatre. The principal problem, apart from the fact that he's confined to crutches and has crap eyesight, is that he's totally deaf.

Nicole is nodding gravely, a portrait of total concern. She appears to be deeply affected by the fact that Sylvana's father is thus misfortuned.

'So what he does is this,' my friend continues, encouraged. 'He buys the play first and reads it, commits it to memory and follows it on the night from the actors' lips.'

Nicole is now shaking her head in awe, chanting what a

wonderful achievement this is for Sylvana's father at his age, adding at the last minute that age shouldn't matter at all.

Sylvana, clearly, is deeply impressed by Nicole's demonstrated human qualities. So she launches into the topic of her father full whack – telling her about his devotion to learning despite his disabilities, his interest in everything around him, his kindness, his infuriating habits such as picking his ears in the middle of the city's auditoria.

Nicole should be a nun – she's the perfect listener. She is nodding and smiling, and shaking her head where appropriate. She's a better listener than I am, though I have to say she's not too hot on irony. And let's face it, anyone who can paint grass without green in it has to be a few sandwiches short of ironic.

Fifteen minutes later Sylvana has told Nicole something which it took her three years to confide in me: that she was adopted. She says she has recently made strides to locate her birth parents. She says she hopes she won't be too disappointed when she does manage to locate them: she's terrified they won't turn out to be multimillionaires.

She's scared from another angle too: that if she ends up a multimillionaire in her own right, she'll be destined to spend the rest of her days fending off alleged relatives.

But her worst nightmare of all, she says, is this recurring dream of hers, which she refers to as a 'backward premonition'. In the dream she meets a sturdy woman in her early fifties who informs her that she, Sylvana, was conceived in the back of a Morris Minor outside the Top Hat disco in the early hours of one morning in August 1970.

'I mean,' she drawls laconically, 'when you think about it.'

Nicole is frowning, getting very involved.

Now it's Sylvana's turn to ask Nicole about herself. And so, in the minutes that follow, we get a rundown of Nicole's life, her art, her music, her obsessions in general. The topic of Ronan is discreetly avoided.

Just ten minutes later we have established that Sylvana felt closer to her father than Nicole did to hers, but that Nicole hated her mother only slightly less than Sylvana hated hers. The main point is that both have gained a thorough appreciation of each other's feelings in regard to the emotional traumas they endured as small girls in families respectively racked (like my own) by dissension and plate-smashing.

All I can do is glare viciously at Sylvana whenever possible.

Now, Nicole is showing Sylvana the gold necklace Ronan got her. She flips it out over her top and points to a small shiny pendant. She says it's a *Mayan* ball, which she bought separately.

'They're great if you're in a difficult relationship. Also, if you hang it from the rear-view mirror of your car it reduces accidents. I tell everyone to do that. It works.'

Me, sarcastically: 'Have you tried it out?'

Sylvana leans forward for a closer look at Nicole's *Mayan* ball. I am beginning to hate my so-called best friend intensely. She can't seem to grasp the meaning behind my spiteful glares. I'll try a few Indian smoke signals instead.

Carelessly, I blow several rings of smoke into Sylvana's face. There's no reaction: she just sweeps it away with her hands and continues her exclusive with Nicole, who is so full of talk and enthusiasm that it doesn't seem even to occur to her that I might wish her an early death. Doll-like, she sits across the table in her own dreamworld, blissfully zombified by Sylvana's attentions.

I shouldn't worry – it will all be over in about half an hour.

'Tell me about Ronan,' says I, blowing smoke in her face.

Sylvana eyes me warily.

But a genuinely happy smile beams across Nicole's countenance. She shrugs as if she can't think where to start. She runs her fingers through her long, golden hair. 'He's very romantic.'

'Romantic.'

'And thoughtful.'

'Aha. Listen to this, Imelda.'

'And he's so generous.'

'Is he?'

'He used to send flowers to where I worked every few weeks. I kept telling him not to, but he wouldn't listen.'

Ronan hasn't given me so much as a petal in the last year. Before that he'd given me flowers all right, but usually the service station variety. For instance, the time I severely sprained my ankle playing chess with him at home – I had to go to hospital for tests and I stayed in overnight – Ronan brought me flowers, which he almost fooled me into believing weren't from the lobby shop downstairs. They were shrivelled begonias.

'Also,' Nicole says, 'he gave me these bangles. They're gold.'

She stretches out her wrist. Four thin golden bangles with tiny intricate designs tinkle against one another like wind chimes.

'When did he give you these?'

'Last March, on my birthday.'

I sit back in my seat and blow a few more smoke rings, one at Sylvana, one at Nicole and one into empty space. 'I wish my husband were as generous with me.'

'I'm sure he is, Julianne,' she says, tilting her head sympathetically towards me. 'What did Helmut give you for your last birthday?'

'*Helmut*?' says our Imelda, incredulous.

'Let's not get hung up on names, Imelda. He gave me a book.'

Audible gulp of sympathy from Nicole: she has grasped my misfortune. What was the book about, she wonders.

'Bumblebees.'

Yes. Not very romantic.

'Once we were watching a documentary about elephants,' I explain, 'and I told him that I loved animals . . .'

'*You*?' Sylvana grins.

'. . . and a month later he gave me a book about bumblebees. It was the best he could come up with. He was probably trying to give me a hint about my deadly sting or something. The idiot can't give you a present without making it symbolic.'

Nicole: 'That sounds a bit like like Ronan.'

It's nearly three o'clock.

We're walking along a path bordering a lake, approaching the monkey enclosures. These are large cabins with glass fronts through which you can spy (if you're so inclined) the inner details of these primates' lives.

First are the colobus monkeys, each of which sits alone on a small length of knotted rope suspended from the ceiling. Their heads are bowed, their eyes closed as if in prayer. Buddhist monkeys. They are black, with a white tufty tail and a cloak of white hair on their backs. Nicole tells us about them off the top of her head: diet, group life, mating habits. And their religious obsessions, naturally.

The spider monkeys next. Black as coal, they hang down limp as a wet shirt on a clothes line, attached to the branch by a tiny fist and a spindly tail – the other limbs hanging loose. Perched on a thick branch at the far end are three of them snuggling up close together like a large coil of shiny black rope. Soon something moves and a tiny black face separates itself from the folds, wrinkled and old-looking. The monkey in question scratches his head and yawns, bewildered.

We stop at the glass enclosure housing the Celebes macaques, dark monkeys who seem to be tearing each other apart, under the bored, benign gaze of the elders of the tribe.

I'm still feeling annoyed at Sylvana's warmth towards Nicole, so I tell her that Nicole plays piano. Chopin, to be precise.

'Really?'

'Yes,' Nicole admits. 'I'm really into Chopin.' (She pronounces it 'Cho-*panne*'.)

Sylvana and I exchange meaning-loaded glances.

Nicole says that when she found out how much Ronan liked Cho-*panne*, she went straight out and bought the notes to his favourite nocturne in C minor. She finally got to play it for him last Tuesday evening. In Paris. On the hotel piano before going out for dinner together. She was a bit rusty, she apologizes, but Ronan loved it. 'It's a really soul-stirring piece,' she explains.

What do you bet poor Cho-*panne* rotated in his grave?

'The piano is wonderful,' she adds. 'It's a great stress reliever.'

'Like the sex.'

'Sorry?'

I shrug at her. 'How is the sex between you?'

'Don't ask!'

This issue is one I worry about. For months, Ronan has shunned just about every erotic procedure imaginable. For him, oral sex has come to mean talking about sex. Foreplay has come to mean fumbling with condoms. And orgasm has come to mean annual pilgrimage. If you're lucky.

My point: is it different for Ronan and Nicole?

'You can tell us, Nicole. Sex should be a meaningful experience.'

'I agree with that,' she says.

'Is it meaningful for you and Ronan?'

A smile slowly and temptingly spreads across her wide mouth, as we cross a narrow bridge over a small stream and head towards the orang-utan enclosure.

'The sex is . . .'

She falters.

'Go on, Nicole. We don't mind.'

'It's wonderful.' She says this almost nostalgically.

This issue has been nagging away at me, really plaguing me.

'What about foreplay?' I ask her.

Sylvana groans.

Nicole turns to me and smiles. 'You mean . . . ?'

'For instance, do you and Ronan build up slowly?'

Her green eyes are presently dilating in their orbits. She glances at Sylvana for moral support. But my pal is staring into space, exhaling cigarette smoke into the surrounding shrubbery.

'Take Helmut, for instance,' I deviate, to ease her gently into the topic. 'With him, the definition of foreplay is the time it takes for him to get from the shower to the bed. You have to whip him to get him going and even then it's a battle against nature.'

Nicole is nodding quietly as if I've just told her my husband died recently. Any minute now she'll tell me how sorry she is for my loss.

I repeat my question about whether or not she builds up slowly with my husband. The corner of her mouth is now teetering on the brink of a grin. Incredibly, she asks Sylvana for a cigarette. Sylvana obliges and offers her a light.

Nicole lights up, inhaling deeply. She exhales, staring ahead into blankness. 'With Ronan . . .' she marvels, 'foreplay is an art form.'

'You paint him first.'

She clicks her finger. 'He can bring me to it just like *that*.'

'That's not foreplay, Nicole.'

'Or he can drag it out. To the very, very . . .'

'Bitter.'

'. . . *very* end.'

'That might be foreplay.'

'All he has to do is go near me and I've suddenly got G-spots all over my body. It's amazing.'

'And how is the orgasm?' I ask her, like I'm referring to a well-known brand of washing detergent.

'*Don't talk to me about orgasm!*' she chuckles, reddening.

'Sorry to be harping on about it.'

'Actually,' she confesses, 'I get multiple orgasms when I'm with him.'

'Factor fifty?'

Sylvana: 'She's not talking about suntan cream, Julianne.'

'Factor sixty-nine?'

'Ronan is amazing.'

'I adore multiple orgasms myself,' Sylvana comments. 'Especially since you don't need a man to give you one.'

'That's all very well, Imelda,' I shoot back, 'but when you've got this implement at home – a fully accessoried male – it's a pity when it stops doing what it was put on this world to do.'

I have both of them roaring with laughter.

'I mean, would someone please describe the multiple-experience thing to me? *Please*? Helmut is a drip. He couldn't satisfy me if you bloated him with Viagra.'

'Oh no,' she says earnestly. 'Ronan always stays with me. He never rushes. He's very affectionate, very sensitive.'

'He must really love you so.'

As we walk on, I'm desperately trying not to appear too shattered in front of them. I must focus on the positive: the three o'clock rendezvous with my future.

At the orang-utan precinct, Nicole is transfixed. The orang closest to us, rust-coloured and reminiscent of a red-brown rug on legs, is moving slowly in our direction. You can just about make out the tiny gentle eyes darting through flabby cheek pads, which remind me of huge black puddings stuck to her face. In her arms is a tiny baby orang.

Nicole is over the moon. She stands there, spellbound, for several minutes as we all watch mother and baby messing around in this primeval-ape compound.

She turns to me at last. 'Julianne?'

'Yes.'

'There's something I've been meaning to tell you.'

'What?'

'I've been keeping it to myself up to now.'

'Right.'

'Nobody else knows. Can I tell you?'

'Yes. *What?*'

She looks at Sylvana, then back at me. 'Julianne, I'm pregnant.'

51

My days spent visiting zoos are over.

Never again can I look at an orang-utan.

Especially not an orang-utan bearing young.

At first I thought I'd misheard what Nicole had said. I asked her to repeat herself. She just smiled and told me and Sylvana not to look so worried, that she'd get through it fine.

'How long have you known this?' demanded Sylvana.

'Several weeks,' she replied, startled.

'When are you due?' Sylvana inquisitioned.

'Mid-November.'

'That means you started it last February.'

Nicole nodded, confused.

'What makes you think it's not Harry's?' darted Sylvana. She was watching me like a hawk.

She shook her head. 'I am absolutely sure: Harry used those things. Besides . . .' that's when she pulled out the letter from her bag '. . . read this. Ronan sent this to me at work. You can ignore the third paragraph – he's just being silly.'

She handed it to me. Sylvana read it over my shoulder.

Dear Nicole,   *3 March*

I want to see you again. Last night was amazing. You were very good indeed, better than I'd expected. It's the longest session I've had in years. I felt like I was going to explode.

You mentioned that you weren't comfortable sleeping with me because I'm married and I told you that my marriage is on its last legs. Nicole, we barely know one another; let's not make any decisions about one another yet. Let's just take things slowly at first. We can build up gradually; what is required will then become obvious.

It's important to be philosophical about this: either it will work out between us or it will not. I think it would help to see it as a chemical reaction. Two elements from the Periodic table will either combine with one another or they will not combine. The capacities of chemical reactions are determined in advance. That's the way I see it with us: it's already decided in advance, therefore there's no point worrying.

Enough of that. All I can think of right now is being with you again, just like last night.

I have decided not to give you my mobile number yet; it's too risky. I'll call you. How does Thursday sound, after work? Thursday is a busy day for me, so it would be nice if you came to my surgery again, say, at about six thirty. The secretary will have gone home then. I'll call you that morning to confirm.

Ronan

'That was the day I became pregnant,' she said proudly.

Broken-hearted, I handed the page back to Nicole.

'Julianne, you've gone all white.'

'I haven't.'

'You have! Are you okay?'

'It's *you* that's having the baby; it's *you* that has all the . . .'

I wanted to say luck, fortune, happiness, love . . . but the words dried up.

Nicole started protesting: 'Julianne, don't worry about me – I'll be fine. Childbirth isn't *that* bad, is it Imelda?'

Sylvana snorted.

'Anyway, Ronan will be there for the delivery – I'll make sure of that. It's his child, after all. Don't worry about me.'

I couldn't help it: I burst into tears. Nicole was mortified. She put her arm round my shoulder and started fussing over me, apologizing, asking me in urgent, high-pitched tones what the matter was.

Then something dawned on her. 'This is about Helmut, isn't it? Oh God, I shouldn't have said anything – I wasn't thinking. It's just when I saw those orangs . . .'

I started moving away. Nicole kept up, walking beside me. 'Julianne, I'm really sorry, please don't hold it against me. It's what I was trying to tell you the whole time: part of the reason he's so important to me is that he's the father of my child. It wasn't planned that way.'

'No,' remarked Sylvana. 'It was the Immaculate Conception.'

'Does Ronan know about this?' I wondered weakly.

Nicole shook her head, saying she didn't want to alarm him.

'Well, perhaps we'll tell him today,' Sylvana suggested.

Nicole pleaded with us not to say a word to Ronan about it; that when the time was right she'd tell him herself. Besides, she added, she wanted to keep it a surprise.

Sylvana was inspecting me like a magnifying glass. She asked me what I wanted to do. I told her I didn't know. She offered to take me home. I said no.

When we got to a fork in the path I veered right. Nicole reminded me – pained – that she was meeting Ronan very shortly in the aquarium, which was to the left. I muttered something about going to the public toilets alone, that I would be back in a few minutes. I made Sylvana wait with her. Nicole told me to take my time.

I hobbled, crying, in the direction of the women's loos. I wanted to find a temporary hole into whose muck I could sink, to bury that grainy, heavy, totally fucked-up feeling inside. The closest equivalent I managed to get was the toilet. I entered a small cabin and was repelled by the stink of urine. I went in nevertheless and spent five minutes regurgitating my breakfast into a soiled toilet bowl.

Washing my mouth out with Listerine and patting my cheeks with tissue, I got the hell out of there, my face a mess on account of there being no mirrors, but I wasn't too bothered.

And I went straight through the turnstiles.

I just couldn't face Ronan and Nicole. Not today. A baby changed things. Drastically. I had to go home and be alone and think.

I took a bus into the city centre and another bus home – my marital 'home'. One and a half hours in total, but then what else would you expect from the bus services?

At four thirty I got back. Mother was knitting woollen socks for a friend's grandchild in the kitchen. I sensed something was up, something was not right. On impulse I went into our bedroom.

The wardrobe was open. There were large spaces in his section, gaps where his clothes should have been. I flung open his drawers. They were half empty. I scrambled through them. They contained non-essential items. But Ronan's passport, his documents, his professional papers – everything important was gone.

On the bed was a folded note.

Julie,   *Thursday, 2.30 p.m.*

I am going away for a while. I have been forced to leave because of your clear desire to bring this relationship to a standstill through your suspicious and destructive behaviour, which has cost me thousands of pounds.

So I am going to live by myself for some months. A break can be a healthy thing. It will give us both time to reconsider things.

A major reason for my decision is your mother. It is impossible to cohabit in the same enclosed space as that woman and I don't intend to repeat the experience. This might sound like an excuse, but it's not. She has made it her principal aim in life to sabotage calm, ever since she moved in with that ridiculous piano of hers. I'm sure she has her virtues (not that she aggressively advertises them) but she seems to seek out subtle and ruthlessly efficient methods of irking people.

For instance: she plays her out-of-tune piano, but only when it is calculated to cause maximum offence. It would not be so bad, of course, if she could actually play. Another technique she has perfected is to storm into the lounge while you're reading and turn on the television at full volume, only to disappear for ten or fifteen minutes to make herself a snack. She makes you think: is this woman deaf? Or blind? Or a mysterious combination of the two? She's certainly not dumb: her voice box seems to run on a permanently rechargeable battery.

The fishpaste episode suggests psychotic leanings. Its sheer deviancy is surely unrivalled, considering your mother's age. She has turned molestation into an exact science, and you yourself are proving a worthy successor.

Of course, an old woman deserves her little pleasures in life. And indeed, pleasures she has had: was it not the very same Whip Chick *I caught her watching yesterday afternoon from the comfort of our leather suite, when I returned from Paris? Of course, I'm the first to defend her inalienable right to enjoy pornography in the privacy of someone else's home. I just thought you should know.*

I trust that in the event of my possible return this woman will have been relocated to a place of her own. With her piano.

As for my future plans, nothing is as yet determined. But it is likely that I will sell off the practice now that I have a good excuse. I have potential earnings in lecturing, or in the art world, other than those I acquire through being what you quite rightly refer to as a professional 'cranial-pothole filler'. And time will tell whether I decide to exploit these possibilities.

I have put the secretary in the building in charge of forwarding any business-related mail to my new PO box. So should any arrive for me, please forward it to the surgery address.

I should be in touch at some stage.

Ronan

I ran from the apartment, wailing, past my mother who stood immobilized in the hall. Cascading down the stairs, I switched on my mobile and called Sylvana. She said she'd been trying to get me but my mobile was powered off.

I screamed at her to f*** herself about my mobile. I told her about Ronan's letter. She cursed. I demanded to know what happened. She said that because I hadn't returned from the loo she'd left the zoo herself, just before Nicole met Ronan.

'Where is she now?'

'I haven't a clue; I'm back in my office.'

I screamed and cursed at her for letting them get away. I flung at her a string of names so inappropriate and foul that if my mother had heard me she'd have stood up and cheered.

Sylvana, though, whose voice did not betray the slightest rufflement, pointed out that it was by no means certain that

Ronan was taking Nicole with him, wherever it was he was going. She also sensibly suggested that I should call Nicole, then Ronan. And if I got no satisfaction I was to call her back at once and we would meet at Nicole's B&B.

Neither Ronan nor Nicole was contactable by phone. I flew to the B&B in my MG. The lady of the house told me Nicole had left a while ago in her 'funny little yellow car' with all her bags, accompanied by a 'good-looking, professional-type man'.

Nicole had told her they were going to Paris. On the four thirty sailing between Dun Laoghaire and Holyhead, to drive through England to Dover and thence to Calais.

I flew back outside, updated Sylvana and ordered her to meet me at the Stena Sealink terminal in Dun Laoghaire.

52

The rusty railings were cold against my sweating palms.

My eyes burnt, my stomach was a rod of hot iron pounding spasms of pain throughout my body. Tears trickled down my face, cooling in the light breeze, the late-afternoon sun burrowed warmly into my scalp.

I stared at the huge white mass of the catamaran, floating barely fifty metres away on the bright-blue engine-simmering water of the harbour. I pestered Sylvana to explain why this was happening to me. She just kept replying: 'You don't deserve this, Julie.'

She urged me to accept the statement of officials at embarkation point that a yellow Fiat Cinquecento with registration plate 99D-54597 embarked just fifteen minutes previously. They refused to allow us on. I tried everything, short of telling them the truth. First I tried to calm down as they sensibly suggested. When that didn't work I tried tears, pleadings, explanations. When that didn't work I treated them to a lecture on public service and the priority of the customer, and one of them smiled infuriatingly and calmly repeated that the gates were now closed.

Sylvana, a dragon in most such situations, just stood there, thick and dumb as a pillar box, letting me take all this shite on my own. I informed both idiots that I was a barrister and could report them to their superiors for such ape-headed treatment of people who through no fault of their own were prejudiced by circumstances entirely beyond their control – too complex to discuss in any detail other than to say that my intention was merely to try to avoid a family tragedy.

'We can have an announcement made,' one suggested.

'No!'

The second man shrugged: 'Do they have a mobile phone?'

'They're not living in the dark ages.'

Stupid answer – they advised me to make contact with them.

We left, heading slowly towards the pier. I watched helplessly as the huge white craft shuddered, ready for departure.

'Come home, Julie,' Sylvana urged, tugging at my right arm. 'We'll think of something – it's not over yet.'

But in her mind it was over: in her mind this was a painful but necessary and permanent expulsion of marital baggage.

On the pier, I clung like gridlock to the railing, mute, staring at the catamaran. The huge foghorn bellowed. The blue strip at the base of the craft began to wash with sea water and the thing started to grumble like a vast rectangular fridge.

On impulse I phoned Ronan.

He asked me where I was. I told him I was changing our bedclothes. The catamaran had begun to move now. It was making a low, machine-like hum.

'Julie . . . I'm sorry . . .'

'Don't tell me you're sorry, you bastard.'

'I couldn't tell you directly. I didn't want to upset you.'

'Oh, well now.'

'More than was necessary.'

'Is *this* necessary?'

'Julie, you smashed my surgery. You can't just expect . . . That's not a small thing.'

'I told you: I did not smash your surgery. It was probably that woman's partner. I smashed everything else but not your surgery.'

Silence.

'Whatever.'

'You don't believe me.'

'It doesn't matter.'

'I know; you'd go anyway.'

He didn't reply.

'Where are you going?' I asked him.

'I can't say.'

'I suggest you look at your ticket.'

'Julie . . .' He sighed 'How do I put this . . .'

'This is how you should put it: "Julie, screw you for all the times we've had together because I never loved you, I was just using you as a trolley while I shopped around for someone else."'

'That's not it at all.'

'How is it, then? You're bored with me. Is that it? I don't give you a kick any more?'

'Of course you do . . .'

'Maybe it's the way I'm kicking you that's all wrong?'

'Julie, my plane is about to leave.'

'What did you just say?'

'My plane. Cellphones are counter to regulations on planes.'

'You're trying to tell me that you are sitting on a plane?'

'I'm quite entitled to travel on a plane.'

'Mother's right. You're a fraud.'

'Whatever.'

'She thinks you're contemptible.'

'Who could blame her for thinking that?'

'And totally insensitive. Those things you wrote about her in the letter – it just proves it.'

'I'm not afraid to be blunt.'

'You're doing so well it'd be a shame to end it on a soft note.'

The craft emitted a deep-bellied foghorn roar, which resounded throughout the harbour.

'Julie, I have to go now,' he said after a while.

'Of course. Your Stena Sealink catamaran is just about to take off into the air.'

'What?'

For the first time I noticed the sounds of the harbour. The wind whirring through the narrow gaps in the pier wall. The splash of water licking and lushing the seaweed-bedecked stone, the yacht ropes whipping and tinkling against their masts like Christmas chimes.

'Julie, where are you?'

Pause.

'I'm flattered you would want to know.'

No reply.

'Are cellphones still counter to regulations?' I laughed bitterly. 'Have you fastened your seat belt? And extinguished your cigarette? Are you enjoying the oxygen-mask drill? Have you taken off yet?'

Still no reply.

I started walking in the direction of the harbour mouth, towards which the huge craft was zooming.

'Or is taking off something you do in the back seats of cars, or in conference hotel rooms, or public restrooms, or in wheatfields, or in kitchens? Or on desks? Or in my bedroom when I'm away?'

'All that's over, Julie.'

'Yes, it's history.'

'She means nothing to me.'

'Well, don't you think you should have the courtesy to tell her? What if she has feelings and needs herself? And hopes for the future? Have you considered that possibility? She'll need you to be gentle with her when you break it off. I'm sure she's not a shaggable piece of meat that you can just dispose of when you've had your fill. Unlike me.'

'You still think I'm with that woman, don't you?'

A huge, angular, fearsome seagull hovered above me in the light breeze, not moving, squawking for some reason. Calling its mate, perhaps, to one of these rare, roller-coaster experiences that seabirds are born to enjoy.

Pedestrians were stopping on the pier to look out at the Stena craft, rumbling through its channel.

'Enjoy Paris,' said I idly.

'Cannes, actually.'

'Oh, so it's Cannes now? You know, it's funny, Ronan. We were happy then. You and me. Don't try to tell me you weren't. And don't even bother trying to tell me that people change. They change far less than you imagine and when you discover this it'll be too late for you.'

'I didn't mean it to happen like this, Julie.'

'I hadn't planned this send-off myself. Goodbye, Ronan.'

'Wait.'

The ferry passed through the harbour mouth and disappeared from view behind the high wall of the pier.

'Look, Julie . . .'

'Unless you tell me *now* that you're returning on the next ferry, it's over between us.'

No reply.

All that remained in the harbour was the troubled rush and surge of the ship's wake, the memory of cataclysm. And an eerie quiet, like the peace after a storm. I climbed the steps to the top level of the pier and peered out to sea. The craft was suddenly much smaller.

'Did you hear what I said? Unless you tell me that you've made a mistake and you're coming home, it's all over. I mean it, Ronan.'

'You destroyed my means of livelihood, Julie.'

'I'm warning you, Ronan. If we don't resolve things now, they will never be resolved.'

Nothing for several seconds.

'Julie', he says with irritation, 'as I tried to explain in the letter . . .'

I pressed the 'off' button.

53

It's five thirty. I am leaning with my back against the french windows on the balcony of my marital home, staring out to sea, a burning cigarette in one hand and a brandy in the other. Musing about my sorry, useless life.

Mother is presumably at bridge. She hasn't a clue what's happened. She should be in shortly. Sylvana is in the lounge behind me, reading another vampire book. She wants me to tell Mother everything. In Sylvana's mind, this will accelerate the painful process of acceptance.

Thick, wintry clouds are gathering over the bay and a warm, restless breeze is fluttering against my hair. On the horizon is a thin, sunlit band of bright-blue, receding with the advent of dark clouds. The world wants to rain. Soon it will scatter its teardrops on road and rooftop, brush against tree, cry rivulets down window-pane.

I want the rain to come.

Safely departed, the Stena Sealink has now well disappeared over the horizon, skiing over the seas to Britain. Thief of the man I love.

I can see them on the rear deck staring out to sea back towards Ireland, hypnotized by the giant milk churn of the jets gushing white foam backwards for fifty metres. They are sailing east in the floodlit sunshine, enfolding them both in its heat and hope.

I fill up my glass with another brandy from the bottle on the plastic table beside me. I wash it down.

On the table are some cards I discovered in Ronan's denuded drawers. Cards I once sent him. One features two teddy bears wearing straw hats, sitting on a bed of roses. It's a birthday card in which I personally wrote the following: 'All the happiness I've found in life I've found in you. Have a wonderful Birthday. All my love'. The bottom of the page is covered in Xs.

Another card I sent him is a blotch of reds and violets surrounding a love heart. I wrote: 'You make the good times we spend together the best times ever. I'm so glad I married you. Happy Valentine's Day.' Then my name, with a heart over the 'i' and Xs everywhere.

The first few spearheads of rain fall like a mass of pin-tips fleeting against the dark-shadowed daylight.

I stare at the cards again. I rip them both up and throw them back on the table. Waste of a life that they were. I move to the far side of the balcony in case anybody is watching me in my present state.

My mother has just returned. She and Sylvana are in the lounge, talking about me. Sylvana is telling her everything that happened. I can hear them through the gap in the french windows. In between earnest silences they are making cool judgements about my case. Between them, they are deciding my fate. Mother's harsh voice is dispensing common sense like a doctor's cures. Sylvana's is firm and low, and quietly agreeing.

I should let him go, Mother says. Now I hear her telling Sylvana about the time my father returned home and how, like a fool, she took him back. She doesn't want me to make the same mistake.

Has she forgotten what it's like to be in love?

I must be beside myself, she says. I resent this. She is speaking as if I am suffering impaired judgement, as if I am somehow unable to see reason. Above all, as if I am no longer able to decide anything for myself.

Sylvana appears to agree with this diagnosis of my unfortunate situation. She says that what I need most of all at this point is peace and quiet to come to terms with what's happened.

Angrily I stride through the french windows and across the living-room, ignoring them totally. I slam the front door of the apartment behind me, wondering if they'll try to follow. They don't. So I go straight to my MG, get in and drive to my new apartment, making sure to power off my phone.

I don't have to come to terms with shit if I don't want to.

The first thing I do when I arrive back in my apartment is dump the keyring Nicole gave me down the kitchen rubbish chute.

The next thing I do is go out to the balcony and smash the easel against the floor until small bits of wood come off, then I fling the loose skeleton into a heap in the corner.

I go around the apartment with a plastic bag now, looking for every sniffable item I can find. In four minutes flat I've come up with a jar of hair lacquer, anti-perspirant spray, nail varnish, nail varnish remover, hair spray, Tipp-Ex, shoe conditioner, a bottle of surgical spirit, a can of Brasso, a small bottle of paint remover and a tiny tube of superglue.

Everything goes into my sack of death.

Paint. Nicole's oils. I storm out to the balcony and grab a handful of her tubes. Her tubes. Ha!

And, silly me for forgetting, the good old cigarette lighter.

I go straight into the kitchen, sit down at the table and start experimenting.

The hair spray and the anti-perspirant are more of a nuisance than anything else. Being new to the technique, I aim the nozzle up my nostrils but end up blasting my brains out instead. I get an old dishcloth then and spray a corner of it until it's damp, and I start sniffing. I need something stronger.

I pull the hair lacquer out of the bag, twist open the cap and sniff that, but after a while it makes my skull feel like it's on lift-off.

The shoe conditioner? Unpleasant smell.

The paint remover is too sharp: one inhalation and it feels like the lining of my lungs is on nuclear meltdown. Nicole's paints are okay, but I can't get the colour green out of my head.

And why, oh why did they have to make Brasso so sickening?

The butane gas is okay, but I'm put off when the tip of my nose gets burnt.

At the bottom of the bag is the nail varnish.

At last I am home. Even the superglue doesn't come close. It's that super scent I have known since I was a small girl, watching my mother paint her fingernails and her toenails red; that sharp, pungent scent which bespoke beauty, glamour, power.

Like an undernourished dog, I sniff away at my discovery. At first I draw in several deep breaths but this makes me dizzy and light-headed. I go more slowly after that, inhaling at a more normal rate.

After a few minutes my nerve endings are beginning to dull. I'm finding it a little hard to breathe. I could topple off the chair on to the floor and not feel a thing. I start sneezing. Nausea fills my mind like thick, black, odourless smoke and I put my head between my knees.

I want to die.

I open my eyes. I'm surprised to find myself lying on the couch in the living-room. Mother is sitting in a chair near me, reading a magazine. I ask her what she's doing in my apartment and she says Sylvana brought her here.

Which doesn't exactly answer my question.

Now I remember everything.

My arms are aching and I have a thunderous headache. I feel torn apart as if a tornado has somehow managed to get into me and whirl me round like a ferocious demon, ripping away every ounce of strength and resilience I had inside me. The poisonous spores of germ warfare have invaded my body and sucked its strength dry, leaving it as it is now: a shell, empty and broken. I

302

never thought love could hurt like this. I want a heart transplant. I want someone to donate me a muscle that beats in my chest and keeps me alive, something without feeling or memory, something new and dull and clinical. I don't know how long I can stand this.

Ronan is everything to me.

He's my lover. He's my protector. He's my best friend. He understands me. He listens to me, in his own way. He loves me. He's good for me.

I should have listened to Sylvana, that Thursday by the pool. I should have confronted them. At the hospital, when her face was all punched up. Or at her place in front of Harry. I had my chance. Each time I met her I could have come clean. I could have threatened her. I could have punched her in the gob.

I did nothing.

I fucked up.

'He's gone,' says I, whimpering.

'I know, dear.'

'What did I do wrong?'

'You did nothing wrong.'

'Mother.'

'Yes, Julie?'

'I've disappointed you, haven't I?'

'Don't be silly.'

She turns away and I am amazed and alarmed to see a tear emerge on to her cheek.

'Mother!' I cry out. 'I'll be okay.'

'Of course you will.' She sniffs. 'I didn't bring you up a softie.'

She takes out a handkerchief from her sleeve, pats her eye and stuffs it back in.

I so badly wanted to protect her from the truth. I wanted her to think I was a success in every aspect of my life. I wanted her to be proud of me. Not just in my career, but in my personal life. I wanted to show her I'd made the right choices, that our joint experience of the same man – her husband and my father – had made me discerning. That her painful marriage was not all in vain – after all, look how sensible and wise I was with the men in *my* life.

I failed.

There is a sad, vacant expression on her face, which I haven't seen in years.

'You were right about Ronan all along,' I tell her.

'I shouldn't have interfered,' she replies.

'But you were right. I should have listened to you. Trouble is, when you love someone you don't want to let go.'

'Don't I know it.'

'Do you remember the time Father returned home, all those years ago, and you let him back?'

'I remember.'

'Do you remember what I said?'

'What did you say?'

Pause.

'I told you you were crazy to have him back. I told you I'd have handled things differently.'

Understatement of the century, Julie. You told her you hated her for being a coward. You told her she was weak. That you couldn't respect her. That you would never take a man back if he did that to you. You told her she could never be your role model. You knew it all.

'Do you remember I said that?'

'It was a long time ago,' she murmurs finally.

'Not that long ago.'

'When people are in love,' she replies, 'they do things for reasons the rest of the world doesn't understand. I took your father back. I loved him: it's that simple.'

'That's what I could never understand.'

'You were only a child.'

'I know.'

She says that only *I* know what is in Ronan's heart and in my own heart. She adds that if I want to take Ronan back, she won't try to put me off. I tell her I desperately want to take Ronan back, but I don't see how I ever can.

But for Mother, I'd be wandering in outer Mongolia, lost, lonely, hungry, cold, bewitched, bewildered and bolloxed.

'Whatever you decide, dear, I'll be behind you. And so will Sylvana – she's a sterling girl, she really is. And you know how wonderful I think you are, how beautiful and intelligent and pretty and principled you are, and I think that in the end there is nothing in life that you can't get through when you put your mind to it.'

'*Principled*?' I choke, crying.

54

Later that evening, after a mixed grill prepared by Mother during which we discuss what I'm going to do with my new apartment now that Ronan has eloped, I call Aer Lingus.

With my Visa card I book two tickets to Paris for tomorrow, Friday, boarding at four thirty p.m. I dial a number for international information. Eventually I get put on to Tourisme France. Four minutes later I have booked one night's accommodation for two at the Hotel Cadet in Montmartre.

'Does that mean I'm going to Paris, Julie?' she enthuses.

'No, Mother. I'm taking Sylvana.'

Friday, 24 June, Paris

55

We descend from our plane at seven p.m. on to the sun-warmed concrete of Charles de Gaulle Airport. We are led into a bleak, modern area, eerie as an abandoned hospital. Signposts in French and English goad us up stairways and along lengthy conveyor-belt corridors, which transmit us eventually to Terminal One, a huge round concrete building filled with shops bustling with a multi-racial, multi-class cast of characters and eventually we locate a sign saying *bagages*.

Recovering our bags finally from the carousel, we pass through the nearby arrivals gates into the arrivals hall. There, we locate some empty seating beside the thick glass walls forming the outer perimeter of the circular building.

Bursting, I rush to the toilets.

Once inside a cubicle I slam across the lock. A minute later it occurs to me that I should phone Nicole. I flip out my cellphone and input her number.

'Julianne! Is it really you?'

'You could say that.'

'You'll never guess what happened!'

'Try me.'

'Julianne,' she gushes, breathless, 'I don't know where to start. I'm in Paris.'

'Go on.'

'When I met Ronan at the zoo at three he said we were going to France. Just like that. We had to leave immediately because he'd just booked tickets on the catamaran from Dun Laoghaire – completely without warning. He was a bit annoyed because he'd been trying to get in touch with me but I had my mobile switched off. I was never great on technology.'

'You're more of an artist.'

306

'I told him I couldn't leave without telling you first. He said there was no time. We had to leave there and then. I drove in my car straight back to the B&B where I packed my bags.'

'I take it there was no time for a quick shag.'

'Julianne, I'm really sorry we missed each other when you went to the loo in the zoo.'

'Don't mention it.'

'Ronan said he couldn't stand it at home with his wife and her mother any more. He was furious at what she did to his surgery. But I think what really did it was when she destroyed *Chi*. Still, that doesn't matter now because I've just finished my new copy of *Chi* and I think it's actually quite good, although Ronan isn't so sure. Julianne, my life has suddenly changed beyond recognition. Do I really deserve this? Do I really deserve Ronan?'

'You do, actually.'

'I didn't mean to upset you like that, Julianne, when I told you I was pregnant. I didn't realize . . . Imelda told me you wanted a child of your own – it was really insensitive of me and I'm sorry . . .'

'Yes. I want a child of my own. But for various reasons I can't have one.'

'I'm really sorry for bringing it up in the zoo.'

'Forget it.'

'I'd love it if you came and visited us here some time, although I know you probably won't.'

'I'd like that. Where will you be tonight?'

'Tonight? We're going out to eat soon, to a place called the Café de Flore.'

'At what time?'

'Well, Ronan plans to have a stroll before dinner. He wants to walk from the Hôtel de Ville across the river to Notre-Dame and across the river again to Place St-Michel, then up Boul Mich, then up Boulevard St-Germain. So I suppose we'll arrive at the Café de Flore for about nine. We did the shops today – they're amazing. It's my second time here in a week. I can't believe it! Ronan bought me this jacket today, right? We went into . . .'

'Where exactly is the Café de Flore?'

I speak a little louder on account of the toilet in the cubicle next to me being flushed.

'It's actually on Boulevard St-Germain too.'

Which Métro, idiot.

'Which Métro?'

'I think it's called St-Germain-des-Prés. It's great to hear from you, Julianne. It's a pity you're not here.'

'Yes.'

'Anyway, when we get settled here in an apartment or something I'll send you the address. It'd be nice to . . .'

'Send Ronan my best,' I interrupt.

After a slight halt in the conversation she agrees to send Ronan my best. 'I've told him about you,' she avers. 'He says you sound fun.'

'He doesn't know the meaning of the word.'

'Is everything . . . okay your end?'

'See you later.'

Dude.

'*Julianne*?'

Coldly, I press the 'off' button.

56

I feel as if I am moving through a silent film.

We are on the Métro, which connects the airport and the city, fleeting through space and time towards the centre of Paris. The train tracks gallop underneath, a calming rhythm. Sylvana is seated opposite, face resting on the palm of her hand, elbow stuck on the narrow window ledge. We don't speak. You can see her reflection in the window, her silent, almost grim-looking profile, which forbids disturbance. I wonder what she's thinking of. The meeting she missed? The employee she meant to fire? Ronan? Nicole? Me?

Sylvana never feels the need to discuss her inner life.

Outside, the sky and the fields glow in a hue of red. The clouds, which seemed puffy and white from the exterior, are now light purple. It's the tinted glass.

Inside, it's as if the carriage is woven out of the French flag: everything is blue and red and white. And clean, modern and stylish. Sitting across the aisle are two Arab women, heads covered with black veils. There's a black man in a suit, with briefcase and glasses. Everyone has bags. We're the only ones in here who look even vaguely European, which is nice for a change. You get so tired of meeting white people your whole life. It's like the only bread you're allowed to eat is white sliced pan. So refined it becomes banal.

The train stops and starts and stops again. It begins to fill up. Some passengers read their *journaux*, others books, others stare blankly out of the window. One man with a pole-thin head and short, curly hair puts his head back and closes his eyes. Tired people stand up and queue, holding on to the straps or the bars, jostled from side to side by the lurching motion, waiting to get out. Once the train is stationary, the doors clank open, the exchange of sombre human beings is made and the doors clank closed again.

I try to think a little of the evening ahead. Of what I should say, or what approach I should take. But soon I give up. I will know at the time. I lose myself instead in the hypnotic whirr of train motion.

We change Métro at Châtelet Les Halles. We fly through the remaining Métro stations to our destination: Cadet, where our hotel is located. Around the corner, past a *boulangerie*, a *pâtisserie*, a *pharmacie* and an *épicerie*, is the entrance to the Hotel Cadet.

We pass through the automatic sliding door into a narrow reception area with a pale marble floor and thin columns supporting the high, slanted white ceiling. To our right are three black leather seats surrounding a low table, a display cabinet with crystal glass objects for sale, a revolving shoe polish machine and a door to the left-luggage room. To the left is a high reception desk shaped into a tall round island, a kind of outpost with a deep hole in the middle. Standing inside the hole is a man in uniform, presumably from North Africa.

He greets us with a cheeky smile, bright white teeth and two twinkly eyes. He hands us forms to fill in. Name, address, nationality, passport number. Luckily my passport contains my maiden name – it was issued before I was married. O'Connor: this is how I shall henceforth be known.

The man points to a rack of leaflets just beside the entrance where we will find maps, museums, opening nights, cinemas, clubs and anything that two fancy-free ladies could hope to find to titillate them on a Friday night, as if that's why we've come to Paris. He is full of good humour and polite laughter, but all we are in the mood for, really, is shutting him up with a smile, which of course he seems to appreciate.

A teenage boy with short blond hair and perfect skin brings us up in the elevator to the second floor. He leads us through a chic, grey-carpeted corridor with ceiling spotlights and modern art prints, and shows us into our room. It is small but impeccably clean. More grey: the headboards and the long narrow dressing-table on which stands a small television. Beneath this is a tiny fridge, concealed in a varnished wooden cabinet. More modern art prints on the walls. I squeeze past the two beds, pull back the white net curtain and open the window. No air enters: we are sheltered by a small courtyard.

I hand the *garçon* a two-hundred-franc note, which he takes with an oddly formal, boyish '*merci*'. When he leaves us to our nightmare of cramped space, Sylvana informs me that I just handed him roughly twenty pounds.

'I bags the bed by the window,' she says.

'That's unfair – you'll get all the fresh air.'

'Yes, but you'll be closer to the bathroom.'

'You make that seem like an advantage.'

'It is if you've got a hangover.'

'Thanks for the vote of confidence about tonight.'

'Okay, you take the bed by the window, then.' She sighs.

'No,' says I affably. 'Go ahead. You generally get your way.'

So she dumps her case on the bed by the window and starts unpacking. She has no respect for people who don't kick and punch and scream for what they want. I'm in no mood for kicking and punching and screaming. At least not yet.

She starts stripping. She's planning on having a shower. Before me. But I beat her to it. Sylvana will now have to make her face up in a condensed, fogged-up mirror.

Fifteen minutes later (after a hot shower which dispenses the maximum amount of steam) I come back out swathed in a flimsy white towel – the largest in the bathroom. She ignores me completely. She undresses and walks into the bathroom seemingly indifferent as to who might see her voluptuous and perfectly naked curves, namely me, and after spending a whole hour inside she walks back out in her black silk lingerie like she's actually planning on going to Club Zed tonight.

She sits down at the narrow dressing-table and begins applying foundation and eyeliner and mascara, indifferent to the fact that she's blocking my view of the TV, as I lean back against my bedhead watching Clark Gable speak French with those odd mouth movements.

I'm in my power-pinstriped suit. I feel I can accomplish things in it. I'm relieved to see Sylvana getting into a downbeat brown suit and dark-green polo-neck sweater. At nine we are ready to embark into the still bright Paris evening.

57

At a quarter to ten I follow Sylvana through the awkward double doors of the Café de Flore. Inside is like a busy tea party. The place is glaring with bright yellow light. The atmosphere in this large, box-like, open room is noisy and bustling and intellectual, and I am immediately struck by the soft, bright-red banquettes on which Parisian life is happily chattering. These are fitted in between low wooden partitions on top of which lie salt cellars and baskets of hard-boiled eggs. The yellow-painted, aged walls are almost completely covered with huge old decaying mirrors.

Ornate chandeliers hang from the high, sculpted, dirt-yellow ceiling. In the left corner a wooden stairway curves its way round, upstairs, presumably to the restrooms.

The wooden rectangular tables are patronized by the trendy twenties and thirties. But there are the old regulars too, one tableful of whom is engulfed in a bellyful of conversation with a bow-tied waiter in black and white who has just rolled a pencil from his ear and taken a small notepad from the black pouch attached to his belt.

We are told to wait until a seat becomes available so we stay where we are just in front of the entrance. Recent arrivals are already forming a queue behind us.

'It's nearly ten and they're still not here.' I peer around the large room.

'Knowing him, they're probably on a café crawl.'

Soon we are led to a small red banquette in the far right corner. I climb into the inside seat. Sylvana grumbles a little because she gets to face the wall, so I remind her of who snatched the bed by the window. She orders a 'café espresso special Flore' from the menu and just to be different I order tea.

And wait. From here there is a clear view of the door on which my eyes are fastened like bolts.

Our order arrives and we sip in silence.

Nothing happens. Everybody seems lost in conversation. Nobody is taking any notice of Sylvana or me, which makes a welcome change. Everybody is too beautiful in here. I watch one slender woman with large eyes animatedly engage her friend whose long arms are folded on the table and who keeps nodding in earnest. At another table sit a group of students in heated debate.

There's a guy with black leather jacket, scruffy dark hair and a dark half-day stubble sitting reading a book. At the table next to him is another guy with long greasy hair but stunning Brad Pitt features, staring at length into the distance. Every so often he dips his head and scribbles something meaningful in a note-book.

'I'm a bit peckish,' Sylvana says.

'You should have thought of that on the plane. The two of them could walk in any minute.'

Sylvana: 'You expected me to eat that chemically refined chicken and carrot paste, and those gherkin droppings? I don't think so. What about an *omelette au crabe*?'

She's reading her menu again.

'That's a crab omelette.'

'I know that, Julie, but do you think it's any good?'

'It's one dish I wouldn't touch with an oar.'

I idly scan my own menu. On the front cover is printed '*Saint-Germain-des-Prés*'. Beneath this is printed '*rendez-vous au . . . Café*

312

de Flore', a quote attributed to J. P. Sartre from his *Les Chemins de la Liberté*. Beneath this is a heavy sketch in pencil of a coffee table on top of which lie a cafetière, a cup and saucer and spoon, a newspaper, a letter, a packet of cigarettes and an ashtray.

I'm getting this tingling sensation in my gut. I desperately want a smoke so I light up. I start inhaling vigorously. I still don't know what I'm going to say to them when they walk through the door. Perhaps I'll just leave it to instinct.

'I think I'll have the crab omelette,' Sylvana says. 'I have yet to watch an egg crawl.'

The waiter comes over and she points to what she wants, then flips the page of the small booklet-menu and points at something else. And in an excruciatingly doggish French accent she says: '*Et: haricots verts frais en salade, s'il vous plaît. Oh, et un bière – un Tuborg s'il vous plaît. Merci.*'

'*Oui madame.*'

'*Et pour moi, un café espresso double s'il vous plaît.*'

On impulse, I take out my phone and hold it for a second, and stare at it. I put it back down on the table. Frustrated, I grab the menu and start reading: *Croissant au beurre, brioche au beurre, pain aux raisins, pain au chocolat, blinis, tartines beurre* . . .

Soon Sylvana's *omelette au crabe* and her *haricots verts frais en salade* arrive, together with the glass of Tuborg beer and my *café espresso double*.

She starts delicately gobbling the pukish-looking stringy omelette mix. I pull back from the sea smell.

She's munching away, now, into her dish, trying to guess the meaning of the various entries on the *Les Pâtisseries* page. She's scoffing her crab omelette like a starved dog and simultaneously she is quoting disapprovingly from the dessert section, mock contempt etched on her brow: will she choose a *gâteau au chocolat Macao* for her dessert? Or a *millefeuille*, whatever that is? Or a *tarte tatin (en saison)*? Or the *pâtisserie du jour*? Or the *cake frais*? None of these, of course, will do much for her figure.

I slam down my cup, twirl the mobile towards me and input Nicole's number. It's so noisy in here that when she answers all I hear from her is a squeak that vaguely reminds me of my name.

'Where the hell are you?' I shout.

Pause.

'How do you mean, Julianne?'

'How do I mean?'

When I repeat my highly complex five-word question she says she doesn't really understand.

'You're supposed to be in the Café de Flore. You're late.'

'But we *are* in the Café de Flore.' She giggles, unsure.

I pause.

'What are you doing in the toilet?'

'What?'

'Have you finished in the toilet?'

'Julianne, we're not in the toilet.'

'Are we talking about the same establishment? The big café on Boulevard St-Germain? With the red benches and the large mirrors?'

'Yes. We're upstairs.'

'There's seating upstairs? I thought there was just a loo?'

'There *is*, but there are tables also. It's lovely here, Julianne. We're having a really nice drink together. He's having – would you believe it – a crème de menthe and I'm having a beer with crème de cassis. We've just eaten prawns and garlic sauce. They were great, though I'm glad Ronan didn't tell me what they were until we'd finished. They have a funny name in French. I'll read it out to you. Listen to this . . .'

I punch out and put my phone away.

'We're going upstairs, Sylvana. Leave your revolting mobile egg where it is and follow me.'

Holding on to the curved wooden bannister rail we climb up the narrow squeaky wooden stairs past paintings of Paris hanging on the stairwell. We squeeze sideways to allow a waiter to pass, an empty tray at his side. We twist round and are now on the first floor. Straight ahead, to my surprise, is a long, narrow room full of people at tables: a banquet of liveliness.

At once I spy Nicole. She is seated on a curved banquette underneath the stained-glass window in the far right corner. She looks wonderful: soft, innocent, glowing, arms folded loosely. She's almost in a kind of watery daydream. Obviously dotty with happiness. She's wearing a loose shirt, the colour of pale-green grass, which accentuates her wonderful suntan. She's in cream slacks. I can see her feet. Enclosing them are sandals with woven gold straps. I can even make out her light-purple toenail varnish.

Her long, goldeny hair is back off her shoulders, exposing her long, dangly Rue de Rivoli earrings.

I advance. Now I can see Ronan's profile. He's reading his paper. Wouldn't you know it: *Le Figaro*. The paper for the intellectual. The paper for Ronan, the pseudo-intellectual bullshitter.

Sylvana: 'This should be fun.'

Nicole says something to him and laughs. He smiles, takes a sip of his green drink and returns to his paper. Nicole hasn't seen us yet, though she's facing this way, still daydreaming.

I advance slowly.

She looks around.

Then looks up.

She sees me. Her eyes are very large and her mouth is slightly open, teetering on the brink of hesitation. She looks like she's about to break out into a great big smile but she doesn't quite manage it. She glances at Ronan doubtfully, as if requiring reassurance. Who can blame her for her amazement? We've just beamed in here like two apparitions from *Star Trek* without the fancy gear.

She touches him lightly on the arm. But he's stuck deep in his paper. She should realize by now that she is located way below the *Figaro* in his order of priorities. She nudges him harder. He raises his crème de menthe and takes a sip and, as he lowers his drink, he glances in our direction. When he sees me his glass halts in mid-air.

I think he goes white, though I'm prepared to concede it's a pale shade of grey. As we approach, the vibe is so thick you could cut it with a baguette.

Nicole snaps out of her daze. She jumps to her feet and throws her arms around me shrieking, 'You had me fooled right up to the very last minute! What are you *doing* here? How come you never said? I had no idea.'

I respond to her hug like a stiff, rolled-up carpet, although to

315

my credit I do say hello. Disengaging myself from her arms, I stand back to let her hug Sylvana if she wants to and I just glare at Ronan.

They disentangle themselves and Nicole squeals at Ronan how *amazing* this is and in high frequency she demands to know what brings us here at no notice.

I don't respond and neither does Ronan: he is in puzzled concentration. This is how he looks when he's been taken for a ride and isn't quite sure who has ridden him, or hasn't yet worked out how best to ride back. As he attempts to get a hold on the situation his eyes flicker around the three of us like a lizard's.

'Oh my God! I can't believe you're here,' chants Nicole, staring happily at me the whole time, head tilted, figertips touching the side of her face.

She starts jabbering now, a useful release of tension for all. 'Ronan do you remember I told you about Julianne and Imelda? They're my two new, very good friends. Julianne's the one that brought me to the hospital – you know – after that thing? Come on, Ronan, of *course* you remember. I told you about her. She's the one who's really into *Feng Shui*. Remember? No, he doesn't remember – he's not into *Feng Shui*.'

He opens a pack of Gitanes.

'Ronan.' She nudges his shoulder. 'Julianne is the one who moved into a new apartment with her husband Helmut recently; that's the place where I started repainting *Chi* yesterday morning on the balcony. And this is Imelda, her friend. I met her at the zoo yesterday.'

She would have to put it like that.

'Ronan, is something the matter, love?'

Love.

Nicole is frowning down at him. 'Ronan!'

But he has turned away.

He is withdrawing into himself, considering the equation, measuring the vibes, preparing the perfect word. And he will not be lost for the perfect word.

'He's not listening.'

Nicole is all sighs.

Me: 'He's not a great listener.'

'Anyway, this is Ronan, folks.'

What an embarrassment. She stands there, her hand opened out towards her lover like he's the next guest on a chat show, grinning away like she's just escaped some institution.

An appropriate response from Ronan is still not forthcoming. All he can do is smoke, very calmly, exhaling to the side. Nicole's orgy of joy is becoming progressively more forced. The smile is fast draining from her cheeks. She frowns, eyeing each of us in turn.

'Talk about an anticlimax,' remarks Sylvana.

'Hello there, Ronan,' says I suavely. 'I must say, Cannes is a lovely city. A little cool, though, for July.'

Only his eyes move. Slowly across. They burn into me like two hard, deep, smoking gun barrels. Sylvana is glaring at him. Hatefully. Loyally.

Ronan consults Nicole: 'You have no idea who this is, do you?'

Nicole's mouth opens, but no sound comes out. *Sure* she knows who this is, the poor thing craves to say: these are her new friends Julianne and Imelda.

But sometimes one is afraid to state the obvious. One is afraid that if one repeats the self-evident, the heavens will suddenly open and a swarm of frenzied forked-tongued demons will break out in a chorus of deafening cackles, deriding one for one's asinine stupidity in missing the insanely obvious. It's an old school thing. Perfectly understandable.

Finally, Ronan sniggers. 'Congratulations!' he says. 'Julianne and Imelda! I especially like the Imelda part. Very suitable.'

Nicole frowns: 'Do you, like . . . *know* one another?'

'You could say that,' I reply.

'What's going on, Julianne? Has this to do with Helmut?'

'No. It's nothing to do with Helmut.'

'Helmut!' Ronan sniggers.

'You people are freaking me out! What is going on here?'

We sit down. Sylvana and I on two stools opposite Nicole and Ronan. He takes another drag of his Gitane and smiles, shaking his head, sitting back in his seat. Then he takes a further sip of his crème de menthe, cigarette-end brushing against the glass. And he replaces the glass on the table.

Now he takes a second cigarette from his box, perches it on his lips, strikes a match disdainfully against a Café de Flore booklet and exhales deeply, spreading white smoke up into the ceiling. He relaxes his weight back against the banquette. His old confidence and superiority are returning. He has got the measure of the situation.

'You're cleverer than I thought, *Julianne*.'

He says this while staring into the distance.

Sylvana: 'It's just that you're stupider than we thought.'

Nicole, by now, is a monument to the totally bewildered. She is desperate for somebody to clarify the situation. But we are all sitting caged in deadly silence, all the deadlier for occurring bang centre of probably the noisiest, busiest café in Paris.

I turn to Nicole and address her in my most elegant voice: 'Nicole, there's something you ought to know.'

'What?'

'Shall I tell her, Ronan?'

'Be my guest.'

'Thank you.'

I draw in a breath. 'Nicole, the slice of whaleshit to your left happens to be my husband.'

I can't even begin to explain to you the sense of utter, profound satisfaction and exuberance I am presently feeling, having finally got this little matter off my chest. It's been excruciating, bottling it up for so long.

'Would that be a fair analysis, Sylvana?'

'Which part? The husband part or the whaleshit part?'

'Both.'

Sylvana (trying not to grin): 'Yes, I think that would be fair.'

I feel totally liberated.

You want to see Nicole's reaction. It's straight out of a horror movie: the flesh on her face has turned practically *green*, though not from jealousy. No. It's the visage of someone who's just discovered, for instance, baby roaches in her yoghurt. She is a tremoring, shaking mass of flesh, palpably on the verge of emotional collapse.

Hands against her cheeks, she turns to her dear love, distraught. 'Is this true?' she stammers.

'Their little ploy won't succeed,' he says in her direction. 'Yes, I went through a marriage ceremony with this woman two years ago.'

'He thinks it was a tedious, forgettable experience,' I tell Sylvana, who's got this great expression on her face.

'I know,' she replies.

'I wouldn't quite put it that way,' he counters eloquently.

Nicole: 'I don't believe this is happening.'

Me: 'I've been meaning to tell you for some time.'

'The deception is despicable,' Ronan says calmly.

Sylvana: 'That's laughable, coming from *you*.'

Nicole: 'I don't believe this is happening. I . . .'

Her mouth is trembling. Her mascara and make-up are running together in black and white streaks down her cheeks.

'. . . I trusted you, Julianne!'

'I trusted my husband, you bitch!'

'There's no need to upset Nicole,' says Ronan in a natural voice.

'Oh, please excuse me for upsetting you, Nicole. Please excuse me for being cheated on. Please excuse me for coming home one day and finding both your clothes all over the kitchen floor and our double bed slept in by you. An appalling indiscretion on my part. Please excuse me for informing Harry and thus getting you beaten up. Please excuse me, let me see . . . oh yes, please excuse me for smashing up your living-room . . .'

I'd give anything for you to see their faces now.

'. . . although I have to say there was something about that festive experience which was particularly fulfilling – especially the tropical marine aquarium.'

While Nicole is gaping at me like a frightened tropical fish, Ronan is examining me objectively. Suddenly I remember the cat. I'm dead scared they're going to bring up Max.

'And lest you think I have one ounce of decency in me, Nicole, I want to state categorically that I think that your *Feng Shui* obsession is a lump of codswallop for the mentally under-nourished.'

'Don't forget the Porsche, Julie,' remarks Ronan.

Sylvana: 'Try some Viagra to compensate.'

Ronan again: 'Or your highly original fish recipe, a most civilized way for people to behave.'

Sylvana, raising her eyes, mutters: 'You deserved it, you prat.'

Ronan: 'And Nicole's painting, which you . . .'

'*Chi*?'

'Yes. *Chi*.'

'Please don't call it a painting, Ronan. It was a muck transplant. Nicole, I have something to tell you about your "art". Please read my lips: *you are one crap painter*. I saw the stuff in your attic. It was laughable. And as for the *Chi* replica you did on my balcony, that was ludicrous. I'm sure Ronan agrees, though he's probably too polite to tell you straight.'

Ronan: 'Somehow, the Parisian art world manages to think differently. Let's go, Nicole. I have no intention of going back home with her.'

'You think I came here just to haul you back home?'

Pause.

I want to grab the nearest wine bottle by the neck and smash it against his skull to see which breaks first.

'Then why did you come?' he wonders, at the edge of his seat.

Sylvana: 'She wanted to alert poor Nicole here that you're as big a scumbag asshole as I always suspected.'

'Who asked you?' says Ronan calmly.

'One doesn't require an asshole's permission to state obvious facts.'

But there's barely a flicker from him.

'Then why did you come here, Julie?' he inquires.

'You think I came here to bring you back.'

He shrugs arrogantly. 'Then why?'

I look at Sylvana and she looks at me.

'Ronan, you are mean and vindictive and deceptive, and even now you seem to enjoy hurting me. I only hope Nicole doesn't have to go through what you've put me through, because in a funny way I think she's not a bad person. Even though she has done me a terrible wrong.'

She is staring mournfully at me now, upset, eyes coated in a film of water. Every few seconds her body shudders minutely.

Ronan: 'All the way here – just to tell us that Nicole is not a bad person?'

320

Something inside me snaps.

Coolly, I tell him that our marriage is over.

'That's fine,' he says, draining his glass.

I stand up now. Sylvana follows suit.

Something occurs to me just before I turn to leave. 'Oh – and Ronan, congratulations.'

'For what?'

'I believe you've achieved one of your central ambitions in life.'

'What?'

'To be a father.'

I sense that somehow I've said the wrong thing. Ronan's reaction is stony. He turns to Nicole, but she just lowers her eyes.

I turn on my heel and Sylvana follows me past several table-loads of people who have been tuning in to the drama.

We exit the café and walk down the crowded, lit pavement towards the corner. Passing the Deux Magots café on our left, I suddenly stop. It's bright inside. I need something strong. Dumping your husband out of your life is not an everyday occurrence and it should be appropriately celebrated. Cognac, since we're in France.

Besides, to abstain for another minute would be sheer hell.

We go inside and sit down at a table close to the window, and Sylvana orders two cognacs. We sit wordless, staring through the glass at the clientele outside who are seated at round tables under the red awning, chatting.

After a few minutes we spot Nicole passing by in her grass-green chemise. The two of them are walking quickly past the café, Ronan slightly in front, his head down. They don't see us. They're having an argument but Ronan doesn't want to know. You can just make out the streaked mascara on her cheeks. I feel a sudden surge of pity for her as she pleads animatedly with him.

They proceed to the pedestrian lights at the corner and stop. She grabs him but he pulls away scratching his neck, sliding his hand through his hair.

Now they disappear round the corner.

I stare through the window for a long time.

When I look down, there's a glass of cognac sitting on the table in front of me.

Saturday, 25 June, afternoon

58

When we arrive back in Dublin airport, guess who's waiting for us at the arrival gates, smiling from ear to ear?

She's already heard of my marital tragedy: I told her by phone from Paris this morning. I told her that what I suspected would happen is now a reality: my life henceforth will be a Ronan-free zone. She was delighted by the news.

She asked me what time my flight was due back in Dublin. I told her it wasn't necessary for her to meet me at the airport. She said it would be nice for me to be met, so I told her that I was going straight back to my new apartment, where I needed to be alone for some time, and that therefore meeting me at the airport would be illogical. She started arguing, saying she loved airports. I told her I'd take her to the airport next weekend, and we could sit in the bar together and lick ice creams together and watch planes landing and taking off, and she said no, she loved airports *today*. I replied that I wanted to be alone and she inquired what was I doing with Sylvana.

I commanded her not to be at the airport to meet me.

And what does she do? She comes to the airport sporting a smile the width of a runway.

The reason she's happy, I suspect, is because now that Ronan is gone, she imagines that she will be able to retire permanently to my apartment.

After hugging me and informing me that I am coming home with her because she is tired of cooking for herself, she hugs Sylvana who is a good bit taller than her, practically having to climb on top of her to get a proper grip.

'It's nice to see you again, Gertrude,' Sylvana cackles over her shoulder, rubbing her on the back.

They are both thrilled I have permanently spewed Ronan out

of my life. I, however, do not share their delight. All I want to do is go back to my new place and weep.

I suggest as much to Mother.

Not a bit of it! She's not leaving the airport without a snack in the cafeteria, she announces. Plus, she hints, the best close-up relationship post-mortem she's likely to get this side of hell.

Up the escalators we go.

While the two of them queue, I sit down and keep a table.

Ten minutes later Sylvana strides back complaining about the inefficiency of the management system of this café. She is bearing aloft a tray laden with coffees and cakes and Coke for three. Mother in her smallness is leading the way, still smiling, handbag swinging.

One huge slice of redcurrant-custard tart is shoved in front of me and I apply the usual protests. Mother advises me not to be silly, that I am very thin and I need to eat up. And that it's not healthy to starve oneself like my forefathers.

As if chastened by this thought, she digs immediately into her Black Forest gateau. Sylvana dives into her own chocolate fudge cake. For several minutes they chomp in silence, watching and listening to the moving plethora of life all around us, the voices, the announcements.

Not one inquiry about how I'm coping in my newly separated state. No: 'Will you be okay on your own from now on?' No: 'How will you cope, Julie?' No: 'Is there anything you need?' Not even: 'Is there anybody you're particularly interested in having murdered?'

Nothing. Just munching and gentle slurps.

Mother, in brief, appears indifferent to my suffering. Which is strange, considering she was all over me before I left for Paris. She's like that. When I appear to be coping she ignores me. But when she sees me crapped with woe she turns into this bathtub of Southern Comfort.

'Well, Julie,' she says, but not before she's finished her final forkful. 'You've hardly told me anything about this Nicole person.'

So I give it to her on a plate. The whole turkey, skin and bones and teeth and ears and . . . earrings. I fill in all the missing gaps in her mind: Nicole's background, Harry, her painting, her *Feng Shui*, how Ronan met her, his plans to represent her in Paris as an original new artist, what I really did to his car and to her place, what I didn't do to his surgery although I was tempted.

Mother is fascinated. She's most impressed by my arch deceptiveness. She is totally into the way I handled things, drawing things out to the very last before I finally confronted the situation. (Sylvana decides to nod her head at this point and agree, then she sips her Coke.) She also says I've been very thoughtful for not wanting to worry her. She says she understands why I didn't tell her sooner about what was happening, especially about my new apartment – and she doesn't hold it against me.

She thinks Nicole is 'a bit dumb' for not copping on to the fact that I was Ronan's wife. But she says if she's dumb, then Ronan is a real 'thick' for not copping on to the fact that the Julianne woman, about whom Nicole spoke so well, actually put a ring round his finger two years previously.

I, of course, find all this unsolicited support most comforting.

'One question, Mother. How did you find out Ronan was having an affair?'

'I found a half-burnt photograph – from your wedding collection. On the balcony.'

'Oh, no.'

'When I couldn't find the wedding photos anywhere I knew something was up. So I rang Sylvana last weekend and she confirmed it for me.'

'I had to tell her, Julie,' Sylvana says. For the first time in years, vulnerably.

'Is that why you fed Ronan the fishpaste, Mother? Because you knew what he was up to?'

Mother, grinning: 'Yes. But also because young men like him need to eat good, wholesome food.'

'But what I find incredible, Mother, was that you *told* him.'

'It was the best part, I admit.'

Amid the general merriment, Mother lays into my redcurrant-custard tart. I point out that it's mine. She points out that I said I didn't want any. And she just keeps on eating.

'Have a bite, Sylvana,' she says. 'I don't want to be greedy.'

Sylvana calmly steals a forkful.

You know, it would be almost amusing if it weren't such a delicious-looking tart. My appetite is beginning to return and Mother dear is monopolizing my dessert, stuffing herself with it like this smiling greed machine. She feels she's lived and suffered long enough in this world, and the time for depriving herself of its luxuries is now over. So she has to deprive me of them instead. But she eats in such a civilized way you'd never guess we're touching base animal instinct here: slowly she separates a modest piece from my plate, slowly she raises the fork, slowly she places the fork in her mouth, slowly she chews. So slowly, you'd swear she was born into nobility.

Still, mothers are wise beings who have suffered so much torment in this life that mere minutes in their company can make you jolly again. Let her, I tell myself.

The three of us spend the next hour lambasting men.

Definitely one of life's coolest pastimes.

In the end, Mother manages to coax me back home with her. When we get inside and she puts me sitting at the kitchen table, I burst into floods of tears because I can still smell Ronan everywhere around me. She pours me a cup of tea and while I am drinking it she makes this huge racket washing some plates in the sink, just as if she's drilling a hole through a granite quarry. When she's finished she dries her hands and pours herself a cup of tea, brings it over and sits down beside me.

A fixed, determined look has appeared on her face. 'Julie, I want you to make a decison here and now.'

'What kind of decision?' says I, beginning to panic.

She sighs.

Feel free, she advises me, to weep my heart and lungs out. Feel free, she prods, to bang my head for three hours against the wailing wall and curse my very existence and have an extended stamping tantrum. Feel free, she lectures, to weep despairingly into my pillow and mourn the loss of the person I used to call my husband, and feel free generally to steep myself in my own soggy, mournful bath of misery and hopelessness and self-beatery, and feel free to desire death from a broken heart . . .

Provided, she warns, I confine the woe-is-me session to the next thirty-six hours.

'Why?' I ask fearfully.

I mean, considering that one gets such a kick out of being miserable, why on earth would one want to confine it to a limited edition of thirty-six hours?

'Because on Monday morning you're going back to work.'

'Hold on a second, Mother.'

Monday morning at seven thirty sharp, she announces, will be the beginning of the rest of my life. She will haul me out of my bed by the toenails if she has to, she says.

So between now and then, I have thirty-six hours to rant. Ronan is worth that, she says, but certainly no more. She refuses to allow me to eat my heart out when it's his heart that deserves to be eaten out. She says that she herself wasted too many years deciding that Father wasn't worth wasting so many years on, and she really doesn't see why I can't learn the lesson in one and a half days.

I know she's right. Working is good because it gets your mind off things. It keeps you strong. It reminds you that even if your life is breaking down and your marriage up – nevertheless you're not a total dump site.

And I'll admit that I enjoy certain aspects of the law, especially personal injuries. It's mostly males who suffer. Seeing men in pain is a welcome distraction from the tragedy of life.

Maybe I haven't woken up yet, maybe it's going to hit me. I don't know. Maybe Mother is just lowering a rope ladder down the pit to me, so that when the enormity of what's happened kicks in properly, I'll have something to cling on to.

'And by the way, dear, I've been thinking.'

'What?'

'I'm going to make you an offer you can't refuse.'

'Go on.'

'Two hundred thousand for the apartment.'

I stare at her, aghast.

'*This* apartment?'

'Take it or leave it,' she says.

326

A day in December

59

There's no doubt about it.

It is who I think it is.

Ambling through the park.

Here I am, standing on the roof garden of my apartment, hanging up clothes to dry on this cold and breezy winter morning. I'm extracting damp shirts and tops, and other exquisite articles, from a basket squatted on top of a stool. When suddenly this apparition drops from the sky.

Everything stops. I was just on the point of attaching a peg to the second trouser leg, so right now an idle peg is sticking from my fingers like a duck's beak ready to bite.

It seems to be a pattern in my life: things are cruising along just nicely when without warning I'm struck by an avalanche of bad luck.

I am jinxed from birth. I must be. In my body is a constellation of stellar minerals whose cumulative magnetic effect is to attract all the woe of the world – but precisely at that point in time when things in my life appear to be running nice and smoothly.

Suddenly the avalanche of bad luck starts waving.

Feeling like I've just been shot at, I turn my back and pin up the second trouser leg like I didn't notice a thing, hoping the move looked convincing.

Will I ever be free?

First, the innocence and peace of your childhood destroyed by your father's affair. Then you and your mother together pick up the pieces, worn and brittle and blood-and-tear-stained, and you live out the rest of your adolescence in a meteorological depression of the soul – but at least without a man to stymie it up on you.

Then you go to college and meet one.

You meet one and marry your addiction, and live on a high for a few years, plan babies and suddenly you discover he's been doing the dirty on you. You take a nosedive. You try to cope, to rehabilitate, to forget – and what happens?

Your front doorbell rings.

I don't want to know.

I extract a soggy white top from the basket and attach it to the line by two further pegs. I like pegs in winter: they don't carry tiny spiders that spin webs on your clothes line to trap unsuspecting miniature airborne wildlife. I have a phobia about cobwebs and all they imply.

The bell rings again.

I don't want to know.

I feel like a seagull with a broken wing, but that's okay. That's okay because my wings are getting stronger by the week and even if I can't yet spin in the air, or do a loop, or a roll, or a dive, or astronavigate the heavens like an eagle, I can at least parachute to safety if I get a sudden blackout and hide in a corner like a fragile kitten, and Sylvana and Mother will be there with their conjoint fat feline tongues to wrap me in a protective layer of their dripping saliva.

The very knowledge that this particular contribution to my emotional welfare is at all times forthcoming makes me certain that I will make it through this dark night of the soul.

Saint Julie of the Cross.

But still.

Still, I'm not strong. I'm still not fully myself. I might be strong enough to cruise in the sky, but only at low altitude. I'm still in constant danger of getting splatted against a chimney, or sprangled against a TV mast, or sliced in half by a cable, or scraped by a treetop or cymballed by a satellite dish (*Feng Shui* is quite right about the negative effects of satellite dishes). I am still fearful of getting nauseous and passing out as I fly through the septic urban air but my parachute fails to open, so I just get splodged on to the pavement like a grave of dogshit and never reawaken to immortalize the memory.

This, precisely, is the reason I do not want to answer the door.

The bell rings a third time.

I just want this interference to go away and leave me in peace. I will survive just fine, provided people whom I'd rather see frozen in a glass cabinet and dispatched to Mars would not decide suddenly to reappear in avalanche form.

I extract a clump consisting of three pairs of frilly white knickers from the washing basket and hang them up in turn, deeming each one no more deserving than a single peg.

It's been truly awful for the last six months. Why do you think Sylvana and Mother still take it in turns to sleep over? Because I'm back on the rails?

Clearly it's because they still don't trust me not to end it all in a bubble bath. I have been a burden on them, a blight in their lives. Like a street littered with misery, they've been picking me up whenever I was down. At one point it got so bad that I begged Sylvana to leave me alone and not stay over any more. Because if I hated what I was doing to myself, I hated even more what I was doing to her. But, like all great friends, she refused to listen.

Mother, too, was an angel, in her very own inimitable way.

But a suicide trough there still was. I had a lot of good ideas about how to do myself in. But the most obvious idea of all – flinging myself off the terrace in front of the park – never quite materialized. I suppose I didn't want to upset Sylvana – considering she often stayed over to thwart precisely that result and she'd have ended up blaming herself.

Or perhaps it was because in my heart I didn't really want to do anything stupid – I just wanted to contemplate death from another angle to prove to myself that life was still worth living.

Or possibly the real reason I didn't jump off the balcony was that it would finish Mother off. Now Mother is bad enough in a confined space like an apartment or a car, but can you imagine what it would be like sharing a grave? A sheer nightmare. Yes, she's the ultimate reason I resolved to stay alive.

But close to death I did come one day. I had been drinking, that old reliable excuse for everything in the world that is excessive, to which I gratefully resort when rational behaviour becomes a burden. I wrote a suicide note to Ronan, care of

Lucien Morel. In it, I blamed him for driving me to my death. Tripping over myself with inebriation, I posted it in the local postbox for early collection the following morning. Then I drove round the suburbs looking for something blank to crash into.

I could not find a suitable wall.

Either there were children playing tennis or football against it, or there were lamp-posts or cars in the way. Or dogs (cf. my innate fondness for wildlife). Or someone was in the vicinity: it was important to me that nobody would be ogling me in the process of bleeding to death, slumped over the wheel, body crushed, face smashed, wheezing my last blood-curdled breath. I did not fancy being trapped in gyrated metal, surrounded by people combing my hair and foundationing my face and snapping cameras at me for a complimentary front-page grin in the *News of the World*.

Finally I found a wall.

But.

It was situated at the end of a housing estate. It was perfect but for one thing: I had only thirty feet to accelerate up to eighty miles an hour. The worst I could do to myself was give myself a painful whiplash and a bit of light bruising.

I was desperate.

I gave up and came home.

Then I remembered the letter.

That whole night I did not sleep a wink. No way was Ronan getting that letter. The following morning I took up sentry duty at the postbox from six a.m. – though the first collection wasn't until eight. When the postman finally arrived I begged him for the return of my letter.

'I'm not permitted to return a letter, miss.'

'It's a suicide note,' I said quite calmly, though still treacherously drunk and whacked with fatigue.

'It's still not permitted, miss.'

I screamed at the poor man and after a brief interlude I asked him politely to consider whether I was or was not dead.

It did not take him long to take out a bunch of letters and start flipping through it for one addressed to Ronan Fitzgerald.

Which he handed me.

Which I promptly burnt in the sink. Washing the last ashes down the drain, it suddenly occurred to me what a dumb fool I was not to have searched out the docklands: there, there were literally hundreds of walls to choose from, walls of all shapes and sizes and colours and degrees of blankness.

Doubly grief-laden, I went to bed (in my marital home) for two whole weeks, despite Mother's valiant efforts to motivate me through pep talks, coffee, chocolate cake, bribery, threats, starvation, Xanax, prayer. She was so worried she even tried piano therapy.

Then one morning Sylvana came to me with coffee and Danish pastries. I felt sufficiently strong in myself to tell her about my suicide exploits. She attempted to comfort me by insisting that the impulse to destroy myself was not a permanent feature of my being but more of a 'temporary blip in my sanity'. I thanked her for her enlightenment, I remember, turned over on my other side and told her to buzz off.

There was this deathly silence from the far side of the bed that made me actually want to turn round and see if I'd hurt her feelings – but I was too proud to do so. That's when I realized I wanted to live.

I am now over this sad period in my life. Thanks in large part to my wonderful friend who refused to abandon me even when I begged her to. And thanks, of course, to Mother.

The bell rings a fourth time. This is bordering on harassment.

I twine down the spiral staircase with my empty basket.

I can't face it.

I can't.

I *will* face it.

60

I open my front door and press for the lift.

I travel down the four floors. When the doors open I see the intruder on the other side of the security door, in profile, stooping slightly over the intercom. Her hair seems more blonde than before, but it's probably just Parisian highlights. She's wearing a lemon-yellow anorak, a cream sweater and brown trousers, and she's holding a small package in one hand.

I walk up to the glass door and push it open, and she jumps, turning to face me. Relief washes over her face and she places a hand on her chest.

'It's you, Julie!'

'Yes, you can call me Julie – it's short for Julianne.'

'You gave me a fright.'

'I seem to make a habit of it.'

I lean against the open door to signify that I haven't got all day.

She doesn't react to me the way she used to. Her face isn't lighting up happily and she's not nodding her head enthusiastically. There's something different about her. Her head is slightly bowed, her pensive, downcast eyes surrounded by black circles. She looks disconsolate and washed-out.

I suppose that having stabbed me in the back discourages jollity. 'What are you doing here?'

'I just ... came because ... I called your mobile – but the number's been changed.'

'I was trying to shake you off.'

'I need to talk to you.'

Something occurs to me. 'You've come here for your cat, haven't you?' I give her a sly look.

'No, I haven't,' she croaks.

'You've come for your easel, then,' I accuse, somewhat relieved that she has not come here for her cat.

She insists she hasn't come here for her easel either.

'Why, then? Oh, I know: you've come to tell me you're sorry for wrecking my marriage. That you're not proud of what you did. That you're a dreadful bitch. Is that what you want to tell me? You want me to let you off the hook so that you can go back to Paris with a good conscience?'

With an uncertain grimace somewhere between a smile and a weep, she holds out both hands. In them is an object wrapped in soft white paper.

'What's that?'

'I brought this for you.'

'What is it?'

She steps forward and offers me the wrapped object. I just stand here staring at it.

'They're my mandarin ducks,' she clarifies.

'The orange ones?'

She nods.

'Oh, I forgot. I'm not supposed to know they're orange.'

'It's best to keep them on a table in the south-west corner of your bedroom. They symbolize fidelity and happiness. They bring good luck to a marriage.'

'Do you want me to hit you?'

She opens the paper to reveal two protruding-beaked, bright-orange porcelain ducks. 'They're for you and Ronan,' she insists. 'I wanted to give them to you before I go to Amsterdam. I won't be needing them any more.'

Folding my arms, I bore steel into her. 'What do you mean, before you go to Amsterdam?'

'I'm not going back to Paris, Jul . . . Julie.'

'Why?'

'I'm going to live in Amsterdam. I'm staying with my brother Joel and his wife in their apartment. He's arranged a job for me there in his English school, teaching English as a foreign language.'

'Sounds riveting.'

'I'm catching the plane to Schiphol Airport this afternoon at three – in a few hours' time. I left my bags at the airport. I'm not staying.'

'What about Ronan?' I wonder, beginning to feel very unsettled.

'It's over, Julie.'

Pause.

I try to take in the enormity of what she's just said. 'What's over?'

'Me and Ronan.'

'Since when?'

'Three days ago.'

'Give it a while.' I laugh. 'In a few days his libido will Rise Again.'

She shakes her head and looks like she's about to cry. 'We had a huge argument. He accused me of abusing his credit card account. His statement from last June didn't reach our Paris apartment until last week because we'd moved apartment. I was able to account for just under four thousand pounds, which included some purchases I made in Paris. And a lovely Raymond Weil watch I bought him specially to thank him for organizing the exhibition for me there. But he accused me of lying, because there was still about fifteen hundred pounds unaccounted for. Really expensive women's clothes purchased in Brown Thomas.'

'I get you.'

'He was really furious about the money. I told him it must have been . . . someone else. But he didn't believe me, because I admitted I'd bought that peach dress on the same day. Things came to a head then, but Ronan was already getting restless. The *Chi* replica which I painted was a flop. My career went downhill after that. It's my own fault, Julie – I don't blame you for doing that to *Chi*.'

'Thank you.'

'I think that's the real reason Ronan dumped me. Also, he couldn't handle the idea of a baby; he was probably just staying around until it was born.'

She informs me that Debbie was born last week.

She has a baby girl.

Nicole is saying something to me about her beautiful baby girl now, but I'm barely listening. I put my head back against the glass door and take a deep breath. A baby. I'm beginning to feel this dread, this utter desolation, an inkling of the huge chasm in my world, of the giant empty treasure chest inside me.

I try to distract myself by focusing on her gift.

'Aren't those the very same ducks that brought you and my husband together?'

She nods reluctantly.

'So now that it's all over, you just dump your ducks on me.'

'It's not like that.'

Her fingers curl slowly back over the bright-orange ornaments, enclosing them like a cage.

'Ronan never really loved me anyway,' she mourns. 'I thought when he came to the birth and saw his child, it might be different. But you were right: you're the one he loves.'

'I hope it was sheer murder,' says I.

'I . . .'

'The delivery. I hope it was sheer murder.'

'It wasn't easy.'

'Good.'

'Julie, listen to me: it's *you* he loves. He really does.'

I crack up now. 'Amn't I so lucky? He loves me. Hurray! What am I supposed to do with that useless piece of information? I've gone through hell. Have you gone through hell?'

She just stares at me. 'He wants to see you.'

'I'll send him a photograph.'

'He told me himself that he wanted to make his marriage work.'

'That was just an excuse to get rid of you.'

'He really meant it, Julie. He repeated it on the plane from Paris this morning.'

'He was on your plane?'

'Yes.' She nods earnestly. 'He's coming back for good, Julie. He's going straight to your home this afternoon.'

'This is my home. I hope you didn't give him the address.'

She swears on her mother's grave that she didn't.

'Good. Now you can go.'

'Julie, I know that nothing can make up for what happened.'

'You heard me.'

'I just want to say . . .'

'Go.'

'I just want to say that I'm sorry about everything.'

'I don't want to hear it.'

'*Please.*'

'I'm not interested. You've messed up my life. Now just take your stupid ducks and leave, and this time don't come back.'

She stares at my wall of hardness, mouth trembling, as I point to the car park. I feel no pity. She deserves no pity. She's had my husband's baby. She's a whore. I want this disease away from me.

She bursts into tears before me.

I stand and watch, cold and unfeeling. I want to be cruel. I want to see her in agony. She ripped through my life and caused me such pain, and she thinks everything will be okay again if she comes here and says sorry and gives me a few ducks and walks away again. Just like that. I hate her.

I hate myself.

There's something else. Something inside me. A feeling within that makes me scared. I am frightened, repulsed by what is on my mind. I am staring at the misery of another woman and all I can think of saying is: 'Well, when you've finished crying you can get the hell out of here and never come back.' Is that not revenge? Is this what all these months have been about? Revenge? Is this what I want? To make her suffer because she robbed from me a priceless gold chain I had no idea contained a permanently weak link?

Face to face, looking into her pained eyes, it's not so easy to hate. I can feel it beginning to evaporate in the wash of her tears.

I tell her to stop crying. I tell her to come up to my place for a cup of tea and something to eat.

No, she says, I'm right; she should never have come. She's only making things worse. She'll call a taxi immediately on her mobile phone. She will leave now and never bother me again. She's sorry for bothering me in the first place.

And I'm standing beside her ordering her to come up to my place before I create a scene.

She puts her ducks into her pocket and suddenly turns round and walks away. I take a step in her direction, then halt. She stops at the low wall just outside the entrance, semi-concealed by a conifer in a huge earthenware pot. She takes a small rucksack off the wall and swings it on to her back, and now she lifts something else off the wall.

At once I recognize what it is. It's a baby's carrycot. Turning to face me again from a distance of about twelve feet – her cheeks running – she says she's sorry about everything and she hopes that one day I will have it in my heart to forgive her. Then she turns on her heel.

'Nicole!'

She stops. She doesn't turn round.

I command her to, in effect, get her and her baby's sorry ass up to my place before I throw a temper tantrum.

She turns slightly, head lowered, baby-bearing, forlorn.

'I've already put you through hell,' she says, weeping.

'At least,' I say, uncertain, 'let me see the baby.'

She turns slowly and reapproaches me.

'Step inside or else the door will lock.'

She comes into the lobby. The door bangs shut behind us. She lifts up the carrycot and my heart literally skips a beat. The tiny baby's dazzling eyes. Her minute, cherubic, snow-white face. As I stroke her cheek, little Debbie's expression now smudges up like a wrinkled glove.

I poke my small finger into her left hand, which curls round it like a baby crab. Her infant odour is upsetting me. Nicole is smiling sadly at me now. She says Debbie likes me.

'Do you really think so?' I wonder, my heart falling. I gently stroke her tiny, light, fawny head and now she starts wailing like a siren. Is she hungry? That's what babies do when they're hungry, isn't it? Wail? Either that or she's allergic to me.

Nicole hands me the carrycot and while I'm holding it steady she lifts Debbie out of it and cuddles her. Then, because she must see how attached I am to events, she asks me if I'd like to hold her.

I could easily have said no. I could have said: I'm useless with babies; I drop them like a bad juggler (of course, the whole point is I haven't dropped even one yet). I could have said: babies make me nervous. They make me unbalanced. Neurotic. Cantankerous. They bring out the psychopath in me. They're not safe with me, I mass-murder them in my spare time. Give me the mandarin ducks instead – way safer.

I could have said: *Please go away, you wagon, and take bambino with you and die of disease.*

But no, like a fool wallowing in a pool of misery I willingly accept her offer to cradle in my arms the result of my husband's fornications.

I can just picture Sylvana admonishing me with raised finger: 'This is the best it gets, Julie. They might look nice dolled up in a cradle but the truth is other. Truth is, babies represent being pissed on, squawked at, puked over and shat upon for three years, and thereafter the very same, metaphorically, for a generation.'

But.

It doesn't seem to matter any more; I love holding Debbie. I want to go on holding her for ever. I am amazed at how light this wailing noise box is, wrapped in her tiny pink shawl. I stare at her cute wet eyes and can't help feeling fantastic.

In minutes this wailing dream has turned my upper arm into a soggy handkerchief. I'm rocking her gently to and fro, and stroking her beautiful little head. I'm all over her, shushing and purring and murmuring and humming to her like a primeval Italian mama. Soon she calms down.

'She's taken to you already.' Nicole smiles.

'Do you think so?'

I don't want to let go of her. This beautiful, fleshy, talcum-powdered, baby-smelling creation is knocking out a hole in my heart. I have both arms wrapped round her, protecting her just underneath my neck, this tiny being who is presently chortling and dribbling and scratching my left ear (does my maternal manner please her?). She's burrowing her tiny warm head into me, so I kiss it and I am speaking to her, rocking her to and fro very slightly, stroking her forehead ever so gently, smoothing down the thin strands of her fair hair and now I kiss her ever so softly on the cheek and nose, and she's making a chuckling, breathy, coughing noise, which might well be an infant's version of a pleased laugh, and I respond by making these cooing noises in her ear.

Now Debbie's face contorts into a smile, rather like that of a wrinkled old man.

Perhaps this is my vocation? Motherhood. Perhaps being a barrister never really was for me? All the struggle, the aggressive competition, the discipline, the rigid cold reasoning. What's it all for in the end? Money? Status? Power? Authority? The latest MGi? The penthouse apartment with the greatest sea view? The best holiday locations? The best restaurants?

But with whom? With a man who no longer wants to be with you? What do these things matter when you come home each day an emotional wreck, only to be supported by an emotional bankrupt? What do these things matter when you feel trapped? When the most beautiful things in this world are so simple to achieve, so possible, available practically at the ring of a bell?

Debbie.

I turn away from Nicole now because, pathetically, my eyes have filled with tears. I lead the way over to the lift.

The elevator doors open and I walk in. Nicole follows me, bearing the carrycot. A middle-aged woman who has just entered the main door comes in after us and presses number four for the whole party. The woman spends the whole joyride smiling slant-headed at the baby in my arms, telling me how beautiful she is and how lucky I am to have her, and me standing here, agreeing, craving the fourth floor, secretly wanting to believe it's true.

The woman exits first and walks down the corridor. As soon as she's disappeared Nicole giggles at the mistake. And when I giggle back at Nicole it's not because I'm necessarily having fun or anything incomprehensible like that, but more because I'm feeling this total resignation, this helplessness.

Outside my door I hand Nicole's baby back to her. A vacuum, an empty and cold longing now enters the space left vacant by Debbie. I rummage in my pocket for the keys.

Nicole's eyes are beginning to reveal their old merriment once more. She and Ronan have split up, but things aren't so bad now that her good friend (me) is showing her some humanity.

And she's got Debbie.

Me, I've got no one.

After several cups of coffee and an orgy of chortling over Debbie and what a wonderful gift to life she constitutes, etc. etc., Nicole wonders if she might take her into a bedroom to change her nappy. I show her into the spare room facing the road, forgetting completely that there's a copy of *Your Baby and You* on the bedside table. I put it there recently just to annoy Sylvana when she last stayed over.

While she's removing Debbie from her wrap, I'm standing behind her, watching her glance at the publication from time to time.

'I ripped that baby magazine off in your place,' I confess, just to break the tension.

'Oh, it's no problem,' she says quickly and she starts humming a tune like it really isn't a problem.

'I also ripped off that small *Feng Shui* handbook of yours.'

She just shakes her head as if it really isn't a big deal.

While Nicole is powdering Debbie's bottom, the phone goes off. It's the landline. I run out. Mother, wouldn't you know.

'Julie, dear, something has come up.'

'What?'

'Ronan's in the kitchen; we're having tea together.'

It takes me just a few seconds to grasp this point. 'That sounds very civilized,' I say.

'He's very respectful for a change.'

'He's up to every trick in the book.'

'He's actually talking to me. He's telling me all about Paris, he's practically cataloguing the whole interior of the Musée d'Orsay for me. It's as if nothing happened. Do I take it that you don't wish to see him?'

'Does he want to see me?'

'He does.'

'I'll be there soon, Mother.'

'I understand. Oops! Here he is now. I'll pass you over.'

Pause.

'Julie?' he says.

'Yes.'

'Julie, the situation has changed somewhat. I need to meet you.'

'What for?'

'It doesn't have to be here, it can be somewhere else. I need to talk to you.'

'But there's nothing to talk about, Ronan. I'm quite happy with my life. I am financially independent, I've got my own apartment, I have my car, my friends. I'm even thinking of getting a cat. What more could I want?'

There's a brief hiatus at this point.

'We still need to meet. The two of us.'

'I object to that phrase.'

'Julie, I'm not leaving this apartment until we talk.'

I consider this point. 'Fine. We'll meet there, so.'

'I don't want your mother to be a part of our marital conversation. What about dinner in town?'

'I don't think so.' I laugh. 'I'll see you in half an hour.'

I replace the receiver and go back into the bedroom where Nicole has just finished fixing Debbie's new nappy. I tell her I'm going home for a short while, but I'll be back to bring them to the airport.

'Is it to see Ronan?' she asks apprehensively, sitting down on the bed.

'Yes.'

I turn to leave.

'Julie, it's the best thing you can do, to go back with him.'

'You think so?'

'I really do. He's changed, he really has. I saw it in him. For the last few weeks he's been miserable with me, really unsettled. I could tell he was thinking about you. I know in my heart he loves you. I think he's sorry for what he did, even if he doesn't have the courage to admit it to you. Julie, you're doing what's best, don't be too angry with him, please . . .'

'I have to go now.'

'And it doesn't matter that he's Debbie's father. He doesn't want to be involved with us. I mean, he didn't even show up for her birth and anyway he dumped me after she was born, and that says a lot, doesn't it? All Debbie needs is a mother who can love her and even though I'm probably too messed up to be a proper mother, I can at least try my best to bring her up on my own. Look at me! *I* never had a proper father – but I've turned out all right, haven't I? *Haven't I?*'

'Yes.'

Before I step outside the hall door on to the landing, I take a brown envelope from the top of the bookcase in the hall.

It's twelve fifteen. Nicole's flight is at three.

'You stay here, Nicole. I'll be back at about two o'clock, and I'll drive you and Debbie to the airport.'

Slipping the envelope into my jacket pocket, I close the door behind me.

61

When I reach the Dun Laoghaire pad, I go straight into the kitchen. Sure enough, Mother is seated at the table holding a cup of tea between both hands. But I wasn't expecting Sylvana to be there, seated beside her.

'She's only just arrived,' explains Mother.

'He's inside,' says Sylvana, nodding her head in the direction of the living-room.

'I assumed as much.'

'I'm saying nothing,' she adds.

Which, translated, means, 'Don't you dare take that bastard back or I will hang you from the balcony railings by the neck.'

'Don't worry, Sylvana, I have everything under control.'

Mother explains that she invited Sylvana here because she didn't want my friend to miss any of the action. Sylvana raises her hand in mock annoyance, as if to slap my poor mother on the arm.

'Anyway, dear,' she says, serious now. 'You do whatever it is you have to do.'

Sylvana: 'If he gives any trouble, just call us.'

I exit the kitchen door into the lounge and shut it behind me. I'm glad she finds it so funny.

'Julie, I've been thinking . . .' He squeezes his nose suddenly.

'In between copulating?'

Ronan is seated on the white leather couch, leaning forward with his hands clasped together over the glass coffee table. He's in a grey jacket and trousers, and a wine-coloured polo-neck sweater. He's fresh and immaculate as always. But beneath his eyes are black shadows.

He lowers his eyes to his shoes.

There's a notable improvement in his attitude since we last met: his tone is conciliatory, regretful, humble even. It must kill him to have to come here and crawl.

'I'm serious . . . I've been thinking.'

'You spend too much time thinking. That's your problem. You

have no time left to feel. Nicole was right about you: with you it's all intellect. You live in your head. In your books.'

I'm sitting cross-legged on the white leather armchair, at an angle to him, holding aloft a G&T.

'Where *are* my books, by the way?'

The emptied bookcase is half filled with Mother's small collection. Cookery, landscapes, stately homes, travel, raunchy novels.

'I've put them into storage.'

I avert my eyes.

'You got rid of them, didn't you?'

I take a sip of G&T. 'Well, if you must know, I hired a skip. But the men were very careful. They didn't tear a single page on the way down.'

A therapist assured me recently that the violent onslaughts of my recent past constituted a promising development in my growth towards autonomy and spiritual healing. I must stop apologizing for my violent tendencies, she counselled. If I feel violent, she advised me, repression is no answer.

This therapist was my mother.

Mothers can be so supportive.

The next day I ordered a small yellow skip into which I flung roughly five hundred books, all his remaining clothes and mobile possessions. Sylvana was delighted to help me transport them down in the lift and out to the car park in large fruit boxes and bin bags.

Red fingers have flushed up Ronan's cheekbones. Lowering his head, he starts stroking his chin meditatively. When he's satisfied himself that I've binned nothing priceless he simply lowers his head, eyes closed. 'They're not important,' he says.

'Must you always take the good out of things?'

'I can understand why you did it.'

'Thank you, but I'd much rather you cursed and blinded a little, and admitted that it's making you hopping crazy inside.'

He stands up suddenly and goes to the drinks cabinet.

'Yes, have a drink, Ronan. You'll be less nervous.'

'I'm not nervous,' he brags, annoyed-sounding. 'I'm merely caught up in the dramatic possibilities of the situation.'

Taking a bottle from the drinks cabinet, he says that he acquired a penchant (French accent) for vodka while he was in Paris. He compliments my very full drinks collection, which is in actual fact Mother's very full drinks collection.

'I see you've become quite self-sufficient,' he says.

'As I intend to continue being.'

'Your mother told me she was still residing here.'

'And will be for the foreseeable future.'

He pours out the vodka, adding some tonic.

'I suppose she didn't phone you,' he says after a while, 'to let you know what has happened?'

'Mother?'

'Nicole.'

'That's the first time you've mentioned her name. Quite an achievement. Are we coming to terms with things at last?'

With his drink in hand, he starts pacing by the window. 'Julie, I'm going to get to the point. I'm coming home.'

'A logical impossibility.'

'I admit I've made mistakes.'

'Oh please, spare me the dribbles. And take off your shoes before you walk on that authentic sheepskin rug. It's Mother's.'

He orbits around it instead. It gives me a warm, happy glow inside to be able to boss him around in what used to be his apartment before the recent legal conveyance to Mother.

'That woman and I are over,' he says.

'That's a familiar phrase. Where have I heard it before?'

'I mean, well and truly over.'

'How *over* does someone have to be before they become *well and truly over*? Is there a decisive moment in this eternal petering-out process, this dying flame?'

'Splitting up takes time.'

'So I've discovered.'

'We have separated for good.'

'Yes, we have.'

'No – I mean, that woman and me. She never meant anything.'

'In which case I clearly meant less.'

'She was only a symptom of deeper issues.'

344

'But a sexually gratifying one.'

'It was a bad misjudgement on my part, I admit it.'

'What about your child?'

'That was an unfortunate error.'

'That's how you regard children.'

'It would be different with you, Julie.'

'So you want children now?'

'I'll seriously consider it.'

'You must really be desperate.'

'Not at all. I thought of having a child while I was in France.'

'It's not you who would be having it.'

'I thought, it mightn't be such a disaster after all . . . Okay, I might lose my freedom and you might lose your figure, but only for twenty years or so.'

He's trying to be funny.

'You're pathetic. You come back here with your tail between your legs, promising to give me a child. I don't even believe you. It's just an excuse to worm your way back in. You're a wimp.'

'Whatever you say, Julie.'

'You're a laughing stock. A buffoon who pretends to be so urbane and sophisticated.'

He doesn't like this. He sips his vodka, turns to the windows again, hand in his pocket, and peers out at the cold afternoon. 'The whole point is I have finished with that woman now. I have no interest in her.'

'Just her body.'

'It was so-so.'

'And her art.'

He makes a noise with his nostrils. 'Is *that* what you call it?'

'It was you who encouraged her.'

'It's expressionistic kitsch, it's . . .'

'How did it do in Paris?'

He eyes me quizzically. 'The revamped *Chi*? It was a disaster. As for her other work, there was minor interest. She won't make it anywhere. Hasn't got the application.'

'You needlessly raised her expectations.'

'By burning *Chi*, I think you needlessly dashed them.'

A point, of course.

'Anyway, Ronan . . .' I stand up and help myself to another G&T. 'I don't share your pessimism about her work. Nicole, unlike you, is able to *feel*. She puts her heart on her canvas and I respect her spontaneity. There's emotion in her paintings.'

He smirks.

'Besides,' I add, sitting down again, 'what about those excellent sketches she made of you?'

'You saw the sketches?'

'I saw them all, even the nude ones.'

'A very poor likeness.'

'Rubbish! I could have recognized your arrogant leer in them a mile away.'

Ronan starts pacing again. 'She tore them up.'

'The fewer reminders of you the better.'

'I offered to buy them off her. And still she tore them up.'

'You're despicable. And vain.'

'She needed the money. She sold her Fiat.'

'And you pretend to despise commerce. In reality you put commerce higher than aesthetics.'

'That's very good, Julie.'

'Oh, get out.'

'I have no problem with commerce. That woman and I were never more than a mutual business venture.'

'With a bit of hot sex added.'

'The sex wasn't great, strange to say.'

'Not even in our bed?'

'We never slept in our bed.'

I take another sip. 'You've been digging your grave for quite some time, Ronan. Slowly but very efficiently. Every time you open your mouth, it seems, you scatter away another shovelful.'

'Julie, this has been a bad period in our relationship. Something of a disaster, actually. What some people might call the lowest trajectory of a learning curve, or what others might call . . .'

'Please, leave now.'

He paces around a bit more, stops and stares at me. 'What do you want me to say?'

He's acting like I'm being unreasonable. Like he expects me to dismiss his liaison with Nicole as so much adolescent swagger.

'Try saying sorry.'

'I have no problem with that.'

'Right then; say it.'

He sighs.

He has a problem with it.

'*I'm sorry*. Now. Are you happy?'

We fall silent. Just the wind through the slightly open french windows. Mother and Sylvana are obviously still in the kitchen, but they have stopped talking. Knowing them, they're tuning in to every word.

'I don't want you in my life any more, Ronan.'

I'm fingering the envelope in my inside jacket pocket, ready to pull it out.

'I accept that going to France was an overreaction on my part.'

'I gave you your last chance. Remember? That day on Dun Laoghaire pier?'

'I made a mistake and I'm coming home now. My bags are outside.'

'It's gone.'

'What's gone?'

'Home.'

'What do you mean, gone?'

'The apartment is no longer yours.'

'Please explain, Julie.'

'I sold it.'

'You sold it?'

'Precisely.'

He's turning white before my eyes.

'Okay,' he says, nodding. 'You sold our apartment ... We'll get over that. When did you ... ?'

'To my mother.'

'*What?*'

He's turned grey now. Concrete-grey. Mushroom-soup grey.

'Surely you prefer to keep it in the family?'

'You sold it to *her*?'

'Watch your tone.'

He runs a hand through his hair and glares at me, and when he's finished glaring he stalks over to the drinks cabinet.

'This is our apartment; you had no right.'

'I'm a lawyer. Don't talk to me about morality.'

'I signed nothing.'

'You didn't have to. I had the place transferred into my name first.'

He gapes.

'How did you manage that?'

'It wasn't easy, though learning to forge your signature helped.'

'I can have it tested.'

'I'm being kind to you, Ronan, so don't fight me on this. After deducting the mortgage, I technically owe you forty-two grand. I'll be sending you a cheque for twenty-two grand next week. I've made a small deduction for nervous suffering.'

'Julie, we're getting ahead of ourselves. Let's discuss this rationally.'

'Hadn't you heard? I'm not rational. *Mother*!'

'What are you doing?'

'It's over.'

Mother walks into the lounge. 'Yes, dear? Did you both want a cup of tea?'

'Julie, I'd like to talk to you in private.'

'We've said all we have to say.'

Ronan turns to face the window and starts to stroke his chin again. Now Sylvana silently enters the lounge and stands quietly behind the aquarium, chewing something.

'I can't talk with your mother here, Julie.'

'Don't mind little old me.' She grins.

'I am moving my things back in, Gertrude,' he says, addressing the window.

'After all the nice things you said about me in that letter?'

'Yes, well . . .'

She sits down on the couch. 'I meant to tell you, Ronan,' she says. 'Julie sold this apartment to me. We had no idea you were returning.'

He's just nodding to himself, arms folded.

'Anyway,' she continues, 'this place is working out a treat. I've turned your old bedroom into a kind of safety-deposit vault for my valuable nineteenth-century furniture.'

'And your antique lawnmower, Mother.'

'Oh, yes – I had it specially polished; it's the one my father used to use in the thirties. And there's an easel in there too, which Julie was good enough to give me, though it was in a pretty worn state. I've been painting during those long weeks, when Julie refused to call out and visit me. I find I have a small talent for art. I never realized it before.'

Sylvana is grinning away at me behind Ronan's back.

'I've dreamt of living in a place like this,' Mother continues, 'with the balcony and the wonderful sea view, the marble floor in here, the leather couches and, of course, the jacuzzi. You put such an amount of thought into the interior design, Ronan, it's truly lovely.'

Cutting a relaxed pose as he stares through the window, Ronan is trying to pretend this isn't bothering him. 'So where are you living, then, Julie?' he says. 'Flat-sharing with that large friend of yours, I take it?'

'I'll thank you not to speak about my friend like that.'

'Your slim friend.'

The face on Sylvana.

'I am renting a penthouse apartment in another part of town.'

'Where?'

'That's a permanent secret.'

'I assume the rent is extortionate.'

'Actually, I managed to purchase it recently.'

'Oh, I see: from the sale of this place.'

'Selling the Porsche helped.'

He inclines his head slightly towards me. 'You sold my Porsche.'

'It took a ride.' (Mother.)

'It had a strong sex drive.' (Sylvana.)

He jumps around to see Sylvana for the first time. He glares at her and very politely asks her to leave the apartment, because we are having a family discussion. She refuses to budge. She just stands there staring cheekily at him, chewing peanuts from the palm of her hand.

'You can hardly blame me for selling the Porsche, Ronan. Remember, I had come home one day to witness Nicole's lemon-yellow brassiere on the front doorknob.'

Sylvana: 'Hanging loose.'

Mother: 'You know, yellow is a good colour for the hall; it's far too dark as it is. I put sunflowers there last Tuesday and I must say they were lovely.'

'Yes, Mother, yellow is nice. But not on the front doorknob in the form of another woman's Wonderbra.'

Ronan: 'She hung it there herself.'

Sylvana, grinning: 'I should think that exonerates him, Julie.'

'What you were *thinking* of when you took her home, Ronan. You've never answered that. What was going on in your head? Did you think that little of me? Going out with Nicole under my very nose, every second feeding me a pack of lies? Telling me you were extracting teeth in your surgery when you were sunbathing with her by the pool? Denying it when I brought it up. Lying about the fantastic state of the apartment after Nicole cleaned it, about the tropical fish, your wristwatch, the conference in Paris . . . Telling me she was history while she was sitting beside you on the boat, or should I say the plane. History!'

Sylvana: 'He's a historian as well as a dentist.'

'Was it worth it? Destroying our relationship like that?'

'I don't blame you for reacting this way.'

'*Get out.*'

'Look . . .'

'And take this before you go.'

I flip the envelope out of my jacket pocket.

'What's that?'

Everybody is staring at the envelope in my hand. No one knows.

'Mother and Sylvana, are you listening?'

They tell me they're listening.

'I just want to say – with Mother and Sylvana as witnesses – that our marriage is over. For good. This is not a threat. It's a fact. There is no possibility of reconciliation between us, Ronan. Does everybody hear this?'

Mother and Sylvana both murmur their agreement.

I hand the envelope to Ronan.

'I think it's time for you to leave now, dear,' Mother tells him softly, getting up. Sylvana follows her back into the kitchen.

Ronan has taken the divorce petition out of the envelope. As he reads it, the paper makes crinkling sounds.

This is it.

I am calm. I feel confident.

The tangled filaments of history are now quickly unravelling into a pattern of meaning, encompassing me and my mother before me, joined by our triumphs, our joys, our sorrows, our failures.

With Ronan, I am now doing what I have made it into a life crusade to do – should history ever repeat itself. What I desperately wished Mother had done, that night when Father returned home the second time after two years' absence.

I remember that night. I was doing homework upstairs in my room and I heard voices. I sat on the top step and peered down into the hallway. It was him. He and Mother were whispering. They moved into the living-room. I went downstairs and listened.

There were long periods of silence behind that door, interrupted by questions from her, and explanations and denials and professions of love and sincere apologies from him. 'You wouldn't be saying that if I hadn't caught you,' I heard Mother say. I could hear my father's soothing promises.

I wanted to burst in there and tell Mother he was a liar and a cheat, and she wasn't to believe him and she should throw him out. But she let him back, after everything that had happened.

And I was right: it did happen again.

She suffered, almost, so that I would be strong.

I can hear her now, in the kitchen. Pottering and clinkering with cups and saucers and plates, crinkling open a packet of biscuits. I can hear the gradually augmenting whoosh of the electric kettle. Coffee. I could do with a cup of strong Colombian coffee. Colombian anything, in fact. I am beginning to feel totally exhausted.

I walk slowly up to Ronan. He is still reading the divorce petition, page by page, intent, concentrated, unblinking. He doesn't look at me, although I am now right in front of him. He is concealing emotion, although his eyes seem glossy, moist, soft. They tell me that he's taken aback, upset. But he won't communicate with me, acknowledge openly that things haven't gone as he'd expected. It would, I suppose, be an admission of defeat.

I touch him on the arm, to reassure him, almost, then I say goodbye and start walking away. I stop at the glass door to the hall and look back once, but he doesn't turn round.

It is the last time, I know, that Ronan and I will be in this room together, with the view we know so well: the blue sea and the harbour, and the boats docking and embarking, and the horizon, the sunrises and the sunsets, the seagulls flitting about in the high sky.

The lounge where he makes his last stand is a tomb. Encasing two happy years of married life.

Just a souvenir.

Mother will turn it once more into a paradise.

Ronan's head is still tilted over the document. Not once does he turn round, not even after I whisper goodbye one last time. I walk out of the front door, leaving it resting on the latch, quietly. Then I begin to run, down the stairs, as fast as I can go, tripping, jumping, racing down, floor by floor, repeating over and over in my mind something I wanted to tell Nicole but couldn't, not before I'd cleared the slate with Ronan first, a proposal I must put to her at all costs, before she leaves the country.

I burst out through the lobby doors and sprint across the car park, and dive into my car and accelerate out of Ronan's life for ever.

62

When I get back home – my *real* home – I close the door behind me and place a jasmine plant on a chair in the hall.

I purchased it on the way back here, in a local garden centre. It's for Nicole. I remember what she said about jasmine. She said it was the plant of friendship. I couldn't find any reason *not* to buy it for her. So I bought it.

Standing in the hall, I listen through the stillness. There's no sound. She must be having a rest in the bedroom. It's a quarter to two. Her flight to Amsterdam is at three. I will have to drive her and Debbie to the airport immediately. As I promised.

Nicole would understand how I'm feeling right now. She has gone through so much. Her life has been a whip hide of pain. Only she knows what it's like to love Ronan. And separate from him. She is a beacon of light through all this bleakness, this grief.

In the hall mirror, I look like a dirty window-pane slashed by rain. I can't let her see me like this. She'd only become all caring and sympathetic. That, I know, would finish me off.

When I walk into the lounge, there's a note on the dining-table, lying adjacent to the two mandarin ducks.

Dear Julie,

Please forgive me for leaving so suddenly, but I thought it best to call a taxi just in case you were delayed with Ronan.

I'm so unhappy, Julie. I've hurt you so badly. I've only ever wanted people around me to be happy, but all I've done is gone and destroyed people's lives. I should have finished with Ronan the second you walked into the Café de Flore. But I didn't have the guts because of Debbie. Now Ronan has dumped me and it serves me right. I know what it feels like. I'd forgotten how much it hurts.

I wanted to tell you all this today, face to face, but it's easier in a letter. I took away from you the person you loved, the person who loves you. I made you leave your home. When I saw you today in your new apartment it made me so sad, to think that you were all alone. It's not right that you should have to live like that.

That's why I'm so glad you went back to see Ronan. I know it sounds foolish, but I really want things to work out between you both. All I can do is hope and pray that things went okay just now. I know you and I know him (at least I think I know you both, just a little) and I know you were made for each other.

I don't expect you ever to forgive me. I'm sure that you will want me out of your life for good and how can I blame you for that? I don't blame you for anything, Julie. I didn't listen to a word of what Ronan said about you being underhand. You weren't. You were trying to protect your marriage and all the time I was destroying it.

I know you won't want to contact me again, but to me you're still a friend no matter what. I just wish we'd met in different circumstances, because to tell you the truth, it always felt good talking to you.

I won't bother you again.

Love from
Nicole and Debbie

I stuff the letter in my pocket, dash into the kitchen, grab a plastic bag, run back out into the hall, lift up the jasmine plant carefully and put it in the bag. Crying, I race back out of the front door and slam it behind me.

At two thirty I arrive at the airport, having taken every short-cut known to woman. I park my car in the multi-storey car park, a giant cold graveyard, and race with my jasmine plant towards the terminal building. I cross the road and enter the sliding dark-glass doors.

A security guard sticks a vibrator-like thing into my jacket, then nods at me like I'm free of infection. People are scurrying hectically across the floor, scrambling up and down escalators, dragging suitcases, staring at notices, pushing trolleys, queuing up at car-hire stalls and check-in areas. At every point you have to step aside to avoid being bashed.

Loud noise echoes up to the giant ceilings of the huge rectangular departure lounge. At one end of the area is a fifty-foot Christmas tree with red, green, blue and gold baubles and flickering lights, and on the metal wall behind it is Santa Claus holding the reins to his reindeer, with a colourful pile of presents in the trunk behind him. Everywhere there is bunting and mistletoe, with red berries and Christmas cards suspended on long lines of string. Just above the Alitalia and Lufthansa booths is an exhibition of figures – one yellow Christmas cracker with purple feet skiing down a makeshift ski slope, a penguin jazz band, jiving Christmas trees, oranges hopping on coloured stilt-legs, waltzing bananas.

Powerful bright lights have turned the place into a vast stage. Everywhere are yellow signposts and red digital messages, and blue TV monitors screening arrival and departure times. I check for the three o'clock flight to Amsterdam. Manchester, Madrid, London Heathrow, Edinburgh, Brussels. Amsterdam! – boarding at two thirty.

It's two thirty-five.

I can't see them anywhere.

I rush around the back of the escalators towards the departure gates. I stick my head into a narrow brasserie but she's not there. I duck in behind a vast seating area, check through a tie shop, a newsagents, a souvenir shop.

Still no sign anywhere.

The man on duty at the departure gates . . . he would surely have remembered Nicole and baby if they'd passed through?

I rush to the front of the queue and give him their description. Long, wavy, golden hair, lemon-yellow anorak, carrying a baby in a carrycot, wearing brown trousers and boots.

He says he doesn't remember, but I shouldn't take that as a guarantee.

Desperate, I scour the departure lounge once more. Toilets, baby facilities, Burger King, Burger King toilets, the bar and restaurant down the escalators in the arrivals lounge, everywhere.

And then suddenly I catch sight of her. I stop to steady my breath and wait until my pulse subsides. She's in the bookshop, standing beside a revolving rack, checking out the best-sellers. I approach her from the side: her left profile. She's reading from a book with the name Cathy Kelly printed in large purple letters. On her back is the small red leather rucksack. At her feet is Debbie in her carrycot. She is gurgling and humming and prattling in that newborn language of hers like no one I know.

When I walk over to Nicole her face lights up like a lantern. With joy, but also astonishment.

'Julie! What are you doing here?'

'I don't know.'

She eyes me carefully, replacing the book on the rack. She touches me on the arm.

'Is everything okay with Ronan?'

'Yes.'

'I'm really glad to hear that, Julie, I really am.'

She's stroking my arm now.

'We're getting a divorce.'

At once she picks up the carrycot with Debbie in it, puts her arm round me and leads me out of the bookshop to the big window overlooking the pink runway, not far from the departure gates where travellers and their companions are congregating, giving one another the final farewell. I stare out at the planes preparing to take off, the minibuses, the vans, the luggage carts.

'But you love each other, Julie!'

She stands facing me, attentive, urgent, upset. I'm just staring out of the huge window. She offers me a handkerchief, which I accept. Now talk is pouring from me like an unstoppable torrent, out of the blue, a complete surprise.

I'm telling Nicole everything. About me, about Ronan, about how we met, fell in love, lived. How I believed in him, in us, in our future, but at the same time how distant that future felt because, eel-like, he seemed to keep slipping through your fingers. I'm telling her how different we were. How – in his mind – I was just *there*. A fixture. Therefore, he no longer wanted me, because life, for him, was a launching pad to someplace else. His life was an airport, mine more like a private garden.

I'm telling her about how I missed Ronan all these months, how I still miss him. I'm telling her about the good things, how kind he could be, how warm, how funny and playful he could be at times. And the bastard had to go and destroy it all.

I tell her I can't get him out of my head. I don't know if I will ever be able to get him out of my head, although I don't bother telling her that.

'No one really understands.'

'I understand, Julie.'

A plane is coming in to land. It seems to hover in the air, motionless as a bird against the wind. Nicole pulls down the light shade over Debbie's eyes to protect her from the glare.

We stand like this for a long time, saying nothing. It's easy, not to have to say anything. It's her presence. It soothes. I can talk to Sylvana for hours and she's great to be with – but with

356

Nicole it's more than that. There's something passive, almost, about her that opens up a space which is safe, where I can feel totally at ease when I talk, where she makes no suggestions, no condemnations, no judgements. She's just there. She doesn't even seem too worried about missing her plane.

This is the first time I've been able to speak like this to anybody since the whole thing started. You know, it's so strange, the fact that she's here listening to me like I've known her for years and yet I know hardly anything about her except that she's a scattered, messed-up girl who experiments with various ways to find happiness in this turbulent life including falling in love with the man I once thought I couldn't live without.

The plane has now landed. You can hear the roar. Its nose has straightened itself as it passes the terminal building, half a mile out, a bullet of shining silver gliding in slow motion through the soft pink light of the runway.

'I'm so sorry, Julie,' she says, her lovely eyes peering through the window, perplexed.

'It's okay, Nicole.'

She shakes her head as if she doesn't deserve my understanding.

'I feel bad, having to leave like this . . .' She falters.

I blurt it out now: 'Nicole, why don't you both stay with me?'

She stares at me. She thinks I'm just being nice. Thinking of her feelings.

'I'm serious. You and Debbie. For a while.'

Shaking her head, she says she doesn't deserve anything nice. She says she deserves what she got: losing Ronan, losing her career as an artist, losing her tropical marine fish, losing the love of her father and stepmother, having had an awful love life. Given everything she did to me, she says, she got her just deserts.

She says she doesn't even deserve Debbie.

'Please, Nicole, don't do yourself down. You deserve the best of everything and I consider you a friend. Stay with me. I mean it, Nicole. You can't take Debbie to Amsterdam. Do you think your brother wants a squawking baby in his house? Do you want Debbie to grow up a Dutchwoman? Selling flowers or chopping cheese? You're not Dutch. You belong here.'

357

I want to tell her: *I like you, Nicole, I really do. You're fun, you're gentle, you're sweet, you're kind, you're good to be with.*

But across Nicole's sympathetic face there has fallen a dark shadow of unhappiness. I want to see the sunshine gleaming once more from her eyes, I want to see her sad countenance dancing once more with laughter.

There's this silence between us now. The surrounding buzz of the airport has faded away like dying music, there's the distant sound of a loudspeaker making an announcement, it contains the word Amsterdam but I don't care, it doesn't matter. All that matters is that Nicole agrees to take Debbie home with me where we can all at least discuss things.

But she's resisting. I know it.

'Come back to my place, Nicole. You can stay for as short or as long as you like. There are two spare bedrooms. If you want you can use the second spare bedroom as an artist's studio. I still have your easel from that time you painted the park. Mother's minding it for you. It's a little scarred but it's basically okay. Think of it, Nicole, you could paint the park every day if you wanted. You could even use a little green! And you know, despite what I might have told you in Paris, I think you're actually a *very* good painter . . .'

'Thanks, Julie,' she says, sheepishly shaking her head.

'. . . And you wouldn't have to pay rent. The place is easily big enough for three. And you'd love my roof garden during the spring and summer: in just ten hours, you can get a three hundred and sixty degree suntan. Stop laughing, Nicole, I'm serious!

'Well? What do you think? Stop saying that, Nicole, of *course* you deserve it, it's not as if you can't do anything in return, I mean, what about those *Feng Shui* consultations you told me about? I was hoping to redecorate my apartment and I could do with some ideas about colour and design . . .'

She laughs at this.

'I've got that *Feng Shui* book which I consult from time to time – I'm keen to learn more about energy flows and furniture positioning. Oh, and by the way, when I told you that time in Paris that *Feng Shui* was a whole lot of codswallop, I didn't mean it, Nicole. I was simply . . . I *know* you don't hold it against me. It's just that I was a bit annoyed at the time . . .'

'Sometimes I think I took all that *Feng Shui* stuff too seriously.' She smiles weakly.

'And I'm mad about tropical fish too. I actually miss having an aquarium: Mother insisted on keeping ours. She had this strange idea that the fish weren't safe in my hands . . .'

Nicole laughs in that tinkly, musical way of hers.

'. . . I was thinking of buying a proper goldfish bowl – I suppose I've built up a kind of debt to fish over the last few months. You could come and help me choose some – oh, it's just an idea . . .'

She agrees that it would be wonderful if I had a goldfish bowl.

'Besides.' I laugh. 'Aren't goldfish supposed to improve your finances? Not that I'm doing too badly right now, but I could always use another million or so.'

And again I'm looking through her eyes and she through mine, and she is semi-laughing at me, semi-sobbing, and she says she can't understand why I'm being so nice to her. I should be pulling her hair (she says). I reply that I wouldn't in a million years dream of pulling her hair because I think she's a wonderful person, because she's been hurt more than I have, but still there is not a cynical bone in her body. She is incapable of hating, of being snide, ruthless, harsh.

Compared with me? I stand here and admit openly to her that I have destroyed things she loved. I have plundered her living-room like a born-again Vandal, stolen her books, liquidised her already dead fish, burnt her art, destroyed her loving relationship with Ronan who only happened by an odd quirk of fate to be my husband. (I find myself painfully unable to tell her the truth about Max.)

And what kind of person does that make *me*?

And not just that: I tell her how I have insulted her intelligence, slagged off her looks, taken pleasure in her misfortune, taken her for a ride, been cunning and deceptive and spiteful, and for the most part totally nasty and horrible.

'Oh, no!' she urges. 'Please don't say that.'

Nicole refuses to allow me to say these things about myself.

She is trying to tell me I'm a good person. How can everyone be so deceived about me? How can everybody fly so blatantly in the face of the most obvious, quadruply corroborated, damning character evidence?

Nicole is beseeching me to speak well of myself. At the same time, there are tears trickling from the corners of her eyes. I put down my plastic bag, take a handkerchief from my jacket pocket, raise it to her face and pat it over her cheeks and dry her eyes, holding her shoulder. Despite all the awful things I did to her, she lets me do this. Despite everything, she still looks upon me with kindness, in a way that forgives me completely – that's assuming she ever blamed me for my atrocious behaviour in the first place.

She's like a dream, a mirage. Do people like her really exist? Am I staring at an illusion? An illusion like Ronan was an illusion?

'Stay in my place, Nicole. You and Debbie. Sylvana – that's Imelda – thinks you should stay as well. She said she thought you were a howl. And my mother can't wait to meet you. You'll like her a lot. She's a total fruitcake, a true original. Also, she's crazy about babies and has been for quite some time. She plays the piano. You could play duets together. I was thinking of buying a piano for my new place. And having it installed on the roof garden. You could give concerts to people in the park below. Why not? You could play Chopin on it all day if you wanted. Prudence . . . Max loves the piano. I swear he does. He used to sit right on top of the strings and lick himself.'

'How is the poor thing?' she wonders.

'He's great,' I reply very quickly. 'He misses you a lot, Nicole. Anyway, as I was saying, if I do go ahead and buy a piano, you could always give me lessons. And you needn't worry about Debbie. She can roam free, subject, of course, to the french windows being closed at all times in case she falls out. I shouldn't have said that. And if you wanted to go out alone I wouldn't mind babysitting. I actually like babysitting, you know, I used to do it at college. And of course I was married for two years – that counts too. Anyway, I'm quite good with babies. Did you see me back there with Debbie?'

360

I bend down and take Debbie's tiny hand and shake it and say how do you do, and Debbie gurgles something uninterpretable. The feeling surges through me once again that I want to pick her up and smother her with love, so much so that she won't ever want to let go of me. Ever.

When I stand up again I can't help feeling like breaking down. Nicole is holding my arm again.

'So look, Nicole, if you're coming with me I think you'd better come now.'

I'm looking down at Debbie, the bundle of love sleeping peacefully at our feet. When I raise my eyes again, I find Nicole staring at me with concern, speechless, crushed.

'I'm fine,' I reassure her and I must look like a right idiot wiping the wet from my face, trying to tell her I'm fine.

'All I'm saying is . . . none of what happened has to matter. It doesn't have to matter that the most important person in my life and in your life will no longer be around. It doesn't have to matter that I haven't a husband any more, or that you don't have Ronan, or that Debbie doesn't have a father, all I'm saying is . . . all I'm saying is . . .'

Nicole doesn't want to stay with me. I know it.

I trail away, miserable, and stare out. A plane is moving very quickly across the runway. It whizzes past us at an astonishing rate. Still its wheels are in contact. Now it's poking its nose into the air. Now it's airborne . . .

'You'd better go now, Nicole. I'm just being silly. Go.'

She comes to me with this beautiful smile on her face, puts her arms around me and squeezes. My head is pressed into her shoulder. I can feel my nose running onto her bushy apricot-scented hair, which expands to fill every last crevice and I'm holding on to her very tightly, but I don't care and she doesn't seem to care either. There's a tenderness emanating from her that seems to enclose me like a soft boiler jacket, and isn't Nicole really dumb? I mean a real softie to let me weep like a deluge on her shoulder like this, because there's all this make-up and mascara smudging on to her cream sweater and she's going to have to send it to the dry-cleaners after me, which is a fine way to begin her time in Holland. But she doesn't seem too worried about this and she's still stroking my back and telling me to shush, *shush* and I don't mind this at all because, like I said, it's almost as if Nicole understands.

When I pull away from her I notice that Nicole's cheeks have tiny wet tracks running down them, and for no particular reason I kiss her on the forehead and then I hug her, and I'm biting my lip hard, telling her to have a lovely time in Amsterdam, not to worry about me, that I'll be fine, telling her that she's to take care of herself and Debbie, and she's to drop me a line any time she wants, if ever she's feeling lonely or things aren't going well.

Suddenly Nicole pulls away from me and picks the carrycot off the floor, and she doesn't ask me for my new mobile number and for some reason I am unable to give it to her, and I just hold out the plastic bag containing the jasmine plant and she takes it off me and seems touched by my present, although she doesn't yet know what it is and now Nicole is gone, gone, gone, running, running to the departure gates fifty metres away with Debbie in the carrycot and the jasmine plant in the plastic bag. She flashes her boarding card and without looking back once she proceeds to the electronic metal detector where she drops her small red rucksack on the moving belt. Then, with extreme caution, she places the jasmine plant on the belt as if there's a bomb inside when in actual fact all it is is a celebration of friendship, not a devotion to airborne terrorism . . .

And I rush across the departure area right up to the thick glass wall to wave at her, but she doesn't look back, she goes through the electronic door, collects the rucksack and the jasmine from the conveyor belt and I'm holding my hand up against the glass. It's crazy but all I want is for her to turn round and give me one last wave, but she doesn't. At all. Not once. I watch her disappear towards the duty-free shops illuminated with names like Ralph Lauren and Armani and Givenchy, running, running quickly because now her name is being called out on the loudspeakers saying that the flight gate is just about to close and I wonder if she'll miss her flight, and now she's disappeared.

And as I stare through the glass partition at the place where Nicole was, an illusion vanished, my heart fills with longing and emptiness, and a terrible, dragging pain in my chest.

I stand there for a long time.

Eventually my hand slides back down off the glass. I walk back slowly through the airport and, although it's still bustling with people, it feels as if the rush of excitement is going on in another dimension of space and time outside me, which I cannot access, which cannot affect me.

Inside it's as if I'm about to cave in.

I stop to look at the huge green Christmas tree, decorated with red, blue, green and gold baubles and flashing lights. Underneath are large presents wrapped in Christmas paper and tied with bows. Behind the tree, Santa Claus is flying across the sky. 'Wish I was at home for Christmas' is playing from a hidden source, the bugles bugling the trumpet sound of joy. All around me the world seems lit up by smiles.

I walk out into the cold afternoon.

63

Winter!

How well the slump in the seasons gels with my disposition.

I am the winter! The outer branches of my being are shivering with frost. The overlocked, brooding sky is wetting the face of the earth with its salt-free tears, the sun is a passing ghost casting its dreary, uncaring light onto the world. My heart is locked like a bulb underneath the ground.

The park has emptied itself of its few quiet strollers, wrapped stiff with thick coats, hardly delaying to observe its denuded frailties. The trees are bare prick-clumps, the lake leaf-clogged, the grass uncut, the place will have to wait out its three long months of bleak purgatory.

Sunday.

The slump of the week.

On the other side of my roof garden is the street below, with its closed shops and restaurants, and apartment blocks. Like a curfew, Sunday has shorn the world of its life. There's nothing to do. Where have all the people gone?

I know: to early-evening Mass. As I stand here alone, a good chunk of Dublin is presently praying to the Lord to forgive them their sins, to bless their loved ones, to prepare their way to heaven and while He's at it, to make them choose the correct numbers in the next Lotto.

God must be driven demented on Sundays with all those church services to attend, all those special intentions to honour, all those prayers to flip through. What a hectic social life He has on this day of rest. I haven't seen much of it, though. Let's just say, he's not exactly making his presence felt.

Mother rang me just now, dying for me to reassure her that Ronan was now truly rid from her poor tormented life. After congratulating me for my star performance with him this afternoon and demanding that I fill her in on anything she might happen to have missed, she requested that I drive her to evening Mass.

I smelt a rat. Under pressure of cross-examination, she was forced to admit she'd already been to Mass this morning. I polished her off with the remark: 'Why, then, Mother, do you need to go again?' Truth is, she imagines that the only way to cure my marriage blues is for me to enter the house of the Lord and take Jesus into my heart.

I asked her if Ronan had left yet. She replied that he stayed in the lounge for a long time, while she and Sylvana remained in the kitchen hogging the biscuit tin.

'Then he came in to say goodbye. He was very graceful about it, I must admit. He was polite and friendly for the first time ever. A good boot up the arse. It's what he always needed.'

'Did he ask for my number?'

'No.'

It surprised me and kind of annoyed me to learn that Sylvana was still in the kitchen with Mother instead of over here comforting me with her arm round my shoulder, which she has been known to do on infrequent, strictly necessary occasions.

Then again, she's crazy about old 'Gertie' as she calls her behind her back. She says she's one of the only women in life she truly relaxes with and she adores her sense of humour. She made a comment about Mother, the same evening that she served Ronan the fishpaste. 'You know, Julie,' she said, 'your mother is a real howl.

'Whatever you do,' she added, 'don't sell her to Oxfam.'

At least they have each other.

Sylvana rang me then. She announced that she wouldn't be leaving me on my own tonight. I replied that I wasn't alone; I'd hired a rent-boy for the evening.

There was a pause on the line.

'I'll be fine, Sylvana,' I said then, a little sheepishly.

She was persuaded I'd survive till dawn. Then, my trusted alarm clock would do the rest.

Truth is, I needed time to myself.

I've decided to take a soak.

The warm water is lapping round my shoulders, the foam bubbles sparkle against my face. My knees are sticking up in the air – cold and bare like a twin Matterhorn – so that I don't burn my feet in the thin water column of the hot tap.

I have solved the bath problem: how to maintain the same water temperature despite the law of nature which says that heat left to itself must turn to cold but not vice versa. The solution is to keep a thin column of hot water running into the bath. Nothing worse than waking up in a bath, freezing.

I want to feel the warm arms of this heat hugging me for ever.

I could call Ronan now. I have his number though he does not have mine. My mobile sits on the toilet seat, condensation-dewed, within easy reach.

But what would be the point? What could I say to him? Reassure him that what I did was the best thing for us both? Tell him we can still be friends? No. I refuse to pick up the phone and quote meaningless verbiage at him.

What then? Tell him I forgive him? And give him one last chance to wind himself slyly back into the heart he has so bruised, a heart he surely still needs? I don't think so.

Besides, *do* I forgive him? What does it mean to forgive? Does forgiveness begin when the crushing need to punch him in the teeth abates? Or is it possible to forgive first and then, as a small consolation prize, go punch him in the teeth?

We speak a different language. He speaks Chinese and I speak Irish. Communication is by indicating things and naming them. Points of contact are on the exterior only; inside, there's nothing to unite.

So no, I will not call Ronan. Ever again.

I will programme myself to forget his mobile number.

I'm moving up and down in the bath now like a sea monster bathing in some great geyser, to distribute the heat of the water around me. I soak the sponge in the foamy rinse and squeeze it over my head so that it trickles past my ears and spreads heat over my face. Around me is a dulling haze of steam. I sink down into the depths, submerged, warm like the womb, the water a mother, comforting, nourishing. I could give myself to it now and never re-emerge . . .

Sylvana.

Her life philosophy: nobody can make you happy because life is the meaning you give it yourself. Take responsibility, for nothing is impossible. The world is full of possibilities.

But is that real? Is the mind so free of the heart? The mind, surely, is bound to the heart like a mother to its baby. When the child demands attention, can the mother wander? But with Sylvana, there is no baby. She can feel, yes, but she will never be bound by feeling.

That's why she can't understand what this is like. She's never been hurt in love. She has stripped all need out of love. For Sylvana, a woman is already in possession of the benefits a man can supposedly afford her. Therefore a woman can experience complete enjoyment of these benefits without him. Money, sex, companionship. Above all, intelligent conversation.

She's lucky.

I, on the other hand, am cursed by an emotional marrow. I feel emotion like a jagged saw across a live tree trunk. Weakened, cheated. I am strong, yet I need a man to help make me strong. I yearn for a reason to live, yet I am without baby. I am a space shuttle that has just run out of fuel, floating precariously in the stratosphere, oxygen dwindling, any minute now threatening to fall, fall, fall, down like Alice fell down, tumbling head-over-heels, life flashing past me into the vortex, the void of heat and hope-loss.

I don't have a piano on whose velvet sound I can key in the minutiae of my woe!

Most pathetically, I yearn for the innocent company of Max.

I drag the bar of green seaweed soap across my scalp and build up a lather with my fingernails. I sink down gorgeously into the hot bath again.

Nicole.

She would understand, but what use is that now? She has her sights elsewhere. She refused even to consider staying here. I feel stupid, now, for suggesting it.

I allowed myself to be carried away. I deluded myself, fooled myself into imagining I was someone special in her book, someone whose friendship she valued. I am even naiver than she. She would have confided those things in whoever was prepared to listen. My own vanity postulated her friendship. The gift of the mandarin ducks. What do they prove? Her guilt, merely. To soothe herself with a token gesture, so she could return to the Continent in good conscience.

Not that she was insincere. She meant what she felt, yes. But still, it was gross of me to put faith in a weathervane.

Why would she need me anyway, when she has Debbie?

Mother.

She's the only one who really cares.

There's no meaning in her life apart from me. I am her Debbie.

Suddenly the doorbell rings.

It must be them. I warned Mother and Sylvana to leave me alone. I don't want to talk to them. I don't want to talk to anybody. I'm not answering. They'll get the message.

A minute later the bell rings a second time.

Why can't people just leave me to grieve in peace?

It rings a third time almost immediately and this time it is a long, sustained, obnoxiously rude gesture. Clearly, this is Sylvana. I stick my wet arm out into the freezing air and grab the phone off the toilet. I input her number. I am asked to leave a message. I ask her to bugger off from my front door and leave me alone. To quote.

You do things like that when you're not in the best of form.

Silence.

She's gone. She must have got the message. Thank God I took the key back off her.

I settle once more into my bath.

The bell rings again.

I curse and blind, haul myself to my feet and step over the bath on to the slippery floor, water cascading all round me and I wrap myself into my bathrobe, the bathmat soaking up my wet feet. I storm out into the hallway, tear off the intercom receiver and scream, 'Sylvana, What do you want?'

'There's a special delivery for a Julie O'Connor,' says a man's voice.

'What do you mean?'

'It's from a woman called Summers. Can I bring it up?'

Automaton-like, I press the buzzer and through the receiver you can hear the main lobby door click as he pushes through. There's a rumpus now in the elevator shaft next to the apartment. I can hear the doors clank open outside my door. I run into the bathroom and put on my slippers. The bell rings again and there's also a knock on the door. Quickly, I towel my dripping hair and rush back out over the water-discoloured woodblock floor.

I open up.

It's a thin, spidery-looking man with a very pale, sickly face and a moustache. He's holding a large object about a foot high, contained in a blue bag with red bubbles on it and a scrawl in yellow writing: *Fishmania*.

That's that aquarist down the road in Dun Laoghaire.

'Bring it in here, please.'

I lead him into the kitchen.

'No. On second thoughts, leave it in the hall. Fish are supposed to be kept in the hall – near the entrance.'

He says he doesn't think it matters too much, provided I feed them every day.

He clearly hasn't heard of *Feng Shui*.

He puts the large object down carefully on top of the low bookcase in the vestibule. He lifts up the blue plastic bag. There is revealed to me the most beautiful goldfish bowl I have ever seen, swimmering with the loveliest small goldfish, fluttering orange and gold over a sparkle of multicoloured crystal stones that resemble boiled sweets.

The man says that this Nicole woman is something else. She rang him an hour ago from an aeroplane, just as it was about to take off. She was in a desperately worried state and told him that she needed to have eight goldfish delivered to a friend, and one had to be either a black fish or a carp of similar size. To stimulate *tea*, he added, observing that he was under the impression that tea grew on trees and not in fish tanks.

The poor ignorant man hasn't heard of *chi* either.

Then, he recounts, she kept him on the phone for fifteen minutes and gave explicit and detailed instructions: she wanted him to prepare a glass bowl at least twelve by twelve inches, round, and with a large air surface; there were to be multicoloured stones at the bottom, in particular plenty of green, there had to be a plant of some sort and he was not to include goldfish with a reputation for bullying.

He hands me a letter now. 'Then she dictated this letter over the phone. Excuse the handwriting, I couldn't get her to slow down.'

I take the letter from him and open it.

'She took ages to remember her husband's credit card number,' he observes.

I've already started reading.

Dear Julie,

Please forgive me for writing to you in this way but I had no choice. After I said goodbye to you I opened up the plastic bag you gave me and took out your wonderful jasmine plant. Julie, it means so much to me. I realized there was so much more I wanted to say to you, but I couldn't because I didn't have your number. So much has happened between us that it would be wrong to let it go. Julie, I want you to come to Amsterdam to visit me and Debbie soon. Will you come to the christening? Please, please do! I must go. Here's my number: 086/8577646. Please call me – I'll keep my phone switched on all the time. Life is so crazy!

Love Nicole

The man is saying something to me about changing the water once a week and feeding the fish once a day with a small amount of flakes, but I'm not really paying any attention. He's saying something to me now about a balanced diet, about how overfeeding can kill fish, but it goes completely over my head. I am staring at one goldfish on the outer edge, shimmering orange in the hall light, almost motionless except for the slight paper-like flutter of his wisp-thin fins in the water, and the gills opening and closing like they're munching plankton, and the flickering of the tiny protruding black button eyes, and each fish seems so alone in his (her?) own little world and yet I'm sure each partakes of what is undoubtedly a bat-wild social life. And I read the letter once more just to be sure. She's invited me to Amsterdam. Not a mention of Ronan, he's out of the picture. Not a mention of Sylvana, just the two of us and Debbie, and does she really want me to attend the christening, is she serious? I want to call her to tell her yes, I'd love to, but I think I should give it a day or two to let things calm down a little, and I can't believe she really went to all that trouble to get these wonderful fish to me. I really can't . . .

. . . and at some point I sense that the man has quietly left the apartment because the door recently made that closing sound doors tend to make when people leave rooms . . .

. . . and I'm feeling this inexplicable feeling. I just adore her fish, I adore the harmonious way they move, the peaceful way they pout and trip through the water like they're on marijuana. Perhaps this is what *chi* is all about, perhaps this is what Nicole meant by *chi* being narcotic, or let me see . . . was she referring to rhododendrons?

It's not often in life that I get crazy ideas.

No. And now is not a bad time to start, is it? Crazy ideas don't generally occur to one when staring into a fish bowl, but then I've always thought fish were totally underrated.

I'm going to call Nicole after all.

I go back into the bathroom, retrieve my mobile and dial her number.

It's ringing. My heart is thumping madly.

I get her voicemail.

on't panic. It doesn't matter.

This is Nicole Summers, em, if you'd like to leave a message, please do so after the bleep.'

'Nicole? Hi, it's Julianne. Nicole, I got your beautiful aquarium with the wonderful goldfish. I don't know what to say, so I won't try . . . Nicole, Sylvana and I have just booked a holiday for four in New Orleans for a fortnight, to start next week. Oh, and by the way, you and Debbie are coming. You won't have to pay a penny. Don't you dare say no: the money's already paid, so if you even think of selling out, you're dead. Have you got that? Sylvana says that if you let us down she'll personally go to Amsterdam to drag you both on to the plane. So both of you are to keep a space free in your hectic social schedule. I'll call you tomorrow with the details . . .'

I punch out.

Now I call Sylvana. As usual, I get her voicemail.

'Sylvana – Julie. Please disregard my last message. I've booked a holiday for four in New Orleans for a fortnight. To start next week. With me, and Nicole and her baby. She says she's thrilled by the idea. She says we'll have an amazing time. She says if you let us down she'll personally go to your place and drag you on to the plane. I *know* you're tied up. I *know* it's impossible. I *know* you will lose business and will have to quell rebellion on your return, but *please? Just for once in your life?* I'll love you for ever. If it's any consolation, I booked it on Ronan's Mastercard. Oh, and if you dare say no I will seriously consider taking him back into my life. Be in touch. Bye.'

Immediately I call Trailfinders. It's just ten minutes before closing time. I demand a fortnight's package in New Orleans in the top hotel, to begin next Saturday, very approximately.

'No problem, madam,' says the gent on the phone.

Ten minutes later he's located four seats on Virgin Atlantic on next Thursday morning's flight from London to New Orleans, via New York, returning on Christmas Eve. With carrycot thrown in.

They do a range of hotels.

Book the most expensive, I command.

Do we want rooms with balcony? he asks.

Yes, I reply: we never take less than superior de luxe.

Do we wish to avail ourselves of a fascinating city tour of t[...] historic city and an escorted tour of the Deep South, which take[...] in the historic plantation mansions?

Book every tour in sight, I reply.

Do we wish to avail ourselves of a dinner jazz cruise on the *Creole Queen* paddle steamer?

Jesus, I say, book it, book it.

He takes our names and books us into the Hotel Sainte Marie, a hotel with every luxury you could ever dream of, right in the heart of the French Quarter, just half a block from the cafés and jazz clubs of Bourbon Street.

Is that *real* bourbon they're talking about? I ask the man.

'Also,' I add, 'we want a four-wheel Chevrolet Blazer. And if you wish to throw in a chauffeur for an additional charge – young and hungry and built like a lust-god – that would be entirely acceptable.'

It comes to almost five and a half thousand pounds, he says, laughing. And are we happy with that?

'Perfectly,' I reply.

Then he asks for my credit card number.

Now let me see.

What *is* his number?